THE
RETURN
OF THE
CONTEMPORARY

ILLUMINATIONS:
CULTURAL FORMATIONS
OF THE AMERICAS SERIES

JORGE CORONADO, EDITOR

THE
RETURN
OF THE
CONTEMPORARY

THE LATIN AMERICAN NOVEL
IN THE END TIMES

NICOLÁS CAMPISI

UNIVERSITY OF PITTSBURGH PRESS

Published by the University of Pittsburgh Press, Pittsburgh, Pa., 15260
Manufactured in the United States of America
Printed on acid-free paper
10 9 8 7 6 5 4 3 2 1

Cataloging-in-Publication data is available from the Library of Congress

ISBN 13: 978-0-8229-4839-1
ISBN 10: 0-8229-4839-7

Cover photograph: Pablo Ernesto Piovano
Cover design: Melissa Dias-Mandoly

CONTENTS

ACKNOWLEDGMENTS

The question of the contemporary posits the need to build a "we" in an era of global emergency. The writing of this book was a collective effort and, as such, proof that the contemporary only becomes visible through dialogue with a chorus of voices. Michelle Clayton was the first interlocutor and the person who, with her usual intelligence and generosity, encouraged me to undertake this journey. At Brown University I am also indebted to Felipe Martínez Pinzón, Julio Ortega, and Nelson Vieira for their insights and encouragement. Brown's Department of Hispanic Studies offered me the tools to thrive as a professor and a researcher. I am grateful to Laura Bass, Erica Durante, Jill Kuhnheim, Stephanie Merrim, Iris Montero, Mary Oliver, Silvia Sobral, Sarah Thomas, Mercedes Vaquero, and Esther Whitfield. At the Center for Latin American and Caribbean Studies, I received the Sarmiento Fellowship, which allowed me to write surrounded by brilliant colleagues.

The generosity I encountered in the Providence community shaped my vision of the contemporary as a co-temporality, a time shared with countless others. I am indebted to my friends Nicolás Barbosa, Claudia Becerra, Mateo Díaz Choza, Sean McCoy, Regina Pieck, Lowry Pressly, Tess Renker, Miguel Rosas Buendía, Ian Russell, Carolina Tobar, and Carlos Yushimito. Ralph E. Rodriguez turned the COVID-19 pandemic—the latest version of our end times—into a period filled with exciting possibilities. At Harvard University, Mariano Siskind offered invaluable support and conceptual clarity in key moments of the writing process.

My colleagues at Georgetown University's Department of Spanish and Portuguese have supported this book project from the day I met them. I am especially grateful to Molly Borowitz, Emily Francomano, Tania Gentic, Gwen Kirkpatrick, Adam Lifshey, Vivaldo Santos, Alejandro Yarza, and my colleagues in the Linguistics track for offering advice and lending an ear. Sophie Heller was my writing buddy and fellow teller of DC stories. Beyond the department, Ricardo Ortiz has been a coffee companion and a constant source of support. I would not have finished the book in time without a fellowship from the provost's office. I want to thank Elena Silva and Lisa Krim for coordinating a year-long seminar for this fellowship program and for jumpstarting my career at Georgetown. Thanks also go to Carole Sargent for her valuable advice in putting together the prospectus. The book benefited enormously from Sofie Brown's detective work and her keen eye for small details and large ideas.

At Tulane University, I found an engaging community that accompanied the writing of this book. Special thanks go to Idelber Avelar, Sarah Dowman, Christopher Dunn, Borja Gama de Cossío, Antonio Gómez, Enrique Gonzalez-Conty, Yuri Herrera, Alejandro Kelly-Hopfenblatt, Carlos Juan Lozano, Fernando Rivera-Díaz, Pamela Sertzen, and Dale Shuger.

Throughout the years, I presented the arguments of this book in several scholarly venues. A list of the myriad people who helped me refine what I mean by "the contemporary" includes Francisco Álvez Francese, Catalina Arango Correa, Ignacio Azcueta, Sarah Booker, Valeria de los Ríos, Carolyn Fornoff, Gabriel Giorgi, Gisela Heffes, Héctor Hoyos, Jessica E. Jones, Luis Felipe Lomelí, Benjamin Loy, Lucas Mertehikian, Gesine Müller, Matías Oviedo, Luigi Patruno, Julio Premat, Ignacio Sánchez Prado, Emilio Sauri, Alejandra Uslenghi, and Maxwell Woods. This book would not exist without the luminous ideas of Elena Deanda, Donald McColl, and Shawn Stein, who helped me become the scholar I am today.

Thank you to Jorge Coronado and Joshua Shanholtzer for offering a home to this book in a stellar catalog whose authors I admire and consider guiding lights within the field.

Most of these ideas emerged in passionate conversations with Mariajosé Rodríguez Pliego, loving companion and thinker of worlds within this world. As our beloved Leslie Marmon Silko once put it: "storytelling continues throughout one's life." This is only a fragment of a much longer dialogue that I am excited to continue in the years to come.

I dedicate this book to my parents, Marta Rosa Gibelli and Antonio Gerardo Campisi.

Portions of chapter 1 appeared as "El retorno de lo contemporáneo: crisis e historicidad en *El año del desierto* de Pedro Mairal" in *Cuadernos LIRICO* 20 (2019). Chapter 2 draws on "Tiempos extraños: comunidad, supervivencia e imaginación sostenible en *El huésped* de Guadalupe Nettel y *Distancia de rescate* de Samanta Schweblin," which appeared in *A Contracorriente: Una Revista de Estudios Latinoamericanos* 17, no. 2 (Winter 2020): 165–81. Part of chapter 4 was published as "O silêncio das ruínas: cosmopolitismo, posmemoria e historicidade contemporánea en *A resistência* de Julián Fuks," in *Chasqui: Revista de Literatura Latinoamericana* 49, no. 1 (May 2020): 240–56. I want to thank these venues for allowing me to reproduce in the following pages revised and translated versions of these journal articles.

THE
RETURN
OF THE
CONTEMPORARY

THE RETURN
OF THE
CONTEMPORARY

I am only the imaginary contemporary of my own present: contemporary of its languages, its utopias, its systems (i.e., of its fictions), in short, of its mythology or of its philosophy but not of its history, of which I inhabit only the shimmering reflection: the *phantasmagoria*.
—**Roland Barthes**, *Roland Barthes by Roland Barthes*

The idea that a writer should be contemporaneous is itself modern, but I should say it belongs more to journalism than to literature. No real writer ever tried to be contemporary.
—**Jorge Luis Borges,** *Borges on Writing*

It takes just one awful second, I often think, and an entire epoch passes.
—**W. G. Sebald,** *The Rings of Saturn*

A massive weather event hits Argentina at the turn of the millennium, transforming Buenos Aires into a desert and causing time to move backward. The event is called *la intemperie*, a noun without an exact English equivalent that could be translated as "the great outdoors." Argentina ceases to exist and its citizens are left out in the open, without institutions that protect them from the violent attack against the modern social contract. La intemperie is an event characteristic of the twenty-first century, when our different crises (social, economic, political, and environmental) cannot be considered isolated phenomena. Told in Pedro Mairal's 2005 novel *El año del desierto* (The year of the desert), the story of Buenos Aires turned desert embodies the setbacks that Latin American societies experienced following the embrace of neoliberalism, whose origins in Augusto Pinochet's Chile (1973–1990) united the "shock therapy" of economic austerity with a militarized state that used torture and disappearance as technologies of repression.[1] "In 2001 the curtain fell and reality became clear," Mairal remarked about the socioeconomic crisis that shook Argentina after the neoliberal reforms of the previous decade. "We had lived under the illusion that we were in the first world. The stories of deterioration accelerated. Everything ended up breaking down."[2] While the novel's protagonist travels to the past and loses her rights as a human being and a woman, Mairal rewrites the most important landmarks of Latin American literature to make sense of a rapidly deteriorating present and the vanishing of a future. *El año del desierto* represents how Latin American novels of the twenty-first century conceive the contemporary as a paradoxical temporality. While social time harkens back to the origins of humanity, writers work with the ruins of modern history and literature to imagine alternatives to our neoliberal end times.

In this book I analyze a series of turn-of-the-twenty-first-century Latin American novels that enable us to frame the continuous search for names, aesthetic genres, and temporal models upon which our era is built. Although it seems evident that literature has always been contemporary with its times, it is essential to acknowledge that, beginning some decades ago (a critical moment that scholars have traced to the end of the Cold War and the turn of the millennium), the grand narratives of modernity have perished along with the notion of a stable future. Meanwhile, postmodernism still gave in to the category of the modern. The postmodern strategies of pastiche, citation, or reevaluation of the past have become inoperative in representing our era of apocalyptic catastrophes. Although postmodernists denounced literature's implication with power through narrative self-consciousness, their critique of representation still promoted the reader's moral and political indifference toward the value of truth.[3]

More than a style or the death of style as such, the contemporary is a renewed inclination toward the present, a need to formulate the question about what it means to live under conditions of global emergency at a time when humanity has jeopardized its survival as a species. That contemporaneity is the privileged mode of twenty-first-century aesthetic searches is not to say that these searches reproduce the contingency or temporal homogeneity promoted in societies under neoliberalism. It means, on the contrary, that writers respond to neoliberal conditions by proposing new temporal orientations. The return to the past is the most distinct aesthetic and political device of the literatures of the present; authors work with remains, material traces, and residual objects to weave new filiations and invent original genealogies after the arrival of the end times. Introducing fractures in the linear conception of time, the contemporary is also co-temporality, the coexistence of various times and places, and the possibility of a collective dwelling in the face of an unprecedented temporal crisis.

In this book I address the question of what it means to be contemporary when the present is felt like a succession of apocalyptic catastrophes. I consider the contemporary to be a time of impassioned reflection concerning our current moment of crisis and I track the different ways in which Latin American writers are resisting the neoliberal present through post-national returns to the foundation of modern nation-states, ecocritical returns to the sustainable knowledge of Indigenous communities, archival returns to the sites of slavery and the cultural practices of Afro-Latin Americans, traumatic or post-traumatic returns to the last state-sponsored military dictatorships, and post-historical returns to a time when it was still possible to build utopian visions of the future. These aesthetic and political returns show us that modernity, understood as progress or telos, is no longer helpful when we are describing the essence of the contemporary world and its models of time. For these Latin American writers, returning to the past serves as a strategy of resistance to the generalized and omnipresent sense of crisis that shuts down all possibilities of critical thinking and utopian desires of change. Some of the twenty-first-century novelists I examine in this book put forward archeological returns to the past to cast the present against the grain, understanding that it is through anachronism that we can arrive at an antidote to the tyrannical here and now of neoliberal societies.[4] Other novels plunge into the future and return to the present with invaluable information about what our world can become or with the desire to create something new when history appears to have ended.

The present that these fictions oppose is traversed by the main symptoms of the contemporary crisis of time: presentism, temporal acceleration, programmed obsolescence, amnesia, and the mediatization of culture. François Hartog coined the term "presentism" to refer to this time of memory and debt, daily forgetfulness, uncertainty, and simulacra that is dictated by life under late-stage capitalism.[5] Unlike the futurism that characterized the political projects and artistic expressions throughout much of the twentieth century, presentism is aligned with the feeling that, no matter how hard we try project ourselves into the future or immerse ourselves in the past, there is no way to flee the confines of the present. According to Paolo Virno, the world today is unfolding under the sign of déjà vu: no activities are worthwhile because they all seem to have been extracted from a script that is familiar to the point of exhaustion.[6] The present turns in on itself and surrenders to the reign of the immediate, the fleeting, and the ephemeral, to the rapid obsolescence of technological artifacts and the tyranny of neoliberal time. On the other hand, these writers are creating untimely presents: presents overloaded with time that—by shattering the chronological order, gathering scattered fragments, and exposing the noncontemporary—turn the aesthetic form into a logbook of unprecedented orientations, where it becomes possible to lament melancholically over what has been lost or to restore forgotten trajectories, which transform the present into a material that can be transmitted to new generations.[7]

How are Latin American writers resisting the time out of time of contemporary societies? In the chapters of this book I approach the question of the contemporary from the aesthetic, temporal, and sociopolitical imaginaries through which Latin American authors are narrating our neoliberal end times: socioeconomic meltdown, ecological apocalypse, memory or postmemory, the cosmopolitanism of migrants and political exiles, and the failed emancipation of Black Latin Americans. In each chapter I examine the work of two authors from different parts of the region. Through their mutual dialogue I demonstrate that the contemporary is a battle over this century's historical identity, which becomes visible when the voices of a multiplicity of actors are heard on a global scale or, in this case, on a hemispheric one. I examine works by Pedro Mairal, Rita Indiana Hernández, Samanta Schweblin, Guadalupe Nettel, Juan Cárdenas, Itamar Vieira Junior, Julián Fuks, Verónica Gerber Bicecci, Valeria Luiselli, and Alejandro Zambra. These authors use the strategy of temporal return as the privileged device to open historical becoming to the possibility of conceiving other worlds and other circulations of meaning. Returning does not mean repeating specific moments of the past but, rather, producing a brief appearance that brings with it the promise of a different future—a future that is always on the verge of ensuing. Returning is, in other words, a way of politicizing the present, an aesthetic and political mechanism to combat the advent of the end times and the sense of impotence that neoliberal measures have brought as an intrinsic part of their structure of feeling.

These writers bring to light issues linked to the effects of Latin America's inscription on the global economy. The type of crisis that emerges in these turn-of-the-century novels such as economic recession or global warming replaced the post-dictatorship testimonial poetics, which focused on the restitution of justice, the battle against oblivion, and human rights abuses. The unstable formal conditions of these works are a direct response to the neoliberal precariousness of Latin American societies, in which large sectors of the population fell into unemployment and were left out of social protection networks. Unlike the totalizing ambition of post-dictatorship cultural production or long-range aesthetic projects such as Roberto Bolaño's, the works of these writers are short novels or novellas that are inserted into a literary market opened by authors such as César Aira and Mario Bellatin since the 1980s. For instance, the novels of Alejandro Zambra and Valeria Luiselli contradict and correct themselves as they go along, reflecting the experience of the present as a precarious and transitional period. A sense of erasure prevails in relation to their aesthetic procedures and to the interchangeable names of their characters. As one of the characters in Alejandro Zambra's *Bonsái* (2006; trans. 2008 as *Bonsai*) says about the novel of the same title that he is writing: "Practically nothing happens in *Bonsai*. There's enough plot for a two-page story, and maybe not even a good one."[8] The creation of a pruning procedure gives rise to works in which not a single word seems to be left over, whose precarious texture summons us to meditate urgently on the contemporary and the worlds to come. These are literatures that, like the temporal models of the new millennium, are in a state of sketch, calling the reading public to move the words from one side to the other, as if they alone could not account for the time out of time of present-day societies.

These aesthetic-political concerns also appear in Anglophone novels by authors such as Tom McCarthy and Ben Lerner. These novels are populated by precarious characters who walk through big cities in search of moments of communion with other citizens and with forgotten voices from the past and who continually question the possibility of having "a profound experience of art" amid the omnipresent crisis of the contemporary world.[9] U., the narrator of McCarthy's *Satin Island*, is an ethnographer who works for a corporation on a tentacular project (a Big Report on our times) that compiles all the information available on the web about every aspect of contemporary life. Immersed in a 24/7 temporality and surrounded by screens, U.—a figure of return whose name implicitly refers to the reader (you) and the U-turn—develops his own field of study, the anthropology of the contemporary. He seeks to dissociate the notion of epoch from the traditional division between historical periods and return it to its original meaning: "a place from which one looks at things."[10] The same stance of distancing from the contemporary appears in Lerner's *The Topeka School*, a novel that returns to the 1990s, in which he weaves a prehistory of the present of Donald Trump's presidency. Against the backdrop of global warming, post-truth politics, and xenophobic and racist policies against migrants, Lerner delineates the discourse on the end of history as a fantasy of white liberal technocrats. Literary practice becomes a search for temporal models that resist the irreversible race of progress and the teleological conception of history, because, as one of the characters says, "history [is] not over but paused."[11]

Similarly, the novelists I analyze in this book create aesthetic devices to capture the present and open future horizons when causal relations between temporal orders have become excessively blurred. Unlike these works of world literature, however, these fictions pose their version of the crisis and form a communal map of Latin America, where neoliberal measures of privatization, free-market capitalism, and austerity have led with a great impetus to a decomposition of the social fabric. These authors imagine Latin America as a web of continental concerns about large-scale extractivism, the battle of the feminist movement against patriarchy, and the void that the new generations feel in relation to a violent past they did not experience and which therefore never ceases to pass.

In the first decades of the twenty-first century, Latin American litera-ture has become fertile ground for dialogues and critical interventions be-tween authors from different parts of the continent that would lose much of their symbolic force if they were analyzed from a national or subconti-nental perspective. After all, critical vocabularies are formed collectively, as is reflected in several of the terms that appear repeatedly throughout this study: intemperie (meaning "to be out in the open, at the mercy of the elements"), "secondary characters," and "literature of the children." These visions show the dialogic matrix of the contemporary moment and the at-tempts made by Latin American authors to draw a collective map of our situation of global crisis or emergency. The recent critical adoption of the concept of world literature in the field of Latin Americanism is indicative of the interest in forming a transnational canon that transcends Cold War geopolitical binarism and center–periphery relations.[12] I will not overlook that many of the dialogues between these Latin American authors come from the circuits established by the cultural field: book fairs, independent publishers, literary magazines, and creative writing workshops. However, the focus of this book will be on temporal imaginaries and the existence of various contemporaneities lying at the heart of the contemporary. In this sense, as Terry Smith points out, *con tempus* refers to the multiplicity of relations between being and time that exist in the same historical period, so that the contemporary, under our current geopolitical conditions, must be thought of as a series of simultaneous temporalities.[13] Besides inhabiting the same epoch, these writers share a distrust of a homogeneous temporal-ity marked by the global circuits of capital: the diachronic temporality of progress as accumulation and improvement.

LITERATURE IN THE EXPANDED FIELD

One of the decisive characteristics of the literatures of the present is their capacity to cross the borders between aesthetic fields and posit a third space that conceives the literary as an interdisciplinary practice.[14] It is a matter of knotting a new "in-between" and enabling other forms of hearing and visi-bility of the common that make the contemporary a time of collective par-ticipation in the reconfiguration of the public scene.[15] By incorporating var-ious aesthetic fields into their making, these writers aim to build a collective present at a time when acceleration, discontinuity, and fetishistic obsession with the past prevent the critical elaboration of a shared experience. These novels travel along the edges of generic conventions to confront a time when our historical experience has been suspended. In this sense, the tendency of these Latin American authors to use procedures of contemporary art gives way to open-ended works that, instead of promoting passive contemplation on the part of the reader spectators, summon them to collaborate actively in the construction of meaning. While rejoicing in the assembly of formats coming from diverse arts and in the conversation with figures of the artistic tradition, these writers destabilize the position of the authorial subject to activate a collective presence that, through its impersonal character, counteracts the neoliberal exaltation of the individual self.

Mexican writer Verónica Gerber Bicecci describes herself as a "visual artist who writes." In *Conjunto vacío* (2015; trans. 2018 as *Empty Set*), her first novel, she introduces Venn diagrams and visual schemes to refer to the formation of emotional ties between the children of political exiles of the Southern Cone's last dictatorial regimes. When the characters in *Conjunto vacío* visit a contemporary art museum, the narrator does not limit herself to duplicating in writing the abstract artworks of Ulises Carrión, Mirtha Dermisache, or Marcel Broodthaers but, rather, draws her own version of the paintings on display, blurring the boundaries between original and copy, between literature and the plastic arts. Like the trajectory of the artists whom she analyzes in the essays of *Mudanza*, Gerber Bicecci inscribes literature in the realm of words and the "expanded field" of actions, propitiating a displacement "from page to body, from word to space, to place; from sentence to event, to action; from novel to staged life."[16] In Julián Fuks's *A resistência* (2015; trans. 2019 as *Resistance*), the narrator visits museums of memory and carefully examines photographs and identity cards of disappeared persons. For Fuks, the active contemplation of these photographs becomes fundamental in the exercise of questioning the supposed neutrality of the representational technologies of the last military dictatorship in Argentina, which conceal the state's responsibility for the disappearance of citizens and show that photography helped to legitimize the structures of military power. Other novels, such as Rita Indiana's *La mucama de Omicunlé* (2015; trans. 2018 as *Tentacle*), narrate the formation of aesthetic projects in which literature intersects with conceptual art, participatory art, and electronic music. One of the characters in *La mucama de Omicunlé* is a DJ who delineates the writer as a collector of common production and a programmer of the artistic tradition.

In this sense, most of these works respond directly to theorizations of the contemporary arts, such as those of French curator Nicolas Bourriaud. Bourriaud has coined a series of terms that account for these shifts in turn-of-the-century aesthetic practices: "relational aesthetics," "postproduction," "exform," and "radicant." The concept of relational aesthetics points to the need to reflect on the artistic manifestations of a present characterized by the fall of the modern project of emancipation and the urgency to propose new models of "possible universes."[17] The exform conceives aesthetics as "the site where border negotiations unfold between what is rejected and what is admitted, products and waste."[18] Whereas postproduction reconfigures the idea of tradition no longer as "a museum containing works that must be cited or 'surpassed,'" radicant aesthetics sets "one's roots in motion, staging them in heterogeneous contexts and formats."[19] The term "altermodernity" encompasses all the above. Bourriaud defines altermodernity as a period in which thinkers acknowledge that modernization has become inseparable from colonial and imperial enterprises.[20] Mairal's *El año del desierto*, for example, rewinds Argentinean history and rewrites the fundamental milestones of its literary tradition within the framework of the precarious economies and barter clubs that emerged after the 2001 crisis, making the writer a "semionaut" who invents "protocols of use for all existing modes of representation and all formal structures."[21] In Samanta Schweblin's *Distancia de rescate* (2014; trans. 2017 as *Fever Dream*), the characters' conversation in the context of pesticide poisoning questions the readers and establishes an "unlimited discussion" that gives rise to "the collective elaboration of meaning."[22]

Other contemporary works expand the book into different formats. These works take to the streets, reconfigure public space, situate themselves in the museum, and establish democratic ties with other institutions (the factory, the publishing house, the theater). *La historia de mis dientes* (2013; trans. 2015 as *The Story of My Teeth*) by Valeria Luiselli—one of the authors whose work I study in the following pages—belongs to the format that Lionel Ruffel has called "exhibited literature," which transcends the modern paradigm of the book and produces new interventions within the cultural industry. In the contemporary moment, according to Ruffel, publishing has become both an action and a practice, returning the word to its original meaning: "making public."[23] *La historia de mis dientes* was commissioned by the Fundación/Colección Jumex for the catalog of an exhibition entitled "The Hunter and the Factory" (by curators Magalí Arriola and Juan Gaitán). The writing of the novel followed a specific procedure. Under the pseudonym Gustavo Sánchez Sánchez, which is also the name of the novel's protagonist, Luiselli sent the chapters to a reading group made up of workers at the Jumex juice factory (located in the municipality of Ecatepec de Morelos). The workers provided Luiselli with ideas for writing the next installment and photographs that were part of the novel's final section. The first version of the work appeared in the bilingual Spanish-English exhibition catalog under the title "La historia contemporánea de mis dientes y algunas parabólicas sin moraleja" ("The Contemporary Story of My Teeth and Some Parabolas without a Moral") and only later in book form (published by Sexto Piso in Mexico and Spain). However, the book as a format also becomes an unstable object, since the English version of the novel, translated by Christina MacSweeney, presents several differences with the two Spanish editions. Among them, there is a change in the quotations that precede each chapter and in the characters' names—references to well-known figures of the Mexican and world literary tradition.

Through these points of contact between art and literature, aesthetics and politics, in this book I trace how twenty-first-century writers are devising strategies of resistance to the referential void that materialized after the fall of genealogies and grand narratives. It is no coincidence that the contemporary as an aesthetic category—a marker of contemporary art museums—emerged following the Second World War. During the war, humanity witnessed events that forever altered the traditional conception of the work of art as a critique of the outrages of capitalism and a vehicle for utopian change. History was no longer a process directed toward the emancipation of human societies.[24]

In the post-1945 world, the new generations had to appropriate the traumatic history of their ancestors to access a legacy they inherited incompletely. This predicament was similar to the one faced by the children of the disappeared and political exiles after the last South American dictatorships. Contemporary artists have become increasingly aware of their limitations in effecting radical changes in the social fabric, which does not mean that their works have ceased to serve as a platform for reflection on the ontology of the present. Andrea Giunta points out that contemporary art has begun to return to the past critically, not as a "naïve, pastiche operation" but as "a return that involves criticizing postwar society and convoking new publics."[25] This attempt to appeal to a more significant number of people is at the core of the notion of an expanded field. Like participatory aesthetics, as theorized by Claire Bishop, contemporary artists "engage in dialogue and creative negotiation with other people: technicians, fabricators, curators, public bodies, other artists, intellectuals, participants, and so on."[26] The elaboration of the present is the domain of a set of actors: the contemporary becomes a world of contrasts, contradictions, and antinomies that cannot be described by universal generalizations.[27] These novels of the expanded field remind us that there is no longer a single contemporaneity but various simultaneous ones.

LITERATURES OF THE PRESENT

I argue that the historicity of the literatures of the present is to be found in anachronisms and nonlinear temporalities. The notion of "timeliness" that contemporary writers work with is not equivalent to the presentism prevailing under capitalist conditions, as in the fashion industry's cycles of novelty and obsolescence. Paradoxically, literature becomes contemporary by returning to specific moments, artifacts, or figures that demand their place in our present. These novels are prophecies in reverse, because insofar as they make it possible to illuminate the blind spots of our inheritance they open

11

possibilities for transmitting part of a lost heritage. The contemporary is a historical investigation into the different temporalities that are part and parcel of our time. Like any question about the links between past and present, the contemporary derives from a discontinuous and asynchronous notion of history. As opposed to chronological conceptions of time, the question of the contemporary assumes the coexistence of different temporalities in any given historical moment: a condition that distinguishes each present from other present moments of the past and that summons critics, historians, and thinkers from various disciplines to unravel these temporal orders.[28] The contemporary implies the development of a historical consciousness about events, places, and figures that haunt the present and destabilize it. These events include the acts of barbarism at the heart of Latin American nation-building projects and the conception of land as *terra nullius*, which served as justification for neoextractivism. Instead of undertaking returns that foreclose our capacity to act, Latin American authors capture the energies that coexist within the contemporary: anachronism, heterochrony, and survival of the past. In the face of a future that is increasingly closed in on itself, contemporary writers establish new circulations of meaning, form a historical consciousness of our times, and participate in the collective elaboration of the present.

Just as these authors imagine literatures in the plural, in the following study I insist that, if the contemporary is to be conceived as a montage of latencies and discontinuities, then history must be considered a choral discipline representing events in their plurality. This notion of historical knowledge as a site of temporal complexity comes from the work of Reinhart Koselleck, for whom historical episodes accumulate at different speeds and form temporal sediments, never a singular history. Koselleck contests the tendency of historians to create teleological versions of history and to draw a picture of time inherited from the Enlightenment: the model of a single history, history as an arrow pointing forward or as *magistra vitae* (a lesson for the future). In contrast, Koselleck argues for finding "possible histories" at the center of historical becoming and conceiving "a multilayered theory of time."[29] The authors studied here resist the presentism of contemporary societies by capturing a plurality of histories. In some novels they bring to the fore anonymous lives and secondary characters. In others they uncover minor events, temporal imaginaries, and memory sites located on the flipside of the neoliberal present. In most of them, they juxtapose heterogeneous temporalities that break away from traditional notions of linearity and teleology. Representations of grand narratives have given way to portraits of anonymous lives, buried histories, and the minute details of everyday life. Writers weave filiations with forgotten artists, not with influential figures. These are some of the strategies through which Latin

American authors at the beginning of the new century imagine alternative presents, glimpsing in the montage of genealogical causalities the emergence of other histories and other possible kinds of literature.

I will outline three facets of the work with temporality carried out by these novelists: (1) the debates about our neoliberal end times, (2) the deliberate use of anachronism, and (3) the question of what is contemporary. The concept of the end times captures the difficulties that contemporary writers face when situating the present in continuity with past and future eras. As a result of the inadequacy of linear history and representational forms, these authors resort to anachronism and return to the past to slow down history and open up the possibility of extracting knowledge from it. In this way, they reconfigure debates about what is contemporary in societies where the present follows the dynamics of capital and the rhythms of nonstop productivity.

NEOLIBERAL END TIMES

Neoliberalism is traditionally defined as "a political order" that champions economic measures such as free trade, deregulation, and the privatization of state institutions.[30] Historians have traced its origins back to the interwar years in Vienna, where two economists—Friedrich Hayek and Ludwig von Mises—advocated for the freedom of market forces to develop without regulatory control.[31] Latin American histories of neoliberalism begin with the work of the economists who studied at the University of Chicago under Hayek and Milton Friedman, known popularly as the Chicago Boys. Friedman and his disciples would go on to shape the economic program of Augusto Pinochet's military dictatorship, which ruled in Chile from 1973 to 1990 and applied a "shock treatment" that left Chileans scrambling to adjust to a profoundly unequal capitalist model.[32] Latin America thus became a laboratory of neoliberal policies whose consequences continue to be felt today, especially in Chile, where the constitution promulgated by the Pinochet regime in 1980 is still in effect despite recent attempts by the people to rewrite its fundamental clauses.[33] Following massive protests in 2019, Chileans voted to draft a new constitution to undo the neoliberal measures of the Pinochet regime and to acknowledge the rights of people who are invisible to the state.

In Latin America, free market capitalism and the repressive techniques of dictatorships went hand in hand, so long as we understand both as analogous forms of shock therapy that dispossessed citizens of their human rights. The rise of neoliberalism came with full force in the 1990s, after the fall of the Berlin Wall and the opening of former communist nations to the reign of capitalist economics. It did not matter that dictatorships like Pinochet's were no longer in power. Both Chile's problematic transition to democracy (with the first democratic government partly made up of former Pinochet officials) and Argentina's embrace of corporate politics (followed by the pardons granted by President Carlos Saúl Menem to former military commanders) confirmed that previous forms of economic and political violence continued under the sign of the neoliberal market. In Mexico, the Zapatista uprising in the Lacandon jungle of Chiapas, in response to the passing of the 1994 North American Free Trade Agreement (NAFTA), became a symbol of resistance to the empty promises of neoliberalism and globalization. It remains to be seen whether the neoliberal order has come to an end with the Great Recession of 2007–2008, the rise of new right-wing politicians such as Bolsonaro and Trump, or the onset of the COVID-19 pandemic and its confirmation that governments are the only institutions capable of mitigating our socioeconomic and epidemiological crises.[34]

In this book I conceive the neoliberal era as a historical period characterized by a series of returns and setbacks in the modern conception of time as progress.[35] Instead of taking 1989 as the historical marker of our globalized era, I take the year 2001, considering that, in Latin America, this was a year in which the dreams of economic freedom, social mobility, and cultural exchange symbolized by globalization crumbled through the advent of a temporality of crisis.[36] In Argentina, the 2001 economic meltdown meant that large swaths of the population fell into unemployment or underemployment. The turn of the millennium marked our realization of the emergence of a planetary temporality: the time of the Anthropocene.[37] Suddenly, stories of dispossession surfaced in the press, returning us to a time before the nation-state was defined as the guarantor of collective futures. I take my cue from Mary Louise Pratt, who refers to these recycled archives through the notion of "demodernization": the spectral reemergence of the narratives of the castaway, the captive, and the slave ship, not as "dramas of triumphal homecoming but [as] tragedies of no return."[38] Demodernization results from neoliberalism's erosion of education, health care, and transportation systems due to austerity and privatization measures. The nation-state stops being an inclusive actor since its democratic networks do not apply equally to all citizens. As a response to these setbacks that deprived people of their most basic human rights, I argue that post-2001 Latin American novels use the strategy of temporal return to politicize the twenty-first-century present, exploring the roots of these interlocking crises in the long-term temporality of environmental devastation and the short-term temporality of dictatorial violence.

In the first part I explore neoliberal rationality's roots in modern nation-building projects, which failed to create policies of belonging and inclusivity. I am inspired by the temporal setbacks of novels such as Mairal's *El año del desierto*, which narrates the 2001 socioeconomic crisis by rewinding the nation's history from the present to the colonial era, its female protagonist growing old while losing her constitutional rights. The novelist stages the temporality of neoliberal reversal through the erosion of the democratic networks of the nation-state, the transformation of the individual into an entrepreneur (or *homo economicus*) and of the proletariat into the precariat.[39]

However, by rewriting important milestones of Argentinean history and culture in light of the temporality of crisis, Mairal posits the strategy of return as a recycling of the collective dreams of emancipation, opening the present to a new sense of futurity. Other writers share this critical strategy by throwing into relief the conditions of social inequality amplified during the neoliberal era, such as the persisting bonds of slavery suffered by Black farmworkers or the commodification of women's bodies in parallel with the exploitation of natural landscapes. Instead of merely pointing out the continuities between the colonial era, the nineteenth-century past, and the neoliberal present, Latin American writers combine different periods in a non-hierarchical manner to create a new image of history. In this way, their narrative art is influenced by the temporal elasticity of Afro-diasporic religious practices and the emergence of alternative systems to capitalism such as recycling and barter economies.

The second part is centered on the last military dictatorships' lingering effects on the generation of writers who grew up during this period or following their country's transition to democracy. By foregrounding the figure of children who came of age during times of social, political, and environmental unrest, these authors explore the role of memory in second-generation exiles or the sons and daughters of political activists. I argue that the writers of this new generation use the figure of children to appropriate the traumatic history of their predecessors and to access an incomplete past. The narrator of Julián Fuks's *A resistência* grew up in Brazil because his parents managed to escape Argentina's dictatorial regime. He asks himself whether he inherited their exile and can also be called a political refugee. Inheritance also comes to the fore in a chapter about the notion of literature after the end of history. Instead of giving in to the depoliticized temporality of the end of history, which heralded worldwide acceptance of liberal democracy and market economy following the demise of communism, I argue that the writers in this group represent the past not as a mere repetition but as a critical rearrangement that showcases its gaps and absences.

The concept of return underscores the combination of heterogeneous temporalities as a literary strategy that is necessary for critically elaborating the present. As a direct response to the reemergence of repressed moments in the continent's history (what Pratt calls the return of the monsters), Latin American writers travel back in time in order to understand the incompleteness of the present and the waning of the future, to make sense of the crisis of historical transmission, and to fill in the gaps of a partial inheritance.[40] In doing so, they reformulate the temporal models of literature in the new century. As citizens of Latin American countries during neoliberalism's attack on the modern social contract, the writers discussed here perceive themselves as orphans of history and victims of the temporal dispossession of contemporary societies, which according to Jacques Rancière, create "a hierarchy of temporalities . . . [a] distance between those who live in the time of knowledge that delivers justice and those who live in the time of ignorance and error."[41] By combining short-term and long-term temporalities, these writers reveal an unconscious of the contemporary and posit the manipulation of time as the only hermeneutical tool that can undermine the highly unequal world created in the wake of neoliberalism.

IN PRAISE ON ANACHRONISM

Hannah Arendt's *Between Past and Future* (1954) is a fundamental book for the prehistory of the contemporary. Arendt's book inaugurated the post-1945 present as a period of in-betweenness—a gap between past and future that throws individuals into a battlefield between antagonistic forces. Drawing on an aphorism by René Char ("Our inheritance was left to us by no testament"), Arendt examines the wasted possibilities of the French Resistance to establish a "public space" in which freedom predominated, a "treasure" that members of these movements had discovered and possessed for a brief period but did not know how to pass on to new generations.[42] Arendt reflected on the European postwar present through a parable by Kafka, "He," which tells the story of a man who feels threatened by two enemies: a past that has not lost its relevance and a future that unfolds before him an infinite range of possibilities and expectations. In Kafka's parable, becoming "an umpire" of the present would consist of extracting from the gap a latent truth, creating the conditions of possibility for thinking about the contemporary.

Since the turn of the century, contemporaneity has come to be experienced as a multiplicity of simultaneous times. French theorist Georges Didi-Huberman has developed a philosophy of heterochrony and anachronism to think about art history in a nonlinear manner.[43] In his works he pays attention to the assemblages of heterogeneous temporalities constituting all images since these "are bearers of survivals . . . essentially montages of heterogeneous meanings and temporalities."[44] Didi-Huberman dismisses the debates on the end of history and the end of art—which, according to him, "are crude and ill-conceived"—since they follow synchronic and non-dialectical temporal models, overlooking the cracks, the dislocations, and the interstices in which images are inserted.[45] In other words, these debates disregard the idea that an artist can set himself up against his own epoch through temporal manipulations that seek to reveal "an unconscious of history."[46]

In *The Surviving Image* (2018), Didi-Huberman exemplifies this anachronistic art historical model through the work of Aby Warburg, who, in his *Mnemosyne Atlas*, complexified the temporality of images via a conception of history as survival (*Nachleben*). The Atlas was a constellation of images of Antiquity randomly arranged by Warburg to activate the imagination and perception of viewers, an encyclopedic project based on an impure model of time and images. This project made any attempt at periodization impossible and deconstructed linear history by blurring the boundaries between before and after.[47] Through a reading of Warburg's *Mnemosyne Atlas* vis-à-vis Walter Benjamin's theories on the dialectical image, Didi-Huberman derives a philosophy of history in which the artist is in charge of revealing the discontinuities of historical discourse, of producing a model of time as a hieroglyphic with layers of archaeological density, and above all, of creating an interval in which the latencies, residues, and impurities of historical time can be perceived. The notion of return that I use in this book owes much to what Didi-Huberman calls "the tempo of the *revenances*," the temporality of "ideas which return, except that they never return completely, a circumstance which constantly incites him to make renewed attempts."[48] Instead of reproducing the presentist obsession of contemporary societies, the novels I study in the following pages work with dialectical images that engage readers in the search for future perspectives when a sense of apathy characteristic of the post-historical era still prevails.[49]

In Latin America, Josefina Ludmer has insistently considered contemporary literature a sphere replete with anachronisms and temporal cracks. In *Aquí América Latina* (2010) she interrogates in depth the methodological resources that literary critics have at their disposal to produce histories of contemporary literature. Attentive to the need to adopt dialectical paradigms of history in an era of presentist organization, Ludmer chooses the model of speculation because, faced with a "new world" that forces us to change "the molds, genres, and species" we use to apprehend it, this model offers us access to "the factory of reality."[50] The neologism "realidadficción" (reality fiction) that Ludmer uses throughout the book conveys the interweaving between the public and private spheres, literary and aesthetic genres, and categories such as author and style. For Ludmer, this intertwining between different orders constitutes a "cognitive map" of the contemporary.[51]

Despite reflecting extensively on the notion of post-autonomous literatures, critics have neglected Ludmer's insights in the first section of her book, where she deals with the question of temporal perception in times of crisis. In "Buenos Aires año 2000: el diario sabático," Ludmer traces the symptoms of temporal disorientation and the mutations of the cultural landscape after the failure of the neoliberal modernizations that defined the 1990s throughout the continent and particularly in Argentina: a sense of "temporal lacuna," of "the beginning of the end," as "the present is memory and déjà vu: a duplication of the past."[52] Ludmer's encounters with a group of Argentinean writers convince her that, in the face of this apocalyptic panorama of presentism, museification of memory, and de-temporalization of the present, literature has the necessary tools to think against the grain, return to the past, and ensure the transmission of a heritage that was experienced as a void. These conceptions of a paradoxical, outdated, and untimely contemporaneity are at the heart of the strategies of critical return that I propose in my reading of the literatures of the present.

NEW JOURNEYS TO THE SEED

The writers studied here are not the first to return to critical moments in Latin American history and literature in order to confront the archive's voids and absences. They are not even the first to describe themselves as orphans of the literary tradition.[53] In *Myth and Archive* (1990), Roberto González Echevarría examined the modern Latin American novel's recycling of the continent's foundational narratives. According to him, novelists such as Alejo Carpentier and Gabriel García Márquez disassembled the scientific constructs culled in the nineteenth century and the colonial period to create "a form of the beginning," a new starting point for the Latin American novel. "The Archive is an image of the end of time. . . . The Archive is apocalyptic, it is like a time capsule launched into infinity, but without the hope of reaching eternity."[54]

González Echevarría's definition of the archive resonates with the task facing contemporary writers after the end of the modern understanding of history as progress or telos. For these authors, contemporaneity derives from their attempts to reconstruct history after the end of historicity and the fall of modernity's grand narratives. As opposed to the modern Latin American novel, contemporary works do not feature "oracular figures" or "living archives," either because these figures have perished alongside modernity's utopian discourses (think of the victims of the last military dictatorships who cannot testify to political catastrophe) or because these works attempt to make sense of large-scale phenomena such as climate change.[55] More than an archivist, the writer becomes a figure of the bricoleur, the DJ, or the pirate who traffics with heterogeneous sources from the literary tradition and recycles discontinuous moments of the continent's past.

Latin American writers conjure the region's forgotten past through the figure of the specter. Spectrality plays a central part in discussions of the contemporary because, according to Ruffel, it questions linear history and conceives the present as "a resurgence of the past of the *longue durée*."[56] María del Pilar Blanco argues that haunting is not always linked to the logic of trauma and mourning but, more extensively, to the "anxiety surrounding the possible shape and location of the events of an *after*-life."[57] Contemporary novelists depict an extended present haunted by various repressed moments from Latin American history, including the colonial period, the nation-building past, and the recent military dictatorships. Some works, such as Schweblin's *Distancia de rescate*, return to many of these periods simultaneously: the present of environmental contamination brings back the past of demographic whitening and the Mothers of Plaza de Mayo's searching for their disappeared children during the last dictatorship. Sometimes, narrative strategies evoke Carpentier's 1944 short story "Viaje a la semilla," which adopts a regressive structure to contrast the chronological time of white Europeans with the mythical time of Afro-Cuban religions.

By embracing the end of modernity's grand narratives and conceiving history as incomplete, writers conjure suppressed historical moments and activate political possibilities that have remained dormant in the past. Other contemporary works, such as Valeria Luiselli's *Los ingrávidos* (2011; trans. 2014 as *Faces in the Crowd*) search for the ghosts of the avant-garde in order to find minor cultural materials and forgotten artistic trajectories, blurring the boundaries between original and copy. These aesthetic returns seek to combat the condition that Borges described in "La biblioteca de Babel" (1941) as the burden of written culture: "The certitude that everything has been written negates us or turns us into phantoms."[58] For these writers, being contemporary means finding collaborators among history's silent witnesses, conjuring their shadows to create a new ethics of representation: although it is impossible to fully depict this repressed history, it is the writer's task to show how it continues to haunt our twenty-first-century present.

Insofar as they return to foundational moments in the continent's history, these writers seek to express their discontent with the status quo rather than to escape the confines of the neoliberal present. Although we live in a culture in which the hypertrophy of memory produces nostalgic pictures of the past, I argue that literature can revisit history as an active rebuttal of market-driven discourses hailing the promises of the future. As Svetlana Boym demonstrates when setting the opposition between restorative and reflective nostalgia, there are ways of returning to the past that foreclose its multiple meanings (which she links to nationalist returns to the homeland) and others that capture its cracks and imperfections. "Restorative nostalgia manifests itself in total reconstructions of monuments of the past," Boym observes, "while reflective nostalgia lingers on ruins, the patina of time and history, in the dreams of another place and another time."[59] Latin American writers assemble fragmentary constellations to point to the discontinuities between past and present and make history susceptible to further elaboration. The narrator of Luiselli's *Los ingrávidos* explains the novel's fragmentary and ghostly structure: "What's happening is that you can remember the future too."[60] The rest of the authors I study share this belief in the capacity of memory discourses to rescue the past and imagine a different future, conjugating the previous century's obsession with the future and our fixation with the past to reformulate the needs of the present.[61]

In addition to conjuring the figure of the specter, these writers turn to the metaphor of plants to find new foundational roots for history and literature in the new century. As Lesley Wylie observes, plants have played a significant role in Latin American culture so long as they "articulate submerged histories, often at variance with those expressed by the central narrative." Patrícia Vieira also highlights the need to hear plants speak through their inscription in cultural texts, a practice she calls *phytographia* or the "encounter between writings on plants and the writing *of* plants."[62] Some contemporary novels dramatize the foundational violence of Latin American nations through emblematic plants like the *ombú* in Argentina and the ceiba in the Dominican Republic. Mairal's *El año del desierto* and Indiana's *La mucama de Omicunlé* travel back to the roots of the modern nation to reveal the erasure of Black and Indigenous cultural histories. The plant horror in Schweblin's *Distancia de rescate* shows that the agricultural model based on soybean production has not brought progress and modernization for the Argentine countryside as the foundational fathers envisioned but, rather, regressions to the premodern past. Juan Cárdenas's *Elástico de sombra* (Shadow games, 2020) and Itamar Vieira Junior's *Torto arado* (2019; trans. 2023 as *Crooked Plow*) are plantation novels that link the act of writing with knotting, invoking the origins of storytelling in women's oral narratives and calling readers to unravel the nation's memory knots.

Other works foreground the portable plants of the globalized world, such as the bonsai in Zambra's eponymous novel and an unnamed dry tree in Luiselli's *Los ingrávidos*. As Cristina Rivera Garza observes in *Autobiografía del algodón* (2020), which mixes her family's past in the United States–Mexico borderlands with the *longue durée* of the cotton plantations in the Mexican state of Tamaulipas where her ancestors once worked: "A book is a form of return: a refamiliarization and a reparation."[63] Contemporary writers take up the call to narrate the present in the deep time of the planet's history or across the artificial borders of modern nation-states. They conceive nonlinear histories of Latin American nations, restoring the broken continuity between past and present in times of generalized oblivion and forgetfulness.

WHAT IS THE CONTEMPORARY?

After all, what do we talk about when we talk about the contemporary? Critics have approached the concept from multiple perspectives that account for the temporal models of twenty-first-century literature. Julio Premat has written extensively on the subject, focusing on narrative beginnings and the question of origins as well as on the outdatedness, anachronisms, and resistances of contemporary literature.[64] Premat's *Non nova sed nove* (2018) is particularly revealing of the vocabulary used in debates on the contemporary, insofar as it shows the recurrence of aesthetic terminology and temporal imaginaries that were already present in the work of authors such as Borges and Barthes (the inscription in the contemporary via "an exteriority, a differentiation, a distance, as the only ways to think about it and to participate in it").[65] In *Cronografías* (2017), Graciela Speranza refers to the "time without time" in which contemporary artworks are inscribed. Speranza shows that the artistic imagination is a laboratory of original articulations of pasts, presents, and futures, "configurations still inaccessible to other languages."[66]

In one of the most comprehensive studies about this concept, *Brouhaha: Worlds of the Contemporary* (2017), Lionel Ruffel makes an archaeology of "the worlds of the contemporary," which comprises debates about historicity, the mediatized experience of time, the multitude, the spatial turn, publishing circuits, and artistic sites. Sarah Brouillette, Mathias Nilges, and Emilio Sauri opt for the term "the global contemporary," referring to non-contemporaneous positions that counter the "neoliberal now" across the globe.[67] In line with these critics, I conceive of the contemporary as a notion that questions the uniformity of temporal becoming under capitalist conditions, emphasizing the anachronisms and counter rhythms that detach us from the perpetual present of neoliberal politics.[68]

The debate on the contemporary gained new momentum after the publication of an essay by Giorgio Agamben, "What Is the Contemporary?" in 2007. Agamben's essay establishes a direct dialogue with Friedrich Nietzsche's *Untimely Meditations* (1876), especially with its second chapter, "On the Uses and Disadvantages of History for Life," in which Nietzsche argues that an age oversaturated with history results in servility and the inability of people to build their own future.[69] For Agamben, therefore, someone becomes contemporary when they relate to the present in an untimely manner, against the grain of the dominant discourse. A contemporary is an anachronistic person who arrives "too early" or "too late."[70] Absolute coincidence with the present is tantamount to the critical incapacity to perceive it, even more so when it unfolds according to the presentist dynamics of contemporary societies that Hartog diagnoses. A skeptical distance is necessary to establish a genuine relationship with the present. By reading Osip Mandelstam's poem "The Century," Agamben derives the hypothesis that "the contemporary is he who firmly holds his gaze on his own time so as to perceive not its light, but rather its darkness." Agamben borrows this metaphor from the neurophysiology of vision in order to claim that the contemporary is "he who knows how to see that darkness, he who is in a position to write by dipping his pen in the darkness of the present."[71] Other concepts such as Benjamin's dialectical image, Michel Foucault's archeology of knowledge, and Fredric Jameson's archeology of the future underlay this idea of the contemporary.[72]

Despite its significance in spearheading discussions about the arts of the present, Agamben's conception of the contemporary lacks a historical and geopolitical dimension. The prophetic character of the text stems from its overdependence on metaphors rather than on concrete readings of historical events or artistic literary artifacts. Agamben evades the question of the ethical-political ramifications of what is contemporary in the twenty-first century, especially under the current conditions of temporal crisis, when the links between past, present, and future have become extremely fragile.

Moreover, it remains to be asked what Nietzsche's meditation has to say to us today when we experience the sense that "one is a latecomer and epigone" and that we have fallen prey to an impulse to archive every action we take (the antiquarian subject, Nietzsche remarks, possesses "a blind rage for collecting").[73] In the absence of grand narratives and the suspension of historical consciousness, people are prone to invent new genealogies in "an attempt to give oneself, as it were a posteriori, a past in which one would like to originate in opposition to that in which one did originate."[74] Contemporary writers are responding to the collecting fervor of the times through fragmentary books resembling the present of the early twenty-first century, which unfolds in the form of a spiral: the sensation that it renews itself and begins again in ever shorter cycles. These are novels of beginnings, tentative approximations, and open-ended forms susceptible to further elaboration. Rather than delineating the contours of a definitive plot, these novels make the hypothetical a central part of the contemporary. Instead of concealing the archive, they unfold as an accumulation of fragments that display its precariousness.

LATIN AMERICAN INSCRIPTIONS

The publication of three books on the contemporary in Latin America proves that it did not take long for the debate spearheaded by Agamben to spread beyond disciplinary boundaries. The first of these, *Moderno/Contemporáneo: un debate de horizontes*, is a volume edited by a group of art historians and published in 2008 by Colombia's Universidad de Antioquia. In the introduction, the editors ask whether the contemporary is perhaps "a historiographical concept (like 'Baroque' or 'Renaissance') with methodological implications" and whether it is "more flexible and useful than 'postmodern,' used to characterize a kind of overcoming of modernity."[75] The second book, *¿Qué es lo contemporáneo? Actualidad, tiempo histórico, utopías del presente*, is a compilation of critical essays edited by Chilean historian Miguel Valderrama and published by Ediciones Universidad Finis Terrae in Santiago, Chile, in 2011. As in the art historians' volume, the debate on the contemporary becomes a critique of the present as a homogeneous time and a call to conceive it as "a mosaic, a kaleidoscope of deferred times."[76] The third book, *Indiccionario de lo contemporáneo*, appeared in 2018 in Editora UFMG, the press of Universidade Federal de Minas Gerais (Brazil) and in 2020 in EME Editorial (Argentina). The notion of the contemporary as a communal and intermittent period is reflected in the book's structure. The authors recognize that knowledge production is an inherently collaborative endeavor and embrace possible contradictions between the chapters. For the authors, the contemporary is a choral experience of the present through aesthetic practices that privilege ideas such as anonymity and the multitude.[77]

The volume edited by Héctor Hoyos and Marília Librandi-Rocha in the March 2014 issue of the *Revista de Estudios Hispánicos*, "Theories of the Contemporary in South America," addresses the question of the contemporary in the context of debates on Latin American literary production, the teaching of twenty-first-century literature in academic institutions, and the insertion of discussions on the contemporary in the field of world literature. In the volume's introduction, the editors point out that the contemporary, "as a critical category and an object of study," is often overlooked in academic discussions, despite the fact that numerous institutions offer courses with the term "contemporary" in their educational programs. While English seems to be the language of the contemporary, as the English-speaking translation market shapes the maps of world literature, Hoyos and Librandi-Rocha argue for a transnational or multidirectional model that conceives the contemporary through the dialogue between different localities.[78]

I seek to join this chorus of voices through a hemispheric model of literary analysis. I recognize the plurality of perspectives and locations of the contemporary and, therefore, oppose the idea that history has come to an end and that humanity is a homogeneous whole moving in the same temporal direction. My task has been to sharpen my ear so that the novels themselves dictate the terms of the debate and the conversation with voices from across Latin America. In my approach to the concept of the contemporary through discussions about our neoliberal end times, I seek to show how literature, in an age of systematic attacks on the modern social contract, offers points of connection between an unfinished past and a potential future.

In the structure of this book I seek to reflect the optical model of a kaleidoscope, that childhood object in which Benjamin saw a figure of the dialectic. For him, the kaleidoscope emerges as a temporal paradigm during periods when the connections between past, present, and future are blurred and when it becomes necessary to interrogate the structures of historical time.[79] Philosopher Ernst Bloch described the interwar years as a "kaleidoscopic period," during which artists become assemblers capable of configuring new formations from different temporal strata.[80] Through the kaleidoscope we can glimpse new arrangements and alter the chains that link historical events. In the early years of the millennium, the writers I study here acquire a glimpse of the imagination, improvisation, and ingenuity with which children combine images in a non-hierarchical way, creating relationships that escape any linear or teleological ordering. Although in each chapter I deal comparatively with the work of two Latin American writers, readers are invited to establish their own connections between authors, works, and ideas to form a dialectical image of the contemporary.

The book is divided into two sections: "Deep Histories of the Present" and "Returns of History and Memory." The focus of the first section is on novels in which our contemporary crisis of time is framed within national histories of resource extraction dating back to the nineteenth century and the colonial period. In chapter 1, "The Return of Nature: The Novel of the Crisis," I examine *El año del desierto* by Argentinean writer Pedro Mairal and *La mucama de Omicunlé* by Dominican writer Rita Indiana. Mairal uses a strategy of literary recycling and evokes the work of the *cartoneros*— the waste pickers who came to prominence in the wake of the 2001 financial meltdown—to travel back in time throughout Argentinean history and to rewrite the literary mediations that shaped the imaginaries of the modern nation. Indiana resorts to the temporality of Afro-Caribbean rituals and queer subjects to create a seamless collaboration between the sixteenth and the twenty-first centuries. Both writers propose relational alternatives to Western binaries through a dynamic conception of the relationship between the human and nonhuman (the human body as an entity that is always already entwined with the natural world) and the creative process (tradition as a network of cooperation between artists rather than a line of predecessors and heirs).

In chapter 2, "A Toxic History of the Present: The Novel of Ecohorror," I analyze Argentinean writer Samanta Schweblin's *Distancia de rescate* and Mexican writer Guadalupe Nettel's *El huésped* (The host, 2006), considering the temporality of climate change and ecological crisis. Both authors conjure up apocalyptic scenarios through returns to repressed moments in the history of their respective nations: the civilizing fantasies of nine-teenth-century Argentinean politicians and the sustainable project of Indigenous communities in Mexico-Tenochtitlan. By theorizing what I call "ecohorror," an aesthetic category that builds bridges between literature and ethics via the role of negative emotions such as anxiety and disgust, I argue that Schweblin and Nettel repurpose the form of the novel to remain attentive to the dizzying temporality of the Anthropocene. Whereas Schweblin puts together a suspenseful dialogue that imitates the effects of pesticide poisoning and builds parallels between the novel and other aesthetic genres, Nettel recycles the gothic tradition of the parasite or the body-taken-over to reflect on the biotechnological intervention in peoples' lives. Both novels serve as a platform from which to reflect on large-scale processes of ecological decay, weaving connections between local and planetary conditions.

In chapter 3, "The Contemporary Plantation: Memories of Slavery and the Oral History Novel," I read Brazilian writer Itamar Vieira Junior's *Torto arado* and Colombian writer Juan Cárdenas's *Elástico de sombra* as novels concerning the persistence of the bonds of slavery for Black plantation workers. I argue that both authors destabilize the privileging of the written over the oral by rescuing oral history archives of the African diaspora and little-known cultural practices such as the syncretic religion of Jarê in northeastern Brazil and the Afro-Colombian martial art known as *grima* practiced in the country's Cauca region. Beginning with Sylvia Wynter's argument that the novel developed alongside the market economy, in this chapter I chart how contemporary writers undermine the novel's historical implication with the capitalist system (and, therefore, with the plantation economy) by incorporating the oral tradition of Afro-Latin American populations. Both Vieira Junior and Cárdenas engage with the Black Atlantic oral history archive—the myths, jokes, proverbs, and folktales that enslaved peoples brought from Africa aboard the slave ships—to endow our neoliberal present with ancestral temporalities. Both authors reproduce the temporal elasticity of Afro-Caribbean syncretic practices by introducing the perspective of nonhuman deities who speak against the destruction of Black bodies and territories.

In the second section, "Returns of History and Memory," I study the so-called literature of the children, novels about recent Latin American history written by authors who grew up during the last military dictatorships and the subsequent neoliberal democracies and who inherited an incomplete picture of the present. In chapter 4, "The Children Return: The Novel of Postmemory," I consider the figure of the children of political exiles of the last Southern Cone dictatorships through readings of *A resistência* by Brazilian writer Julián Fuks and *Conjunto vacío* by Mexican writer Verónica Gerber Bicecci. In these novels, the notion of return acquires a spatio-temporal dimension, reflecting the geographical dislocations and aesthetic quests of a generation whose access to the past is mediated by documents, objects, and photographs from family and state archives. The narrators in both novels are children of political activists who grew up in Brazil and Mexico and who return to their parents' home country of Argentina in order to investigate their recent family histories. Whereas the narrator of *A resistência* questions the supposed neutrality of the representational technologies of the last military dictatorship, such as the state ID of the *desaparecidos* (disappeared), Gerber Bicecci's alter ego in *Conjunto vacío* represents the names of the characters through Venn diagrams that dramatize the formation of affective bonds between the children of political exiles. Thus, both authors resist the waning of affect in the neoliberal era by forming alternative communities to the family and the nation-state.

In chapter 5, "Ways of Being Contemporary: The Novel after the End of History," I continue to think about the literature of children through the analysis of *Los ingrávidos* by Mexican writer Valeria Luiselli and *Bonsái* by Chilean writer Alejandro Zambra. Against the eclipse of the notion of the future, Luiselli and Zambra delve into family genealogies and literary traditions to activate a historical perspective on the present and to imagine potential horizons. In this chapter, I foreground theorizations about the end of history to show how writers like Luiselli and Zambra are conceiving the end as the urgent need to reassemble the competing temporalities of the new century, not as a déjà-vu of previous eras that prevents transformative action in the present. Although contemporary societies alternate between amnesia and the desire to remember each moment of the past, Luiselli and Zambra focus on characters who experience the past as an unsolvable mystery, reproducing this ontological instability in the precarious subjectivities of their characters and the fragmented condition of the novel form. My aim is to examine a series of turn-of-the-century novels in which our present is defamiliarized through fractures in the linear conception of time. In doing so, I find that these novels reach the critical distance required by any attempt to seize historical knowledge.

PART I

DEEP HISTORIES OF THE PRESENT

CHAPTER 1

THE RETURN
OF NATURE

The Novel of the Crisis

"Crisis" is an important keyword in understanding Latin America circa 2001. In December of that year, Argentineans witnessed on live television the resignation of President Fernando de la Rúa and his escape from the Casa Rosada, the house of government, via helicopter. The people of Buenos Aires immediately took to the streets under the chant of "Que se vayan todos" (All of them must go). Under the spell of the 2001 socioeconomic recession, Argentineans were suddenly faced with a new vocabulary of crisis: words such as *corralito* (the diminutive of corral or animal pen) to refer to the economic measure of freezing the money in people's bank accounts or *cacerolazos* as a form of protest by banging pots and pans.[1] As the crisis worsened with the rapid succession of five Argentinean presidents in less than two weeks, the citizens faced what seemed to be a series of returns to precapitalist society. Suddenly, they saw the nation's founding fathers' utopian dreams of Argentina as an agro-exporting country return in the shape of a dystopian nightmare. Whereas people in most provinces started to use alternative currencies (*cuasimonedas*), other people turned to a barter economy (*trueques*) to exchange goods in response to the currency and food shortages. Meanwhile, the province of Buenos Aires suffered extreme flooding that left entire populations underwater and increased the damages caused by the recession.

The case of 2001 Argentina stands as a perfect example of how history, after the turn of the century, started to move backward, and how the idea of crisis in the twenty-first century involves the entanglement of the economic, social, political, and ecological. A few months into the new millennium, the notion of global progress and utopia that had animated most of the twentieth century began to fade away, especially in Latin America, where large sectors of the population were left out of the narrative of a collective future. The umbrella term that appeared to encompass all these crises was "neoliberalism," meaning the new stage of predatory capitalism that involved privatization and economic austerity, which took shape in 1970s Chile under Pinochet and soon spread to the other military regimes that rose to power across the region.

Latin American writers delineate 2001 as the year of *intemperie*: the return of a series of events, signifiers, and images that remained buried in the political unconscious of the modern nation. The term "intemperie" refers to being in the harsh outdoors, but it is a word that, according to the dictionary of the Royal Spanish Academy, also means "temporal inequality."[2] Latin American novelists writing about the turn of the millennium reveal, in significant ways, the flip side of the time of equality, the struggles for emancipation and social justice, tracing in the temporal dispossession suffered by contemporary citizens other forms of life and coexistence in space and time. In this sense, intemperie is a call to think in an untimely fashion.[3] In the midst of a crisis, people become bricoleurs who build with the materials they have at their disposal without drawing distinctions between highbrow and lowbrow culture, between means and ends. One could think of the informal economies and precarious jobs that emerged because of the 2001 crisis in Argentina, emblematized in the figure of the *cartoneros* and the commercialization of apocryphal brands in the Mercado de La Salada, the largest black market in Latin America. In addition to being the name given to the temporal setbacks experienced by the social fabric in the wake of the neoliberal era, intemperie is also a *modus scribendi* that combines different times and spaces to resist capitalist dispossession.[4]

In this chapter I focus on two novels: *El año del desierto* (The year of the desert, 2005) by Argentinean writer Pedro Mairal and *La mucama de Omicunlé* (2015; trans. 2018 as *Tentacle*) by Dominican writer Rita Indiana.[5] Both writers take the year 2001 as a departing point for a historical time that is emptied out of the promises of emancipation and social justice or what I call (following Pratt) a time of *demodernization*: the process by which the state stops being the guarantor of inclusivity and belonging.[6] As they turn to repressed moments of the continent's history such as the plantation economy in the Caribbean or the genocide against Indigenous populations in the Argentinean pampas, these authors reveal the vulnerability and the temporal dispossession that characterizes life under neoliberalism. The narrative strategies of regression in *El año del desierto* and the temporal palimpsest or juxtaposition in *La mucama de Omicunlé* show the obsolescence of the dreams of progress and insatiable modernization that drove the cultural and political imagination of the twentieth century across the Americas. Against the disenchanted nihilism of end-of-history narratives, these novelists in their fiction produce a new distribution of times and spaces that restores the voices of the subjects excluded from the constitution of the modern nation-state. Through an aesthetics of remix and bricolage, reproducing the informal economies that emerged in the wake of the 2001 socioeconomic crisis, Mairal and Indiana conceive of the writer as a pirate who introduces new frameworks and protocols to revisit cultural and literary traditions, casting the contemporary as the time of repetitions: a time that is incomplete and therefore always ready to be built from scratch.

As a response to the precariousness of the social fabric and the proliferation of postindustrial waste at the turn of the millennium, these novelists derive their aesthetic procedure from the figures of the ragpicker and the bricoleur that have their precedents in Charles Baudelaire's poetry and Walter Benjamin's critical theory. Whereas Baudelaire's ragpicker collects and catalogs the rubbish scraps of the great cities, Benjamin's bricoleur gives waste a new meaning through constellations that reconstruct the forgotten lives of the defeated and create alternative journeys through history. However, both Mairal and Indiana inscribe this tradition within different regional contexts. In *El año del desierto*, Mairal uses the procedures of the baroque economies of the 2001 socioeconomic crisis in Argentina: the work of the cartoneros and the trafficking of counterfeit goods in Buenos Aires's Mercado de La Salada. By rewinding Argentinean history from 2001 to the colonial period, Mairal rewrites the literary and artistic mediations that shaped the modern imagination and organizes an original journey through the nation's cultural tradition. In *La mucama de Omicunlé*, Indiana turns to Afro-Caribbean rituals in order to trace the kinships between human and nonhuman beings and the pluriverse of queer subjectivities that simultaneously inhabit multiple bodies and worlds. This montage points to the tradition of buccaneering on the island of Hispaniola and the Dominican Republic's *cultura del corso* (buccaneering culture), the political corruption and trafficking of influences that determined the nation's modern history. Through the art of citing without quotation marks, writers such as Mairal and Indiana capture the spectral return of the distant past and build bridg-

31

es between the past and the future. In doing so, they forge the necessary historical consciousness to avoid accepting the future as a mere repetition of our neoliberal present.[7]

THE TEMPORALITY OF CRISIS

Halfway through *El año del desierto*, which can be placed within the category of cli-fi, or climate fiction, the regime of historicity that organizes experiences in time vanishes completely, and even the fortune tellers are unable to predict the future of their clients: "The fortune tellers held our hands and could tell us all the details about our past, but they could not even tell us if we were going to die the next day."[8] The agent of crisis is called *la intemperie* (here, possibly translated as "hostile environment" or "the exposed outdoors"), which in the novel is a natural phenomenon that operates through a logic of spatiotemporal regression. On the one hand, la intemperie causes the desert gradually to invade the city of Buenos Aires; on the other, it causes time to move backward from the twenty-first-century present to the colonial era, in such a way that the streets of the city lose their names as the people stop recognizing the country's national heroes. The narrator, María Valdéz Neylan, is condemned to grow old as she returns to the past as an orphan of history and relives in her own flesh the anguished narrative of her Irish ancestors. Over 365 days, María experiences not just one year but all Argentinean history in reverse. Symbolically, she turns twenty-three on the day la intemperie is set in motion, which lays bare the social workings of time in the novel: the gap between personal aging and collective regression, between the history of the individual and the time of the nation.[9] Simultaneously, in *El año del desierto* Mairal proposes a rereading of the literary tradition, a new ordering of the canon, in a cultural context in which apocalyptic discourses about the end of literature are the lay of the land.[10] In contrast to the progressive order of genealogical novels such as Gabriel García Márquez's *Cien años de soledad* (1967), which is a pervasive point of reference throughout the narrative, Mairal builds *El año del desierto* with the remains of Argentinean literature and returns to the past in order to find literary filiations to make sense of the crisis.

El año del desierto begins in a vague historical context that corresponds with the eternal present of the crisis. In the first chapter, "Maps," María is slowly recovering her speech, native language, and the memory of events she will experience throughout the narrative. Mairal dramatizes the impossibility of influencing the course of history since human actions cannot project into the future. The beginning of the novel evokes the context of the national crisis experienced in December 2001: the *cacerolazos*, the climate of street violence, the looting of retail chains and small businesses, the outflow of capital, the emergence of alternative currencies, and the volatility of the peso (which María, after going to the supermarket, sees in the "superimposed prices" of each product).[11] If neoliberalism means the privatization of companies and public goods, la intemperie is a phenomenon that blurs the boundaries between public and private, as in the scene in which the walls of the building where María lives with her father collapse and a communal dwelling is set up.

However, the term *intemperie* also means the loss of collective belonging, especially María's emotional ties with her boyfriend and her father. Her boyfriend, Alejandro, is drafted into military service, which evokes the context of the last military dictatorship and the Malvinas (Falklands) War, and María's father goes into a catatonic state from compulsively watching the news on TV. The loss of her status as a daughter runs parallel to the erosion of her rights as a citizen and a woman. After working at the Hotel de Emigrantes (an inversion of the tenements where European immigrants stayed from the nineteenth century onward shortly after arriving in the country), María becomes a sex worker in the port of Buenos Aires. She is taken as a captive by an Indigenous tribe (the Braucos) who speak a dislocated version of the slum sociolect. After María joins the ranks of the Ú Indigenous community, the reader realizes that the modern nation has ceased to exist, that Spanish as a national language has evaporated, and that on the ruins of the nation's capital there still stands the Garay tower of the investment company Suárez & Baitos, whose members, in the absence of a currency with which to speculate, have reverted to cannibalism.

El año del desierto stages the main symptoms of the contemporary crisis of time and Mairal's position of non-contemporaneity with which he responds to it. The temporal logic mobilized through la intemperie translates into the continuous updating of all the moments of the past and the fall of the future as "grammatical time" or horizon of change. According to George Steiner, "the future tense came relatively late into human speech . . . [and] looks to be specific to *homo sapiens*."[12] Mairal highlights the mood brought about by the turn of the millennium: the feeling that the crisis means "a point of metabolization of all the pasts and all the futures."[13]

Following Henri Bergson's writings on durational time, Virno argues that we currently inhabit a post-historical condition whose dominant pathology is "false recognition" or déjà vu—that is, the feeling that the contemporary moment is a faithful replica of an original that never existed as such. According to Virno, the state of mind that derives from déjà vu is one of apathy and indifference because the future is already predetermined and people "become *spectators* of their own actions, almost as if these were part of an already-known and unalterable script."[14] As an embodiment of this fatalism in the face of a future that has already occurred, María is swept along by the current of history and becomes a spectator of her own life. Mairal conjures up the figure of the contemporary writer as an orphan or disinherited heir, someone who blurs the differences between copy and original, between continuity and rupture, by appropriating all the codes, forms, and protocols of literary history.

The first chapters of *El año del desierto* reflect the neoliberal present through the transformation of the contemporary citizen into *homo economicus* and the glorification of the individual over the collective. Among the harmful effects of neoliberal rationality, Wendy Brown refers to the lack of guarantees of security, protection, and survival to which we are subjected as we are left in the hands of firms, organizations, or states whose only concern is "their own competitive positioning."[15] When she is fired from the investment company where she works as an administrative assistant, María experiences both symbolic and material dispossession or *intemperie*. The second chapter of the novel is entitled "Suárez & Baitos," the name of this financial conglomerate that has its headquarters in one of the city's tallest buildings, the Torre Garay. The tower's name points to the founder of Buenos Aires (Juan de Garay) and casts the novel as a journey to the seeds of what María calls "savage capitalism," which, contrary to chronology, has its starting point in 2001 and its climax in the colonial period.[16] After all, the tower's street is called Reconquista (Reconquest) and is blocks away from the Plaza de Mayo, the city's foundational site. The Torre Garay (as opposed to the urban landscape being erased by la intemperie) remains intact.[17] The tower becomes a dialectical figure as the city's origin point and the last bastion of the neoliberal model.[18] The image of one of the senior partners, Baitos, resorting to cannibalism summarizes the neoliberal ethos of the financial conglomerate as "a throng of hungry men."[19]

The implosion of the neoliberal model is also apparent in the sphere of interpersonal relationships, since social class becomes an insurmountable obstacle in the formation of affective bonds. María is attracted to her boyfriend, Alejandro, in large part because he occupies a socioeconomic position that is antithetical to hers: he is a "dark-skinned man with strong features" who works as a motorcyclist in a courier service and who calls her "Mery" (a creolization of her English name).[20] In this sense, their relationship allows for an X-ray of the "mirage years" that took place between the democratic transition and the mid-1990s.[21] As the upper political and social sectors indulged in the consumerist fantasy of the shopping mall, boasting a lifestyle that they conceived as a "lasting phenomenon," the lower classes lost fundamental rights until they fell into destitution.[22] At first, María confines herself in this petit bourgeois bubble as she stays away from the demonstrations against la intemperie, reminiscent of the *cacerolazos* that took place in the wake of the crisis and following the resignation of the nation's president. Alejandro attends the demonstrations and disappears after being called for compulsory military service, but María devotes all her attention to an expensive dress she intends to wear for New Year's Eve. Before the crisis, the couple experience the present as a dead end or a time out of time, although María is aware that "someday [the relationship] was going to end because it could not last with the two of them being so different."[23] As María becomes a likeness of her Irish great-grandmother, Alejandro turns into a barbarian who joins the military ranks of Juan Martín Celestes (an inverted figure of the nineteenth-century caudillo Juan Manuel de Rosas). Moreover, the fact that Alejandro is a *motoquero*-cum-gaucho who drives a black motorcycle immediately brings to mind Julio Cortázar's short story "La noche boca arriba," whose narrator is a biker who turns into an Indigenous *moteca* (a play on the words "motorcyclist" and *azteca*). Through these regressions in historical time, Mairal represents the effects of demodernization imposed by the crisis, to the extent that the upper social spheres were secluded in walled neighborhoods while the lower classes were subjected to the intemperie of the shantytowns.[24]

In this context, *El año del desierto* depicts the present of the 2001 crisis as the eternal return of previous catastrophes. When María takes up the role of a nurse in a public health clinic that has ceased to receive state support, it becomes impossible to think about the body politic through its inscription in the nation-state: "I felt that the bodies I washed and cared for were always the same body. The same body that I helped to cure so that it could leave, and came back sick, shot, humiliated, dirty, and once again it had to be cleaned, disinfected, cared for so that it could go out again and be sent back out again, destroyed."[25] Underlying this description is the question: If the social body is always the same, how does one account for a present that does not admit generational change? Or better: How does one think about the concept of the nation against this present that passes by in a loop and in the face of the continuous deterioration of the body of the people? On the one hand, her sense of fatigue is an indication of the apathy that Virno associates with the end of history, with the state of mind of the millennial generation that can no longer draw distinctions between before and after and which, therefore, is condemned to relive all the moments of the past as if they were the stuff of the future.[26] The present is experienced as a series of repetitions of a false original, as a temporal receptacle that, in Ludmer's words, "contains all the pasts and also the future, which 'already was.'"[27]

On the other hand, this scene shows how the 2001 crisis undermined the state's role as the warrantor of a future for the body politic. As Beatriz Sarlo points out, "when a body suffers, it leaves the time of history, loses its possibility of projecting itself forward, erases the signs of its memories."[28] In this sense, Mairal in his novel draws "a map of indolence" in which the body politic and the very concept of the nation-state have fallen, tracing parallels between the deterioration of state institutions and the obsolescence of Argentina as a meaningful category.[29] As time moves backward, the nation becomes an obsolete symbolic structure: the immigrants turn into emigrants, the Spanish language transforms into a *cocoliche* (a slang that mixes Spanish and Italian) and then disappears as such (the last chapter of the novel is entitled "En silencio" or "In Silence"), and the city goes from *gran aldea* (a big village, a reference to Lucio Vicente López's homonymous 1882 novel) to terra incognita.[30]

Mairal's regressive logic in the novel evokes Ezequiel Martínez Estrada's theory of "historical invariants," which was based on his vision of Argentinean history as a continuous reincarnation of the social types described by Domingo F. Sarmiento in *Facundo* (1845) and, in general, as a reappearance of dynamics that had their roots in the colonial period. Martínez Estrada carries forward a "meditation of the old in the new, of old age in the contemporary," by considering the gaucho as a "fallen conquistador" and the modern public servant as a nineteenth-century caudillo, in such a way that the conquest seems to have established a series of "hidden tectonic forces" that are in a permanent state of metamorphosis.[31]

Mairal sheds new light on the historical invariants or déjà vus of the nation by displaying them in an inverted manner (capitalists, for example, become Unitarians and then cannibals) and by positing regressive forces as tectonic plates that can resurface at any moment: "Underneath the city, the vacant lot had always been latent."[32] But he exhibits the logic of these repetitions as they allow him to reflect on the "broad present" of the crisis—a present that gathers remnants of other times and spaces and reactivates social structures that seemed to have been buried but which, on the contrary, still remain in force.[33] For example, María goes through a descending scale of social standing throughout the novel: first, she is a secretary at a multinational corporation, then an untrained nurse, a sex worker in the port of Buenos Aires, and finally, the captive of an Indigenous tribe. This gradual loss of her rights as a woman, rather than serving as a mere historical recounting, is a direct critique of "the gray zone" of the informal tertiary sector that was established during the neoliberal era in Argentina and that worsened in the postcrisis period.[34] Progressively, the Argentinean middle class lost its purchasing power and its centrality in the discourse of the nation.

THE DECLINE OF THE NEW

In *El año del desierto* Mairal pushes the limits of the metaphor of a postcrisis Argentinean society "devoted to searching through its trash."[35] The materials of the 2001 present are recycled in different contexts and historical periods: the leader of an Indigenous community, a former bus driver, builds an Indian camp with parts of a Buenos Aires city bus; Indigenous peoples fight with modern Tramontina barbecue knives. The delirious trajectory of these nonhuman materials shows an alternate side to the absolute present, to presentism as the regime of historicity of late capitalism, to work as a 24/7 temporality of duration without pauses, and more important, to the role of objects as merchandise that is part and parcel of an industrial chain of production.[36] Mairal questions the association of the contemporary with presentism and innovation, showing the underside of a neoliberal capitalism that produces ruins, fossils, and obsolescence. In this way, the natural phenomenon of la intemperie as a geological force of desertification corresponds with the logic of the Anthropocene, insofar as nonhuman temporalities both reveal the anachronism that underlies the contemporary and also disassemble the narrative of national history as a series of modernizing processes.

Fashion becomes the main target of this attack on the contemporary understood as presentism. At the beginning of the novel, María tries on a blue dress that exceeds her budget but that she wants to pay for in twelve installments, deferred over a year. If, at the outset, the blue dress symbolized the monetization of the future, in the last chapter the dress has become a piece of cloth that is "unrecognizable, filthy, disheveled."[37] It is only then, after a year has passed and the dress has lost its exchange value, that María can take possession of it. Fashion becomes the metaphor par excellence of a present that devours itself and leaves ruins in its wake. For Agamben, "being in fashion, like contemporariness, entails a certain 'ease,' a certain quality of being out-of-phase or out-of-date, in which one's relevance includes within itself a small part of what lies outside of itself, a shade of démodé, of being out of fashion."[38] In this sense, la intemperie functions as a "temporal device" that unveils the tension between the current and the out-of-date that are part and parcel of the contemporary.[39] The dress goes from being a fetish, a commodity, to adopting a more primordial function: protecting María from the elements. This is a rewriting of César Aira's El vestido rosa (1984), a novel that recounts the comings and goings of a dress through the Argentinean pampas in the nineteenth century and that, according to Fermín Rodríguez, subverts "the constitution of the state as a chronological process that is oriented by the forces of progress."[40] The disparate trajectory of inanimate objects, therefore, widens the lens of what we understand of the present by suspending the linearity of progress and bringing the ruins behind it to the surface.

Mairal thus interrogates the present of technological acceleration by examining its underside of rapid obsolescence. The writer becomes an archaeologist who gathers the debris left behind by the fossilized present of the Anthropocene. As Jesús Martín-Barbero points out, technological acceleration has inaugurated a "continuous present . . . a succession of events in which each event erases the previous one," so that we live in a post-historical era that causes "a sensation of no-exit."[41] Amnesia is one of the most common symptoms experienced by the characters, as temporal regression is accompanied by the inability to distinguish between before and after, between old and new. Amnesia becomes a collective phenomenon as national history is rewound and the memory of the 2001 present is completely erased. This is the case, for example, of a captive who reads household appliance manuals as if they were science fiction novels. When toward the end of the narrative María loses the ability to speak, she seems to suffer from the main symptoms of late capitalism: amnesia and the atrophy of historical consciousness.

In *Twilight Memories*, Andreas Huyssen poses the paradox that contemporary societies are obsessed with the problem of memory at a time of generalized amnesia caused by television and entertainment culture.[42] The "mnemonic fever that is caused by the virus of amnesia [seeks] to slow down information processing, to resist the dissolution of time in the synchronicity of the archive, to recover a mode of contemplation outside the universe of simulation and fast-speed information and cable networks."[43] The title of Mairal's novel can be read as a reversal of the heritage years often promulgated by political or cultural bodies: the year 1980 was decreed *l'année du patrimoine* in France and 2018 was deemed the European Year of Cultural Heritage. Rather than fetishizing the past, in *El año del desierto* Mairal combats the amnesia virus through an endless search of historical and literary origins.

In this sense, *El año del desierto* is a fin de siècle rewriting of the "plague of insomnia" suffered by the characters of García Márquez's *Cien años de soledad*, which does not imply "the impossibility of sleeping, for the body did not feel any fatigue at all, but its inexorable evolution toward a more critical manifestation: a loss of memory."[44] When José Arcadio Buendía in *Cien años de soledad* exhorts the town's inhabitants to find solutions to the sickness of oblivion, his son Aureliano has the idea of labeling each object with its name and utility. The fictional town of Macondo becomes a museum of memory in which objects, feelings, and even deities have their own explanatory label, in a mnemonic impulse that evokes the modality Nietzsche called "antiquarian history": the need for people to preserve their roots, genealogies, and cultures, a need that nonetheless runs the risk of conserving the past as inert matter instead of using it to generate new possibilities in the present. This is the same function of "the memory machine" as conceived by José Arcadio, first to remember the inventions of the gypsies and then to review "every morning, from beginning to end, the totality of knowledge acquired during one's life."[45] Museological fervor is also the disease suffered by Pilar Ternera in *Cien años de soledad*. Like the fortune tellers in *El año del desierto* who can foretell the past in great detail but cannot predict the future, Pilar "conceived the trick of reading the past in cards as she had read the future before."[46] In Mairal's novel, on the other hand, objects traverse a year as if they were traveling through entire centuries. They become false copies of themselves and appear in unusual places, removed from their original context and functionality.

The case of José Arcadio Buendía corresponds to the situation of María's father, in *El año del desierto*, who is so obsessed with television newscasts that he falls into a "cathodic coma," a disorder that affects "compulsive viewers" when the technological apparatus stops working and ceases to be a means of accessing reality.[47] Perhaps another symptom of temporal regression is nostalgia—not for the past or the future but, as Jesús Montoya Juárez points out, a "nostalgia for the contemporary, for a present that adopts the texture of what is on the verge of extinction."[48] More than any other phenomenon, the computer virus known as the Y2K bug of the year 2000 symbolized the fear of losing all the data stored on global networks and a sense of distrust of digital devices as archives of human knowledge. Mairal in *El año del desierto* reflects this collective paranoia in more than one way. For example, the first sign of technological backlash is replacing computers with typewriters in the workplace, which María perceives as a phenomenon condemning "to the graveyard of appliances the entire memory of life."[49] Mairal's novel shows that the new brings with it the moment of its obsolescence and, therefore, that the period we call "contemporary" is increasingly ephemeral.

INHABITING TRADITION

In this context, the question is how to write during and after the crisis, imagining new ways of appropriating tradition in the face of the passive neoliberal logic of consumerism. Mairal foregrounds the procedure of recycling, even piracy, which in pre- and postcrisis Argentina was associated with the work of the cartoneros and the emergence of informal economies such as the Mercado de La Salada. Verónica Gago calls this context "neoliberalism from below"—in other words, "a powerful popular economy that combines community skills of self-management and intimate know-how as a technology of mass self-entrepreneurship in the crisis."[50] Whereas recycling plays a part in repurposing materials whose use value seems to be exhausted, piracy highlights the tense relationship between original and copy, between authenticity and falseness. As Bourriaud theorizes in his book *Postproduction*, beginning in the 1990s artistic practices started to take place in a symbolic "flea market . . . a place where products of multiple provenances converge, waiting for new uses." This aesthetic and socioeconomic context sheds light on *El año del desierto* as a novel whose references encompass all of Argentina's literary history, as if the crisis triggered an aesthetic that takes pleasure in the "nomadic gathering of precarious materials and products of various provenances."[51] Mairal's references to the national canon are fleeting and omnipresent all at once—going from gaucho literature to Esteban Echeverría's *El matadero* and *La cautiva* to Borges's body of work, which appears and disappears throughout the text. This strategy of literary recycling gives the reader the feeling of déjà vu—or even *déjà lu* (of something that has already been read)—and blurs the lines between copy and original.

Rather than an exhaustion of literary possibilities at the turn of the century, this procedure posits a new "narrative of beginning" (*relato de comienzo*, Julio Premat) or "narrative of filiation" (*récit de filiation*, Dominique Viart). Nowadays, to interrogate the narratives of beginning means, according to Premat, "to situate ourselves in a cultural moment marked by instability, superposition, and speed."[52] If the omnivorous present of the crisis has engulfed the contemporary, writing becomes a navigation through national history and literary tradition in order to restore meanings and ways of situating oneself up against historical time. To oppose presentism Mairal blurs the genealogical narrative of ruptures and continuities and encapsulates all literary history in a single instant. This gesture becomes apparent from the first chapter, a prologue that is also an epilogue, a story of a beginning that is, in turn, the anticipation of a denouement. María is writing from a European city—possibly from the Ireland of her ancestors—where she works as a librarian, teaches at a women's college, and oversees the map collection. The cartographic metaphor is significant because tradition has become a "pasture," a tabula rasa that must be populated from scratch, and María is the only person qualified to draw new combinations of planes. "Sometimes, I must lock myself in here to speak without being seen, without being heard; I have to say phrases that I had lost and that now reappear and help me to cover the pasture, to superimpose the light of my native language on this translated light where I breathe every day. And it is like coming back without moving, coming back in Spanish, coming back home. That was not undone, it was not lost; the desert did not eat my tongue."[53]

For Mairal/María, the new lies in the ghostly reworking of tradition. María conceives literary practice through the estrangement of one's own language and the return to the past in an original way—a repetition that, paradoxically, entails a new way of returning home. If Argentina is a colored piece on a map, an empty place, or a signifier that has lost its symbolic weight, the novel works with this truncated heritage to carry forward a "search for traditions," which holds "the promise of a revitalization in contemporary culture."[54] The blurred contours of this historical moment—a dystopian future? a Middle Ages of "cathedrals and castles"? a "time out of time" in which "things do not change"?—reaffirm the tension between the archaic and the contemporary, between the fashionable and the démodé, as a point of departure for the assertion of a new myth of beginning.[55] If Gersende Camenen observes that María is a translator—a job that ends up being essential in her race for "salvation," for survival—it should be added that she is also a translator of the literary tradition, an archivist who has to dust off the stories of origin, a cartographer who draws new maps of filiation in a cultural moment characterized by the prediction of various endings, among them that of literature itself.[56]

In this sense, the image of María as an orphan or survivor of history is that of the Latin American writer at the turn of the century. In the face of socioeconomic and temporal crisis, Mairal proposes ways of blurring the map of tradition and giving a new value to the library through rereadings of the literary past. Rather than a straightforward account of Argentinean history told in reverse, *El año del desierto* is a palimpsest of rewritings of the cultural and literary discourses that shaped the imaginary of the modern nation. There are rewritings of Cortázar's "Casa tomada" through the characters of Irene and her brother; of Rodolfo Enrique Fogwill's *Los pichiciegos*, the emblematic Malvinas War novel, through the profession of the *tuneleros* or tunnel diggers who, like the soldiers in Fogwill's novel, resemble moles; and Juan José Saer's *El entenado* through the rewriting of the colonial genre of the *crónicas de indias* and the narrative of going native (as María becomes a captive of an Indigenous tribe). In addition to building a "national allegory," as Juan Pablo Dabove and Susan Hallstead have convincingly argued, Mairal rewrites the canon to bridge the insurmountable distance that separates turn-of-the-twenty-first-century writers from the literary past.[57]

In Chile, for instance, the young poets who jumped to the literary scene in the 1990s conceived themselves as *huérfanos* (orphans) and *náufragos* (shipwreck survivors or castaways). As Gustavo Guerrero points out, this was a generalized tendency among young Latin American writers during the last decade of the twentieth century: "The image of a generation without teachers, growing up in a sort of symbolic intemperie, or that of a group of immature Robinsons who survive the shipwreck of the twentieth century and have to build everything back from scratch."[58] Born in 1970, Mairal is a member of a generation of Argentinean poets and narrators (Fabián Casas, Washington Cucurto, or Sergio Raimondi) who define themselves by a feeling of not belonging rather than by a set of collective markers: a displaced generation, a generation that arrived too late, a generation without a generation.[59]

In addition to the nautical image of the shipwreck, Mairal posits the act of writing through the metaphor of diving: the exploration of language and the estrangement from one's mother tongue that Damián Tabarovsky has theorized in *Literatura de izquierda*. Tabarovsky conceives fiction writing as the subjection of the original language "to a state of hesitation, of stuttering, of paradox. To a permanent exile, to doubt about the very notion of the original." In other words, Tabarovsky argues for "exteriority as literary experience," for exile from one's own tongue as a condition of possibility for inventing a new experience of language.[60] In *El año del desierto*, as la intemperie moves forward and history moves backward, María loses the faculty of language, exiling herself from the Río de la Plata Spanish of the early twenty-first century until she finally falls into mutism. It is in the first chapter, after all, that she reveals what happens following the loss of her mother tongue: on the one hand, the return of the English spoken by her Irish ancestors and, on the other hand, the process of learning Spanish as a foreign language over a period of five years. María's account can be read as a slow reacquaintance with her mother tongue and as the creation of a new language at the heart of the old one. In turn, the process of learning Spanish as a foreign language is made possible by a rewriting of the literary tradition. In addition to being a translator, then, in the new century writers "are 'semionauts' who produce original pathways through signs[,] . . . project new possible scripts," and propose an "incessant navigation within the meanderings of cultural history."[61] Mairal in *El año del desierto* offers a new journey through tradition based on the distance that separates writers from their mother tongue, on the suspension of the borders between original and copy.

Ultimately, Mairal poses the need to distance oneself from presentism as a starting point for defining the contemporary. If the character of María is read as a figuration of Mairal (a reading that would be corroborated, after all, by the similarity between the names), the novel defines the role of the contemporary writer based on a double negation: the community of those who have no community (a concept that Tabarovsky borrows from Jean-Luc Nancy) and the contemporaneity of the non-contemporaneous (which Virno repurposes from Ernst Bloch).[62] On the one hand, Tabarovsky proposes a "literature of the left" that eludes the mandates of the market and the academy. The contemporary writer would thus be the person who "belongs to the literature of the inoperative community, integrates the community of those who have no community."[63]

In *El año del desierto*, María embodies the figure of the writer who has been left out in the open, since the military forces have plundered her family library. The library contained books from the Anglo-Saxon tradition—Shakespeare, Woolf, Faulkner, Hawthorne, the Penguin Classics collection—that María had inherited from her mother and grandmother. Faced with the loss of the genealogical narrative, María is forced to invent a new account based on filiation, on the appropriation of her lineage, responding to what Premat calls a "disinheritance" from tradition.[64] María's narrative establishes a present-past or a future-past that opposes the tyranny of clocks, the presentism of the contemporary world, by building her trajectory with the ruins of the literary tradition.

On the other hand, the exhaustion of the genealogical narrative is reflected in the phenomenon of la intemperie as a reversal of the hurricane with which *Cien años de soledad* comes to an end. The very title of Mairal's novel indicates that what in García Márquez's novel takes place over a century is encapsulated within a single year in Mairal's. In *El año del desierto*, the whirlwind that shatters the story is the point of departure, not arrival. Mairal carries out a paradoxical operation, for he conjures the literary tradition in order to free himself from it; he quotes the masters of the Latin American novel in order to move past them. The writer's role at the turn of the century thus becomes working with the fossilized remains of tradition, as if the grand narratives of Latin American literature had been erased by a computer virus and had to be reconstructed from scratch. María's story begins at the moment of its enunciation, when she gives herself to the task of fabricating an origin—understood as *oikos* and *arché*—since the relation of continuity with previous generations has been broken. This is what Ludmer calls "fabricating the present" after the rupture of the grand narratives and what Virno calls "the contemporaneity of the non-contemporaneous," a historiographical praxis that engages "with the enduring interconnection between pre-history and actuality (that is, with the condition that makes history possible)."[65] The mnemotechnical procedure of the novel is framed within the extended scales of the literary tradition to combat the culture of amnesia, atrophy, and claustrophobia generated by the media at the turn of the century.

This approach to literary praxis turns the writer into an archeologist of the contemporary who searches in the past for the meaning of a disorienting present. Over the course of the novel, María becomes obsessed with the figure of the *ombú*, the national tree of Argentina, which serves as the source of the country's foundational narratives: "I would have wanted for the *ombú* to swallow me, for its roots to close over me, as in a children's book. . . . I wanted to stay in the tree, to make the tree my home."[66] *Ombú* was one of the first Indigenous words to appear in Argentinean literature in Echeverría's *La cautiva*. The name of the title's captive woman is María, and like Mairal's narrator-protagonist, she slowly becomes a figuration of the desert. In the poem's epilogue, María's grave is crowned by a cross—the same journey toward Catholicism that Mairal's narrator sets out on—and lies beneath an *ombú* planted by an anonymous hand, which serves as a sign of hospitality in the middle of the desert.[67] In the novel, however, the *ombú* as a figure of Argentina becomes an uninhabitable space and designates the opposite side of the modern imagination, which saw time as an arrow pointing forward, as a grand narrative with moments of continuity, novelty, and rupture. Unable to inhabit his or her own genealogy, the contemporary writer has to reappropriate the literary tradition's codes, figures, and forms to find filiations in the precarious present of the crisis.

A TENTACULAR NOVEL

Whereas Mairal in *El año del desierto* conceives of time as a dialectical image (his characters grow old while social time returns to its origins), in Rita Indiana's *La mucama de Omicunlé* time is a tentacular entity: past, present, and future are part of "an erratic system" that presupposes neither beginnings nor endings.[68] This is how Édouard Glissant defines a poetics of relation, in which history is not conceived as a forward movement but, rather, as a coexistence of different times, places, and lives that intertwine and form the image of a mangrove (an important figure for Indiana's novel). In *Caribbean Discourse*, Glissant alerts us to the dangers of a single History with a capital H that serves as a functional fantasy of the West. He calls Caribbean writers to put together what he terms "a prophetic vision of the past," reconstructing the nonhistory or "tormented chronology" of Caribbean nations by channeling the "creative energy of a dialectic reestablished between nature and culture."[69] By bringing together the seventeenth-century culture of buccaneers, the turn of the twenty-first century, and a postapocalyptic future that is dealing with a global pandemic, Indiana shows that the island has become a key space to measure the scales of the environmental crisis—the points of contact between the local and the global, the plantation economy, the extinction of countless native species, and modern extractive enterprises.[70] In fact, at the center of *La mucama de Omicunlé* lies an endangered sea anemone that serves as a portal to other times and places, which reflects the temporal elasticity of Afro-Caribbean cosmologies.

By combining the cosmological order of Afro-diasporic religious practices with contemporary concerns about global warming and the end of the world as we know it, Indiana moves the novel seamlessly between three temporal planes. It begins in a dystopian version of Santo Domingo in 2027, three years after a tidal wave has laid waste to the island's ecosystem, leaving behind "a beach contaminated by unsalvageable corpses and sunken junk" and turning the Caribbean Sea into "contaminated chocolate."[71] Along with environmental degradation, the country suffers from the tyranny of its politicians who are perpetrating a systematic massacre of the island's inhabitants. They target especially the Haitian immigrants who are fleeing to the Dominican Republic because of a quarantine imposed on their side of the island. They are being murdered by waste collectors who detect the virus in their bodies. In these episodes of biopolitical control over the Black bodies of Haitian immigrants Indiana reveals the continuities between the imperial, colonial, and neoextractivist projects that have taken place throughout Dominican history. She thus stages the "acts of erasure" that Dixa Ramírez refers to as "ghostings" and that are "part and parcel of colonial, imperial, and many nationalist projects that have produced not so much actual silence as other unwieldy and recalcitrant presences."[72] As Lorgia García-Peña points out, anti-Haitianism is a "colonial ideology" deeply entrenched in the border history of Hispaniola.[73] Indiana plays with these ghostings of Dominican history as many of her characters reappear in other historical periods under different names. For example, a slave in seventeenth-century Hispaniola becomes Malagueta, an Afro-Dominican performance artist who continues to be an invisible subject even at the turn of the twenty-first century.

The novel's title character is Acilde Figueroa, who has abandoned her former job as a sex worker in Santo Domingo's port to work as maid for Esther Escudero, the *santera* (or priestess of the Santería Afro-diasporic religion) of the country's president. Esther is called Omicunlé because she is the person in charge of protecting "the cloak that covers the sea" or "the house of Yemayá," the orisha goddess of the ocean and maternal love—and also a figure of virginity, since in Afro-Caribbean religions she is known as the Virgen de la Regla.[74] Esther has a sea anemone that in 2027, after the tidal wave has permanently harmed the island's ecosystem, becomes vital for the planet's future. In fact, in 2027, marine species are trafficked on the black market because the contents of the biological weapons that Venezuela had donated to the Dominican government were emptied into the Caribbean Sea, causing the immediate extinction of a significant portion of the island's marine life. One of the traffickers, Morla, wants to convince Acilde to steal Esther's sea anemone in exchange for Rainbow Brite, an injection "that promised a complete sex change without surgery."[75]

The episodes in the first chapter lay the ground for the trans-historical dialogues in the novel. Morla kills Esther Escudero, Acilde kills Morla and escapes with the sea anemone, becoming an embodiment of Olokun, the orisha god of the bottom of the sea who possesses a fortune and is both a man and a woman. After completing the sex change via Rainbow Brite, Acilde travels to turn-of-the-twenty-first-century Santo Domingo and turns into Giorgio Menicucci, a Swiss Italian immigrant who becomes a millionaire by marrying Linda Goldman, heiress to her father's economic empire. Together they establish the Sosúa Project, an initiative combining contemporary art and sustainability to form an eco-friendly sanctuary dedicated to preserving marine species. Enter Argenis Luna, a painter in residence at the Sosúa Project who comes into contact with a sea anemone while swimming in the Caribbean Sea. A severe allergic reaction to the sea anemone plunges Argenis into a fever dream that transports him into seventeenth-century Hispaniola, where a group of French buccaneers take him prisoner. This plotline is reminiscent of Samanta Schweblin's *Distancia de rescate*, since both novels represent ecological pollution through ecstatic temporalities that defamiliarize the logic of capital accumulation.

Argenis Luna embodies the apathy toward a present that is experienced as a time outside of history (recently divorced, he works in a call center and spends his time fantasizing about the women around him) and demonstrates an intense communion with other historical periods, becoming an inhabitant of two eras. Bedridden at Playa Bo, the ecological reserve that serves as the base of the Sosúa Project, Argenis is taken captive by the French buccaneers along with a Black slave and a Taino Indian. According to Hartog, since the turn of the millennium the present has been experienced as a "broken continuity," so we must constantly weave relationships between past and present to derive historical knowledge.[76] Through the figure of Argenis, Indiana illustrates how we experience the anachronistic and hypertrophied present of the early twenty-first century. In addition to being the result of his contact with an ocean-dwelling anemone, Argenis's temporal journey is a recovery of the unresolved fragments of the Caribbean past, remnants of a shipwreck that come to the surface from time to time and reconfigure our image of the present. The tidal wave of 2024 thus serves as a figure of spatiotemporal recycling that Indiana uses as a narrative procedure.

In fact, the artistic objective of the Sosúa Project is to activate the sediments of the past so as to open alternative futures, moving viewers to engage in creating sustainable energies. Through the study of Goya's work, the group of artists aim "to complicate the notion of contemporaneity in art and analyze the ways in which Goya, two centuries ago, had articulated his philosophical and formal observations, divorcing himself from the expectations of the work he was commissioned to do and thus inaugurating modern art."[77] It is not a coincidence that this narrative arc takes place in 2001, a period between centuries whose structure of feeling oscillates between melancholy in the face of an irretrievable past and the anxious anticipation of an ecological catastrophe that can unfold at any moment. Just as the novel shows that the beginning of the Anthropocene should be traced back to the extractive enterprises that razed the island to the ground in the colonial period, the rescue of the figure of Goya as a precursor of modern art suggests that contemporaneity is a relationship of multiplicity with the historical present: a contemporary is an artist who creates an anachronistic, outdated art, outside of the prevailing temporality. This anachronistic figure of the artist becomes evident when Argenis adopts the pseudonym Psychic Goya, which both references the destruction of imperial enterprises portrayed by a painter such as Goya and anticipates a future that can only be imagined as a landscape filled with ruins.

The tentacles of the sea anemone evoke the relational, trans-historical, and multispecies thinking that Indiana posits as the only possible way out of the contemporary climate crisis. The notion of "tentacular thinking" is at the center of Donna Haraway's theorization of what she calls the Chthulucene, which she proposes as an alternative to notions such as Anthropocene and Capitalocene that are focused exclusively on the agency of human beings and ignore the kinships between human and nonhuman forces. As Haraway points out, the term does not refer to H. P. Lovecraft's "racial-nightmare" monster of the same name but to the "tentacular powers and forces" with names such as Gaia, Pachamama, or Spider Woman.[78] Haraway borrows the name of a spider, the *Pimoa cthulhu*, which lives under the earth and, therefore, possesses the "chthonic powers of Terra" (the idea of deities that live under the earth inevitably refers to the figure of Olokun, the orisha spirit that lives at the bottom of the ocean). For Haraway, as for Glissant, the tentacular beings need to tell the story of our present catastrophe, as they allow for "the patterning of possible worlds and possible times . . . gone, here, and yet to come."[79]

This interchange helps explain the central role of coral reefs in the novel, especially the giant Caribbean sea anemone (*Condylactis gigantea*), which serves as a portal to different times and places and establishes kinships among the marine beings that inhabit the bottom of the ocean. As Indiana claims: "Caribbean identity has been coagulating for the last 500 years and continues to absorb elements. It is a spongy and living matter."[80] This description recalls the main attributes of coral reefs and Glissant's theories of the Caribbean's rhizomatic identity: a constellation of roots, languages, histories, and times that gives way to a fluid, open-ended identity.

However, Giorgio Menicucci and Linda Goldman's Sosúa Project proves that the same tools that guarantee environmental sustainability can be put to the service of primitive accumulation and the expansion of extractive industries. Acilde Figueroa, locked up in La Victoria prison in the Santo Domingo of the future, returns to the colonial past as Roque and to the 1990s as Giorgio in order to become part of a neoliberal culture that rejects all possibilities for long-term change. While Esther Escudero had recruited Acilde to save the Caribbean from the environmental holocaust that began in the colony and ended up materializing with the tsunami of 2024, Acilde in fact becomes a messiah of primitive accumulation by reincarnating in different versions of buccaneer characters who act outside the law. Indiana distinguishes between participation in Afro-Caribbean rituals that seek to intervene in the flow of history and the passivity of virtual worlds in the digital age. For example, Acilde manipulates the historical timeline via remote control, "as though he were playing a video game, accumulating goods, trophies, experience, enjoying the view, inexistent in that future of acid rains and epidemics in which prison was preferable to the outside."[81] The task entrusted to him has become so titanic that Acilde decides to immerse himself in a culture of presentism and the exaltation of the (alter) ego instead of authentically undertaking the journey to the seed of capitalist disaster.

The Sosúa Project begins as a laboratory of tentacular assemblages that combine diverse orders of knowledge, as a community of artists, biologists, and environmental activists who put their expertise at the service of preventing planetary collapse. However, as the plot progresses and the storyline recedes, the project becomes an institution promoting the commodification of the landscape and the art world, as seen in the decision to sell the Côte de Fer engravings to private collectors instead of donating them to the Dominican state. The name Côte de Fer (iron coast) points both to the creolization of Caribbean culture and a Dominican coastline littered with postindustrial waste. At the end of the novel, the members of the Sosúa Project organize a party that privileges the culture of presentism and neoliberal networking over their initial intention to promote sustainable knowledge. Giorgio's ambition ends up turning him into the figure of the amnesiac citizen who succumbs to the hypertrophied historical consciousness caused by neoliberal culture: "In a little while, he'll forget about Acilde, about Roque, even about what lives in a hole down there in the reef."[82]

In *La mucama de Omicunlé* Indiana mobilizes negative emotions such as apathy and horror through the inextricable link between bodily and natural damage. If the inhabitants of dystopian Santo Domingo experience post-traumatic stress disorder as a product of the end of nature, Giorgio's wife, Linda Goldman, suffers from pre-traumatic stress through her fight against the bleaching of coral reefs. In front of coral reefs, Linda feels "like an oncologist standing before her patient's body," an environmentalist agenda she undertook after watching filmmaker Jacques Cousteau's documentaries about the pollution of the Caribbean Sea. However, her own family history reveals the continuities between colonial and extractive projects on the island of Hispaniola. Her father arrived in Sosúa with hundreds of Jews who escaped from concentration camps when the town was "a jungle, the abandoned lands of the United Fruit Company."[83] The parallel between the extermination of bodies and the devastation of the natural world should not be overlooked, as Linda embodies the physical and affective impact—the anxiety, depression, and trauma—that the degradation of the island has on the people who feel most attached to it. Linda has written a thesis on "coral reef diseases," spent entire nights without sleep, walked naked through campus, attended her graduation sedated with pills, and been diagnosed with bipolar disorder. The novel shows how Linda inflicts on her own body the material damage that humans are dispensing in the natural world. Before establishing the Sosúa Project, Linda personifies the sense of apathy that contemporary citizens suffer in the face of a panorama so gigantic it comes to paralyze action on an individual level, feeling "that the end of the world was irreversible and widespread ignorance would continue to prevent her from saving the ocean."[84]

Indiana stands against this generalized sense of apathy and inaction through her conception of history as a chaotic arrangement of repetition and difference. She bases the structure of the novel on the creative reenactment of multiple spaces and times, which form a kaleidoscopic image of the present in the manner of tentacles that open and retract as they respond to ocean tides. The metaphor of historical returns comes from Antonio Benítez-Rojo's influential book *The Repeating Island*, in which he theorizes Caribbean identity through the notions of natural chaos and meta-archipelago: "a chaos that returns, a detour without a purpose, a continual flow of paradoxes." Indiana immerses the reading public in her search for homologies between historical processes of natural resource extraction. Instead of the temporality of progress, where history is conceived as an inexorable race toward the future, her novel unfolds as a swarm of species, affects, stories, and practices advocating collective action in times of capitalist dispossession. For Benítez-Rojo, the Caribbean is "the natural and indispensable realm of marine currents, of waves, of folds and double-folds, of fluidity and sinuosity."[85] Indiana's novel replicates the sinuosity of the ocean through a cartography of temporal folds that are like islands repeating themselves, sinking and then resurfacing. The narrative universe becomes a kaleidoscope reflecting the collective and improvisational nature of Caribbean culture.

The novel's temporality follows the designs of the orisha divinity Olokun, a "marine creature . . . [that] could travel back in time . . . very Lovecraftian."[86] Sharae Deckard and Kerstin Oloff describe *La mucama de Omicunlé* as a novel that inscribes H. P. Lovecraft's weird fiction in two conflicting timescales: "the mythic temporality that emanates out from the age of the gods and the cyclical periodicity of the 500-year durée of colonialist capitalism."[87] Indeed, the novel is framed by the long history of colonialism and resource extraction on the island of Hispaniola from the pasts and futures of nonhuman forces, the "earthly forces" that, according to Donna Haraway, "travel richly in space and time."[88] In the Chthulucene, the past is not a hologram or a set of specters outside of history like the illusory eternity projected by the machine in Adolfo Bioy Casares's *La invención de Morel* (a work that Argenis reads at the Altos de Chavón School of Design) but, rather, is presented as an incantation, a fabulation, or a speculation that is capable of modifying the structures of temporal causality. The novel is thus inscribed in the "ongoingness" that, according to Haraway, defines the urgencies of our geological era, an "ongoing temporality that resists figuration and dating and demands myriad names."[89] Rather than proposing a concrete name for our climate predicament, in *La mucama de Omicunlé* Indiana unfolds the powers of collective action in a time of environmental precariousness when nature, because of the devastating actions of extractive projects, is rapidly turning against us. Indiana shows that, unless humans establish long-term alliances with the nonhuman forces that populate the planet, the coming catastrophe will find us out in the open, without swarms or tentacles to protect us.

MANGROVE POETICS

Whereas in *El año del desierto* the rootedness of the *ombú* serves as an image of the Argentinean cultural tradition, in *La mucama de Omicunlé* the ceiba tree is the exact place under which the Dominican national treasure lies buried: the engravings that Argenis creates in the colonial past under the pseudonym "Côte de Fer." According to García-Peña, the ceiba is "the tree of life" whose connection to tradition serves as an antidote to the colonial orphanhood of the Dominican Republic. The Dominican Republic's colonial history reminds us of its brotherhood with Haiti rather than the neighboring country's stigmatization as a "colonizer-invader."[90] In Lydia Cabrera's *El monte* (1954) about the traditions of Black Cubans, the ceiba tree is cast as a meeting place between "all the spirits, the ancestors, the African 'saints' of all nations brought to Cuba, and the Catholic saints."[91] Simultaneously, the ceiba is linked with the colonial past since Columbus allegedly used the trunk of this tree to moor the *Santa María* when arriving in Santo Domingo.[92] Given that his father is a corrupt Dominican politician who stopped speaking to him years ago, Argenis's relationship with the past is that of an orphan who is bound to reconstruct from scratch the dislocated history of the Caribbean—which, according to Glissant, "came together in the context of shock, contradiction, painful negation, and explosive forces."[93]

Whereas the ceiba tree posits a relationship with the past marked by chronology, Argenis embarks upon a journey that is interrupted by shock and dislocation of the historical continuum, which Indiana symbolizes through the figure of the mangroves. In the mangrove, the earth devours what is buried, with no possibility of future rescue. It is a site that lies between the river and the sea, where the traces of human presence do not survive for posterity. "Memory fails in the mangrove," remark Natasha Ginwala and Vivian Ziherl, "just as the marking of claims becomes impossible."[94] Instead of being buried in the ground, the roots of the trees come to the surface and intertwine with all kinds of plant and animal life.

The image of the mangroves helps account for the novel's narrative procedure because, rather than restituting the Caribbean past through a chronological narrative, Indiana seeks to reveal how past and present form a palimpsest of juxtaposed times, in which the contemporary has become a "present that only made sense when dealing with other people in other times."[95] As Charlotte Rogers points out, Alejo Carpentier's *El siglo de las luces* (1962) features mangroves when he is narrating the construction of the agora on the island of Guadeloupe, which serves as a symbol of the author's "baroque recycling" since it becomes an open-air market where goods are smuggled.[96] In *La mucama de Omicunlé*, the mangroves are the refuge of pirates, whom the novel represents in a double sense: both as buccaneers who traffic in products they exchange with other smugglers and also through the figure of Argenis as the contemporary artist who makes use of procedures that oscillate between the legal and the illegal, the quotation and the copy.

Evoking the figure of the mangrove, Indiana leaves the novel's roots in the air, in full view of its readers, devouring different traditions to adapt these influences to a new territory. She thus rewrites several narrative genres of the Latin American literary tradition: the existentialist account of the conquest (such as Antonio Di Benedetto's *Zama*), dystopian or postapocalyptic fiction, the bildungsroman, the *novela de la tierra* (such as José Eustasio Rivera's *La vorágine*), and the sci-fi novel. It is a form of writing proper to the island as a place of encounter and clash, embodying what Glissant calls "creolization," the process of transplantation and survival of populations that represent "the tangled nature of lived experience."[97]

Mangroves embody this uncontainable nature, which evolves in an undisciplined, nonlinear way, like the roots of a tree hanging in the air. Bourriaud used Glissant's theories on creole culture and the idea of exoticism formulated by Victor Segalen to coin the notion of radicant art, a type of art that behaves like "an organism that grows its roots and adds new ones as it advances."[98] Bourriaud's and Glissant's concepts are helpful in elaborating a theory on the role of the mangroves in *La mucama de Omicunlé*, in which Indiana uses wandering formats to refer to the flows of people and products throughout the history of Hispaniola as well as to the precarious condition of identities traversed by transplantations and adaptations to new territories.

The ceiba may suggest rootedness to the national soil, but the mangroves resemble the tentacles of the sea anemone, in which fish entangle themselves to take refuge from other predators. Mangroves hide and reveal in equal parts. They have the capacity to adapt to diverse contexts and pose problems to the human ambition to leave visible traces in each of the territories where they set foot. Alexandra T. Vazquez coined the term "mangrove aesthetics" to refer to the performative works of Cuban exiles in Miami who inhabit a porous temporality where antiquity and futurity coexist in a versatile way: "A rousing impression of intense rootedness, of a transition toward an abyss, and a tidal undertowing to a new place, all at once."[99]

In *La mucama de Omicunlé*, when the workers hired by the Menicuccis at the turn of the millennium dig up the engravings composed by Argenis supposedly five hundred years earlier, the relationship between the anemone and the ceiba becomes evident, as "they pulled out years of dirt and cow shit from among the ceiba's enormous roots, which had grown like tentacles in the Antillean summers." It is then that the pirates emerge from the mangrove in which they were hiding, in a simultaneity of temporal planes that dissolves the differences between past, present, and future. "A few miles from the place where the vultures are circling, the buccaneers advance uneasily, hesitating over the mangrove roots while below in the muddy stream hundreds of crabs open and shut their pincers. Argenis made a superhuman effort to move his legs in both places, no longer asking himself why this was happening, and follows the others like a zombie."[100] For a novel that combines the Hispanic, creole, and Afro-Caribbean traditions, the image of finding a balance with a foot on the watery ground of the mangroves and the other on the roots of the ceiba tree evokes the tension between the liberation of colonial oppression and the continuation of this past through phenomena such as racism, xenophobia, and environmental violence.

These resurrections of the colonial past are confirmed through the reference to the figure of the zombie. The Haitian tradition of the zombie grapples with the subjugation of African slaves on the island of Hispaniola and their rebellion during the Haitian Revolution, when the press described them as antinatural monsters. Like the mangrove, the zombie is a liminal figure that oscillates between the living and the dead and threatens the stability of subjects and objects.[101] Glissant describes the poetics of relation as "latent, open, multilingual in intention, directly in contact with everything possible."[102] Through the figure of the mangroves in *La mucama de Omicunlé*, Indiana mixes times and places to make an X-ray of our contemporary crisis of time and to transform the here and now of late capitalism into a true archive of planetary destruction.

To read *La mucama de Omicunlé* is to be thrown into a process of immersion. Argenis is a person who, like the roots of the mangroves, finds his perspective turned upside down because his future lies in the ongoing exploration of the colonial past. The mangroves oppose the inherited narratives and rigid borders imposed by the nation-states on the island of Hispaniola, which created historical divisions between the Dominican and Haitian populations.[103] In contrast to the myths of absolute belonging to a territory, mangroves are twisted trees with overhanging branches that, when touching the ground, take root and become intertwined. Mangroves, as opposed to the ceiba, defamiliarize tradition. The type of anemone described in the novel, the *Condylactis gigantea* or giant anemone of the Caribbean, is one of the so-called hosts, which give shelter to other species and carry out symbiosis with each of them. As biomes in which the ecological components are in tension, mangroves can host migratory birds and diverse marine species. Faced with a present broken by all kinds of pasts and futures, readers are forced to dive into a territory without borders, putting down their roots and formulating new forms of belonging to a tradition.

THE WRITER AS A PIRATE

In *El año del desierto* piracy is a technique of the subjectivities of the 2001 crisis, and in *La mucama de Omicunlé* the buccaneering tradition of the Caribbean serves as a backdrop for an aesthetics of quotation, trafficking, and appropriation based on the constant modification of original materials as they are introduced into new contexts. The word "pirate" has several ramifications throughout Indiana's novel. The artists of the Sosúa Project accuse Dominican politicians, including Argenis's father, of "piracy" (in Spanish, *la política del corso* or "buccaneering politics") by legitimizing the practice of theft and peddling among public officials.[104] Upon hearing this accusation, Argenis recalls "Osorio's devastations," the measures taken by Antonio de Osorio, the governor of Hispaniola in the early seventeenth century, to eliminate the smuggling of goods on the island. Osorio's policy of depopulating western Hispaniola harks back to the parallel world inhabited by Argenis, in which a group of French buccaneers in the seventeenth century flee persecution by the Spanish.

In addition to detailing the historical circumstances for the separation of Hispaniola into two independent countries (the Dominican Republic and Haiti), this narrative arc introduces the practice of trafficking cultural goods, which reappears slightly modified at the turn of the millennium when digital technology allows for the manipulation of preexisting materials. The novel opens with the image of garbage collectors in post-apocalyptic Santo Domingo, at the turn of the twenty-first century, but it is the artist who has become a collector of the common production in contemporary culture's flea market. As Benjamin indicates about the allegorical mode, artists turn backward to exhibit the fractures in historical becoming and to restore the instants of possibility hidden in the past.[105] Indiana thus stages an aesthetic of the privateer, the pirate, or the smuggler that corresponds to the temporality of the end times, when a journey to the seed (to borrow from Carpentier's landmark "Viaje a la semilla") is required to recover the sense of openness and multiplicity of potential futures that has been lost in the current scenario of generalized crisis. However, as the narrative unfolds in the

Sosúa Project, the novel's somber tone raises questions about the capacity of art to produce long-lasting change when financial interests voraciously corner all aesthetic projects. As Carlos Garrido Castellano points out, Indiana's novel "can teach us about how culture works in neoliberal conditions, and more particularly what hope remains when subaltern creativity and marginality seem to be fully colonized by neoliberal reason."[106]

At the Sosúa Project, the colonial plane begins to intervene in the trajectory of the artists in residence and the seeds of predatory capitalism begin to corrode the utopian projects of contemporary art. Little by little, works of art become pieces that cannot escape the dictates of the market economy and their own status as fetishistic commodities. The intentions of Giorgio Menicucci and Linda Goldman obey the interests of financial speculation: Giorgio because he asks artists to make their works conform to the neoliberal values of personal consecration (whose parallel in the art world could be the work of the American sculptor Jeff Koons) and to the documentation of Dominican poverty; Linda because she suffers from a white savior complex, whereby she agrees to sponsor the artists only "because her husband had assured her they would recover their investment and the profits would help them push forward her environmental protection project for Playa Bo."[107]

The character of Elizabeth Mendez, a DJ who ceases to be a video artist to devote herself entirely to synthesizing music, provides concrete clues to the poetics of remixing that are pushed forward in the novel. Expanding traditional ideas about compositional work, Elizabeth's practice privileges collaboration over individual creation and process over finished work, which is how Terry Smith defines the concept of artistic composition at the turn of the twenty-first century.[108] At a time when the circulation of images has saturated virtual space, contemporary artists conceive compositions that focus less on producing new content and more on adopting original frameworks for existing forms. In addition to her aural experiments, Elizabeth's work is composed of "a constellation of references" that she has accumulated throughout her stay in Playa Bo, including "papers, photos, notes on napkins, clippings from newspapers and magazines, songs, ideas, feelings, and pieces by Goya."[109] Behind Elizabeth's artistic output hover Benjamin's *Arcades Project* and Warburg's *Mnemosyne Atlas*. Warburg's project preceded Benjamin's by a few years and set out to trace the survival of antiquity in the modern era through the erratic combination of Renaissance images. Indiana, through Elizabeth's aesthetic practice, offers clues on how the novel makes visible the persistence of lost temporalities and forgotten lives, showing that the concept of the contemporary consists in managing to perceive which moments of the past demand to be recovered.

In this sense, the novel develops a prehistory of the present through the proliferation of figures from the art world who anticipated the citational procedures of contemporary art. Elizabeth's practice locates in Goya a precursor of modern art, specifically for his portrayal of the monsters of progress, and in Giorgio Moroder a pioneer of the procedure of inventory, sampling, and remix through which, according to Hal Foster, certain contemporary works reorganize the order of the archive and unfold as "promissory notes for elaboration" or as "enigmatic prompts for scenarios."[110] In fact, the event where Elizabeth will inaugurate her work as a DJ is named *Caprichos*, a homage to Goya's series of engravings that are inserted in the pictorial tradition of *capriccio*—a type of Renaissance composition that combined buildings, archaeological ruins, and other architectural monuments in a fantastical or whimsical way. These are the same engravings that in the novel Argenis appropriates to illustrate the destruction of Hispaniola more than a century before Goya portrayed his *Disasters of War* (1810–1820), placing the precursors after the disciples and showing that in the history of art, as Viktor Shklovsky points out, "it's not the eldest son who inherits seniority from his father, but the nephew who receives it from his uncle."[111]

Once again, Indiana references Carpentier's *El siglo de las luces* through the Cuban author's epigraphic use of Goya's *Disasters of War* paintings, which Catherine E. Wall reads "as an allegorical portrayal of Carpentier's concept of history as a spiraling force."[112] Both Argenis and Elizabeth put into practice a procedure of appropriation whose radicality consists in creating what Benjamin called "dialectical images," in which past and present merge into a single entity and allow glimpses of alternative paths through the history of culture. "Her aural archaeology didn't discriminate between genres. She'd learned from hip hop how to find nuggets of gold in a Rocío Jurado ballad as well as in a song by Bobby Timmons, pieces which, loose and looped, created a new music, divorced from the original sources. She stole, without leaving a trace, whole blocks of songs completely alien to one another, which she'd seamlessly weave with minor chords from the synthesizers, and filled the air with the dark nostalgia of the blues and with Dominican-Haitian gagá, which she loved."[113] Note the comparison between Elizabeth's work and the task of the treasure hunters in present-day Hispaniola, who are after the chests of gold supposedly buried by seventeenth-century buccaneers.

The archaeological work of the contemporary artist is nourished by the same paranoia that drives treasure hunters insofar as it seeks to unearth hidden relationships between minor materials such as quotations, voices, or newspaper fragments, conceiving history as a "dormant presence" from which new knowledge can be extracted.[114] The "dark nostalgia" that Elizabeth perceives in the blues and in Dominican-Haitian gagá reveals how Afro-Caribbean rituals are combined with Western rhythms for the creation of a "new music," which does not aspire to overcome tradition but, rather, to show potential narratives and futures that lie in the interstices of what has already been produced. Likewise, synthesizing music goes hand in hand with the syncretism that characterizes Caribbean cultures, established because of fusions, assimilations, and exchanges between different peoples.

Beginning with Elizabeth's remix strategy at the Sosúa Project, the various temporalities of the novel begin to fold over each other in an ominous way: the voice of Jacques Cousteau in *Haiti: Waters of Horror* mixed with a Donna Summer song falls on the dance floor "like a tsunami," prefiguring the ecological disaster that would ensue in 2024.[115] Another episode of temporal mirroring occurs when the Black slave Engombe and the Afro-Dominican artist Malagueta punch Argenis, the former in the seventeenth century with a weapon he wields "like a bat" and the latter at the turn of the millennium "with his baseball glove-sized hand."[116] Rather than casting readers into the passivity and cynicism of postmodern pastiche, Indiana seeks to engage them in the perception of cracks in the historical sequence as a bridge between an incomplete past and the opening of an alternative future.

Elizabeth's character provides a key figure for thinking about the novel's narrative procedure: the idea of the writer as an "unoriginal genius" (Marjorie Perloff) or a "postproduction artist" (Nicolas Bourriaud) or the literary task as "non-creative writing" (Kenneth Goldsmith) or "quotational practice" (Patrick Greaney).[117] All these theorists highlight the sampling strategies that contemporary artists employ to create original routes through the history of culture. It is no coincidence that the narrative line of the Sosúa Project takes place in the late 1990s, when artists began to conceive of the remake as a foundational gesture and used the strategy of search engines to give new meaning to existing materials, abandoning the quest for the new that had characterized modernist aesthetics.[118]

In *La mucama de Omicunlé*, the figure of the artist as a pirate sets out to establish an original cultural trajectory, making the past a fiction constructed from a multiplicity of presents. However, the intervention of a series of commercial interests—such as launching a Casa Museo Côte de Fer that re-creates "a buccaneer settlement . . . [whose] guides would be dressed as pirates"—leaves open the question about the potential of art to effect radical change.[119] In the face of a nostalgic culture that promotes the passivity of spectators, Indiana proposes a kind of piracy that breaks out of mercantile circuits and activates new uses for traditional objects. By establishing negotiations between artist and spectator and between temporal orders, she stimulates an imaginary of anticipation and reminiscence at a time when our capacity to develop historical thought has been called into question.

QUEER ORIENTATIONS

In addition to overthrowing the binary ontologies that conceive nature and culture as separate entities, Indiana questions the heteronormative time of progress. María Teresa Vera-Rojas has shown how Indiana's musical and literary works are populated by "bodies whose materiality accounts for the instability and possibilities of resistance" to hegemonic discourse.[120] Alexandra Gonzenbach Perkins has read the novel through the lens of "queer materiality," which underscores the connections between the human and the nonhuman via Santería rituals and Acilde's contact with the sea anemone.[121] Indiana's nickname, "La Montra," suggests both a monstrosity that disarticulates identity essentialisms and the visibility of female artists in the Dominican cultural context, which has excluded them throughout history.[122] In *La mucama de Omicunlé*, Indiana shows that revolutionary time lies in the recovery of forgotten pasts that never materialized and that continue to inhabit the unconscious of the modern nation. This conception of history undoes the linear time of heteronormative subjects whose life trajectory obeys a prearranged script: marriage, reproduction, child-rearing, and death.[123] For the dissident bodies of Indiana's novel, the present is a constant becoming (a becoming-with) in which history appears as pure potentiality.

Acilde's body is the target of various forms of exploitation—in terms of gender, class, and race—that signal a return of the repressed of the modern nation, from slavery and the plantation economy to the forms of biopolitical control prevailing in the neoliberal era. His gender-affirmation surgery allows him to escape the linearity of heteronormative time and to fight against the ecological destruction of Hispaniola through the Sosúa Project. After all, there is a tangled relationship between the time of heteropatriarchy and extractive activities. As Rita Segato has pointed out, the extractive projects that settle in Latin America's rural communities are accompanied by brothels in which "the body-thing of women" is offered in exchange for nothing.[124] Indiana's novel suggests that, in the face of intemperie and the expropriation of the body politic, queer subjectivities project futures that exceed capitalism and heteropatriarchy.[125]

There is not one world in which culture and nature are separate entities, as promoted by extractive corporations and modern technocrats, but several worlds in which bodies, objects, and supernatural beings coexist fluidly. Arturo Escobar theorizes the notion of pluriverse as the opposite of the modern binaries that separate nature and culture, body and mind, and human and nonhuman. In the concept of pluriverse, he considers "the fact that all entities that make up the world are so deeply interrelated that they have no intrinsic, separate existence by themselves."[126] In *La mucama de Omicunlé*, Acilde's contact with the sea anemone triggers a series of spatiotemporal transactions that sow the seeds of a post-extractive, relational, and communitarian world.

In this sense, Indiana develops a queer aesthetic, understanding queerness—as theorized by Jack Halberstam, José Esteban Muñoz, and Elizabeth Freeman—as a spatiotemporal orientation that is open to the possibility of building other worlds. Halberstam points out that queerness entails a particular relation to time and space because it opposes bourgeois institutions such as family, reproduction, and heterosexuality. Muñoz reveals how queerness combats the capitalist logic of the here and now and the continuous production of commodities, which gives the idea that nothing exists beyond the present.[127] In response to theorists such as Lee Edelman, who conceived queerness as a time devoid of future, Muñoz points out that it is an ecstatic temporality that allows us to intervene in the past so as to imagine a new future: "a queer time that is not yet here but nonetheless always potentially dawning."[128] Halberstam also makes a connection between queer temporality and ecstasy when arguing that, while the normative logic of the middle-class privileges long periods of stability, individuals who live at a different pace, such as drug addicts, are considered immature and dangerous. The bourgeois state of mind cannot perceive how the playful temporality of drugs (which Halberstam illustrates through William S. Burroughs's notion of junk time and Salvador Dalí's melting clocks) reveals the artificiality of constructs such as time and activity in contemporary societies.[129]

The temporality of queer ecstasy appears in Indiana's novel through drugs that allow time to be conceived as a hybrid entity. Convalescing in a bed in the 2001 present, Argenis is transported back to the seventeenth century by the anemone that stings him in the Caribbean Sea and the strip of Valium given to him by the art curator Iván de la Barra. In a memorable passage, Argenis describes the Dominican Republic's energy crisis in parallel to the use of LSD: "In the Caribbean we live on the dark side of the planetary brain, just like with LSD; the neurons that correspond to our islands are very rarely lit, but when they are. . . ." From then on, the present becomes an ecstatic temporality reminiscent of Burroughs's use of cut-up techniques to convey the experience of ayahuasca in *The Yage Letters* (1963). Argenis begins to inhabit a "night in two worlds" and two bodies: his own body in the region of Puerto Plata at the end of the twentieth century and the body of the colonial painter Côte de Fer at the beginning of the seventeenth.[130]

This is a queer and psychedelic rewriting of Cortázar's "La noche boca arriba," in which the temporal planes of a young man in a modern city and a war prisoner in pre-Hispanic times converge and blur the differences between before and after, reality and dream. The relationship between ecstasy and queerness is reflected when, in a state of delirium that straddles the lines between past and present, "in both his bodies, that of Argenis and of Côte de Fer, he went to the beach muttering, 'Faggot, loco, crazy faggot,' and those words cut him inside with a sharpness like the edges of the reef in whose nooks and crannies he recognized the broad nose and thick lips of his father's profile as if in a paranoid painting by Dalí."[131] Considering that his father is a high-ranking Dominican politician, it is not difficult to interpret Argenis's fear of queerness as a manifestation of the mechanisms of heteropatriarchy that Segato has referred to using the expression "pedagogies of cruelty": the mandate of masculinity, distancing, desensitization, lack of empathy, corporate ideology, and excessive bureaucracy.[132] On the other hand, the reference to Dalí's work reveals the artificiality of the notion of time in an era of presentism: the ecstasy of queer temporality is the only alternative to the "sinister clock," as Linda Goldman puts it, of contemporary capitalism.[133]

Similarly, the reference to the coral reef produces a decentering of the place of humans in the conception of historical time, which is crucial to the idea of "temporal drag" theorized by Freeman. Drag—the deliberate exaggeration of gender through dress or makeup, which challenges binary definitions of identity—is for Freeman an anti-genealogical temporal practice sharply opposed to the structure she defines as chrononormativity: the causality and forward movement of the life histories of heteronormative subjects. Drag introduces a crack in the linear conception of history because it allows us to think of identities and social change across different times and spaces, as "a productive obstacle to progress, a usefully distorting pull backward, and a necessary pressure on the present tense."[134] This relational way of conceiving gender identities and historical periods is key to understanding the temporal scope of Acilde's subjectivity. At the beginning of the novel, Acilde works in the port of Santo Domingo as a sex worker with a body with androgynous features that "passed for that of a fifteen-year-old boy."[135] After undergoing gender-affirmation surgery, Acilde's narrative intermingles with his past as Giorgio in the Sosúa Project and as Roque in the colonial era. In this sense, the novel proposes that queerness is a way of being in time that dissociates itself from the neoliberal logic of capital accumulation. Acilde seeks to flee from this temporal regulation of the body, first when she abandons her job as a sex worker to become Esther Escudero's maid and later when she manages to think of herself as a queer subject who inhabits several worlds simultaneously.

Against "the demolition of an ecosystem that had no resources left to regenerate," the artists of the Sosúa Project think of a relational and regenerative practice that recognizes the intertwining of the human body with the environment.[136] Malagueta, for example, is obsessed with the photos of Cuban American artist Ana Mendieta in which body and earth become one and the same, a becoming that makes him think of the human body as "an elemental and magical fury, like a ball of fire."[137] Mendieta's *Silueta* series (1973–1980) is composed of a set of photographs and films in which the artist leaves the mark of her body in the natural landscape in the form of silhouettes, which point to the ephemeral condition of human time on earth as opposed to the continuous regeneration of natural processes.[138]

In addition to evoking the body of the buccaneers hidden in the mangroves, Mendieta's assemblages, which she called earth-body artworks, are a combination of absence and presence, an image of the telluric forces that facilitate the spectral exchange between time and space in Indiana's novel. Mendieta's earth-body artworks could be seen as reincarnations of the gorgons, the figures of Greek mythology who avenged crimes against the natural order and whom Haraway describes as "chthonic entities without a proper genealogy; their reach is lateral and tentacular; they have no settled lineage and no reliable kind (genre, gender), although they are figured and storied as female."[139] Unlike the heteronormative *anthropos* that conceives of time as a forward motion, the dissident bodies in *La mucama de Omicunlé* project a disorienting temporality that delineates an image of history as a weaving, or a tentacle, of worlds—remote, present, and yet-to-come.

Mairal's *El año del desierto* and Indiana's *La mucama de Omicunlé* were published in contexts in which the ubiquity of the notion of crisis—environmental, social, economic, and biopolitical—gave rise to a sense of a life lived in la intemperie, in the harsh outdoors. Whereas Mairal's novel appeared in 2005, four years after the socioeconomic crisis in Argentina and during a time of massive unemployment and underemployment, Indiana's was published in 2015, five years after the earthquake in Haiti with its epicenter in Port-au-Prince, which left more than three hundred thousand dead and one and a half million people homeless. The narrator of *El año del desierto* is swept away by the spatiotemporal disorientation caused by the crisis; she cannot form a historical consciousness but only instincts of survival and adaptation to the growing precariousness of the public sphere. Despite recounting a process of personal and collective amnesia, Mairal offers hope in the novel's alternative lifestyles to capitalism, such as María's coexistence with Indigenous communities on the outskirts of a devastated city and the recyclers of obsolete materials reminiscent of the cartoneros in postcrisis Buenos Aires. On the other hand, *La mucama de Omicunlé* unfolds in an apocalyptic setting in which machismo, violence against the environment, isolation of vast sectors of the population, and anti-immigration sentiment proliferate. Questioning the capacity of art to generate prospects for change once the interests of capital have subsumed it, Indiana proposes a platform to build new worlds from the fragments of both past and future catastrophes. Both novelists pose ambiguous or dialectical scenarios that oscillate between order and entropy, microscopic and cosmic, and national vis-à-vis foreign (or post-national) languages, undoing the global belief in progress and opening other modes of subject formation that escape the circuits of capitalist consumption.

Ultimately, both novels develop relational aesthetics in which the writer, as a figure of the pirate or the buccaneer, traffics with artistic materials and foundational events of the modern nation to reconstruct the social edifice and the literary tradition from an original vantage point. Both authors oppose the binary systems on which modern narratives were founded: culture versus nature, male versus female, and civilization versus barbarism. Instead, their recombination of signs is aimed at forming a collective persona through the implication of readers in what Bourriaud calls "an interactive democracy": the communal creation of new spaces of sociability and reconstruction of the social fabric.[140] Both writers propose relational alternatives to Western dualistic visions through dynamic conceptions of the human–nonhuman relationship and the creative process. By thinking of history as an entity that transcends chronological narratives, both novelists offer dialectical images that unleash the forces of collective action to elaborate the present and imagine potential futures.

CHAPTER 2

A TOXIC HISTORY
OF THE PRESENT

The Novel of Ecohorror

Throughout Latin America, large-scale extractive projects are appropriating communal lands, displacing local populations, and damaging the biodiversity of regions such as the desert and the rainforest. In complicity with local governments, police forces, and criminal organizations, predatory businesses are targeting environmental activists who oppose extractive capitalism and defend Indigenous territories, making Latin America one of the regions with the highest murder rates of land defenders and Indigenous protesters.[1] In light of global capitalism's perpetuation of colonial policies of natural resource extraction, how is the novel as a genre staging the contamination, toxicity, and ecological risk that pervade contemporary societies? How are novelists reflecting on the ethical and political concerns at the heart of our current discussions on the Anthropocene? The focus of this chapter is on ecohorror narratives that build a tangled relationship between bodily, social, and environmental sickness and that harness literary affects so as to conceive new forms of communal life through the pairing of local and planetary conditions. The emotions that these novels inspire in readers serve as vehicles to raise awareness of the precarious conditions of the environment, but they also serve to turn us into the discerning citizens that anthropogenic climate change calls us to be.[2]

I use the category of ecohorror to refer to works that inspire negative emotions such as anxiety, disgust, and uncertainty in order to delineate landscapes of contagion and toxicity and convey the urgency of determining the origins of bodily and environmental illness. I take my cue from Sianne Ngai, whose notion of "ugly feelings" introduced the politics of negative affects "as a mediation between the aesthetic and the political in a nontrivial way."[3] I also echo Christy Tidwell and Carter Soles's notion of Anthropocene ecohorror as "both a genre and a mode," which includes not only nature-strikes-back stories but also narratives that feature human fear of and for more-than-human nature.[4]

As opposed to these scholars' understanding of ecohorror as a "critique of environmental degradation . . . couched in mere entertainment" and a possible cause of ecophobia, however, I show that these novelists catalyze new forms of political agency and environmental sustainability. In doing so, they stand against the state of apathy, indifference, and "carelessness with respect to human life" that, according to Virno, has invaded all aspects of contemporary life after the turn of the millennium.[5] In the contemporary Latin American novel, writers are thus promoting a sustainable imagination not only through a poetics of recycling of the literary canon but also through the representation of toxic landscapes that make it possible to configure a space of coexistence between human and nonhuman beings.[6]

Negative emotions feature prominently in modern Latin American literature. The region's literary canon cannot be understood without the recurrent eliciting of disgust, fear, and horror as agents of aesthetic discernment and political change. A list of Latin American literary works inspiring negative emotions would necessarily include Echeverría's *El matadero* (1871), in which the hordes supporting the dictator Juan Manuel de Rosas kill a young political opponent in the city's slaughterhouse; Borges and Bioy Casares's rewriting of *El matadero* in "La fiesta del monstruo" (1947) under the pseudonym H. Bustos Domecq, a short story in which the marginal masses marching to the Plaza de Mayo to support the Monster (a political leader who serves as an allegory of Juan Domingo Perón) kill a Jewish man in a grotesque public spectacle; and Juan Rulfo's *Pedro Páramo* (1955), which lays bare the contradictions of Mexican capitalist modernity through Comala's plundered rural landscape and the wandering spirits of abused women. In these works, the negative emotions arise from the marginalized masses, the region's authoritarian regimes, and the traumas of failed revolutions and corrupted forms of government such as *caciquismo*. Disgust, fear, and horror are aesthetic and political feelings capable of immersing readers in a state of alert and historical consciousness. I argue that contemporary works of ecohorror continue this tradition by emphasizing the relationship between the body and the land. As a genre of the climate crisis, ecohorror links the pillage of the earth with the decaying health of its most vulnerable inhabitants, drawing readers to the injustices of the capitalist system and the legacy of five hundred years of colonial plunder.

In this chapter, I analyze *El huésped* (The host, 2006) by Mexican writer Guadalupe Nettel and *Distancia de rescate* (2014; trans. 2017 as *Fever Dream*) by Argentinean writer Samanta Schweblin, two novels of ecohorror that account for an ominous present marked by the state of confusion and the daily acts of survival of the communities who are disproportionately impacted by the climate crisis.[7] Both novels make visible the urgency of the crisis through the enactment of "skin shows," which reflect the gothic concern over "the staging of historical battles within the body."[8] *El huésped* is a gothic narrative about the recovery of the sustainable past of Indigenous communities in a dire present haunted by air pollution and overpopulation. Nettel is concerned less with elucidating the etiology of the illness that affects the protagonist than with instilling a relationship of uncertainty between the bodily and the environmental parasite, opening a space for readers to diagnose the origins of the malaise. On the other hand, in *Distancia de rescate* Schweblin portrays the catastrophic effects and distressing affects brought to Argentinean farms and their surrounding populations by the implementation of agrochemicals and synthetic pesticides. She explores the connections between environmental toxicity, pesticide poisoning, and human sickness. Both novelists show that ecological danger is an invisible and omnipresent phenomenon resulting from historical natural resource extraction processes that have caused social and environmental decay across the Americas.

In tandem with a growing corpus of ecohorror fictions from across the hemisphere, Nettel and Schweblin depict environmental issues in rural and urban ecosystems through the recycling of a repressed past—the sustainable knowledge of Indigenous communities in Mexico City and the civilizational fantasies of nineteenth-century Argentinean politicians.[9] They use the gothic mode to defamiliarize the present and reveal "the ecological unconscious" of primitive accumulation.[10] By deactivating the utopian potential of the modern national project and by activating its dystopian nature (the state as a murderous, accumulating, and expropriating machine), both authors inscribe our contemporary climate predicament within colonial and geological timescales. This widening of the temporal focus of the novel as a genre allows them to weave relationships of historical continuity between processes of resource extraction at a time when our horizons of expectation have succumbed to free-market capitalism and large-scale extractivism.

Contemporary novels that deal with the climate crisis elapse on a timescale far beyond any one person's or society's lifetime. As a crisis that has been developing over many centuries, the degradation of the environment should be framed in the *longue durée* or the deep time of geological scales. The most extreme interpretations of the Anthropocene date its beginnings back to the Neolithic Age, the Pleistocene, or even before, showing that human life itself could be seen as a harmful event for our planet.[11] For Rob Nixon, the concept of "slow violence" accounts for the logic of long-term ecological damages such as deforestation and climate change, insofar as it is "a violence that occurs gradually and out of sight, a violence of delayed destruction that is dispersed across time and space, an attritional violence that is not viewed as violence at all."[12] As Déborah Danowski and Eduardo Viveiros de Castro point out, the temporal acceleration of contemporary societies has given way to "a present 'without a view,' a passive present" in which every discourse about the climate crisis or every action that seeks to counter it feels "anachronistic, out of step."[13]

The novels I analyze in this chapter expand the timescales with which we frame the contemporary by using anachronism as a narrative strategy that makes visible the ubiquity and omnipresence of large-scale ecological damage. This focus on the *longue durée* of geological processes stands against the presentism that Hartog diagnoses as the privileged regime of historicity of contemporary societies. This temporality produces the past and the future while privileging the most immediate present.[14] In *El huésped* and *Distancia de rescate* Nettel and Schweblin raise the possibility of conceiving a historical imagination in a period marked by the presentism of the neoliberal model and the advent of several discourses about the end of nature and the end of the world as we know it.

Recent ecocritical approaches to Latin American novels of destruction, preservation, and sustainability have raised the possibility of conceiving a global community of letters not as a Eurocentric fantasy but through our urgent need to think together about the dangers of the climate crisis.[15] The notion of crisis forces writers such as Nettel and Schweblin to reorganize the canon and the ways of understanding the literary as a result of the shared problems that communities, ecosystems, and territories experience on a planetary scale. By arguing that apocalyptic imaginaries, instead of foreclosing sustainable impulses, in fact promote an environmentalist vision through a call to immediate action, I frame Nettel's and Schweblin's novels within a series of narratives that Heather Houser has called fictions of ecosickness: "This literature shows the conceptual and material dissolution of the body-environment boundary through sickness and thus alters environmental perception and politics."[16]

Similarly, Ursula K. Heise argues that contemporary narratives about extinct species show that affliction, grief, and melancholy can be emotions that are intrinsic to the construction of a long-term sustainable vision. Heise claims that environmentalists "often mourn openly for nonhuman beings, for species, for places, and even for processes (certain kinds of weather, seasonal changes, animal migrations) that might not usually be considered appropriate objects of grief."[17] *El huésped* and *Distancia de rescate* are Anthropocene eulogies that mourn animals, ecosystems, and nonhuman entities whose destinies are entangled in decisive ways with that of human beings.

The Latin American narratives examined here use the gothic to represent temporal imaginaries that have emerged in the wake of our current climate predicament, unlike modern visions that rely on developmentalism, utopia, and the potentiality of human actions to shape the world. The climate crisis has confronted us with a catastrophic temporality that lacks any sense of stability—the immensity of the problem discourages human action and makes it seem as if there is no future. By writing works that oscillate between gothic and horror fiction (two genres that have traditionally been excluded from the realm of serious literature), Nettel and Schweblin capture the derangements of scale when human action is measured through the lens of the global and the planetary, thus responding to Amitav Ghosh's assertion that "the climate crisis is also a crisis of culture, and thus of the imagination."[18] As they incorporate the temporality of nonhuman phenomena such as pesticides and atmospheric pollution, these novelists blur the boundaries between realist and speculative fiction, between local and planetary, and between human and nonhuman, aligning with Debjani Ganguly's theorization of the climate change novel "as a mutant or recombinant form that has as its pulse our catastrophic present."[19] In this sense, *El huésped* and *Distancia de rescate* are mutant novels that question the modern conception of the human as separate from nature by showing its entwinement with biochemical, geological, and technological processes.

Both novels take place within the communities that most clearly suffer the slow violence of the climate crisis, becoming genuine zones of socioeconomic exclusion: the marginalized populations of peasants, beggars, and Indigenous peoples living either in the underground of neoliberal megacities or in rural towns that are far removed from the inclusive networks of the nation-state. Both novels recount the precarious existence of people who, living outside the protection and assistance of modern democracies, are thus unable to cope with the magnitude of the crisis. The authors weave clear links between the appropriation of ancestral lands and the health of each community member, echoing the notion of bodies-territories espoused by ecofeminist movements throughout the region. For ecofeminist activists and scholars such as Gago, "body-territory is a practical concept that demonstrates how the exploitation of common, community (be it urban, suburban, peasant, or Indigenous) territories involves the violation of the body of each person, as well as the collective body, through dispossession."[20]

Nettel and Schweblin focus not only on the vulnerability of marginalized communities but also on their attempts at collective resistance. Such attempts should be framed within the activist organizing that Rob Nixon and Joan Martinez-Alier refer to as "environmentalism of the poor," the local or transnational environmentalism of populations that are at a higher risk of experiencing the invisibility of slow violence (who Nixon, citing Kevin Bale, calls "disposable people").[21] There is, without a doubt, a continuum between the marginalization and structural poverty of the past decades, such as the rural-to-urban migrations that occurred during the Cold War, and the impact that the environmental crisis is having on these communities. Nettel and Schweblin reveal these continuities and inaugurate the contemporary as a critical moment. By proposing an apocalyptic vision as opposed to a revolutionary eschatology, these writers uncover human vulnerability as it is exposed to the powers of nature.

Both these novels feature human protagonists who have lost control over their own bodies. They adhere to the apocalyptic narrative tradition through the zombie trope and show that it is impossible to apprehend our current regimes without considering the relationships between human and nonhuman agents such as animals, minerals, and plants. Both novels are elegies for a decaying planet; they do not prophesize a coming apocalypse so much as narrate in the present tense the anxiety about a future on the verge of extinction, threatened by environmental toxicity, the loss of natural habitats, and the expansion of industrialized monocultures. The zombie is no longer a plague monster that turns people into ghouls or vampires but, instead, an invisible entity that resembles the effects of pesticides and atmospheric pollution as it invades the human body without our awareness.

While depicting a regime of historicity that is closely tied to the logic of neoliberal capitalism, Nettel and Schweblin reflect on how to reconfigure the present through the imagining of other spaces and times that allow for long-term sustainable visions. Or, in the words of Néstor García Canclini (referring to the temporal explorations of contemporary artists and writers), these novels pose the question of "how to open up the instant to history."[22] Nettel opens the contemporary moment to the deep time of geological timescales and the sustainable knowledge of Indigenous communities, laying bare the dark side of neoliberal Mexico City, fraught with overpopulation, air pollution, and the proliferation of toxic waste. Schweblin disconcertingly intersperses the voices of two narrators, emulating the effects of pesticide poisoning and inciting readers to take an ethical stance in the face of an imminent catastrophe. Ultimately, both authors reflect on the future of literature at a time when the surge of apocalyptic discourses raises doubts about the status of the literary—a time, moreover, in which the climate crisis forecloses the historical imagination through the blurring of the differences between past, present, and future.

MEMORIES OF THE PRESENT

Nettel's *El huésped* is the story of a woman named Ana who, in her early childhood, begins experiencing the presence of a parasite, The Thing, which slowly removes her eyesight and forces her to act against her own will.[23] True to the "stories of self-duplication" that the narrator is fond of reading, *El huésped* gives us enough hints to claim that the parasite is a figuration not only of blindness but also of the extractive policies and enterprises that throughout history have devastated Mexico City's urban ecosystem.[24] Nettel shows that humans do not exercise complete control over the natural world—as Western epistemologies claim through the dangerous divide between nature and culture—but that we are toxic remnants of our destructive actions.[25]

Significantly, Ana joins an organization of blind people who meet regularly in the city's underground. Their plan is to recover the sustainable knowledge of Indigenous communities and to fight the rampant capitalism of neoliberal Mexico from below. "I was only hoping that that other thing, THE URBAN THING, would not permeate into the underground, so that at least the city would be able to preserve that space unspoiled just like I would preserve my memory."[26] Nettel tells the story of the climate crisis by uncovering its spectral underside, the sustainable past of the Indigenous communities who inhabited México-Tenochtitlan, against the backdrop of a new geological era (the Anthropocene) in which humans are losing the capacity to intervene in the construction of a collective future.[27]

Critics have examined *El huésped* from various vantage points and highlighted its dissident portrait of Mexican society at the turn of the century. Carolyn Wolfenzon points out that the novel connects Ana's doubling with the existence of two Mexicos (one visible and modern, the other invisible and underdeveloped), identifying the space of the underground with Octavio Paz's category of "the other Mexico," the one inhabited by peasants and Indigenous communities. Inés Ferrero Cárdenas approaches *El huésped* through the connections between urban geography and corporeality, arguing that the transformations undergone by Ana's body throughout the novel parallel those of the Urban Thing: the city grid in times of neoliberal policies.[28] Similarly, Carina González considers the novel a political bildungsroman that tells the story of the narrator's induction into an alternative community fighting against the neoliberal model. Ana's repulsion toward The Thing, seen as a figure of neoliberal rationality, slowly drives her away from her bourgeois origins and into a community of individuals who oppose the forces of the state.[29] I will examine how *El huésped* makes an archaeology of the Mexican neoliberal present to situate the dispossession of contemporary citizens within the large scales of continental history (with the year 1492 as a marker of the primitive accumulation that has caused a socioeconomic above and below) and to bring out the temporalities that survive within the city's underground.

My analysis of *El huésped* is aligned with Wolfenzon's approach insofar as it stresses the novel's contribution to the Mexican gothic tradition. But I depart from her approach by highlighting how the novel builds a critical reflection around extractive capitalism, the depletion of natural resources, and the exploitation of Indigenous labor. Oloff has read Carlos Fuentes's *Aura* and Juan Rulfo's *Pedro Páramo* as gothic novels about the "ecological unconscious" of the nation and the environmental consequences of the so-called Mexican Miracle or the golden age of Mexican capitalism in the mid-twentieth century. According to Oloff, both novels "register the logic of processes that characterize capitalism in its *longue durée*, such as the increasing commoditization and destruction of lands, labor, and communities."[30]

El huésped is an urban refashioning of the homonymous short story by Amparo Dávila, which is a cornerstone in the Mexican gothic literary tradition. Dávila's "El huésped" narrates the story of a rural family that receives the visit of a living creature—the reader is unable to determine whether it is a person or an animal—that attacks one of the children once the father has left to work in the city. "He [the houseguest] was grim, sinister. With large yellowish eyes, unblinking and almost circular, that seemed to pierce through things and people."[31] Nettel inscribes the gothic trope of the uncanny in a context of environmental vulnerability, as the body of the protagonist comes to suffer the threat of processes of natural damage such as air pollution or toxic waste, which materialize in the presence of a parasite living inside the human body. In this way, Nettel sheds light on how people's bodies are entangled in environmental degradation, biotechnological intervention, and biomedical hazard.

I situate *El huésped* within a larger corpus of Latin American novels about environmental collapse.[32] I establish an explicit dialogue with Mark Anderson's work about contemporary nonfictional accounts that depict Mexico City's underground through an apocalyptic lens. According to Anderson, these texts represent the neoliberal invasion of the underground via the creation of the metro, which turned Mexico City's subsoil into an

uninhabitable space.[33] The underground condenses the environmental issues affecting Mexico City, such as overcrowding, lack of recycling, and
subsidence. The apocalyptic threats of twenty-first-century Mexico City are
the direct result of the extractive enterprises that have devastated the urban
landscape, beginning with the hydraulic engineering project of draining
the Valley of Mexico (the Desagüe), which Spanish colonizers undertook
in order to protect the city from flooding.[34] However, Anderson also points
out that the underground is one of the very few urban sites where it is still
possible to find remnants of the Indigenous past and to generate "the sense
of living in a historically dense time that belies the superficial fixation with
the present that rules the surface."[35]

By locating the narrative in the dark passages of Mexico City's underground, Nettel shows the gothic genre's capacity to underwrite contemporary capitalism by evoking the deep time, the *longue durée*, or the prehistory
of the modern nation. The narrator's progressive blindness forces her to
delve into the deep layers of the underground, to stop seeing "timelessly,"
and to store memories "with the voraciousness of a bulimic person, as if it
were the very last time."[36] Here the metro serves as both a spatial journey
(the movement through the city) and a temporal one (survival of the forgotten Indigenous past). The novelist thus reveals the historical layers that
have been obliterated by the narrative of national modernization, which
considers the construction of the metro as one of its watershed moments.

In *El huésped*, the underground takes up two interrelated meanings. On
the one hand, it is the locus of resistance for the people historically marginalized by Mexican society. In other words, it is a literal figure of the space
that Guillermo Bonfil Batalla, in his groundbreaking study about the tactics of resistance and survival of Indigenous communities, has called *México profundo* or "deep Mexico." According to Bonfil Batalla, Mexican society
has been torn between two competing models for the modern nation, the
Western and the Mesoamerican, for the past six centuries. Whereas the hegemonic classes have pursued a process of gradual "de-indianizing" and adaptation to Western values, the Indigenous peoples of the México profundo
have developed specific survival strategies to achieve complete decoloniza-
tion: "The peoples of the *México profundo* continually create and re-create
their culture, adjust it to changing pressures, and . . . cyclically perform
the collective acts that are a way of expressing and renewing their own
identity. They remain silent or they rebel, according to strategies refined
by centuries of resistance."[37] Even though they come from diverse ethnic,
racial, and socioeconomic backgrounds, the individuals that gather in the
underground embody the resistance strategies of Indigenous communities
against the progressive de-indianizing of the modern nation-state, strategies
that include displacement, the founding of alternative communities, and

the recovery of ancestral forms of knowledge. They bear in their bodies the various policies of colonial rule that Indigenous communities have suffered throughout history, as they are blind, crippled, and mutilated. Nettel does not elucidate the causes of these wounds nor the etiology of Ana's parasite but shows the modes of collective resistance of these communities that are invisible to the eyes of the modern nation-state.

On the other hand, it is underground that the repressed past of the nation comes back to haunt the present. In our current context of unprecedented mutations to the geosphere, the emergence of this past reveals the failure of the sustainable policies of the modern nation. Bonfil Batalla points out that the air pollution that affects Mexico City like cancer is only one of the many urban scars revealing "the unresolved contradictions of Mexican society and history." Modern architects have obliterated Indigenous knowledge of urban planning and natural resource management.[38] This denial of the sustainable knowledge of Indigenous communities is not recent but a long-standing phenomenon linked to the colonial state. Following the Spanish conquest, Mexico City suffered repeated floods primarily due to the Spaniards' ignorance of the Indigenous hydraulic system. According to Ivonne del Valle, these issues were not resolved until the colonizers finally understood that the irrigation system was not simply a part of nature but a cultural, logistical, and technical hydraulic complex they had completely misunderstood.[39] Del Valle suggests that the Mexicas chose to settle in the old Tenochtitlan because of the disposition of the lakes and for that very reason created a complex hydraulic system "that protected the city from flooding, made land available for agriculture, and enabled movement onto and off of the islet."[40] Beginning in the colonial period, the relationship of Mexico City's inhabitants with the natural world was marked by the spectral absence of Indigenous knowledge. In *El huésped*, the resistance strategies of the peasants and Indigenous peoples who inhabit Mexico City's underground clearly evoke the conflict over the lack of sustainable urban policies and the erasure of this techno-cultural legacy.

As a space that belies the neoliberal drive to annihilate other worlds, the underground retains this obliterated Indigenous knowledge. The underground community of blind people flee from the overpopulation and air pollution afflicting the city's surface. Ana's body is inhabited by a parasite that takes control of her actions and becomes a figure of the gothic monster that, according to Halberstam, "will make your home its home (or you its home) and alter forever the comfort of domestic privacy."[41] Mexico City has also become a parasitic ecosystem that has turned its back on its own inhabitants: "the threat [of The Thing] was constant, an immutable factor of the atmosphere like the smog or the acid rain that falls in Mexico City during the summer."[42] Ana's internal parasite is the mirror image of the parasitic relationship that human beings have established with the natural world.[43] The parasite proves that the human body is a platform that materializes the violent exploitation of natural resources and the environmental degradation that extractive capitalism has carried out in Mexico City.

Simultaneously, the city is described via metaphors of the human body that reveal, as Houser points out, "the inseparability of our somatic and ecological fates."[44] *El huésped* establishes a close tie between earth and soma, the city and the body, to show the harmful effects that the neoliberal paradigm has caused in the urban ecosystem and the health of its inhabitants: "I, who for several years had been carrying a parasite inside me, knew it better than anyone; the city was also splitting into two, she was also beginning to have new skin and eyes."[45] The mutation of Ana's body is analogous to the degradation of the urban ecosystem, whose levels of habitability drop so dramatically that by the end of the novel Ana makes the underground her home.

Even though the subway system provides a network of urban circulation necessary for the correct functioning of the neoliberal city, the underground is an archaeological space that seeks to restore the ancestral memory of Indigenous peoples. As Anderson suggests, capitalist rationality has conceived Mexico City's underground as "a mere vault, a sub-terra, a non-environment whose only purpose is to store commodities until future demand endows them with sufficient value to warrant extraction."[46] This instrumental vision of the natural world is at the heart of Nettel's ethical and political critique. Although she does not provide specific temporal coordinates, it is possible to locate the novel's plot in the early 1990s, to the extent that Nettel has identified the character of Cacho, one of the leaders of the community of blind people, as a figure inspired by Subcomandante Marcos.[47]

The context of Indigenous resistance evokes the rise of the Zapatista Army of National Liberation (EZLN) on January 1, 1994, the same day that the North American Free Trade Agreement was enacted. By replacing the Lacandon Jungle with Mexico City's underground and Subcomandante Marco's ski mask with the blindness of its acting members, Nettel allegorizes the anonymous forms of anti-capitalist resistance and survival that emerged in the wake of Mexico's economic downturn. However, in *El huésped* she narrates not only the history of Mexico City during the last decades of the twentieth century following the collapse of the Mexican Miracle but also the processes inscribed in the deep history of the modern nation and the stratigraphic history of its geological record. According to Claudio Lomnitz, the destruction of Mexico City and the devaluation of the lives of its inhabitants did not begin during the so-called years of the crisis (1982–1989) but, instead, could be told "in the *longue durée* (beginning, perhaps, with the process of draining the basin of Mexico, which has taken centuries)."[48] By recovering Indigenous knowledge as an antidote to the various centuries of ecological devastation, Nettel renders the pre-Hispanic past not as a remote temporality but as the flip side of a failed modernization, as an unrealized present.

Blindness could be considered a symptom of the novel's relationship with the contemporary. As she gradually loses her eyesight, Ana goes through a process of myopia whereby one of her eyes points to the distant past while the other registers the most immediate present. When she describes the toxic urban scenario of Mexico City, Ana proves that her vision is alert to the "contiguousness with the ruin" that, according to Giorgio Agamben, is typical of contemporariness. Curiously, Agamben elaborates his theory of the contemporary based on a metaphor about the inability to see, when he claims that "the contemporary is he who firmly holds his gaze on his own time so as to perceive not its light, but rather its darkness."[49] According to Agamben, this darkness is another way of designating the archaic, immemorial, and prehistoric temporalities that continue to influence our present. He proposes an archaeological approach to accessing the present that considers the relationship of proximity and not only the distance that binds us to the origin (*arkhé*).[50] In *El huésped*, the contemporary is composed of the spectral and archaic temporalities erased by earthquakes, flooding events, and the Euro-Western urban planning that destroyed the sustainable design of old Tenochtitlan. The community of blind people meeting in the underground of present-day Mexico City embodies an archaic temporality that, paradoxically, keeps them tied to the needs of the present.

Nettel's work is filled with ecopoetic figures that make it possible to conceive of the contemporary through anachronism, untimeliness, and the survival of the archaic. Curiously, the figures she uses are usually nonhuman organisms such as parasites, fungi, and cockroaches, beings living off the waste of others and which can survive nuclear or ecological holocausts. Ana describes The Thing through the figure of mites ("microscopic insects that eat out our fat and will later devour our remains"), showing how human beings are entangled in a sensorium that includes nonhuman agents and dispelling the anthropocentric idea of human autonomy and control over one's body.[51]

The temporal metaphor is more clearly elaborated in another of Nettel's novels, *El cuerpo en que nací*, when the narrator, as a result of the nickname ("cockroach") that her mother gives her when she is a child, forges a symbolic and symbiotic alliance with trilobites: "the oldest inhabitants of the planet. They have survived climate changes, the worst droughts, and nuclear explosions. Their survival does not imply they haven't known suffering, but that they have learned to overcome it."[52] As Lilia Adriana Pérez Limón points out, these symbolic images of nonhuman organisms make visible the nonnormative human body, thus redefining our notion of citizenship and allowing us to reflect on who has access to the Mexican social and political community and who does not.[53] The references to the deep time inhabited by these nonhuman organisms also serve as a way of broadening the timescales of the contemporary and conceiving a sustainable aesthetics in times of ecological precariousness, when the very soil that the characters step on—the soil of Mexico City—is in danger of disappearing.

In *Survival of the Fireflies*, Georges Didi-Huberman also uses the image of insects, which he considers figures of an archaic temporality, to advance a theory of the contemporary. Didi-Huberman examines a series of writings by Pier Paolo Pasolini in which the Italian thinker associates the figure of fireflies with the capacity of the people to collectively resist the abuses of centralized power. Published during the rise of Italian fascism, these texts establish a stark contrast between *luce* (light) and *lucciola* (firefly), hegemony and the marginalized, power and resistance. Years later, in the mid-1970s, Pasolini observed that the disappearance of fireflies from urban centers because of atmospheric pollution served as an ecopoetic metaphor that could be tied symbolically to the triumph of fascism, which continued to exert an influence on Italian society through a phenomenon he called a "cultural genocide," the emergence of a society of the spectacle that erased or assimilated the people's gestures of resistance—though we might also add the rise of a national language (Italian) at the expense of local dialects.

Didi-Huberman, however, uses the concept of "survival" to argue that what had in reality disappeared was Pasolini's capacity to perceive the grey areas of contemporary history, the survival of the "back then" in the "now," which both thinkers designate through the metaphor of fireflies shining intermittently in the dark. Engaging in dialogue with Agamben's essay, Didi-Huberman proposes that being contemporary "would mean giving oneself the means to see fireflies appear in the fierce, overexposed, overbright space of our current history."[54] By situating the locus of the marginalized in Mexico City's underground in *El huésped*, Nettel links the vulnerability of these individuals with the remains of a sustainable urban model whose eradication in the years following the Spanish conquest led to the current scenario of ecological devastation. Rather than gesturing toward their assimilation into the neoliberal society of the spectacle, their blindness points to their ability to perceive the spectral survival of this failed sustainable model. The blind people's resistance is a movement for eco-social justice that critics have referred to as the environmentalism of the poor.[55]

However, in *El huésped* Nettel complicates the association of the community of blind people with a long-term anti-capitalist project, as its initial impulse does not catalyze radical change. The leader of the organization,

Madero, traces a genealogy of the group with other vulnerable communities that have gathered in the Mexico City underground, but he ends up recognizing that blind people do not follow a collective action plan: "The blind people of these movements have always been driven by the force of anger and collective revenge, not by a project."[56] Nettel reveals the paralysis that is a consequence of the state of mind brought about by the end of history, which Virno links to the experience of déjà vu or false recognition: the idea that human actions cannot influence history, as they appear to be copies of an original that never was. "The state of mind correlated to déjà vu is that typical of those set on *watching themselves live*. This means apathy, fatalism, and indifference to a future that seems prescribed even down to the last detail."[57]

The Thing becomes a temporal device corresponding to the neoliberal paradigm because it undermines people's bodies like an internal parasite, even those who take refuge in the underground to fight the extractive model that has invaded most spheres of contemporary life. Nettel tells a gothic tale that interweaves social and environmental precariousness, so long as the blind people become figures of the living dead whose state of indigence is directly tied to the contemporary ecological crisis (as they were expelled from their homes because of overcrowding and now live among toxic waste) and the exclusionary logic of the primitive accumulation of capital (as they have been deprived of the means of production). In her novel she reflects on an extractive logic that alienates citizens from their own bodies while at the same time remaining oblivious to the effects of social and environmental degradation.

The same sense of paralysis caused by Mexico City's apocalyptic present is apparent in Ana's behavior, as she slowly becomes an archivist of her own life. After realizing that The Thing is causing the progressive impairment of her visual memory, Ana gives herself to the task of creating what she refers to as a "recuerdoteca" or memory library: a sensorial archive of the most immediate present, as an antidote to the distressing feeling of living in the end times. "To preserve in my memory as many images as possible, to build a memory library, was to pay tribute to myself."[58]

This is yet another symptom that Virno links to the condition of living after the end of history: the failure to conceive of the day-to-day as part of historical experience as well as the disposition of daily events in a nonhierarchical manner, as if every moment of a person's life had equal importance. In tandem with Nietzsche's notion of "antiquarian history," Virno points out the need for post-historical individuals to record everything they have witnessed, becoming figures of Borges's "Funes el memorioso" who are unable to forget or select memories in light of the future. According to Virno, the post-historical state of mind and the society of the spectacle turn individuals into spectators of themselves, people "who *collect their own life while it is passing, instead of living it*."[59] Ana's memory library shows that the invasion of The Thing is a somatic illness inherent to the post-historical condition, whose most visible symptoms are apathy, inaction, and the impossibility of projecting sustainable futures: the social symptoms that give shape to the zombie. As The Thing takes control of Ana's body, the initial project of recovering Indigenous knowledge and fighting neoliberal capitalism from below falls apart, to the point where the only thing she feels capable of doing is "to collect memories, as someone who stores a stock of supplies, to resist the imminent catastrophe."[60] In *El huésped* Nettel mobilizes an apocalyptic imagination to show the unbridgeable gap between our scientific capacity to imagine the coming ecological catastrophe and our political unwillingness to end capitalism.[61]

Despite the failed attempts of resistance led by Ana and the community of blind people, Nettel builds a sustainable aesthetics by shedding light on how negative emotions and literary affects can turn our attention to the precariousness of the ecological present. The end of the novel shows that blind people, more than restorers of a sustainable past, are the "human debris" or "wasted lives" of contemporary societies, figures who resemble refugees insofar as the nation-state does not want to recognize them as part of the body politic and who live in contiguity to the toxic waste the ruling classes seek to keep away from their homes.[62] The underground that the blind people inhabit contains not only the modern metro system but also the sewer.[63]

The novel ends with the failed sabotage of the local municipal elections, which the community members carry out by filling the voting envelopes with human feces and transporting them to the polling stations. On the surface, this is a subversive act of civic participation when the government's indifference and political and judicial corruption prevent these people from escaping the state of destitution in which they find themselves. However, through this proliferation of landscapes of abjection and disgust, Nettel elaborates a shocking scene of confrontation of the city inhabitants (and therefore the readers of the novel) with their own toxic waste, as the blind people move through the city in the garbage trucks they steal from the local government, preventing the recycling of urban waste for an entire day. As Houser points out, "Disgust slaps us in the face and forces us to confront that which we would rather ignore."[64] *El huésped* demonstrates how disgust is an integral part of a sustainable ethics and aesthetics, allowing readers to confront their own insensitivity toward the suffering of others and to stand against the apathy typical of the post-historical state of mind.

In *El huésped* Nettel conceives of the contemporary through an archaeological or forensic vision of urban design. Especially significant is the narrator's description of Mexico City as "an empty façade that conceals the debris of all of our earthquakes."[65] This vision of the city denounces a specific form of configuring urban space that recalls the category the architect Rem Koolhaas has termed "the generic city" (closely linked to his notion of "Junkspace"): cities that never age because they comply with the needs of the present, spaces without history or where history is supplied to the highest bidder.[66] Ana designates this spatiotemporal configuration with the expression "The Urban Thing," an apocalyptic city in which past, present, and future get mixed up because they have lost influence as distinct temporal markers:

> In the city, the streets are filled with houses, ads, and people, and are nevertheless so empty, painted with that tarnished mold that covers everything. The smells of the city have become a homogeneous, nauseating stench. Constantly, space ceases to exist and people, adamant in denying it, continue to talk about buildings, statues, and movie theaters that have long ago been knocked down; continue to mention certain streets that are no longer streets but road axes or that no longer carry the same name, avenues where the refuge islands are the only collective memory of a more placid and less vertiginous era.[67]

The empty streets of a metropolis such as Mexico City evoke Benjamin's description of the photographs Eugène Atget took on the streets of Paris in the early twentieth century, which according to the German thinker resembled the scenes of a crime: "A crime scene, too, is deserted; it is photographed for the purpose of establishing evidence."[68] The forensic vision of the narrator in *El huésped* points to another type of crime scene, more akin to the precarious condition of the contemporary moment. In this case, the urban apocalypse is of an ecological order. The narrator associates the nauseating smell of Mexico City with two specific phenomena: the excessive traffic in the streets (because, as she clarifies, these "are no longer streets but road axes") and the ongoing flaws of the sewage system ("the constipated waste pipes").[69]

The passing mention of the road axes is a critique of Mexico City mayor Carlos Hank González's system of *ejes viales* built in the 1970s to make the city more car friendly, bringing to the fore the long-term environmental consequences of an infrastructure that was heralded as the pinnacle of Mexican modernity. Even though the streets are packed, the narrator imagines them completely empty, as if she were describing an apocalyptic landscape and gathering evidence for an ecological crime that has been brewing silently for centuries. Through the narrator's forensic gaze, Mexico City becomes a palimpsest that gathers the rubble of ecological disasters both past and future. Language itself reminisces about the past, serving as another type of memory library or as an accumulation of the sediments of a city that must be continually rebuilt because of natural disasters or modernizing policies that destroy its urban patrimony. Nettel outlines the landscape of Mexico City as a great crime scene that brings together competing temporalities in a sensorium proper to the Anthropocene, in which the distinctions between production and waste have become inoperative.

In reflecting the gothic concern over the return of a repressed past, Nettel uncovers the spectral survivals that haunt the contemporary moment. The locations where the blind people come together are all in-between spaces where the waste, fossils, and specters of the national past accumulate: the landfill, the underground, and the graveyard. The novel depicts the clash that exists in the city underground between the ancestral past of Indigenous communities and the nonplace that is the modern subway system, where thousands of people come together regularly. As Juan Villoro points out, "the metro is the new thing circulating in the grotto of origins. Underground, there is a 'no-place' where time bites its tail," which gives way to a symbolic fusion where "a pyramid, a cross, and an electric vehicle are strictly contemporaneous."[70] But instead of focusing on the modern infrastructure of the metro, Nettel traces non-anthropocentric temporalities that harbor other types of knowledge within Mexico City's subsoil: "I would have liked . . . to slowly integrate into the submarine flora as if I were another seaweed; to get to know the baffling happiness of the drowned; to live for all eternity underneath a rock like a snail, like a millenary fossil."[71] In *El huésped* she recalibrates the timescales of the novel by remaining attentive to the temporality of fossils, minerals, and inorganic matter, assembling what Gabriel Giorgi calls "landscapes of survival" in relation to the scalar shifts of contemporary aesthetics: the positing of heterogeneous temporalities that cannot be contained under the categories of subject, nation, nature, or cosmos.[72] In addition to conjuring a new politics of memory in the face of the current ecological crisis, Nettel delineates new timescales that enhance our notion of "the present," timescales that we are only beginning to apprehend.

THE THREAD OF HISTORY

Samanta Schweblin's *Distancia de rescate* is part of a decades-long tradition of literary works that depict the proliferation of industrial monocultures and the use of biochemical pollutants such as glyphosate, whose effects include miscarriages, malformations, breathing problems, and cancer. The beginning of this tradition dates to Rachel Carson's *Silent Spring* (1962), whose influence on the environmental movement and the creation of the U.S. Environmental Protection Agency was primarily the result of its urgent wake-up call about the indiscriminate use of synthetic pesticides, especially

DDT. Though never explicitly mentioning pesticides, Schweblin draws on several public health concerns that have made national and international headlines in recent years, such as the trials faced by Monsanto (now part of the German multinational company Bayer AG) because of cases of pesticide poisoning throughout the Southern Cone, especially in rural villages located next to fields of genetically modified Roundup Ready soybeans.[73] In fact, Schweblin claimed that while writing the novel she faced the dilemma of whether to include the names of multinational corporations or politicians involved in the court trials, as this was the first fictional rendering of pesticide poisoning in the Argentinean context.[74]

Critics such as Patricia Stuelke have read *Distancia de rescate* through the novel's alignment with recent feminist and ecofeminist strikes across Latin America, as well as with the anti-capitalist manifestos written in Argentina by Gago (founding member of Ni Una Menos [Not one less], the movement that spearheaded the feminist strikes against gender-based violence in the Americas) and in Mexico by Sayak Valencia (author of the influential *Gore Capitalism*, which theorizes "necroempowerment" or the profitability of the business of death in the Third World).[75] In *Distancia de rescate* Schweblin delineates this context of poisoning, necropower, and resistance implicitly, without ever mentioning words such as "pesticides" or "glyphosate"—a narrative strategy akin to the invisible nature of this agrochemical epidemic, which Marie-Monique Robin has named "a silent genocide."[76] Schweblin captures what Amalia Leguizamón calls "a conspiracy of silence" and "the elephant in the field," referring to the denial of glyphosate and pesticide drift by the residents of these rural communities whose economic future depends exclusively on the well-being of the agricultural industry.[77] In *Distancia de rescate* she uncovers the inner workings of a system of agricultural exploitation controlled by the invisible hand of corporations that stay far away from the soy fields and benefit from the imperceptible nature of these toxic substances. Through the eeriness of the gothic genre, she conveys the horror of these silent, invisible, ubiquitous poisonings, which pose several representational challenges as they are framed within processes of slow violence.

In *Distancia de rescate*, the primary victims of agrochemical poisoning are the children who grow up in the rural villages adjacent to the vast soy fields. After getting poisoned, they survive in a zombie-like condition that is externalized as a series of bodily disorders and the loss of their affective capacity.[78] Schweblin uses the child-zombie figure to narrate two interwoven stories that both show the limits of motherhood in agrotoxic scenarios.[79] In the novel she narrates, on the one hand, the story of Carla and her son, David, who survived pesticide poisoning in the soybean plantations six years before the beginning of the plot; on the other hand, the story of

Amanda and her daughter, Nina, who have come from Buenos Aires to spend the summer in a farmhouse located near Carla's property. By adopting the form of a dialogue between Amanda and David, Schweblin focuses on "the important thing" and returns to "the exact moment" when the poisonings took place. The narrative depicts the ominous effects of these bodies deprived of their spirit through typographic changes and the length of the characters' speeches. Whereas Amanda's interventions appear in roman type and can stretch for pages as they piece together the voices of other characters, David's phrases are written in italics and are almost telegraphic, as if he could not catch his breath to speak at length. The exchange between the two characters takes the shape of a palimpsest that reproduces the vertigo of agrochemical pollution.

The crucial scene of contagion occurs when Amanda and Nina, before returning to Buenos Aires, visit Carla at the headquarters of Sotomayor, her employer and the owner of the soy fields. While they watch the agricultural workers unload large plastic barrels containing a substance whose name is never revealed, the women sit on a lawn irrigated with pesticides but that Amanda mistakes for dew. Even after re-creating the events that led to her poisoning, Amanda is incapable of realizing that the substance staining Nina's clothes is the glyphosate used in farming transgenic soy—which points to the complete ignorance of city dwellers about the origins of the food they purchase in the grocery store.

In the novel Schweblin plays with the spatiotemporal scales of motherhood vis-à-vis the interests of corporate actors. As Leguizamón insightfully points out in her reading of the novel, whereas motherhood values "*long-term care at close distance*," corporations "push for maximizing both short-term profitability and distance from the farm and the natural conditions that make farming possible."[80] The novelist foregrounds Amanda's incapacity to distinguish between dew and glyphosate and Carla's cultural predisposition to accept the arrival of pesticides as a positive change in the countryside. Schweblin shows that rural inhabitants do not mobilize against the use of pesticides because of both confusion regarding the health impacts and socioeconomic dependence on the agricultural industry. "If the business of GM soy were to shut down," Leguizamón argues, "whole towns could collapse." *Distancia de rescate* puts forward a narrative of failed motherhood because of the influence of corporate ideology in all socioeconomic sectors of Argentinean society.[81]

It is no coincidence that the only male protagonist, David, is the person who decides "what is important" in the elaboration of the story. Schweblin takes up several tropes of the genre that critics have labeled "female gothic," so long as it reflects on the construction mechanisms of a male version of history and the deliberate obliteration of female lineages. As Diana Wallace points out, the language of spectrality "suggests the particular power of the gothic to express the erasure of women in history, something that may not be expressible in other kinds of language or in the traditional forms of historiographic narratives."[82] Other distinctive features of this genre appear throughout the narrative: the dialogue between Amanda and David takes place in an emergency room whose darkness evokes the metaphoric space of a womb or a tomb, and the role of the doctor is fulfilled by "the woman in the green house," a healer who saves the poisoned children under the strict condition of migrating their spirits from and to other bodies, effectively turning them into zombie children. As Ana María Mutis argues, Schweblin considers the eco-zombie figure "an appropriate instrument with which to represent the anxieties around environmental destruction, especially that associated with new forms of agricultural production fostered by neoliberalism."[83]

Toward the end of the novel, soon after the women get poisoned, Amanda's husband travels to the countryside to visit Nina, who seems to be confined with the other zombie children in the emergency room. This temporal framework conflicts with the fact that Amanda died earlier because of her exposure to pesticides, making it seem that Amanda's voice originates from beyond the grave or that the husband's journey to the countryside is a foreshadowing or a hallucination of an irreversible future. When he gets in the car to return to Buenos Aires, the husband finds David in the backseat playing with the stuffed mole that belonged to Nina. This exchange of roles confirms that Nina's spirit, following her migration via the hands of the healer, lives on in David's body.

Referring to the novel's aesthetic format, Schweblin has claimed that the text emerged as "a short story that did not work out."[84] This aesthetic form that does not easily fit the parameters of either the novel or the short story allows us to understand the genre as a monstrous receptacle that mirrors the uncanny effect of the exchange between Amanda and David and that is situated within the expansive field of contemporary literature. Florencia Garramuño argues that several artistic interventions of the last decades stand out precisely because of "not belonging to the specificity of a particular art form, but also, and above all, not belonging to the idea of art as a specific practice."[85] Garramuño's thesis is based on the paradigm of community put forward by Roberto Esposito, who theorizes otherness or alterity as the basis of the common.[86] It is no coincidence that a text about a community of monster children defined by the ominous dissonance between body and spirit, interiority and exteriority, highlights this estrangement by creating a monstrous genre that oscillates between short story, novel or novella, and stage play.[87] The novel's performative quality stems from Amanda and David's dialogue, which plunges readers into these characters' interiority, aligning with David Kurnick's contention "that some of the most formally innovative novels introject the 'theatrical' deeply into their texture." As Halberstam points out in relation to the gothic genre, "monstrosity always unites monstrous form with monstrous meaning."[88]

In *Distancia de rescate* Schweblin narrates a double set of stories that cross-pollinate each other and leave marks in the body of the text through the exchange of roman and italic typescripts. Moreover, the novel mirrors the effects of agrochemical poisonings by suspending traditional generic conventions and immersing readers in a state of uncertainty resembling the characters' predicament. Such formal elements are crucial for the novel's ethical reflection on the use of pesticides in the Argentinean countryside.[89]

The novel's apparent lack of style creates an uncanny historicity in which the now dissolves into a seamless exchange between the foundational past of the modern nation and the dystopian ecological future. It is a narrative device that reflects the "ecology without the present" that Timothy Morton associates with the temporal regimes of the Anthropocene: "*Now* evaporates into a sickening relative motion of traffic between past and future."[90] Lucía de Leone argues that *Distancia de rescate* stages "a new rural narrative, eaten by worms, told in two voices, undercut by different temporalities, marked by the rhythms of poisoning."[91] Indeed, the delirious narrative of *Distancia de rescate* mixes verb tenses, suppresses the coordinates that make legible the cumulative and utilitarian conception of time that follows the rhythms of capital, and thus appears to be happening outside or on the edges of history. Following the logic of dystopian narratives, the dialogue between the two characters is a race against time because contagion is irreversible. In this sense, *Distancia de rescate* develops what Lawrence Buell has called a "toxic discourse" to refer to the mounting anxiety over the threats of a natural world chemically poisoned by human action.[92]

Schweblin raises the question of why to write fiction in times of environmental collapse, when developing a narrative about contagion would seem of less importance than the medical, legal, and socioeconomic aspects of the conflict.[93] The toxic discourse of *Distancia de rescate* revolves around "the exact moment" in which contagion occurred—that is, around the etiology of somatic illness. Nonetheless, just as David pushes Amanda to focus on "the important thing," Schweblin also insists on the need to create a narrative of the ecological conflict free of excess, inviting readers to envision what is essential as well as opening a space of collective awareness.

The temporal models in the novel include not only the pure present of primitive accumulation but also the spectral return of a repressed past. Pratt coined the term *demodernization* to designate the series of returns of a nineteenth-century past that, in the context of the neoliberal policies sanctioned across Latin America at the turn of the millennium, abolished the narrative of progress and made it "turn backward."[94] According to Pratt, this *demodernization* was a direct consequence of the incapacity of Latin American states to ensure democratic networks of communication, education, justice, and transportation. It became visible not only in the rise of territories of exclusion and marginalization but also in the return of a monstrous imaginary.[95] These symptoms of temporal setback are the same as those Ludmer diagnoses in *Aquí América Latina*, where she reads a series of turn-of-the-century Latin American fictions that dissolve the linear time of the nation and inaugurate an apocalyptic temporality in which the past returns like a specter and the future has already occurred—what she calls, echoing Pratt, "the de-temporalization of the present."[96] At the beginning of the twenty-first century, the return of the nation's foundational past as a series of monsters exposed the dark underside of the neoliberal oasis that flourished in a country such as Argentina, where the bursting of the convertibility bubble—the pegging of the peso and the US dollar that prevailed during the 1990s—led to the 2001 socioeconomic crisis.

In *Distancia de rescate* Schweblin reproduces the fantasies of boundless wealth that the Argentinean countryside has embodied since the dawn of the nation, a wealth that is currently symbolized by the genetically modified crop of the soybean. Instead of depicting the fulfillment of the utopian drive of nineteenth-century Argentinean politicians and intellectuals, she shows that in the new century these fantasies have returned in the shape of a nightmare. Take Sarmiento's ideas in *Facundo* that nature should be appropriated by human reason to ensure national progress. Or Juan Bautista Alberdi's point in the *Bases y puntos de partida* (1853) that to govern meant to educate and populate the "empty" zone of the pampas with European immigrants—"we need a policy," claimed Alberdi, "centered on the conquest of solitude and the desert," at a time when several Indigenous communities already inhabited the desert.[97] On the contrary, the twenty-first-century countryside of *Distancia de rescate* is a zone of exclusion where the democratic network of the modern nation is practically absent—the "waiting room" replaces the school, and the healer takes up the role of the doctor—and where, as Pratt points out, even the national symbols have been *demodernized*, given that mate is one of the primary agents of contagion.[98]

On the other hand, the return of a monstrous imaginary can be seen in the representation of the sick body of children. In *Distancia de rescate*, the toxicity of nature directly impacts the networks of cultural development, diagnosing a series of anxieties over a decaying educational and health system. Among the symptoms the children regularly suffer are hallucinations, hair loss, migraine-like headaches, ongoing thirst, fever, and a state of photophobia that forces them to be confined in a dark room throughout the day. But more distinct damages appear at skin level: the red skin that the town nurses wrongfully diagnose as a sign of sunstroke, the itchiness that David associates with the presence of interior worms, and the patches of white and thin skin that peel off as if they were scales. These bodily disorders inevitably influence their cultural development, as the children of the waiting room are incapable of learning how to write: "*they can't write, almost none of them can. . . . Some of them do, they learned how to write, but they can't control their arms anymore, or they can't control their own heads, or they have such thin skin that if they squeeze the markers too much their fingers end up bleeding.*"[99] As part of her gothic critique of the modern nation, Schweblin subverts the idea that whiteness corresponds to intelligence, tact, and civilization. The impossibility of belonging to the community is directly tied to their incapacity to learn the language of social institutions. In *Distancia de rescate*, the fantasy of Sarmiento and other nineteenth-century politicians of building the nation's future by populating the pampas with immigrant populations falls apart through the sick bodies of children who cannot inhabit even their most immediate present.

These zombie children are figures of what Slavoj Žižek has called "the return of the undead," referring to the dead people who were not adequately buried and who now come back to demand fulfillment of a symbolic debt.[100] Following the "migration" that allows his body to be kept alive, which could be read as an incomplete funerary rite through Carla's refusal to accept her son's death, David claims that his mother blames him for embodying ecological damage: "*That whatever has cursed this town for the past ten years is now inside me.*"[101] The use of italics for David's interventions points to the lack of emotion of the zombie child, whose uncanny effect deepens each time he ignores Amanda's questions. Symbolically, the migration signifies the death of David as Carla's son, as it becomes apparent in the sinister relationship that ensues when he stops calling her "mom" and starts using her proper name.

The trope of the zombie also manifests in the descriptions around how the poisonings cause a splitting between exterior and interior, sameness and otherness. For instance, Nina speaks in an ominous plural that makes people laugh and then becomes a symptom of her gradual zombification. Notably, it is the children and not the mothers who become zombies. The zombie is the body that consumes, does not possess a historical consciousness, and inhabits a crowd-like state that estranges it from its individuality and even its senses. But it is the child—whom adults traditionally think of as historically unconscious or as pure potentiality—who is now taken out of the chronological time of the nation. Through this zombification of children, Schweblin reflects on the poisoning of a nation's soil and the *demodernization* of the narratives that the nineteenth-century civilizers had sold as the only way forward.

According to Žižek, the zombie is a metaphor for people who have become habituated to reality and have lost the capacity to be amazed or horrified.[102] David's father, Omar, does not take part in his son's daily life because of his obsession with the stallion to which he has entrusted his financial future: "Omar watched him all day long, followed him around like a zombie to keep track of how many times he mounted each mare."[103] The horror of *Distancia de rescate* stems mainly from this collective inability to cast affective and ethical judgments, this immunization against the zombie condition of children's bodies. Whereas the children are zombies that move around in hordes, adults become isolated to pursue the fantasies of productivity embodied by agroindustry embodies. As Jorge Fernández Gonzalo observes in *Filosofía zombi*, "What unites a zombie to another is that they have nothing to do with each other. . . . This establishes a community of beings that are uniquely segregated, a community of non-community, non-communication, non-union, non-mixture."[104] The possibility that children will become part of any community through education, writing, and reading is immediately lost after the introduction of agrochemicals in the Argentinean countryside. Carla speaks with composure about poisoned and deformed children, invites Nina to play near the pool and the well, and ignores that she and Amanda are both drenched with herbicides. Fernanda Sández coined the term "sick with tranquility" to refer to the people who believe that agrochemicals are "friendly" toward humans and the environment.[105]

A community that does not take any measures to prevent the harrowing reality of agrotoxic contagion feeds the horror of Schweblin's novel. By estranging the supposed tranquility of the sequence of pesticide poisonings, *Distancia de rescate* contributes to raising awareness of the hazardous effects of environmental pollutants in farming communities. The lurking horror derives from the emptiness, silence, and desolation of the soybean landscape. The empty plantations deprived of human labor delineate a scenario of "'dematerialised' capitalism" that, according to Mark Fisher, is a crucial element of fictions that deal with "the eerie underside of contemporary capital's mundane gloss."[106] Fisher argues that the feeling of eeriness is intimately tied to questions of agency, to the invisible hand that governs capitalist society, and it is therefore possible to perceive it in landscapes that have been emptied of all human presence.[107]

Distancia de rescate is a novel concerned with the eerie effect caused by the invisible presence of the agricultural workforce, as it takes place in plantations where we do not see any workers, as if the soybeans were alive and able to disseminate on their own. The novel reveals the invisible hand of corporations as the gothic underside of global capitalism, so long as corporate executives seem to be controlling the soy fields from their remote metropolitan headquarters. The soybean landscape becomes a character with an agency that undoes the rigid distinction between background and foreground, between human and nonhuman forces. There is an ominous divergence between the "dry and hard" ground of the soy fields, as Amanda describes it, and the soy plants that turn out to be suspiciously green to grow in such a barren landscape: "Beyond the soy fields it looks green and bright under the dark clouds. But the ground they are walking on, from the road to the stream, is dry and hard."[108] This description reveals the strangeness of an irrigation system that fertilizes violently, inciting the production of antinatural yields. The feeling of eeriness increases if we consider that the scourge is invisible, perceptible only through its impact on the bodies of children, who are the main victims of a health emergency for which nobody takes full responsibility.

The complicity of the state and the agricultural industry within this network of agrochemical poisonings becomes evident in the virtual absence of male figures. De Leone observes that *Distancia de rescate* shows how agribusiness, while protecting its goods through the so-called immunological crop, abandons individual lives to the power of agrochemicals.[109] Indeed, the concept of immunity, which according to Esposito is the exact opposite of community, frames the role of agricultural workers. While Nina's body is soaked with a liquid that her mother mistakes for sweat or dew, the workers handle the barrels of agrochemicals with plastic gloves and live away from the soy fields. For instance, it is impossible not to ask where the person who leases the house to Amanda is; or why the caretaker of the rental house, Mr. Geser, only appears spectrally through the presence of his dogs. The greatest absence is probably that of Sotomayor, the owner of the fields, who seems to be hiding backstage. When visiting his offices, Amanda wonders "if either of them [the employees] is Sotomayor."[110]

The male figures remain detached from the poisoning of children. Inside his house, David's father has photographs of his racehorses, who have also suffered from pesticide poisoning, but none of his son. When Nina's father travels to the rural village and asks about the origin of her daughter's mental and physical injuries, Omar refuses to divulge the network of agrochemical poisonings, as if doing so would break the contract he has reached with the agricultural sector. In this sense, the passivity of fathers serves as a metaphor for the absence of the state in the village, which has become a town-clinic run by mother nurses. *Distancia de rescate* reveals the complicity of a nation-state that asks to be conceived of otherwise, precisely through the work of mother nurses.

It is a novel not so much about agricultural labor as about raising children under extreme ecological conditions. Although maternal lineages are present throughout, the erasure of male figures is a clear metaphor for the invisible hand that steers agricultural capitalism. The absence of men is strategic in the novel because it allows them to learn how pesticides operate, profit from them, and remain within "rescue distance." The women are responsible for healing the single-crop wastelands and the sick children. The emergency room that quarantines the children and fulfills the role of the family is an institution that depends exclusively on female labor. All the nurses are women, and the director is a person who, as we can gather from Amanda and David's descriptions, has not been formally trained to fulfill this role but does so out of pure maternal instinct. Proof of this is the necklace she carries with the photograph of her three children: "two girls and a boy, the three of them close together, almost on top of each other, squeezed between her enormous breasts."[111] The novel elevates the work of mothers to give another shape to agricultural work in Argentina, up against the invisible hand of corporations controlled by male figures.

The labor of care is embodied in the name of the novel's female protagonists. Amanda, whose name evokes the verb *amar* (to love), is the mother who loves her daughter so passionately that she becomes one of those helicopter parents who worry obsessively about the well-being of their children, thus introducing the notion of "rescue distance" that she has inherited from her maternal lineage. "Rescue distance" is, according to Amanda, the thread that keeps her genetically tied to her mother and grandmother, but it is also "the variable distance separating me from my daughter, and I spend half the day calculating it, though I always risk more than I should."[112] The name Nina oscillates between "niña" (child) and "nena" (girl), even though the fact that it lacks the letter ñ to be a child foreshadows her subsequent transmigration at the hands of the healer. By highlighting the role of mother-child and their impossibility in the context of the soybean plantations, the names of Amanda and Nina seem to fulfill the same role as the epitaph in the gothic poetic tradition. According to David Punter, the names of dead people bear with the living "the perpetually ambiguous relation that names bear to objects: namely, that they represent them while at the same time signifying their loss."[113] The fact that Amanda cannot avoid Nina's poisoning and that the only survivor turns out to be her husband reflects the gothic concern over the obliteration of female genealogies.

In this sense, *Distancia de rescate* is a novel concerned with the fragility of the thread that ties many different orders: the family tree, the female line, and aesthetic genres. The recurring metaphor of the thread shows the abolition of the time limits that characterize the concept of the contemporary and, by extension, the obsolescence of the category of the modern as a succession of historical periods independent of each other: "the word *modern* implies a representation of time based on the idea of a boundary. . . . So time appears like a succession of stations in an irreversible forward journey."[114]

Among the different threads that appear in the novel, one should high-light the umbilical cord that ties a mother to her baby, the rope that the healer uses to perform the transmigration of spirits, the string that ties the family photographs on the wall of Carla's house, and "the fine, dark thread of water" in the stream where most of the poisonings take place.[115] Howev-er, the thread metaphor is more evocative if we relate it to the discursive act that frames the novel. David incites Amanda to find the origin of the in-fection without getting distracted by side issues, and the conversation turns into an act of weaving, treading lightly, and arriving at the heart of the mat-ter. As David points out, "*We're looking for the exact moment because we want to know how it starts.*" At the end of the novel, the figurative rope or thread that has guided the course of the conversation disintegrates into a fuse: "the rope finally slack, like a lit fuse, somewhere; the motionless scourge about to erupt." When Amanda's husband returns to the city, he finds that "there are too many cars, cars and more cars covering every asphalt nerve."[116] The massive flight from the countryside toward the city is an inversion of the nineteenth-century narratives about the conquest of the desert and the es-tablishment of single-crop farming as the motor of the national economy. By granting agency to the vast soy fields, Schweblin conveys how the land is about to get angered because of the excessive use of pesticides and, in the form of a natural disaster, will invade the streets of Buenos Aires.

The affective charge of metaphors such as "the lit fuse" and "the mo-tionless scourge" connects *Distancia de rescate* with the contemporary nar-ratives of ecological contagion that Houser has called "ecosickness fictions," narratives that display the dissolution of the body–environment dichotomy through sickness and that mobilize affects such as anxiety, fear, and para-noia in order to instigate ethical and political change.[117] On the one hand, the prevailing affect aroused by Schweblin's novel is horror, one of the "ve-hement passions" that Fisher links to the genre of the summary, the report, or the outline of a case. Horror forces us to tie the loose ends and actively contribute to the construction of the story: "a universe where things hold together in a frightening way . . . has the most profound aesthetic effect."[118] The horror of an incomplete plot correlates with the dialogue that formally structures the novel, which begins in medias res and incites readers to ask themselves whether the most important information might be that which is conveyed between the lines, partially, or which remains unsaid. On the other hand, an example of the immediate influence that *Distancia de rescate* has had on public debates over the use of pesticides is the fact that Sández, in her 2016 nonfiction book *La Argentina fumigada*, uses a quote from it as an epigraph that embodies this aesthetics of fear: "*The important thing already happened. What follows are only consequences.*"[119]

In *Distancia de rescate* Schweblin uses this aesthetics of fear in order to show Argentinean national history through a fabric of opposing versions. In fact the gothic genre, so long as it reveals the mutability of historical narratives, depends on the revival of other texts behind it that are continually invoked and often distorted. According to Punter, the force of the gothic lies not in its constant adaptation to the historical conjuncture but in its way of revealing the anachronisms of the contemporary moment, in how "the contemporary can in some way be put into relation with the most archaic."[120] The gothic of *Distancia de rescate* unties the seams of the modern nation-state and unravels the foundational narratives behind it, such as the texts of demographic whitening (*blanqueamiento*) or the forced appropriation of Indigenous territory. Through this reemergence of the repressed past, Schweblin reformulates the civilizational fantasies of the white fathers of the nation in the form of a fever dream or an agrotoxic nightmare. While the agro-exporting fantasies have materialized in the monoculture of the soybean, *Distancia de rescate* shows that these have not brought wealth but, rather, disease and death. If critics have compared the style of Sarmiento's *Facundo* with the rhythm of breathing and therefore with the movement of the gauchos throughout the pampas, *Distancia de rescate* is by contrast an intoxicated and claustrophobic narrative that has run out of air.[121] In this way, the temporality of agrochemical substances such as glyphosate becomes part of the novel's formal structure, whose leaps in time delineate an apocalyptic historicity that invites the readers to ask themselves, as Amanda does in the emergency room, "What's going to happen when the time is up?"[122] In posing this apocalyptic conundrum, *Distancia de rescate* transmits the urgency of the current scenario of ecological devastation, inciting readers to move from the search for its causes to immediate political action.

Guadalupe Nettel's *El huésped* and Samanta Schweblin's *Distancia de rescate* represent the state of precariousness and ecological emergency of contemporary societies through the somatic sickness of their protagonists. In both novels, the human body loses agency because of the invasion of parasitic organisms, which figure not only the intervention of the state and multinational corporations in the most vulnerable bodies of the Global South but also the environmental hazards brought about by the biotechnological manipulation of nature. As Michel Serres asserts, "through our mastery, we have become so much and so little masters of the Earth that it once again threatens to master us in turn."[123]

In addition to conceiving the contemporary moment through experiences of dispossession, both novels engender negative emotions so as to engage readers in ethical and political actions. Neither of these works reveals "the exact moment" of bodily and environmental contagion, but both point to the invisibility and omnipresence of geological processes of slow violence.

The protagonists of both novels undertake intense searches around "the important thing" of the climate crisis without shutting down other ways of reaching sustainable solutions, inviting readers to continue the search on their own terms. Instead of providing models of epistemological mastery over nature, these novels show how the contemporary is composed of various temporalities that transcend the immediate present of human action. Both authors explore the temporal entanglements between humans, animals, plants, and chemical substances so as to illustrate how the time of the Anthropocene is not immediately accessible to human perception. These writers offer new models for how literary form can expand the scales of our present and show the human imprint within geological timescales, as opposed to a present that revolves around itself and a future perceived as a constant threat.

In this sense, the two novels display the potential of the gothic to create a sustainable imagination across the Americas. They stage apocalyptic scenarios to collectively reflect on the environmental policies addressing urban and rural landscapes. As Buell points out, "Apocalypse is the single most powerful master metaphor that the contemporary environmental imagination has at its disposal."[124] By inspiring affects such as anxiety and horror, these authors contravene those stances of relativism or, in some cases, complete denial of the climate crisis. Their apocalypticism, however, combines the gothic genre with an imaginary of speculative anticipation via a reformulation of the concept of heritage. According to Hartog, these are times of intense strategies of cultural preservation, which seek to protect not only the things that have been lost in the recent past but also what is about to disappear.[125] Instead of foreclosing a horizon of collective reflection through fatalistic visions of the future, the apocalyptic nature of these narratives reveals the strategies of contemporary art and fiction to create "sustainable flows of survival, cooperation, and growth."[126]

Whereas Nettel in *El huésped* seeks to channel the sustainable past of pre-Hispanic Mexico toward new forms of political resistance and models of environmental thinking, Schweblin, through the suffocating narrative of *Distancia de rescate*, puts literary form at the service of finding both the causes of agrochemical contagion and possible strategies to escape our current predicament. These strategies bring into question the ways of understanding the nation-state as a heteropatriarchy and of understanding the logic of gender domination that drives the accumulation by dispossession of land in places like Argentina and Mexico, where large-scale extractive industries are appropriating communal territories, transforming bodies into machines of labor power, and confining women to a form of reproductive work continually thwarted by the maltreatment of the land. Both novels show that women—as the caregivers of bodies and territories—are the people most likely to denounce the effects of extractive capitalism, such as pesticides in the countryside or atmospheric pollution in the megacities. Ultimately, *El huésped* and *Distancia de rescate* lay out personal and familial dramas that soon evolve into collective predicaments, calling for the creation of sustainable paradigms that allow us to imagine more just planetary futures.

CHAPTER 3

THE CONTEMPORARY PLANTATION

Memories of Slavery and the Oral History Novel

An aphorism by Brazilian satirical author Millôr Fernandes, "O Brasil tem um enorme passado pela frente" (roughly translated as "Brazil has a huge past that lies ahead"), serves as a suitable starting point for an analysis of slavery's afterlives as depicted by contemporary Latin American writers.[1] Fernandes's reversal of Brazil's national motto, *Ordem e progresso* (Order and progress), is a scathing critique of the country's promises of a just future to communities that continue to be haunted by the lingering shadow of slavery. Although most Latin American countries abolished slavery around 1850, Brazil did not follow suit until 1888 when a decree, the Lei Áurea (Golden Law), was signed by Isabel, Princess Imperial of Brazil, that put an end to an already weakening structure but that did not contemplate welfare for the enslaved or a planned transition to a new social order.[2] As a result of this veiled continuation of the status quo, in Brazil and across the Americas the logic of the plantation survives in practices such as the militarized control of Black bodies in shanty towns or the racialized logistics of the prison-industrial complex.

In this chapter, I explore the ways in which slavery has returned to haunt Latin American nations and how writers conjure its specter through an expansive understanding of literary form: the braiding of the novel with the ethnographic essay and the first-person slave narrative. Unlike in North America, however, the slave narrative tradition is almost nonexistent in Latin America.[3] Contemporary writers are thus faced with the challenge of reconstructing slavery from the silence of the written archive, whose methods of classifying and collecting were bound up with the dispossession of Afro-Latin Americans, or through the scattered oral histories and cultural practices that return us to Black ways of resistance via the creation and re-creation of collective memory. In what follows, I explore how Latin American writers rescue forgotten oral histories of Black enslavement and emancipation in order to repurpose the project of the modern nation-state and the form of the novel.

I focus on two novels, *Elástico de sombra* (Shadow games, 2020) by the Colombian writer Juan Cárdenas and *Torto arado* (2019; trans. 2023 as *Crooked Plow*) by the Brazilian writer Itamar Vieira Junior.[4] In the first novel Cárdenas returns to the ancestral past of Afro-Colombian communities through the *esgrima de machete*, or Colombian *grima*, an endangered martial art practiced by a small group of Afro-descended people in Colombia's Cauca Valley, the montane forests located west of the country. In the second novel Vieira Junior allegorizes the specter of slavery through the accident of two sisters who steal a mysterious knife from their grandmother's belongings and put it in their mouths, and then one of them cuts her tongue off and permanently loses her ability to speak. Whereas modernization prompted a change in agricultural methods through advances in artificial intelligence and robotics, these novelists show that the conditions for plantation workers continue to be as precarious and inhumane as in the days when slavery was yet to be abolished.

Each novel foregrounds the dual meaning of the knife as a technology of oppression and a source of defense against the persecution of Afro-Latin American communities. In *Elástico de sombra* Cárdenas considers the machete as an archive of ancestral memories of the African-descended communities of Colombia's Cauca region. The Afro-Colombians' mastery of the art of the machete is a testament to the preservation of an ancestral legacy through embodied memory. Vieira Junior in *Torto arado* casts the knife as a symbol of the return of the repressed in the context of a *quilombola* (Maroon) community and the historical silencing of Afro-Brazilian voices. He paints a grim picture of the survival of social Darwinism in the contemporary plantation, ending with this community's growing awareness of the historical dispossession of their bodies and lands: "On this land, it's the strongest who survive."[5] Both authors point to the inseparable relationship between bodies and territories as sites of communal memory and cultural preservation in the face of neoliberal encroachment.

By staying attuned to the oral counter-histories of Latin American nations, both *Elástico de sombra* and *Torto arado* are novels about the silent witnesses erased by modern technologies of archiving and cataloging. Each writer pays close attention to the materiality of the tongue as a way of redistributing the differential roles assigned in the constitution of the modern archive: the tongue as the ultimate witness to the forced migration, enslavement, and separation of Afro-Latin Americans from their lands and material environments.[6] In *Elástico de sombra*, Cárdenas puts forward an anachronistic figure of authorship by describing himself as a writer of the Middle Ages: the writer as the person who gathers forgotten oral histories and gives them an order, rather than inventing new stories. Cárdenas thus becomes an archaic-contemporary writer whose art is close to that of the DJ as well as to the medieval troubadour—understanding the Middle Ages as a transitional period when capitalism was on the rise and the "fantastic and magical reactions to our nonfantastic reality," as Michael Taussig puts it, were ways of critiquing the new modes of production.[7] In *Torto arado*, the tongue is a powerful symbol of the centuries-old silencing of Afro-Brazilians and their coercion into modern political formations even as they escaped the pre-abolition plantation. Vieira Junior writes from the perspective of a natural deity to widen the temporal scales of the modern nation-state and to restore the memory of these communities as inscribed in their ancestral territories. Both authors invert the logic of the first-person account characteristic of the neoliberal era and the autobiographical slave narrative through the use of free indirect style, which reproduces syncretic religious practices—the interweaving of the written and the oral, the past and the present—and gives way to the collective formation of meaning.[8]

THE ORAL HISTORY NOVEL, BETWEEN THE PLANTATION AND THE PLOT

Sylvia Wynter writes about the clash between a plantation system dominated by the exchange value of people and things (dictated by the market economy) and a plot system that considered human need and was therefore structured around use value. Citing Lucien Goldmann's *Towards a Sociology of the Novel*, Wynter posits that the emergence of the novel as a literary form was simultaneous to "the extension and dominance of the market economy." The novel did not reproduce the values of the society in which it was born, however, but developed precisely as a "critique of the very historical process which has brought it to such heights of fulfillment."[9] Underlying Wynter's argument is the fact that in previous centuries literacy was the realm of a privileged few.

By contrast, the communal creation and re-creation of oral tales, songs, and religious beliefs were instrumental in raising "slave consciousness" within the confines of the plantation.[10] Like the novel form, created as a reaction to the conditions in which it emerged, for Black slaves folk culture became "a source of cultural guerilla resistance to the plantation system." For Wynter, "this plot system was, like the novel form in literature terms, the focus of resistance to the market system and market values."[11] Whereas the plantation served the objectives of the market, the plot was a breeding ground for the emergence of culture. While the history of the plantation, the history told by the forces of the market superstructure, was written and hegemonic, the history of the plot was passed on orally from generation to generation: it was, according to Wynter, "a secretive history expressed in folk [culture]."[12] The abolition of slavery and the end of the plantation as a superstructure of the economy did not bring immediate systemic changes. The struggle between the plantation and the plot continued under similar terms: the divide between the city as the commercial center of the plantation logic and the marginalized urban masses forced to survive with the scraps of industrial capitalism.

Echoing Wynter's call to recover the oral tradition of enslaved peoples, which was one of the only spheres not regulated by slaveholders, Afro-Colombian writer Manuel Zapata Olivella argues that Black Latin Americans feel a deep suspicion of written archives because they have been crafted by white people—that is, plantation owners. Instead of examining written archives, which he considers "dead letters," Zapata Olivella calls researchers to speak with the Afro-Colombian inhabitants of modern cities, who are "living characters of a history that is alive and well." It is a matter of giving voice to the Afro-descendant people who are considered invisible to contemporary societies because of colonial prejudices that continue to cast them as "external to national culture." In colonial archives, according to Zapata Olivella, Afro-descendant people are mentioned only indirectly, through the number of slaves who worked at a given hacienda. In other words, they are considered "brute force," not active agents in the production of culture, science, and technology.[13]

On the other hand, oral history represents the richness of the ancestral stories linked with the logic of the plot. Afro-Colombians expanded the notions of personhood and family to include nonhuman nature through the concept of Muntu, which comes from the Bantu peoples of Central and Southern Africa. "Muntu conceives family as the sum of the deceased (ancestors) and the living, united by the word to animals, trees, minerals (earth, water, fire, stars) and tools, in an unbreakable knot."[14] The influence of Bantu in Colombian literature has been significant. Look no further than García Márquez's Macondo, which comes from the Bantu name for the banana tree (Makondo) and underscores the Muntu philosophy of interconnectedness between humans, plants, minerals, and animals.[15]

Afro-Colombians crystallized this inclusive philosophy by creating creole languages, or Palenquero, to preserve tradition and conjure ancestral legacies. The African diaspora conceived of these languages as subversive spaces excluded from the written word and the lettered city. Through African terms and morphologies, loanwords from European languages, and Indigenous concepts, these creole languages proved that Mother Nature, as Zapata Olivella tells us, "hides many secrets not yet revealed by science." Oral tradition casts identity not as a fossilized narrative but as "survival, history, as well as a creative and thinking force at the time of doing historical research."[16] The writer researcher becomes the person who restores the plurality of voices that was missing in written culture, a conjurer of ancestral spirits.

By the oral history novel, I refer to a corpus of works by authors who seek to undo the cultural and sociohistorical hierarchies that privilege the written over the oral. Caroline Levine has called for cultural critics, especially those working in the field of world literature, to be attentive to "the great unwritten," works that have "circulated for centuries in oral form" and have thus been neglected in the processes of canon formation.[17] Contemporary writers such as Cárdenas and Vieira Junior are turning to the realm of the oral to reconceive what we understand as literature: not the institutionalization of "great books" but the oral traditions—songs, stories, proverbs, jokes, and folktales—that traveled across the Black Atlantic on the slave ships and into the space of the plantation.[18] If we conceive of literature as a realm that includes cultural materials such as these, we might arrive at something closer to the idea of the contemporary: the re-politicization of the present through our attentiveness to archaic and anachronistic temporalities. Moreover, if we conceive the contemporary "as a co-temporality, as a synchronization of multiple times," as Ruffel does, what could be more contemporary than the multi-temporal and more-than-human worlds of the folktale—the domains of the devil and the witch, the demonic possession and the benign deity?[19] Writers have turned to the oral traditions of Afro-descended and Indigenous communities to create counter-memories of their nation's histories.

The question remains as to how these oral folktales, when transcribed on the written page, reconfigure the form of the novel. I argue that writers of novels such as *Elástico de sombra* and *Torto arado* build bridges between oral and written traditions through free indirect style. James Wood describes this style as the fold between omniscience and partiality, between the authorial third person and the characters' point of view. Timothy Bewes, for his part, argues that contemporary novels make use of free indirect style as a mode of thought that manifests itself in the fragility of literary form—the fragility of "the formal principles and qualities of the works, including the presumption of a directionality to the plot, the cycles of suspense and revelation, the 'expressive' element, and even the structure of the sentence."[20] In these novels, the reason for such fragility emanates from the distinct qualities of African folktales, which straddle the lines between life and death, human and more-than-human. Cárdenas describes free indirect style as the failure of third-person narration: "it is not a God like in Macondo," he says about his novel's narrative voice, "it is a kind of ghost, a ghostly voice that does not coincide with any of the characters' voices but is attached to them."[21]

This voice that enters and leaves the novel's characters corresponds with the spatiotemporal malleability of Afro-diasporic deities. In *Elástico de sombra* wind is a character that stirs the direction of the plot, and *Torto arado*'s last section is narrated by a water spirit who walks alongside enslaved people in their transatlantic travels on the ships and follows their lives in the Afro-Brazilian diaspora. By positing an in-between space that reproduces the logic of oral transmission, these novels shed light on a cultural tradition created and re-created ceaselessly through the voice of the community.

BLACK NEW WORLD

The temporality of Cárdenas's *Elástico de sombra* is symbolized by the *timbutala*. This is the name Afro-Colombians from the Cauca region give the whirlwind that forms in rivers and interferes with the transportation of commodities such as diamonds, gold, and timber. The spiraling temporality of the timbutala is synonymous with the creation of alternate dimensions, where racialized bodies are instrumental in the production of knowledge and where lives are not measured by the ebb and flow of the market. The novel follows a white scribbler called Cero (Zero), Cárdenas's alter ego, as he accompanies two Afro-Colombian men to the depths of the Cauca Valley in search of a lost martial arts technique entitled, like the novel, *elástico de sombra* (elastic shadow games). The martial arts game is the *esgrima de machete* (a martial art utilizing sticks, knives, lances, and particularly the machete), an Afro-Colombian machete-fighting cultural practice developed by slaves in the sugarcane plantations of the Cauca region in southwestern Colombia.[22] Based on two real-life *macheteros*, Héctor Elías Sandoval and Miguel Lourido from the town of Puerto Tejada, the Afro-Colombian characters are the elderly Don Sando, who is referred to as "the last great machetero," and his disciple Miguel.[23]

The purpose of the trip, which only Don Sando seems to know, is to conjure up a *duende* (gnome) in order to ask him how to preserve the ancient art of the *esgrima*. When the duende materializes out of the whirlwind that forms in the Guachené River, Don Sando begs him to divulge "that lost knowledge that, as the old people said, you hang onto like a treasure . . . the missing techniques of the esgrima de machete."[24] The elástico de sombra is a mythical game believed to have been brought from Haiti following Simón Bolívar's campaigns for independence. The game is practiced in total darkness, with the fighter's eyes covered by a blindfold. The art of dominating darkness in the elástico de sombra evokes the journey aboard the slave ships, the slaves' confinement in the ship's hold, and their inability to see beyond their own bodies. Given that Colombian grima is an art on the verge of extinction (Don Sando and Miguel count themselves, in fact, among its last practitioners), its vanishment would amount to the extinction of an ancient corpus of knowledge that has been passed down from generation to generation through the spoken word and, most important, through the body.

The origins of Colombian grima are a source of dispute among cultural historians. Some posit that it was brought to Colombia by African slaves, whereas others contend that it stemmed from the European sword-fighting experts who visited the country during the colonial period.[25] The two epicenters of Colombian grima are the towns of Puerto Tejada, where the novel's Don Sando and Miguel are from, and El Patía, which boasts an ancestral tradition around music and dance. There is consensus among historians, however, around its similarities with other circum-Caribbean machete-fighting martial arts. In Cuba, for instance, the members of the Abakuá secret society, who were also known as *ñáñigos*, preserved the Biafran military tradition by defending the community through machete fighting.[26] As in Haitian *Tire machèt*, Afro-Colombians teach this martial art using sticks to create a safe environment. As opposed to other Caribbean fighting practices, Colombian grima is sometimes passed down through written manuals called *cartillas* (notebooks), which in some instances have been lost. This is the case of the technique known as elástico de sombra.

Cárdenas's counter-history of Colombian modernity recovers forgotten events that challenge the version written by white liberal elites. He shows how the Cauca macheteros were recruited to fight for Colombia—a country that in many cases did not recognize them as legitimate citizens—in political conflicts such as The Thousand Days' War (1899–1902) and the Leticia Dispute (1932–1934). The history books written in Bogotá attribute Colombia's victory in the Leticia Dispute to the country's aerial power; they neglect to mention the help of the macheteros. The macheteros learned their guerrilla warfare tactics from the Código Maceo, a cartilla that Colombian General Avelino Rosas wrote after fighting in Cuba's War of Independence. The macheteros' tactics defied the logic of trench warfare because they used a set of techniques known as "shadow games," through which they camouflaged in the jungle and became their opponents' shadow. As Wynter reminds us, when the written culture of the colonizer plays an oppressive role and exterminates the oral tradition of another culture, there ensues a rift between a big tradition and a little tradition.[27] For Cárdenas, writing is a mode of listening to these Afro-Colombian voices that have been doomed to oblivion, to the little tradition made up of oral histories. The authorial voice performs a shadow game by relinquishing center stage and foregrounding the lettered city's complicity in the destruction of entire worlds.

Through the cultural practices of Afro-Colombian macheteros, Cárdenas shows the existence of other temporalities, more ancient and less linear than the time of Western societies. Colombian grima recovers long-forgotten temporalities necessary for building counter-histories of the present. Central to Colombian grima is the *falso diagonal* (fake diagonal) movement: the tilting of the body to prevent an opponent's strike that is said to contain "the lost memory of the body."[28] The movements of this martial arts practice are closely connected with the rhythms of Afro-Colombian dances, conjuring up "the lost memory of the ancestors." Both performative practices keep alive various aspects of Black ancestral knowledge that have survived various attempts to erase the memory of these communities. As the narrator observes, "rhythm is the tremor of human time."[29] Gabriel Giorgi has argued that *Elástico de sombra* opens temporalities that do not fit neatly within the nation-state or the time of capital.[30] Colombian grima allows the Black body, with the contortion of the hips, to remember the various crimes committed against its ancestors throughout history. Like the spiral in the river, the diagonal movement opposes the idea of time as progress, as a straight line leading directly into the future. Through the movement of the macheteros, "the lost world begins again" and a "black new world" emerges out of the ruins of the capitalist present.[31]

According to Cárdenas, the literary novel is a political form devoted to recovering these ancient temporalities. He aligns with theorists of the Black Caribbean such as Glissant, who posits that the novel of the Americas deals with "a tortured sense of time" because of the continent's ever-present colonial heritage. In a description that evokes the spiraling energy of the Afro-Colombian timbutala, Glissant argues that "we are faced with apparent snatches of time that have been sucked into banked up or swirling forces."[32] Glissant is referring to the fragile realities of Caribbeanness: the tension between roots and wandering, the trauma of slavery ("a struggle with no witnesses"), the erasure of collective memory, and an imposed citizenship.[33]

Elástico de sombra contains a preliminary note in which Cárdenas declares the need to revisit the project of the modern nation-state and carve out a space for Black becoming. He inscribes the novel within what he considers "the most urgent project of universal culture, namely, the definitive annihilation of the White Man."[34] The annihilation of the white man is Cárdenas's way of building a counter-history of the present that is different from the notion of a white Colombian nation, a totality that excludes the nonlinear histories and practices of the Afro-Colombian diaspora. In *Elástico de sombra* he grapples with the exploded temporality of Black communities: the erasure of the Afro-Colombian past, the forgotten myths excluded from Western modernity, and the various traumas imposed on the Black body. Like Glissant's Caribeanness, a new notion of Colombianness emerges. There is no single Colombia, just as there is no single Western history.

Cárdenas poses the question of cultural appropriation from the beginning by carving a space for himself through an elusive narrator. His alter ego, Cero, is a "white scribbler, a coffee with milk mestizo," accused by scholars of Afro-Colombia of being a "thief and appropriator of other people's culture."[35] Leaving the white narrator unnamed and reducing him to a mere cipher is a way of reflecting on the faceless and nameless slaves who populated the Cauca's slaveholding past.[36] It is also a counterstrategy of erasure: the white narrator, who seems to be the leading voice at the beginning, through a witch's spell will end up transformed into a cockroach. Cero becomes an example of Cárdenas's call to arms: the white man's annihilation from Colombia's hegemonic history. According to Miguel, Cero is not an appropriator but a smuggler: "someone who carries and brings things from one side to the other, jumping over and ultimately trying to erase the racial borders that the white man invents to guarantee his right of domination, to mark the terrain with his system of measurements."[37] As in Mairal's and Indiana's novels, in *Elástico de sombra* we see the writer's figure as a smuggler of cultural materials. In this case, the writer opposes the plantation logic of exchange value and follows the dynamics of the plot: he does not invent new cultural materials but gives an order to existing oral sources, thus aligning with a culture of use value. Through a counter-poetics of recycling and remixing, Cárdenas remains attentive to the collective matrix of the Afro-Colombian oral tradition.

The Oral Archive

Elástico de sombra is an oral history novel concerned with transmitting a cultural practice that could be dying, agonizing, or in its final stages. The novel marks a transition from a politics of *testimonio* (the genre of witnessing exemplified by Rigoberta Menchú's 1983 book *Me llamo Rigoberta Menchú y así me nació la conciencia*) to new explorations that question what the archive conceals and silences. *Elástico de sombra* shares with *testimonio* the intention to go beyond the lettered city's archives through the subaltern's word. However, the novel's preoccupation is in the obscure stories of the Afro-Latin American archive lying dormant in the collective unconscious, which corresponds to Saidiya Hartman's definition of the Afro-Atlantic archive as "a death sentence, a tomb, a display of the violated body, an inventory of property . . . an asterisk in the grand narrative of history."[38]

Cárdenas is not particularly interested in repurposing written archives to showcase forms of colonial violence—as in NourbeSe Philip's *Zong!* (2008) and its rewriting of the only extant document corresponding to the murder of 150 African slaves aboard a slave ship. Instead, he focuses on the cultural practices that cannot be passed on to the next generations. The irrecoverable traces of oral history are unreachable to the collection, cataloging, and indexing methods that are part and parcel of European archival practices: the archive is "the mystery of the Incommunicable . . . where no computer will ever be able to reach."[39] The focus of the novel is on the esgrima de machete, a cultural practice that is difficult to pass on to new generations since it takes around ten years for someone to become a master. The novel also describes the esgrima as a creole cultural practice that transcends the written archive and is passed down as a secret code through bodies and speech.

Elástico de sombra is an assembly of an archive of forgotten events and cultural practices in the history of the modern nation through the recovery of oral history archives. Oral archives go against linear accounts put forward by history books, and archivists do not seek to reclaim their stable origins so much as to illuminate and interrupt the present with a new knowledge of its absences. As opposed to the bureaucratic nature and the moral boundaries imposed by written history (documents such as plantation ledgers indicating the possession of bodies and territories), the oral folktale, according to Glissant, "outlines a landscape that is not possessed: it is anti-History." Instead of the supposed neutrality and progressive temporality of History with a capital H, the folktale unfolds through continuous breaks in time, repetitions, excess, and without imposing moral solutions.[40] For Afro-diasporic communities, the division of history into different periods was an external idea imposed by the West, and the folktale contains counter-memories that conjure historical trauma and popular knowledge through the connection between body and speech. For Glissant, the folktale is the realm in which history and literature, the individual and the collective, become one and the same.[41] Cárdenas refers to the two macheteros as "living archives where popular memories, accumulated knowledge of political struggles, and stories are deposited. Tales, legends, myths, anecdotes, jokes, décimas, etc."[42] The novel thus becomes a repository of these diverse oral materials, standing against the strict boundaries between the oral and the written.

Oral folktales are archives of Black consciousness and identity, including the forces that threaten to tear them apart. Cárdenas's novel shows how the figure of the devil conveys anxieties about the continuation of plantation logics because it is a reincarnation of the slave owner, and therefore, it is unnamable: characters in the novel refer to it as "El-Que-Ya-Sabemos" (The-one-we-already-know) and "El Señor-Ese" (The-man-over-there or The-master-over-there). The devil is also a figure of the white extractive view, because he kills animals and humans as soon as he touches them. The devil becomes an essential character in the novel when Don Sando encounters the duende, who recounts how the devil condemned him not to reveal his secret knowledge of the esgrima, as a spell could befall the person who possesses it. In his classic book *The Devil and Commodity Fetishism in South America*, Taussig argues that when peasants are deprived of their own land and become proletarianized, the devil emerges as a symbol to replace the godly spirits of fertility.[43] He shows that while they are introduced to the logics of Western modernity, these peasant communities interpret the symbols of capitalism through precapitalist beliefs.[44] The figure of the devil is part of "an egalitarian social ethic" that takes issue with the people who gain more money by prioritizing the individual instead of the collective. The devil is not only a symbol of anxiety but one of resistance, as the slaves appropriated the Spaniards' most fearful enemy and turned it against them. The Spaniards associated African folklore and religious practices with the devil, but for the slaves the devil was not necessarily an evil spirit—it "was also a figure of mirth and a powerful trickster."[45]

The figure of the trickster is closely connected with that of the witch. In the novel, the witch is called Doña Nubia and is responsible for transforming Cero into a cockroach. Doña Nubia is described as one of "those [women] who make stones talk, those who pray backward, those who turn other people's tongues upside down, those who know how to fly and cast spells of love, spells of hate and even spells to win the departmental elections."[46] Another man who falls under Nubia's spell is Iginio, who becomes her slave and accompanies her on nocturnal flights over the Cauca skies. To break the spell, Iginio's brothers hire another witch, more powerful than Nubia, who gives them detailed instructions on what to do, including touching Nubia's left armpit during one of her nocturnal flights. When he falls under Doña Nubia's spell, Iginio works at a bottling facility of the Coca-Cola Company. The witch forces Iginio to quit his job and cut ties with his family: "The thing is that Nubia forced me to quit my job, she forced me to sell a little piece of land I had on the shore of El Palo and left me broke, then she forced me to fight with my family, she forced me to hate my friends."[47]

The fear of witches, as Silvia Federici reminds us in *Caliban and the Witch*, accompanied the transition to capitalism and its attack against magic, which "seemed a form of refusal of work, of insubordination, and an instrument of grassroots resistance to power."[48] Women are perceived in the novel as figures of anti-capitalist resistance because of their association with witchcraft. Iginio's incident with Doña Nubia is a blessing in disguise since he ultimately escapes to a Nasa (Páez) Indigenous community where he learns his two current professions: auto-mechanics and painting. The witch is depicted as the paradigmatic figure for plotting class revolt through sexual transgression, as Doña Nubia prompts Iginio to leave his alienating job for a multinational company (Coca-Cola) that continues to reproduce the logic of the plantation under current conditions.

In *Elástico de sombra*, the incorporation of oral folktales such as these is made possible through free indirect style. The novel's narrator acts like a spirit medium who takes possession of the characters' bodies and speech, which gives the novel the quality of a séance, the ceremony of relaying messages from dead spirits. The transformation of Cero, the white scribbler, into a cockroach dramatizes the procedure of giving voice to the Afro-Colombian people, whose speech is transcribed on the page respecting its spoken variation: "vos" (you) is transcribed as "voj," "para" (for) becomes "pa," and "monstruo" (monster) turns into "mostro," capturing the oral idiosyncrasies of the Cauca region. Thus the novel exemplifies this tension between the written and the oral through a wide array of references to Afro-Colombian speech.

Glissant observes that the novel of the Americas emerges out of this "synthesis of written syntax and spoken rhythms, of 'acquired writing' and oral 'reflex,' of the solitude of writing and the solidarity of the collective voice."[49] The synthesis of the oral and the written in a single text is exemplified through Cárdenas's comparison of writing with the absorption mechanisms of mushrooms, especially their ability to transform adverse living conditions into the proliferation of new life forms.[50] Cárdenas takes his cue from Anna Lowenhaupt Tsing, in *The Mushroom at the End of the World*, who examines the matsutake mushroom's "contaminating relationality" and its "transformative relations with other species."[51] Cárdenas shows that the oral tradition thrives and acquires new life when it is assimilated into other cultures and that the task of recording these oral archives is equivalent to the act of building counter-histories of our neoliberal present.

MEMORIES OF SLAVERY IN THE CAUCA

Cárdenas displays the legacies of slavery in our necropolitical era. Although in the novel he designates via witchcraft "the spells of the market," he also uses the symbol of hands to refer to the contemporary plantation economy and how it is controlled by "the invisible white hand that moves all brown hands."[52] In Colombia's necropolitical present, in which the armed conflict and the plantation economy are two emblems of the state of exception,

Black bodies are likened to merchandise through various regimes of dispossession.[53] The survival of the plantation in the contemporary moment is felt most vividly, according to Katherine McKittrick, "in the sites of toxicity, environmental decay, pollution, and militarized action that are inhabited by impoverished communities."[54] In the Cauca, the ancestral past and the late-capitalist present coexist seamlessly. The Colombian armed conflict appears during the characters' trip throughout the region as they encounter two dead bodies on the side of the road. The bodies have been tortured and dismembered and all three travelers are left in silence, unable to think coherently about what they are seeing: "None of them was able to say anything. Some things are beyond words."[55] For the macheteros, the fact that the two corpses lie at a crossroads is a bad omen for the country's future and an image of the contemporary as a time of interlocking forms of violence, where the environmental, racial, and socioeconomic are part of the same continuum.

The survival of the plantation economy becomes more prominent in the parallels drawn between the dispossession of bodies and territories, especially in the scenes surrounding the Afro-Colombian environmental activist and politician Francia Márquez, who would go on to become the country's vice president in August 2022. The three travelers arrive in La Toma, Márquez's hometown and the site of large-scale gold mining by multinational corporations, on the day of an environmental activist's funeral. As various members of La Toma explain, Afro-Colombians from the Cauca region are fighting two simultaneous wars in the contemporary moment. "In these mountains, we are fighting two wars," they remark, "the one in the nineteenth century and the other in the twenty-first."[56]

Colonial dispossession is deeply entrenched in the landscape of the Cauca, with inhabitants facing the constant threat of land eviction, watershed pollution because of mercury mining, and death threats from the Colombian military and multinational corporations. As a measure to protest the murder and stigmatization of environmental activists and to defend the ancestral territories from neocolonial occupation, Cárdenas follows Márquez as she leads a march organized by an Indigenous and Afro-Colombian *minga*. A minga is an Inca tradition of communal work, construction of public infrastructure, agricultural harvesting, and self-determination via protest.[57] The travelers find out that a minga is not only a blockage of roads, as the hegemonic media regularly report to stigmatize its organizers, but a structure of resistance against human rights abuses and a demand for the restitution of ancestral lands. Márquez's speech highlights the status of Indigenous and Afro-Colombians as protectors and defenders of the earth, the difference between land and territory (the first as conceived by the deadly gaze of extractive corporations, the second as the perpetuation of life forms), and neoliberalism's global machine of death, which inhabits each person's body like a parasite (see the two novels analyzed in chapter 2).

> Brothers and sisters, Francia said, we have fought for these territories for centuries. I have been to the historical archive of Cauca, the Casa Mosquera, several times and have gone through those hefty volumes. And there it is recorded that, at least since 1632, our ancestors managed to settle here to pan for gold in the river and work the land, taking care of the water, the forest, the mountain. . . . We are not the owners, we are the caretakers, the guardians of these lands. We are the ones who know how to take care of life. And that is why they attack us, that is why they persecute us, that is why they displace us, and that is why they kill us. Because they, this Government, where the descendants of those who enslaved our great-great-grandparents four centuries ago found shelter, today are agents at the service of a great global machine of death, an automatic machine that produces death, that subsists thanks to the production of death. . . . And be careful, comrades, this machine of death is not far away, in the capitals of the world, this machine of death is cunning because it works inside each body, each soul. The death machine colonizes our language and dominates us until it manages to speak for us, in our name.[58]

The landscape of the tropical Cauca Valley is traversed by sugarcane plantations and former *rochelas* (Maroon communities). Márquez mobilizes the figure of the vampire to designate the dispossession of bodies and territories by extractive projects, which have expanded the logic of the plantation to include late-capitalist phenomena such as urban marginalization, air surveillance or "overseeing," and the prison-industrial complex. The metaphor of the contemporary plantation as a vampire who sucks the life out of bodies and territories appears earlier in the novel when the narrator describes "an artificial stream, one of those that the sugar cane mills use to irrigate their vagabondage and suck the blood out of the rivers."[59]

Extractivism is a mechanism of large-scale subordination of human bodies and nonhuman landscapes that clashes with Indigenous notions of the earth as Pachamama (Mother Earth), which aligns with Márquez's belief that earth beings such as trees, rivers, and rocks are essential to the reproduction of human life. In fact, in *Elástico de sombra* Cárdenas shows that the landscape of the Cauca has a life of its own, especially nonhuman beings such as the wind, whom Don Sando speaks and interacts with throughout the narrative. Following Gago, I use the term "bodies-territories" to refer to the work of ecofeminist activists such as Márquez, who have denounced the attack on natural landscapes as being simultaneously an attack on the body of each of its inhabitants. Márquez's denunciation of capitalism as a machine of death that inhabits one's body like a parasite is a reversal of the ceremonies of demonic possession through which Afro-diasporic peoples conjured the evils of slavery.

While plantations were powered through the visible hand of Black slaves and the invisible hand of white owners, the capital of the Cauca region, Popayán, is to this day called *La ciudad blanca* (The White City). As Márquez has pointed out elsewhere, the name derives not only from the white paint on the city's buildings but from the long-held belief that its inhabitants are direct heirs to the Spanish crown.[60] Cárdenas depicts the picturesque architecture of Popayán as a façade of colonial violence and dispossession: "A machine of whitewashed façades where for centuries dispossession was legalized, naturalized, and even embellished."[61] Popayán symbolizes the continuation of the large slaveholding estates in our late-capitalist present. Cárdenas refashions the figure of the slave master through the character of Simón, a young white filmmaker from Popayán who pays to film Miguel practicing esgrima. In truth, Simón wants Miguel to fight Don Sando, who has been put inside a cage, has fallen under a spell, and is intent on killing his disciple. Don Sando's spell is an example of the market's spell that obeys the logic of the parasite: the white neoliberal rationality that can inhabit Black and Indigenous bodies and deactivate their social agency. The fight between Miguel and Don Sando, which takes place in a mansion that evokes the planter's residence or big house, is a reenactment of slavery for the white neoliberal gaze. Cárdenas forces readers to acknowledge that, in one way or another, we are all implicated in this spectral return of the plantation economy.

Cárdenas posits women as the ultimate keepers of ancestral traditions, as they are the ones who provide other ways of relating with the territory and the historical archive. The invisible hand of extractive capitalism, which is associated with the logic of exchange value, contrasts dramatically with the hand of the macheteras and the act of weaving and learning to read embroidered threads. A woman named Doña Yasmín Góngora reads an embroidery she has woven to tell the three men they have to visit the women macheteras of La Toma, where a Maroon community is governed by a council of practitioners of the esgrima de machete. By looking for the origins of this traditional practice, the macheteras "keep the flame of history alive" and the voice of their African ancestors.[62] This exercise of historical memory, according to Nina de Friedemann, consists of looking for the "traces of Africanity" in Afro-Colombian cultural practices.[63] According to Fidelia Mina, one of the women macheteras of La Toma, it is a fight "against death and systematic oblivion, against the oblivion imposed from above."[64]

The woman who preserves the secret of the esgrima de machete is called

Doña Lucero Caicedo and when Don Sando and Miguel pay her a visit she has just died. However, she knew ahead of time that two men would come looking for her, and she had prepared an archive about the elástico de sombra, including a cartilla detailing parts of the forgotten movements. The slim volume containing the memory of this martial art contrasts with the hefty volumes in the archives of lettered cities such as Popayán. In this way, Cárdenas expands traditional historiography by looking for the scattered remains of ancestral memories. Instead of replacing the written archive with oral history, he reminds us that it is in the contrasts where alternatives to the modern nation-building project are to be found.

KNOTS OF SLAVERY

In Vieira Junior's *Torto arado*, the logic of use value corresponds to the *roças* (provision grounds), the small plots that landowners gave slaves and indentured servants to grow food crops, which allowed them to sell a surplus in local markets.[65] The novel takes place at a plantation called Água Negra (Black water), a former quilombola or Maroon community where, more than a century after the abolition of slavery, Afro-Brazilian families continue to experience its material sequels through lack of access to basic services such as electricity and the ability to build houses with long-lasting materials.[66] According to Federici, throughout the Americas, women used these plots of land to reconfigure the sexual division of labor—they "marketed the crops" they produced in provision grounds to reappropriate and reproduce "within the plantation system what had been one of their main occupations in Africa."[67]

The plantation of *Torto arado* is located in the Chapada Diamantina region of the state of Bahia in northeast Brazil, whose name derives from the mountainous landscape (an upland plateau) and the large deposits of diamonds that were discovered in the eighteenth century and exploited by *garimpeiros* (miners) who were initially Black slaves.[68] The name of the plantation, Água Negra, is an implicit reference to the vast array of environmental issues brought about by mining enterprises, including water pollution and subsidence. The semiarid qualities of this landscape, an ecoregion that in Brazil is called Caatinga (the Indigenous Tupi word for "white forest"), as well as its isolation from the state's main urban centers contribute to the idea that the characters of *Torto arado* are living outside of history. The novel's lack of historical markers gives the feeling that these quilombola communities have lived a long but unfulfilled emancipation from slavery.[69]

The novel follows twin sisters Bibiana and Belonísia and begins with an accident in their early childhood that haunts them for the rest of their lives. The sisters are captivated by the figure of their grandmother Donana, who speaks to the ghosts of her enslaved past: "She'd talk about beings we couldn't see—spirits—or people we didn't know."[70] As part of their plan to access Donana's past, Bibiana and Belonísia commit a transgression by breaking into her room and opening a suitcase she keeps hidden underneath the bed. The suitcase contains a mysterious knife with an ivory handle whose blade the sisters take into their mouths, a reckless action that leaves Bibiana with lasting wounds on the tongue and Belonísia unable to speak again. We soon find out that Donana stole the knife decades earlier from the *casa-grande*, the big house, as a symbolic compensation for her work as a slave. The knife also evokes a story of women's defense against gender violence as she has used it to avenge her daughter Carmelita, who was beaten and raped by a man living under the same roof.

The accident marks the sisters' lives in ways that become clear throughout the novel. Whereas Belonísia stays in the community, unwilling to interact with other people, her sister, Bibiana, goes to the city to study and returns with solid ideas about "our work and our subservience." She becomes a schoolteacher for the children of the plantation workers.[71] The accident is also an essential milestone in the twins' awareness of power relations within the plantation structure since they were unaware of their status "as workers bound to the plantation."[72] Slitting their tongues is a powerful metaphor for the disenfranchisement of Afro-Brazilian women. It allegorizes the open wounds of the Brazilian neoliberal present.

Just as Cárdenas in *Elástico de sombra* links Afro-Colombian memory with the women who weave tapestries containing ancient folk stories, Vieira Junior in *Torto arado* associates the preservation of ancestral knowledge with the act of unknitting the broken chains between the past and the present. The image of the knot recurs throughout the novel in the knotted hands (*mãos nodosas*) of the enslaved workers and in the notion of knotting a story. The link between text and textile returns us to the context of the cotton plantation. Moreover, as Irene Vallejo reminds us in *Papyrus: The Invention of Books in the Ancient World*, some of humanity's earliest storytellers were the women who found in stories a way out of the confinement imposed by their male counterparts. As I mentioned in the analysis of Schweblin's *Distancia de rescate*, we still speak of literary practice through metaphors that come directly from weaving. "We keep speaking—with textile metaphors—of the warp and weft of a narrative, of spinning a tale, of weaving a plot. What is a text for us, if not a collection of verbal threads knotted together?"[73]

The narrators of *Torto arado* are all women: the first part is narrated by Bibiana, the second by Belonísia, and the third by a water spirit who loses her powers once the rivers of the Chapada Diamantina region become polluted beyond repair. Storytelling is the space for conjuring these interlocking forms of dispossession of bodies and territories, from Belonísia's severed tongue to the water spirit's broken ties with land and water.[74] The novel begins with the act of untangling a knot to find a knife with an ivory handle, whereby the knot serves as a metaphor for remembering and summoning past traumas.[75] The opening scene underscores the uncertainty of whether the blood is coming from the blade of the knife or an open wound, from the immediate present or a distant past that has just been reawakened. Belonísia writes her stories down while working in the fields or mending old clothes: "When I sit quietly to mend an article of clothing, when I raise my hoe and swing it back down, opening gaps in the soil and tearing at roots, all the while the thread of my thought keeps weaving a fabric."[76] Storytelling is intimately tied to the preservation of bodies and territories carried out by the women who follow the logic of the plot and not that of the plantation.

Through the imagery of hands holding onto the remains of a distant past, Vieira Junior builds connections between storytelling and healing. The twins' father—José Alcino da Silva, nicknamed Zeca Chapéu Grande (Zeca Big Hat)—is a healer of Jarê, an Afro-diasporic religious practice from the Chapada Diamantina region. Jarê ceremonies involve channeling spiritual forces, or *caboclos*, the equivalent of the Orishas in Yoruba religion. As opposed to the healers of the Jarê rituals that take place in urban centers such as Salvador, the healers of the Chapada Diamantina focus their energies on healing peasants through the spilling of blood and the use of medicinal herbs and roots. Healers are trained to distinguish between illnesses they can cure through ritual action and others best handled by Western medicine.[77] The hands of Donana, a midwife in the local village, are cast as conduits "of the encantado Velho Nagô," one of the most potent healing spirits of Candomblé Ketu and an important deity in Jarê religious ceremonies.[78] Hands become tools of survival, defense, and justice—they are used not only to work in the fields but also to heal community members.

Similarly, the roots and herbs used in healing ceremonies are metaphors for the cultural recovery of a lost origin (Africa) and the conjuring of historical traumas suffered on the plantation. Donana uses "herbs and roots to make tinctures and medicines for the illnesses that befell folks of all types."[79] Meanwhile, Belonísia compares writing to throwing a fishing net and reaching for the roots of a plant. She interweaves memories of Zeca Chapéu Grande's funeral with stories from his childhood, which took place at the beginning of the twentieth century, not long after the abolition of slavery. Like the mangrove in Indiana's *La mucama de Omicunlé*, the roots used in Jarê ceremonies serve as metaphors for the novel's intricate temporalities, which correspond with the various dispossessions suffered by members of the Afro-Brazilian diaspora—the continuation of the plantation economy under new, though not altogether different terms.

Unlike the nineteenth-century plantation, which was divided into the big house and the slave quarters, the contemporary plantation shows an invisible and unlocalizable power dynamic. The owners of Água Negra are the Peixoto family, who come to the plantation only occasionally to show their face to the workers and collect the profits. Landowners embody the continuities between colonial and contemporary forms of violence by performing their "role of taskmaster[s] . . . remote descendants of the colonizers." Vieira Junior illustrates how the landowners of the Chapada Diamantina region made their fortunes through small- or large-scale mining (*garimpo*), which depended on the labor force of slaves and then freed—but unpaid— Black workers. The Peixoto family symbolizes the colonizers who live in metropolitan areas or more extensive plantations and profit from workers perceived as closer to the earth. Bibiana's husband, Severo, states they are people of the earth: "He was born from the earth."[80] This description evokes José Lins do Rego's novel *Menino de engenho* (1932; *Plantation Boy*, 1966) about the children of slaves who lived in dirt barracks that smelled like urinals: "The boys slept in malodorous hammocks and all the rooms were filled with the horrible stench of urine which rose from the damp floor on which one and all relieved themselves. But we felt entirely at home and satisfied in those surroundings, as if we were in the most luxurious rooms." Lins do Rego inverts the plantation paradigm by casting the children of the enslaved workers as "we from the Big House" to critique the logic of masters and slaves upon which Brazilian society was founded.[81]

In contrast to Lins do Rego's nostalgic depiction of the slave quarters, Vieira Junior represents the precarious dwelling of the plantation workers as graves in which they are buried alive.[82] The workers are subject to a plantation overseer or *jagunço* who tells them that they can build homes out of clay but not brick because they are not allowed to mark soil that does not belong to them. This uninhabitable dwelling built out of mud conveys the feeling that the workers are dead inside their own houses. The presence of the overseer marks the continuation of the plantation logic, since the *jagunços* were militias hired by big plantation owners to defend the land against external threats such as those posed by rural bandits or *cangaçeiros*. By forbidding them to build their homes in the style of the planters' big houses, landowners force peasant families to erase their own presence: "nothing enduring to mark how long a family had been on the land."[83] In fact, before finding a mirror among Donana's belongings, the sisters had looked at their reflection only in the river.

Dispossessed of their bodies and lands, peasant families like the one depicted in *Torto arado* seem to live inside the *grunas* (submerged caves) where their ancestors worked prospecting for diamonds. In the novel, the family inhabits an eternal present imposed by the landowners to their benefit; not looking at themselves in the mirror leads to an inevitable acceptance of the status quo. Through the correspondence between writing and cultural practices such as Jarê, which opens the body to the connection with ancestral forces, Vieira Junior posits alternative temporalities to the progressive time of the plantation economy.

DISPOSSESSED BODIES, DISEMBODIED SOULS

Vieira Junior tells a story of race and dispossession in the *longue durée* of Portuguese colonial settlement in Bahia's Chapada Diamantina.[84] The interlacing of Bibiana and Belonísia's story with the history of mining in the region begins with the discovery of diamond deposits by a Black person who is later falsely accused of killing a traveler from the state of Minas Gerais. The white colonizers took hold of the land through a gift from the kingdom, whereas the Black and Indigenous communities "were pushed aside, or killed, or forced to work for these owners of the land." This long history of land dispossession materializes in the present when the Peixoto family sells the plantation, and the new owners forbid the workers to bury their corpses, arguing that it constitutes "a crime against the forest, against nature."[85]

Vieira Junior shows how losing the right to rest alongside their ancestors dispossesses these communities of the links between past and present, life and death. After all, the community has used these lands to bury their family members' dead bodies and their children's umbilical cords. As opposed to the landowners, who have never lived in these lands, Vieira Junior posits a tangled relationship between body and territory for the Black communities of the Chapada Diamantina region: the body lives in the land and the land inhabits each person's body. As Salustiana, a midwife, remarks about her relationship with the land, "I birthed this land. . . . This land lives in me . . . it sprouted within me and took root."[86] The legal papers that prove that this territory belongs to them are the body itself: their bodies carry memories of dispossession, extraction, and deep roots to the land. Landowners can expel them from the land, but they cannot expel the land from each of their bodies.

The novel weaves a relationship of continuity between bodies and territories through the practice of Jarê. The body of Zeca Chapéu Grande hosts a wide variety of human and nonhuman beings, undermining the idea of human autonomy. An obvious point of reference here is Mackandal, the Haitian Maroon leader in Alejo Carpentier's *El reino de este mundo* (1949), a character based on the Vodou priest François Mackandal, who was thought to possess lycanthropic powers and to have resurrected after being burned alive at the stake. In Carpentier's novel, Mackandal's knowledge of the natural world allows him to take up the form of all sorts of animals to escape the clutches of the slave owners. Similarly, as Belonísia recounts in the novel's second part: "My father, the healer Zeca Chapéu Grande, could do anything. On the nights of Jarê, he'd transform into any of the encantados. He'd speak differently, he'd sing and whirl with wonderful agility around the room, endowed with the powers of the spirits of the forest, the waters, the mountains, the air."[87]

The specter of slavery persists in the collective amnesia suffered by the people that Zeca Chapéu Grande receives in his home and heals—people who cannot remember their identities and who are found wandering without direction in the nearby plantations. This lack of a stable identity derives from the convergence of extractive enterprises in the Chapada Diamantina with their promises of endless wealth. Like the mines that extractive companies have exploited and left behind in postcapitalist ruins, the enslaved people who worked for them are hollowed out inside, having lost ties to their bodies and territories. There are significant parallels with Nettel's and Schweblin's depictions of extractive capitalism as a parasite that tears apart people's bodies and spirits.

> What appeared most often at our door were maladies of the divided spirit—people who had somehow lost their stories, lost their memories, people separated from themselves, people you couldn't distinguish from wild beasts. Some thought madness was so common in that region because the first migrants had mining in their blood. They'd gone insane hunting for diamonds, seeking their radiance in the night, moving on from one hill to start digging in another, moving on from the land to go combing the river. People chasing fortunes who dreamed night and day of some good luck, but grew frustrated after enduring long periods of exhausting toil.[88]

In addition to the work of Zeca Chapéu Grande as the healer who restores the connection between bodies and spirits, Vieira Junior in *Torto arado* casts writing as a technology of remembrance that brings together stories of physical and spiritual dispersal. As an extension of the metaphors of hands reaching into the ancestral past, he traces a link between two objects of Black emancipation: the pencil and the knife. One of Belonísia's first thoughts after discovering the knife among her grandmother's possessions is to use it for sharpening a pencil, even though she has yet to learn how to write. "We could grab that knife and use it to sharpen our busted pencils."[89] Unable to speak following the accident with the knife, Belonísia conceives of writing as a conjuring of the specters of slavery by linking the power of these two objects. The fact that the twins use the knife as a mirror suggests that they might put the pencil to a similar use: writing their stories and faces into the official record.

Knives were important symbols in Afro-Brazilian healing practices, as James H. Sweet's biography of an African healer, Domingos Álvares, demonstrates. A knife represented the power to kill malignant spirits and the ability to forge a path through the forest. The use of a knife in healing rituals was a reference to Gu, the god of war. It "simultaneously represented the power to destroy one's enemies . . . and the power to liberate oneself from the confines of powerful, usually malevolent, forces (slavery, illness, disease, hunger, and so on)."[90] The depiction of the pencil as both a weapon and an instrument of healing illustrates the need to reconcile the written and the oral to enact a process of historical restitution.

The novel's last section, "Rio de sangue" (River of blood), links body and land—not through the trope of the hollowed-out body but through earthly spirits deprived of their ancestral homes. The third narrator is called Santa Rita Pescadeira (Saint Rita Fisherwoman), a recurring deity in Jarê ritual songs. A water spirit who loses her powers after the garimpeiros damage the rivers in their perpetual search for diamonds, Santa Rita Pescadeira is looking for a host body after her last human medium, Dona Miúda, passes away. Through the perspective of this water spirit who witnessed the rivers of blood spilled in the wake of the race toward precious stones, Vieira Junior positions us in the deep time of the diamond fever that comes back to haunt the present in the form of homeless Black workers. "When viewed in deep time," Robert Macfarlane observes, "things come alive that seemed inert. New responsibilities declare themselves. A conviviality of being leaps to mind and eye."[91]

An injured and homeless environmental deity is a fitting narrator for a story of bodily and spiritual dispossession, as her voice can attest to the continuation of slavery under different terms following its abolition in 1888: "The landowners . . . began referring to their slaves as 'workers' and 'tenants.' They couldn't ignore the law completely; it might cause trouble. The owners drummed into their workers just how kind they were for providing shelter to those Blacks adrift in search of a place to live"[92] The ancestral memory of Black people is also forgotten as the new generations stop learning the chants of Santa Rita Pescadeira, because the rivers have been emptied or irreparably damaged and people can no longer go out fishing. Through these spectral connections between past and present, Vieira Junior brings into relief how ancestral memory is tied to the land and, in turn, how the body serves as a tool for understanding environmental damage. As the water deity recounts how white garimpeiros used to cut off Black people's hands after accusing them of stealing diamonds, the twins' accident with the knife suddenly flashes up before our eyes.

THE MUTED SOUNDS OF THE ARCHIVE

In *Torto arado* Vieira Junior raises the question of how to restore the voices of Black people when there are no extant writings of Brazilian chattel slavery reflecting the perspective of slaves. As opposed to North America, in Brazil there is not an ample archive of first-person slave narratives. The only surviving autobiography is the story of Mahommah Gardo Baquaqua, a Muslim person from Benin who related his account of Brazilian slavery to an Irish abolitionist while living as a free man in Canada. In "The Site of Memory," Toni Morrison speaks about the need to fill in the gaps of autobiographical slave narratives, which made the experience of slavery more palatable to the people in power by silencing essential aspects of the enslaved person's suffering and interior life. She thinks about her work as a novelist as "a kind of literary archaeology," because the silence of the archive forces her "to journey to a site to see what remains were left behind and to reconstruct the world that these remains imply." According to Morrison, the creative act is indistinguishable from the exercise of memory, because both acts can be conceived through the metaphor of flooding. "All water has perfect memory," Morrison writes, "and is forever trying to get back to where it was."[93] This exploration of the unwritten lives of Black people corresponds with Hartman's notion of "critical fabulation," a writing practice that restores the voice of the voiceless while foregrounding the impossibility of doing so in its entirety.[94] Both Morrison and Hartman conceive of the exercise of listening to the stories of others by placing writer and reader in the same space of unknowingness, standing among a group of listeners and reconstructing the meaning collectively.

The ethnographic work underlying *Torto arado* reveals the novel's engagement with the tenuous relationship between fact and fiction. Vieira Junior has traced the novel's origins to his work as a civil servant for the National Institute for Colonization and Agrarian Reform (INCRA), which put him in touch with the communities of the *sertão* (backlands) in the state of Bahia. The novel began to take shape during the ethnographic work that Vieira Junior conducted for his PhD dissertation about the formation of quilombola communities in the Chapada Diamantina. In this sense, *Torto arado* can be read through these communities' progressive awakening to their own identity as quilombolas and, therefore, to their struggles to be granted land titles for their ancestral territories. As reflected in Bibiana and Severo's political activism and in his subsequent murder, Vieira Junior chronicles the long history of violence against these communities, foreshadowing their inhumane treatment during the presidency of Jair Bolsonaro, who, upon becoming president in 2018, promoted the encroachment of Black and Indigenous lands. Morrison's metaphor of the memory of water to designate the act of the imagination resonates not only with the earthly forces that serve as narrators in *Torto arado*. The metaphor also addresses the reconstruction of national histories of displacement and dispossession through the voice of forgotten local actors. The fact that Vieira Junior does not provide specific temporal markers delineates the act of reading as a joint reconstruction of modern Brazilian history. By piecing together events such as the arrival of Zeca Chapéu Grande to Água Negra during the great drought of 1932, readers can put the narrators' voices alongside other actors buried in the modern archive, such as the rural workers fleeing this same drought in the state of Ceará who were placed in concentration camps by the Brazilian government.[95]

Vieira Junior allegorizes the silent condition of the Brazilian slavery archive through Belonísia's muted perspective. The novel's title derives from Belonísia's attempts to pronounce the word *arado* (plow). "My voice was a crooked plow, deformed, penetrating the soil only to leave it infertile, ravaged, destroyed." Her inability to pronounce the word correctly becomes a metaphor for a life unfolding on the edge of history, unnoticed by the institutions of the modern nation-state. Unsurprisingly, Belonísia is not interested in learning the Brazilian national anthem, for she could not sing it out loud. The nation's archive does not have a place for history's silent witnesses. Belonísia harbors deep suspicions toward the historical narrative of miscegenation (*mistura*) and the myth about "how we should rejoice to live in a country so blessed" because her family story does not coincide with the image of Brazil as a racial democracy. The plantation's schoolteacher, Dona Lourdes, does not include in her history lessons the perspective of slaves, the history of Bahia, or the story of Afro-Brazilians who have lived for centuries in plantations like Água Negra. While linking the political tools of the nation-state with the title's crooked plow (the institutionalization of modern formations such as the plantation economy, which casts the realm of nature as separate from human cultural practices), Belonísia's narrative associates the archive with other types of knowledge embodied by her father, Zeca Chapéu Grande, who listens to the earth to decide how to plow the land: "Like a doctor listening to a heartbeat."[96]

This description of the earth as possessing the same vital organs as humans bridges the realms of nature and culture and depicts the earth as an alternative archive to that of the modern nation. Moreover, it posits the act of listening to the earth as essential for environmental care and restoration. Belonísia's silence is thus not equivalent to barbarism. As Ana María Ochoa Gautier argues, silence provides another framework to think about Afro-diasporic conceptions of personhood, because "sounding like animals, learning sounds from animals, or incorporating nonhuman entities in sound is not a problem but an objective."[97]

In this sense, *Torto arado* is a novel about the sound of Afro-Brazilians who have been deprived of their voices for centuries and who are fighting to make themselves heard in the present. The novel is filled with an aural syntax and vernacular words that attest to the long history of violence against both body and land in the Chapada Diamantina region. Belonísia's failed attempts to pronounce the word "plow" return us to this ancestral object that was already there when the first Afro-Brazilians moved in, a symbol of the "workers arriving from distant places, workers long since forgotten."[98]

Language is a repository of this archive of dispossession of Afro-Brazilian bodies and territories: it houses the archaic temporality of the first inhabitants, thus standing against land deprivation in the contemporary moment. Like the body of Zeca Chapéu Grande, language is another form of spirit possession. Unable to speak, Belonísia reconnects with the voice of her female ancestors, articulating "words cried out by my ancestors, by my mother and grandmother and the great-grandmothers I never knew, words that came to me to be uttered in my horror of a voice, and thus those words acquired the sad and enduring contours that would keep me alive." Belonísia acts as a mediator between the suffering of her female ancestors and the struggles of women today, such as her friend Maria Cabocla who is repeatedly beaten by her husband and whose bleeding mouth evokes the twins' accident with the knife. Belonísia's "wounded tongue" channels the injustices suffered by her predecessors, who were coerced into colonial regimes and timelines, to stand against the absences in the written archive.[99] An undomesticated tongue such as Belonísia's challenges the colonial classification regimes according to which women, particularly Black women, were understood as belonging to someone else.[100]

In *Torto arado* Vieira Junior lays bare the simultaneous violence against the land and the body of women, two archives cast as silent throughout history. He expands the notion of the archive to encompass the voice of nonhuman beings presumed to be "the mute world, the voiceless things once placed as a decor surrounding the usual spectacles," which suddenly stop being local phenomena and become global forces in their struggle to be heard.[101] The timeless voice of Santa Rita Pescadeira speaks not only to the decimation of natural resources but also to the assault against women. Vieira Junior weaves a relationship between the pollution of rivers and the violence suffered by the women in whose bodies the water spirit becomes flesh. Miúda, who hosts the spirit of water, is a *mulher-peixe* (fish-woman) whose displacement is also shaped by extractive forces. The rivers that cut across the *sertão* are described as the veins of Miúda's body-territory: "The river was an open vein of her body coursing through the woods." Similarly, Belonísia suffers from her community's association of men with culture and women with nature. Her partner, Tobias, beats Belonísia repeatedly and subjects her to domestic slavery because she is unable to conceive a child. Tobias's abusive behavior echoes the actions of "so many other cunning men who'd carry young women away from their parents' houses to turn them into slaves . . . introducing us to the hell that so often is a woman's life."[102] In the plantation's hierarchical social structures men are linked with production and women with reproduction.

By reconstructing the counter-memories of Black women and earth beings who are considered entities without rights, Vieira Junior repurposes the form of the slave narrative to narrate slavery's afterlives in the contemporary plantation. The current revival of the slave narrative, according to Yogita Goyal, points to "an examination of the ghosts of past inequities not yet laid to rest," because "such returns to the past as much speak to a desire to understand history as they frame the possibilities of the present and the future."[103] Vieira Junior takes up various tropes from the slave narrative tradition, such as the equivalence of literacy with freedom and the depiction of internal migration patterns. By repurposing this tradition in the late-capitalist plantation, however, he speaks to concerns about the intersection between "racial capitalism" and the extraction of bodies and territories.[104]

The novel stages the absence of the slave narrative tradition in Brazil. Its narrators are not the slaves but the natural forces that preceded them and these people's descendants who continue to experience similar conditions of dispossession, exploitation, and uprootedness. The fact that Vieira Junior makes a natural deity speak in the first person echoes the self-fashioning of the slaves who at the time were considered a piece of property to be exploited, just like nature today. The first-person slave narrative gives way to a polyphonic canvas of slavery's afterlives, told not with the documentary precision and historical evidence that white abolitionists looked for but with the glimpse into these people's interiority that only the oral tradition can grant. The novel's formal structure derives from the syncretism of religious practices like Jarê, combining the written and the oral to showcase the archive of slavery through its constituent absences.

The action of weaving counter-memories of the slave past is essential in the two oral history novels analyzed in this chapter. The knot as a recurring motif appears in the injured hands of enslaved people, the knotted roots of the trees bearing witness to ancestral times, and the embroidered cloth in which Afro-descendant female knowledge is reflected and passed down from one generation to the next. The interweaving of premodern myths, peasant and slave testimonies, and the linguistic structures of African languages is the procedure through which these oral history novels inscribe Afro-Latin American lives in History with a capital H. The contemporary is "a critical gesture" that politicizes the novel form by opening it to the multiplicity of voices and faces that remained in the margins of these countries' histories.[105] Knitting and knotting reflect the denial of African identity, the "not" embodied by Black and Brown lives, within the idea of Latin America.[106]

Reading becomes an act of disentangling the different threads that make up Afro-diasporic identities and stories. According to Henry Louis Gates Jr., Black people have mastered the art of figurative storytelling because "saying one thing to mean something quite other has been basic to black survival in oppressive Western cultures."[107] When language carries traces of hegemonic power and ideology, readers of novels like *Elástico de sombra* and *Torto arado* are invited to decode these signs and to learn how to distinguish between the masters and the slaves, the plantation and the plot.

By rewriting this foundational dialectic upon which modern Latin American nations were constituted, Cárdenas and Vieira Junior posit the need to revisit slavery's archive in light of the escalating violence against bodies and territories. If "history was made in the form of nation-states," as Azoulay reminds us, these authors delve into forms of knowledge production that escape the methods of collecting, cataloging, and indexing characteristic of the modern archive: the knowledge of the land, the oral folktale, and the embodied cultural practice.[108] Cárdenas makes his intentions clear when he states that national history is an invention of the archive and its mechanisms of forgetting: "Colombian history," he remarks, "has operated based on imposed machines of oblivion."[109] When he turns the white narrator of his novel into a cockroach, he blends two domains (nature and culture) that remain separate in the white neoliberal gaze. Rather than focusing on the human rights offenses of Brazil's recent dictatorial past, Vieira Junior shows that Bahia's Afro-Brazilian communities still await the concession of more basic rights: bodies, territories, and freedom. Both novels weave these different struggles through a knot that is impossible to untie, a metaphor that Zapata Olivella uses to refer to the inseparability between the living, the dead, the ancestors, and the spirits as the shared matrix of Afro-Latin American life. If neoliberal societies are enchanted by commodity fetishism, these novels show that they need to be re-enchanted by the power of the word: the mixture of the oral and the written as the only possible way of making the archive speak.

PART II

RETURNS
OF HISTORY
AND MEMORY

CHAPTER 4

THE CHILDREN RETURN

The Novel of Postmemory

Sebastián and Verónica are the children of exiles from the last Argentinean military dictatorship. Sebastián grows up in São Paulo, Brazil, and Verónica in Mexico City, belonging to a "generation of children" characterized by their incomplete access to the tragic events of the dictatorship and, consequently, to their parents' lives during those years. In this sense, Sebastián and Verónica inhabit "a kaleidoscopic period," as Ernst Bloch referred to the years after the First World War—a period in which history is not shown under the teleological order of "progress" or "decadence" but as an accumulation of anachronistic ruins that interrupt the course of history and that people are forced to order if they want to build future horizons.[1]

Montage was a procedure used by avant-garde artists from the 1920s onward to adopt a position of non-contemporaneity with their own time, underlining the anachronisms that were a constituent part of the present. Montage also creates a dialectical image of history that brings forth the new and that turns past remains into transmissible experiences, giving the reader spectator a new agency in constructing the present. This is how Sebastián and Verónica—respectively, a writer and a "visual artist who writes"—conceive of their aesthetic projects: as a kaleidoscopic montage of a spectral past. Both author narrators propose retracing history by dismantling the order of the archive, an archive that has been filled with black holes and discontinuities, standing in what Benjamin referred to as "the threshold of the present."[2] With this goal in mind, Sebastián and Verónica return to Argentina—he to Buenos Aires, she to the city of Córdoba—and lose themselves in streets that they feel both personal and foreign. They aim to restore an incomplete inheritance and bridge the gap separating them from their familial past.

Sebastián is the narrator of *A resistência* (2015; trans. 2019 as *Resistance*), winner of the prestigious Jabuti (2016) and Saramago (2017) awards, by Brazilian writer Julián Fuks. Verónica is the narrator of *Conjunto vacío* (2015; trans. 2018 as *Empty Set*) by Mexican writer Verónica Gerber Bicecci.[3] Besides the year of publication (2015), Fuks's and Gerber Bicecci's works share many similarities. They are novels told in the first-person whose narrators are alter egos of their respective authors. The genealogy of both narrators is constituted by cosmopolitan dislocations that make them conceive of the contemporary as a period of permanent instability. Sebastián returns to Argentina to investigate the family origins of his brother, whom his parents adopted before fleeing to Brazil. Verónica returns to try to ascertain why her mother disappeared (not during the dictatorship but in her Mexican exile), as if absorbed by a past that did not allow her to move forward. *A resistência* and *Conjunto vacío* are inscribed within the discourse of postmemory, a particular kind of memory connected to its original source "not through recollection but through an imaginative investment and creation."[4] The aimless walks that the narrators undertake through Argentinean cities—with which they have maintained a vicarious relationship based on their parents' memories—fulfill the purpose of authenticating a past of which only remnants survive, what Sebastián calls "the calcified ruins of the events . . . their silent ruins" and Verónica calls "an illegible disorder."[5]

Sebastián and Verónica thus practice an art of memory with the aim being to establish a new disposition of traumatic history, separate from the teleological order and attentive to the survival of the past. This archeological vision of historical becoming is common to the second generation of postmemory, "a generation marked by a history to which they have lost even the distant and now barely 'living connection.'"[6] Fuks and Gerber Bicecci put together exercises with language and form in order to question how to restore the past when it has become an accumulation of scattered fragments. Through heterogeneous assemblages that open the past to the influence of other temporalities, they propose an alternative cartography of time: a provisional ordering of history that fluidly straddles the lines between fiction and reality, literature and document.

On a formal level, the fragmentary and oscillating structures of *A resistência* and *Conjunto vacío* reflect the narrators' concern not to transgress the suffering of the victims through literary practice. This is what Rebecca Walkowitz calls "critical cosmopolitanism," referring to the development of a narrative strategy that is suited to the task of representing the experience of others, especially when dealing with minorities or communities distant from one's own: "a way of thinking about people whose lives are geographically or culturally unrelated to one's own and a way of acknowledging, though not only acknowledging, the ethical or affective compromises that go with that thinking."[7] This notion of critical cosmopolitanism is in tune with that developed by Kwame Anthony Appiah and Susan Sontag, who also call for a thorough reflection on the methods conducive to thinking about the suffering of others. In this sense, the montage technique adopted by both Fuks and Gerber Bicecci delineates literary practice as a permanent work-in-progress that confronts the minor lives consumed by acts of destruction with History with a capital H, combining reflection and invention, search and discovery. For these narrators of unstable national affiliations, literary practice breaks through the restrictions imposed by disciplinary fields, identity documents, and inherited versions of history. Rather than trafficking in hard truths about history, Fuks and Gerber Bicecci write in a manner characterized by the relentless interrogation of the frameworks that give access to the past and shape the contemporary. By putting the linear version of history in suspense, both authors create polyphonic discourses that give voice to secondary actors usually excluded by hegemonic narratives and show the discontinuities at the core of historical becoming. History, in other words, is an entity devoid of a telos or a single meaning.

Ultimately, Fuks and Gerber Bicecci contextualize the quest of their narrators within a new contemporaneity—linked to the work of the memory of children and grandchildren, the formation of alternative communities to the family and the nation-state, and the resistance to the regime of presentist historicity that characterizes neoliberal societies. In contrast to the genre of *testimonio*, which John Beverley described as "primarily concerned with sincerity rather than literariness," these novelists foreground their aesthetic procedure to convey art and literature's limits in capturing the personal and collective traumas of the last dictatorial regimes.[8] Neither author entrusts us with imagining "the violence and the pain of the other as our own" or "vanishing the aesthetic frame that divides the textual witness and the reader or spectator," as Eugenio Di Stefano argues regarding literary works that align with the logic of human rights.[9]

As opposed to the *testimonios* that relied exclusively on human rights restitution, which were cast as "a moral alternative to bankrupt political utopias," Fuks and Gerber Bicecci question literature's capacity to transmit empathy and its complicity in perpetuating the pain of others.[10] Each author assembles an ethics of representation by immersing readers, not in the suffering of torture victims or the families of the disappeared, but in the opacity of meaning experienced by the generation who grew up during or shortly after the dictatorial period. By introducing blank spaces or adopting photographic writing practices that question our voyeuristic relationship with the past, Fuks and Gerber Bicecci reconfigure the novel form to represent the specters of the last dictatorships and their afterlives as absence rather than presence. In doing so, they move the act of writing from representing to conjuring, from depicting historical memory to capturing its enduring legacy in the present.

ARCHIVES OF POSTMEMORY

Fuks in *A resistência* addresses the tense relationship between history, memory, and literary invention. His narrator, Sebastián, is an alter ego of the author who seeks to reconstruct the story of his adopted brother by delving into the lives of his brother's parents. Sebastián is the son of Argentinean political activists who were exiled from the country during the last military dictatorship and who ended up settling in São Paulo. He embarks on a journey back to Buenos Aires in order to elucidate the origins of his adoptive brother—namely, whether his brother's biological parents (whose identity remains unknown to this day) were victims of state-sponsored terrorism. Despite being unable to gather conclusive evidence about his brother's clandestine birth, Sebastián reflects on the mediations that keep him away from the truth, especially that of literary discourse.

The novel's title evokes several references in the context of South America's struggle for human rights. On the one hand, it points to the revolutionary militancy of the 1970s and the act of resistance involved in conceiving a child in a political context that protected the kidnapping of newborn babies. The book's epigraph comes from Ernesto Sabato, the intellectual author of the report of Argentina's National Commission on the Disappearance of Persons (CONADEP), the *Nunca más* (Never again).[11] On the other hand, in the Brazilian context the verb "to resist" evokes the Memorial da Resistência de São Paulo, the former headquarters of the Departamento Estadual de Ordem Política e Social do Estado de São Paulo (DEOPS-SP) and a detention center between 1940 and 1983, which is now a museum.[12] The book's transnational focus allows it to be inscribed within public debates about the culture of memory in both Argentina and Brazil and to provide an unprecedented perspective on the generation of children born in exile.

A resistência is part of a trend in contemporary Latin American narrative that is often categorized as "literature of the children," a term that refers to the work of authors who grew up in the context of the last military dictatorships in the Southern Cone and, in general, had an incomplete or partial understanding of the traumatic events that impacted their private lives. Fuks's novel occupies a unique role within this corpus as it is narrated by the son of Argentinean political activists who were exiled in Brazil.[13] The novel has as its main character Sebastián's brother, who gradually becomes "a schematic character."[14] Throughout the novel, the brother grows progressively thinner. He is the victim of an eating disorder that Sebastián contrasts with the dysfunction of the adopted children who grow fat to feel that they are the legitimate occupants of the family home. Simultaneously, the brother locks himself in his own room or flees the house without warning, losing himself in the confines of "a city that is the very antithesis of his bedroom."[15]

However, the schematic nature of the brother's character is rooted in an ethical-moral crisis of literary representation, for the narrator feels that to make him speak within the framework of a fictional discourse would be to exercise an act of epistemic violence. Thus, Fuks translates the identity crisis of the children onto the literary text itself, in such a way that Sebastián does not know in which discursive mode to inscribe his own story: "I can't decide if this is a story."[16] This literary mode corresponds to Sarlo's critique of the testimonies of the victims of state terrorism. According to Sarlo, *testimonios* produce "a distinct sense" of history since they provide specific details about human rights violations.[17] These texts straddle the lines between law and literature, as they were used as legal documents in the trials against the leaders of the military juntas. Faced with the exhaustion of the narrative mechanisms of the testimonial genre, in *A resistência* Fuks proposes ways of conjuring the past as a fundamental part of the present.

The cover of the Brazilian edition of the novel shows the scattered montage of photographs from a family album. This is the first indication that the work of memory is closely linked to inspecting the family's photographic archive. The novel seems to have the structure of a photographic album composed of black-and-white slides that the narrator endeavors to reconstruct. Sebastián equates the act of writing with translating the photographs in the family album, taking them out of their original context and making them speak in the present: "It's only because the photo stays silent that I am obliged to speak for it, that I insist on translating its rhetoric, on capturing its meandering judgment."[18]

The "meandering judgment" consists in reading between the lines that separate the past of the family album from the narrative present, which forces him to stand against the grain of chronological historicity. At the textual level, this is reflected in a photographic writing practice that rejoices in the length of the sentence, as if Sebastián wants to convey the temporal parenthesis that occurs when we contemplate images for an extended peri-od.[19] By arbitrarily interspersing various temporal planes, the novel's brief chapters reveal an exercise of memory that does not close off the past but opens it up to all its hermeneutical possibilities. As Hirsch points out, "Art-ists and writers have . . . attempted to use the very instruments of ideology, the camera, the album, and the familial gaze, as modes of questioning, resistance, and contestation."[20] Indeed, this is one of the symbolic mean-ings that the word "resistance" acquires throughout the novel, as Sebastián attempts to go beyond the opaque surface of family photographs and ques-tion the various layers that make up his second-degree memory.

Fuks's discursive procedure unveils the mediations that intervene in forming a second-degree memory. A crucial scene occurs when Sebastián finds a photograph of his mother arranging the family album, an image that captures the mechanisms of montage to which all vicarious memory is subjected: "A curious record of memory being assembled, of a remote existence being transformed into narrative through an artful sequence of images; a curious notion of there having been something memorable about the very formation of memory."[21] Fuks weaves an inextricable link between photographic and psychoanalytic discourse. Commenting on Benjamin's writings on photography, Hirsch argues that the photographic camera—just like psychoanalysis—has the potential to unveil "optical processes" that are invisible to the human eye. "The camera can reveal what we see without realizing that we do, just as psychoanalysis can uncover what we know without knowing that we do: what is stored in the unconscious."[22]

These reflections on the optical unconscious are particularly apt in de-scribing the novel's narrative procedure. The rhetorical questions Sebastián asks himself, as if suspicious at all times of the mediations imposed by literary representation, could be framed within psychoanalytic discourse, which he has inherited from his parents. Like the superimposed slides that illustrate the cover of the book's Brazilian edition, the brief chapters of *A re-sistência* invert the structure of the family album by scattering the temporal coordinates that gave it meaning in the first place. Through this procedure, Fuks shows that the manipulation of the archive can make visible the opti-cal unconscious, which remained hidden in the photographic narrative as organized by Sebastián's parents.

These uses of photographic discourse allow us to read *A resistência* as a novel that builds a new archive on the legacy of state violence. Fuks does not attempt to restore the original meaning of the family photographs, the meaning that the participants of the photographic event tried to inscribe on them.[23] On the contrary, he inserts the photographs into a new discourse to examine the blank spaces between them, the gap between the original image and the text with which Sebastián seeks to make sense of it. This photographic writing is framed by what Azoulay has called "potential history"—namely, "the transformation of the past into an unending event, into what Benjamin has called incomplete history, in which our deeds in the present allow us to read the violently constituted achievements of the past in ways that historicize the sovereign power of the past and render it potentially reversible."[24]

In *A resistência*, the incomplete reconstruction of the past is a historiographic method that reflects the nature of state crimes in Argentina, where the number of disappeared is estimated at thirty thousand. The impossibility of finding out the identity of his brother's biological mother, who could be a victim of state terrorism, makes Fuks/Sebastián adopt a system of enunciation that questions the limits imposed by disappearance as a repressive technology, as a death without a corpse. In this context, the novel's literary operation is reminiscent of the film essay or cinema verité, a procedure that Gabriela Nouzeilles highlights in her analysis of Albertina Carri's documentary *Los rubios* about the filmmaker's disappeared parents.[25]

More than proposing a new ordering of the family archive, in *A resistência* Fuks interrogates the photographic organization of cultural memory. Visiting the Museo Sitio de Memoria ESMA in Buenos Aires (located at the former clandestine detention, torture, and extermination center), Sebastián looks closely at the black-and-white photographs of disappeared women. In front of the photographs of these women whose smiles contrast with the tragic fate they faced, he endeavors to reconstruct every trace of their faces. The exercise of reading photographs from the 1970s becomes a way of understanding the bonds of affection between members of human communities that transcend the family, an exercise that Azoulay defines as "the exercise of citizenship—not citizenship imprinted with the seal of belonging to a sovereign, but citizenship as a partnership of governed persons taking up their duty as citizens and utilizing their position for one another, rather than for a sovereign."[26] The restitution of their citizenship is demonstrated by the fact that many of the photographs of these women correspond to the photos of their former DNIs (National Identity Cards), a gesture that restores their inscription to a regime of state belonging, from which they were violently expelled. Recontextualized in the museum space, these "paper monuments" subvert the purpose of state regulation that initially characterized them by becoming documents of denunciation.[27] In *A resistência*, photographic reading is transformed into a civil exercise whose objective is to restore the traces of those completely removed from the historical archive. The notion of citizenship is not based on belonging to a single sovereign power but, instead, on a cosmopolitan responsibility that challenges humanity as a whole.[28]

In this sense, the scene at the Museo Sitio de Memoria ESMA questions the "we" that brings together the viewers of photographs, reflecting on the need to take a stand in the face of the victims' suffering. In *Regarding the Pain of Others*, Sontag questions the civil responsibility assumed by the viewer when looking at photographs that make a spectacular portrayal of war atrocities. Sontag asserts that these graphic representations of war, by aiming to shock, lose the power to guide the viewer toward understanding the suffering of others. This is because the photographs do not evoke the suffering of war victims but, rather, display it in an undisguised way, causing the viewer to remember photographs rather than historical events.[29]

In contrast, the images of the disappeared women account for a repressive technology—disappearance—that does not provide the viewer with photographic evidence of state crimes. The fact that these black-and-white images were taken from the family album of the disappeared women is proof, according to Nelly Richard, of "the latency of the *not yet* (past-past) and of the *still* (past-present) that causes the technique of photography to waver ambiguously in the tension between the absent and the present, the real and the unreal, the tangible and the intangible."[30] The suspension of photographic meaning, although a direct consequence of the repressive method of the dictatorship, opens up new modes of understanding and commemoration in the face of the loss of others. As Sebastián argues in relation to the portraits of disappeared women: "a sensitive effort has been made to catch them in a moment of joy, to capture some glimpse of happiness . . . a sensitive attempt to give them strength and dignity."[31]

However, in Fuks's novel, there is also at stake the idea that looking at photographs of the disappeared can become an act of voyeurism, not because they are insensitive representations of the victims but because of the feeling of violating the intimacy of the person photographed. Fuks questions how to develop a cosmopolitan ethic when empathy is an insufficient, if not inappropriate, response to the suffering of the victims.[32] Sebastián, the narrator spectator, seeks to convey a cosmopolitan sensibility by incorporating new ways of conceiving otherness, not confining it to the immutability of the photographic image but opening a space of continuous actualization of the memory of the victims. Thus, Fuks in *A resistência* develops a critical cosmopolitanism that questions not only national affiliations and fixed identities but also the capacity of language to access the traumatic events of the recent past.

CRITICAL COSMOPOLITANISM

Cosmopolitanism has been connected, from its origins in Stoicism, to the notion of universal citizenship and the discourse of human rights. In "Patriotism and Cosmopolitanism," Martha Nussbaum traces the germ of cosmopolitanism to the Stoic doctrine that envisioned the world as a series of concentric circles composed of family, neighbors, fellow citizens, and so on, giving priority to the circle that embraces humanity as a whole. Nussbaum derives her notion of cosmopolitanism from this doctrine, asserting that where one is born is only an accident and that a true citizen of the world must pledge allegiance to the whole of humanity rather than to a particular nation-state.[33] Appiah, for his part, comments that Nussbaum's vision risks conflating cosmopolitanism with humanism by considering humanity as a single concentric circle. In an essay entitled "Cosmopolitan Patriots," Appiah argues that the cosmopolitan celebrates the fact that there are local forms of existence rather than the desire for "global homogeneity" promoted by humanism. Appiah thus recognizes the importance of the concentric circles closest to oneself—the street, business, profession, and family—as basic sites of moral responsibility.[34]

Viewing the nation as an artificial symbolic construct, Appiah points out that the job of the "rooted cosmopolitan" or "cosmopolitan patriot" is to prevent the state, through its institutions, from trampling on the essential conditions of community life. Appiah argues for a cosmopolitan ethic similar to that of Sontag, who also suggests that we cannot intervene entirely in the suffering of human beings farther away from us because, although we have access to it through photographs, these cannot be considered "a transparency of something that happened. It is always the image that someone chose; to photograph is to frame, and to frame is to exclude."[35] In *A resistência*, Fuks articulates an ethical cosmopolitanism that highlights the role of state institutions as guarantors of the reconstruction of historical memory. However, the novel takes this task even further, conceiving literature as the site of enunciation of a critical cosmopolitanism that questions the capacity to speak for others, not only those distant from us but also those who make up our closest circle.

Sebastián, in his role as the narrator, embodies the cosmopolitan subject in more than one sense. To begin with, he is part of a genealogy that has been dislocated by state violence. His Jewish grandparents emigrated from Romania to Buenos Aires in the 1920s because of growing antisemitic fervor, but his parents experienced the flip side of the cosmopolitan imaginary by living under a dictatorship. In Argentina, his father was forced to adopt a false name and to see his patients in offices lent to him by friends. His mother, on the other hand, had a miscarriage while living in Buenos Aires, as if the impossibility of carrying a baby to term was a physiological reaction to the situation of permanent threat experienced under dictatorship. The couple tentatively emigrated to Brazil, despite their original plan to travel to Spain or Mexico and despite the risk posed by the information exchange system between the dictatorial regimes of the Southern Cone, known as Plan Condor. The transitional place initially occupied by Brazil in the family itinerary delineates the present of the children of political exiles as an intermittent temporality, given that Sebastián's birthplace (São Paulo) as well as his mother tongue (Portuguese, which is not his mother's language) are the fruits of a cosmopolitan accident. He reconstructs his surname's genealogy through its various dislocations, starting with his ancestors' journey from Germany to Romania, which entailed a modification of the surname to adapt to the new language. Even a supposedly stable signifier such as the narrator's last name becomes subject to the intermittences of cosmopolitan dislocation. Sebastián interrogates the paradox that the "incessant displacement" and the "provisional dwellings" of his ancestors might form part of the legacy he has inherited from them. "Can exile be inherited? Might we, the little ones, be as expatriate as our parents? Should we consider ourselves Argentinians deprived of our country, of our fatherland? And is political persecution subject to the norms of heredity?"[36] In *A resistência*, the literature of the children is determined by a double mediation: a second-degree memory and an inheritance of familial exile. The novel conjures these two orders through the figure of the wandering Jew, which manifests in Sebastián's urban wanderings.

Walking the streets of Buenos Aires constitutes one of the pivotal moments of Fuks's body of work. Sebastián mentions a book he has written about the "experience of walking the streets of Buenos Aires and looking at people's faces."[37] This veiled reference to an earlier novel written by Fuks (*Procura do romance*; 2011) delineates the narrator of his books as a cosmopolitan flaneur—half Brazilian, half Argentinean—who traverses Buenos Aires's urban landscape in search of concrete signs that return him to some sense of rootedness. These walks through the city would seem to embody what Mariano Siskind calls a "cosmopolitanism of loss," the cosmopolitanism of contemporary migrants who experience the decomposition of their own identity and cannot establish a new home as an ontological source of meaning. For Siskind, refugees and stateless migrants are "effective catachrestic figures of the end of the world."[38]

As Sebastián observes, "it's me who wants to redeem my own immobility, it's me who wants to go back to belonging to the place where I've never actually belonged . . . nothing will restore me to anywhere, nothing will repair what I have experienced, because it doesn't look like there's anything in me to be repaired."[39] This is a new incarnation of the cosmopolitan flaneur, for cosmopolitanism now implies the impossibility of establishing an *oikos* (home) as a nucleus for the organization of the journey and the exploration of a traumatic past. In *A resistência*, the outdoors and orphanhood are the symbolic conditions for Sebastián's quest to shed new light on the continuities between past and present.

Sebastián's walks through Buenos Aires evoke the counterpart of the figure of the cosmopolitan flaneur: the psychiatric tradition of the *fugueur*.[40] The fugueur originated in France's "dissociative fugue" epidemic during the last decade of the nineteenth century, when this psychiatric disorder was first diagnosed.[41] Dissociative fugue—also known as dromomania, *automatisme ambulatoire*, or ambulatory determinism—is a compulsion to wander in a state of amnesia that can be indefinitely dilated. Ian Hacking points out that the fugueur's journey represents the pathological flip side of flânerie since it is "less a voyage of self-discovery than an attempt to eliminate self." He states that the prototypical fugueur was associated with the figure of the wandering Jew, a sign of the antisemitism that reigned in France at the end of the nineteenth century.[42]

In *A resistência*, Sebastián's walks among the crowds of Buenos Aires lead him to his progressive isolation, not to the cosmopolitan encounter or the sense of national belonging he aspires to. "If I'm lost and I keep going round in circles in such a logical city, I muse as I walk, it's because I don't want to arrive at a central point, it's because I resist reaching the destination I've chosen, it's because I'm trying to escape whatever's waiting for me when I get there."[43] His ambulatory automatism is intimately linked to the intergenerational transmission of trauma. The figure of the fugueur also refers to the psychic condition of his adopted brother, who used to run away from the family home to wander the streets of São Paulo. Fuks shows how Sebastián's flânerie can become an act of vagrancy and, by extension, a pathological disorder that is common among those who possess a mediated memory of traumatic events.

On the other hand, Sebastián conveys a critical cosmopolitanism by questioning language as a means to access the past and the suffering of others. Thus, Fuks raises the question of the relationship between history and literary representation, in the context of the exhaustion of testimony as the privileged epistemological genre for narrating the dictatorial past and its inscriptions in the present. *A resistência* is a narrative built on detours: between reality and fiction, the past and the present, the story of the adoptive brother and that of the parents. Sebastián thus questions the exercise of accessing the past through language, not only because of the vicarious condition of his postmemory but also because his parents' generation was forced to live in hiding. The impossibility of obtaining a complete version of his familial past becomes evident when he tries to reconstruct the clandestine birth of his brother in the outskirts of Buenos Aires as well as the origins of his brother's biological parents, of whom the only thing he manages to find out is that the mother was of Italian heritage.

The writing of a book that accesses the past in a fragmentary manner points, on the one hand, to the inadequacy of the testimonial genre for the narrative project of the children's generation and, on the other, to the erosion of realism as a paradigm for literary representation. As Sebastián argues, "I know I am writing my failure. I don't really know what I'm writing." If the representational failure is due to the fragmentary nature of the archive, he wonders how to prevent language from misrepresenting reality, so that his brother does not become an embodiment of all children of the disappeared when he cannot even assert who his biological parents were: "It's an unfair role I've cast him in, my brother as a hostage to what he will never be."[44]

However, the attempt to account for the past through language, despite the impossibility of accessing a translucent version of the events, constitutes an act of cosmopolitan sensibility. Through these attempts to reconstruct his familial past, Sebastián wants to understand the suffering of his adoptive brother and, therefore, to find new avenues of communication after a "noticeable loss of contact" between them.[45] The novel's first chapter is a meditation on the expressions that situate his brother's place within the family circle, among which Sebastián opts for "adoptive son" since it does not reaffirm the stigma of adoption. To the extent that Sebastián understands that language can become a means of epistemic violence, robbing the adoptive brother of his possibility of representation, Fuks's novel embodies the cosmopolitan slogan that, according to Appiah, consists of seeking in literary discourse the shared values that facilitate interpersonal communication.[46]

The drama at stake in *A resistência* is to find an adequate tone to capture the voice of others—the parents, the adoptive brother, and the victims of state-sponsored terrorism—without transgressing the moral responsibility entailed in all acts of literary mediation. This tone is critical with its own enunciative character and is what Paloma Vidal emphasizes when she argues that the narrative is constructed from a "sensation of illegitimacy": the illegitimate person is not the adoptive son but, rather, the narrator who wants to tell a story based on other people's memories.[47] As Walkowitz states, the articulation of a critical cosmopolitanism (as opposed to a "planetary humanism," which would be in tune with Nussbaum's position) depends on two interrelated characteristics: "an aversion to heroic tones of appropriation and progress, and a suspicion of epistemological privilege, views from above or from the center that assume a consistent distinction between who is seeing and what is seen."[48]

In the novel Fuks does not frame the interventions of the characters with quotation marks, thus creating a space of indistinction between Sebastián's monologue and the free indirect discourse of his interlocutors. On repeated occasions, Sebastián introduces the speech of other characters and then retracts his narrative procedure: "These were not the words, I don't really know what words they were." The critical cosmopolitanism lies in assuming the impossibility of articulating a polyphonic discourse. This aesthetic gesture becomes visible when Sebastián's parents read the manuscript and criticize his supposedly negative portrayal of them, the "detailed description of old scars . . . this public scrutiny of our conflicts."[49] The scene casts the novel as an indefinite work-in-progress because the manuscript contains a similar discussion between the narrator and his parents. *A resistência* thus represents the narration of experience through a continuous negotiation between parents and children, between testimony and imagination.

A HISTORY OF THE PRESENT

The end of the Southern Cone dictatorships inaugurated a new historicity not only for the direct victims of state terrorism but also for the individuals affected in a collateral way, such as the following generations of children and grandchildren. The need to name this period has given rise to various terms that postulate an "after," from temporal markers such as post-dictatorship to concepts from fields outside Latin Americanism (postmemory would be one of them, but also post-history, post-ideology, etc.). However, as Richard has pointed out, the prefix of the word "post-dictatorship" seems to confine to the past the "traumatic adjacencies" that persist in the present—while it participates in the phenomenon of "dismissals and cancellations" that the other "posts" already predicted toward the end of the twentieth century.[50] On the contrary, the terms "recent history" and "contemporary history" were coined in the social sciences to account for the tension, sometimes the opposition, that exists between the categories of history and memory, knowledge and experience, distance and proximity.[51] In Latin America, the emergence of this new discipline became visible with the establishment of professorships, institutions, and research conferences dedicated to studying the legacy of the last dictatorships and the transmission of cultural memory. The Centro de Pesquisa e Documentação de História Contemporânea do Brasil (CPDOC), the Laboratório de Estudos do Tempo Presente of the Universidade Federal do Rio de Janeiro (UFRJ), and the Jornadas de Trabajo sobre Historia Reciente (JTHR) in Argentina are just some of the initiatives that demonstrate the rise of this field of study.[52]

The field of contemporary history provides strategies for countering the historicity of periods of democratic transition, which are characterized by neoliberal policies that established a present devoted exclusively to the logic of the market. The notion that memory is a task, for example, reverses the presentism of the market (the result of the demands of consumption and hyperproduction) by anchoring the past firmly in the present. The study of recent history poses several methodological challenges, however; among them is the temporal delimitation of the field of study. Henry Rousso, former director of the Institut d'histoire du temps présent (IHTP) in Paris, argues that all contemporary history begins with "the most recent catastrophe," which inaugurates a time marked by trauma and the tension between the mandate of memory and the seduction of forgetting. According to Rousso, "the history of the present time as it has unfolded over the last thirty years [the book was originally published in 2012] is rather a form of resistance to presentism, an aspiration to restore, as all historians do, a depth to the near past and to current events, a way of inserting it in time."[53]

In this sense, Fuks in his novel offers an act of resistance to the regime of presentist historicity, first conceiving writing as working with the ruins of historical processes and then discovering the signs of an unresolved past in everyday temporality. The greatest emblem of this resistance to presentism is found in a newspaper advertisement that the Grandmothers of the Plaza de Mayo have been publishing continuously since 1978, in which they demand the restitution of kidnapped children. By way of speculation, Sebastián imagines his parents reading the ad in August of that same year, when they were already in exile, having adopted a child from an anonymous family. "Speculating about how my parents might have reacted, about how they might have read the appeal from the Grandmothers of the Plaza de Mayo, is a fragile attempt to consign this appeal to a specific time, to remove it from time, to exclude it from the present in which its voice still exists. Since 1978 the appeal from the Grandmothers has been repeated: it's in the square where the women walk in silence every Thursday, it's in the papers I've been able to read many times, reproduced in several news articles."[54]

This scene demonstrates that the newspaper, by including the ad of the Grandmothers of the Plaza de Mayo, is the scene of a clash between the immediacy of presentism and the culture of memory. According to Hartog, the need to remove death and the dead from our daily routines is one of the signs of presentism.[55] The ad shows that today we might be experiencing the contours of a "commemorative era," which atones for all past crimes and reinscribes the memory of the dead in the present moment.[56] This reading scene encloses a double operation of resistance to presentism. On the one hand, the Grandmothers' announcement is a daily reminder of the outstanding accounts that the work of memory has yet to settle, not only at the familial level but also collectively. On the other hand, reading the announcement is among the acts that trigger Sebastián's trip to Buenos Aires and his investigation into the original family of his adoptive brother, which implicates him in an alternative community through his commitment to the struggle for human rights.

In this context, contemporaneity implies a relationship not only with time but also with space. Fuks reflects on the role of collective action in the reconfiguration of public space, designing an urban cartography around places of cultural memory. If Sebastián describes his flânerie through Buenos Aires as a series of circular paths, the symbolic center of his journey is the Plaza de Mayo. The decisive event that occurs during his stay in Buenos Aires is the recovery of the grandson of Estela de Carlotto, the Grandmothers' historical leader. The aimless walks through the city lead Sebastián almost naturally to the Plaza de Mayo, where a crowd is gathered at the Grandmothers' headquarters. After joining in "the heat of community," he spontaneously participates in this act of collective reparation through shouts and applause.[57]

This scene widens the margin of people "directly affected" by state terrorism, taking into consideration not only kinship ties but also new forms of coexistence and responsibility in the face of loss.[58] The public intervention inverts the material and symbolic charge of the Plaza de Mayo as the place of the founding of the city and of the May Revolution of 1810. The Plaza de Mayo becomes the emblematic site of public memory and cultural heritage in Argentina, a *lieu de mémoire* or site of memory that needs to be protected from the "acceleration of history" through the civic work of the community.[59] As Huyssen points out in relation to Buenos Aires's Parque de la Memoria, "the memorial as a site of intervention in the present may become an agent of political identity today. For memory is always of the present even though its ostensible content is of the past."[60] Huyssen reveals how the sites of memory demand a continuous updating of the traumatic past—a conjuring of the disappeared as dead who have not yet found proper burial—as a starting point for the emergence of alternative forms of coexistence among people.

The collective feeling of living a historic date, the recovery of Estela de Carlotto's grandson on August 5, 2014, makes it possible for the work of memory to be conceived as an elaboration of the present. Fuks, in *A resistência*, seems to build the politics of memory around the slogan of the Grandmothers of the Plaza de Mayo: "they are and will be present, now and always—*presentes, ahora y siempre*."[61] The meaning of the slogan splits between the evocation of the disappeared and the act of presence that makes such a call possible, referring to both the victims of state terrorism and the political activists. The plural suggests that the present of political action is not an entity folded in on itself but is, instead, composed of a wide array of temporalities that go against the grain of the representation of history as a series of modernizing processes. According to Ruffel, the contemporary is "a palimpsestic or layered representation of time," rather than an arrow pointing forward.[62] Thus, the exercise of memory depends on this conception of the present as a time of coexistence between various temporalities. Fuks's memory exercise posits an archeological gaze that points out the continuities between historical periods that seemed distant from each other.

Fuks seems to suggest that literature, in order to remain anchored in the present, must understand "the most recent catastrophe" as the end of a specific regime of historicity and the beginning of another, reflecting this change of temporal paradigms through aesthetic form. I use here the term "catastrophe" in its Greek etymology, as "ruin" and "destruction," as the action of "turning downward," and finally, as the "theatrical blow" that produces the denouement of a dramatic work. This conception of historicity, according to Rousso, is emancipated from the logic that mobilized revolutionary modernity (time as linearity and an arrow moving in the direction of progress), taking for granted that the present is a provisional entity and that it would be impossible to situate it within a temporal framework of long duration. It is a vision of history that considers the Second World War, and in particular the year 1945, as the starting point of a new regime of historicity, characterized not only by generalized pessimism but also by the difficulty of overcoming the memory of the most recent catastrophes.[63]

In an essay entitled "A era da pós-ficção: notas sobre a insuficiência da fabulação no romance contemporâneo," Fuks points out that ruins constitute the fundamental matter of the contemporary novelist: the dissolution of the boundaries between aesthetic genres, the end of utopias, the distrust of institutional language, the impossibility of making conclusive statements, and the shortcomings of the fictional pact between author and reader. After associating the ruins of post-1945 Europe with the destruction of the novel as an autonomous genre, Fuks wonders "if the novel is constructed today with the remains of its own destruction and whether what is created with remains is only created to be destroyed afterward."[64] The term "post-fiction" designates the ethical commitments of the contemporary novelist in the face of the representation of recent historical traumas, when many of the witnesses are still alive and can refute their version of the events. But above all, it refers to the task of writing fiction in an era that has wrecked the category of truth.[65] In this sense, Fuks's reflections on the contemporary novel resonate with Sarlo's critique of the testimonial genre, whose use of the first person would fabricate a "realist-romantic mode" that was incompatible with the incompleteness of all memorialist work.[66]

This "reflexive imagination" is what Sarlo argues is required to make the traumatic past intelligible.[67] Contrary to the victims' testimonies sustained by "the truth of experience," Sarlo observes that in literature "a narrator always thinks from outside the experience, as if humans could take hold of the nightmare and not just suffer it."[68] Sebastián has this "outside of experience" in mind when he resorts to the metaphor of reconstructing bones, remains, and vestiges to describe the work of memory. The metaphor is evocative not only because in the political background of the novel lies the question of the disappeared but also because it points to the incompleteness of the children's memory. The narrative gradually investigates "the calcified ruins of the event, touch[es] them, move[s] them about, and construct[s] from the silence of those ruins." This archaeological work with the past becomes evident when Sebastián tells the story of Marta Brea, his mother's friend who was kidnapped in the Buenos Aires hospital where they both worked. The mother used to share her "mental stock of images" about Brea's disappearance at the dinner table, giving rise to an intergenerational transmission of trauma. From then on, the children begin to create their own archive of images about the disappearance of the Argentinean psychologist, whose name comes to designate for them "the holocaust in our house, another holocaust, one more holocaust among many, and one so familiar, so close."[69] Three decades later, the family receives a letter informing them that Brea's remains have been identified. Only then does his mother's colleague leave the realm of imagination, as Sebastián learns that her full name was Martha Maria Brea (with an "h" that he had silenced) and that she was murdered on June 1, 1977. This episode demonstrates that Fuks's novel works with a repertoire of names, words, and objects that embody feelings of loss and melancholy, remnants that contain an affective connection with traumatic events.

In contrast to narratives that erect a seamless truth, the first-person narration of *A resistência* seems constructed from the distance that separates it from the traumatic past, in such a way that it establishes an ambiguous pact between the author and the reader. Only in the next to last chapter of the novel does the reader realize that the narrator is not Fuks himself but an alter ego of the author named Sebastián. More than a reminder of the book's fictional character, this gesture problematizes the authority of the first person as the productive subject of the narrative, because the last chapter begins with solid proof of its indeterminacy, as if the narrator had become a residue of himself: "I am and I'm not the man who walks down the corridor." The structure of the novel, on the other hand, is also built based on rubble, questions never asked, uncomfortable silences at the family table, taking the form of a fragile building that could collapse at any moment: "From this immaterial debris I have tried to construct the edifice of this story, on deeply buried foundations that are highly unstable. There is something I don't know about, however, around the limits of this precariousness, something they never told me, and which I still don't want to, or cannot, ask them."[70] The description of the contemporary novel as a receptacle of ruins, residues, and traces of the past delineates a specific archival politics. In *A resistência* the archive does not return an exhaustive version of family history but, rather, a fragmentariness that makes it possible to verify the survivals of the past and, by the same token, to find a new narrative anchored in the present.[71]

A resistência acquired an unprecedented relevance in the post-2018 Brazilian context, where Jair Bolsonaro's election to the presidency marked the spectral return of a wide range of political, economic, and social measures linked to the period of the last dictatorships.[72] In the face of these ghostly returns, Fuks's novel raises the question of how to reconstruct the impulse of resistance and the struggle for truth, memory, and human rights from the ruins of the utopias that mobilized his parents' generation. He vindicates this gesture in *A resistência* by defending a critical cosmopolitanism and establishing a dialogic pact with the reader. In an interview, Fuks highlighted the ambivalent character of the word "resistance" and the role that writing plays in the process of repurposing its negative aspects: "Resistance as something negative, as a refusal to achieve something or, on the contrary, as an act of strength, of taking a position in the face of a situation that demands taking a stance. I like to think of literature as capable of making this transition."[73] To the extent that Fuks invites the reader to take a position in the face of other people's suffering, literature becomes a direct intervention in the present, influencing new forms of community and affective filiation. The novel's fragmentary nature demonstrates that any reconstruction of the past is selective, making it possible for each reader to undertake his or her own exercise of historical enunciation. It is a vision of literary practice that, in the end, proposes the exhaustive analysis of the remains of the past as a fundamental condition for understanding the tensions between history and memory, presence and absence, on which the present moment is built.

ANACHRONISTIC ASSEMBLAGES

In *Conjunto vacío* Verónica Gerber Bicecci raises the question of how to find new temporal models against the grain of linear history. Her novel narrates the story of a daughter, Verónica, who experiences firsthand the holes of memory and the voids of transmission of the children's generation. For Verónica, the past takes the form of portable traces and material remains that never quite forge legible constellations. In this sense, the children's generation must deal with a spectral transmission of their parents' experience, understanding the spectral not as a series of unrecoverable moments from the past but as sediments or temporal layers that form a constituent part of the present and that must be conjured by means of an archaeological procedure. Verónica has only partial access to the past not only because of the irreconcilable gap standing between the twenty-first century and the 1970s but also because of the geographical distance separating Mexico from Argentina, the country from which her parents were exiled after the March 1976 coup d'état and the subsequent establishment of the state-sponsored military dictatorship.

Verónica has a repertoire of images that she does not remember but cannot forget, forcing her to develop narrative and visual strategies to situate herself in front of her parents' experience and to complete a mourning process that has not yet occurred. Instead of restoring the past from a realistic register such as that mobilized by the victims' testimonies, in *Conjunto vacío* Gerber Bicecci creates new frames to make visible what does not easily fit into the linear timeline of history, proposing original points of connection between times and spaces. The first dislocation of the real occurs at the level of proper names, as the narrator designates the characters through formulas that compose Venn diagrams, abstract collections of objects that allow her to reflect on interpersonal relationships and community ties. This procedure reconfigures the past through visual montages and shows that members of the children's generation do not intend to fill in the gaps of transmission through accurate reconstructions of historical events but, rather, to exhibit the gaps and holes of memory as unrecoverable originals.

Conjunto vacío is part of a constellation of contemporary Latin American works that revolve around secondary characters—members of the children's generation who grew up during the last military dictatorships or the subsequent neoliberal democracies and who, therefore, received an incomplete heritage from their parents.[74] The narrator considers herself a secondary character because her mother's sudden disappearance in 1995, many years after she escaped to Mexico, plunges Verónica into a tireless search for her mother's traces. The stagnation of the present is reflected in the state of the apartment where Verónica lives with her brother, "a paleontology lab" where everything continues in the same way as the day their mother disappeared.[75] The narrator and her brother refer to this house as "the bunker" because it remains "suspended in time" and its walls are eaten away by humidity. The house becomes "a time capsule where everything is in a state of permanent neglect."[76] This description of the family home as an uninhabitable place can be thought of in relation to *House*, the work of British artist Rachel Whiteread, a house covered with concrete throughout its interior that at the time showed the unheimlich quality of living in a world without history.[77]

Similarly, in *Conjunto vacío* Gerber Bicecci interrogates how to represent absence through nonmimetic forms, conjuring the mother's disappearance based on the silhouettes, shadows, and traces that still haunt the children's historical imagination.[78] Whereas Whiteread's work represents a world devoid of history, Gerber Bicecci shows that the excess of the past prevents emancipatory action in the present, as the bunker is a nostalgic museum where objects cannot be removed from their inscription at a particular moment in history. It is an exact image of what Fisher calls "capitalist realism," referring to how contemporary societies have transformed culture into a series of museum pieces that promote the passivity of citizens: "the condition of Nietzsche's Last Man, who has seen everything but is decadently enfeebled precisely by this excess of (self) awareness."[79] Through the random assembly of scenes from the past, Verónica seeks to convert these pieces from the family museum into clues that allow her to create an unprecedented relationship with her genealogy.

In *Conjunto vacío* Gerber Bicecci constructs evanescent frames that capture what lies outside motionless images of the past in order to address disappearance as an event and a repressive technology. The notion of evanescence comes from the "Manifiesto Evanescente," a text in the form of a comic strip in which Gerber Bicecci updates avant-garde manifestos for the new century. She posits the impossibility of articulating a collective manifesto in an era of presentism and asserts the predominance of the first-person singular as the privileged epistemological mode, rescuing the verbal form of the gerund to account for a present that does not allow us to look beyond it: "A manifesto should be manifesting itself, in gerund, in its infinite present. For example, it is not the same to disappear as to be disappearing every day, all the time."[80] The text represents disappearance not as a singular event firmly anchored in the past but as a phenomenon that exerts a direct influence on the present of the people most affected by it, who must live with a sense of uncertainty that does not allow them to move on with their lives. Rather than framing specific images from the past, Gerber Bicecci extends the frames to marginal details that can take the present off its axis and establish unthinkable connections between various timelines.

In *Conjunto vacío*, disappearance is a volatile event that cannot be attributed to a specific social or political cause. Gerber Bicecci approaches disappearance literally, emptying it of its links to the Southern Cone's recent sociopolitical history. Verónica's mother disappears when her figure blurs and escapes from the plane of reality; the causes of the disappearance are not as important as the consequences it generates in the lives of the children, who cannot reclaim her in the Plaza de Mayo as a place of memory: "There's no recognizable cause, only effects. Correction: only a frontier in space-time, turbulent flows, interrupted. Inter ruptured."[81] By questioning the limits of representing disappearance through mimetic techniques, Gerber Bicecci dissociates *Conjunto vacío* from the testimonial depictions predominating in the literary and legal discourse during the decades following the last dictatorship. Verónica illustrates her mother's sudden disappearance and the entanglement of time through a drawing that resembles a staircase framed by a painting: the visible Universe(U). However, the staircase continues outside the frame, extending into an invisible universe that Verónica wants to capture through the montage of heterogeneous scenes and the crossing of aesthetic genres. Montage accounts for those events in the novel that float in the present as invisible particles and serve as figures of the untimely, a time open to the appearance of signs from the past that interrupt the linear course of history.

The novel's aesthetic procedure can be understood through the concept of anachronism theorized by Didi-Huberman, for whom the history of images must be considered an assemblage of heterogeneous times and materials. In *Ante el tiempo* (a translation of *Devant le temps*), Didi-Huberman questions the idea that history is a science that works with the past as an immovable entity. Memory is a filter based on temporal assemblages, reconfiguring the past in each new reminiscence. Didi-Huberman's concept of the "symptom-image" illustrates how other temporalities can influence the past through manipulation or decantation: "What the symptom-time interrupts is nothing other than the course of chronological history. But what it contradicts, it also sustains: it could be thought of under the angle of an unconscious of history."[82]

Didi-Huberman shows how images, composed of a combination of durations and temporal strata, disrupt traditional models of time and representation. In *The Surviving Image*, he continues to reflect on anachronism by taking Warburg's *Mnemosyne Atlas* as his object of study, which he interprets as the montage of heterogeneous images that operate at the heart of every memory exercise. For Didi-Huberman, Warburg's *Mnemosyne Atlas* reveals the archaeological density of the present: "an interpretation which does not seek to reduce complexity but instead to show it, to lay it bare, to unfold it in a way which reveals a further, unexpected degree of complexity."[83] In this sense, the purpose of montage is to unfold the gaps and interruptions in the chronological conception of history, which reconfigures our understanding of the contemporary. Montage is located at the intersection of various aesthetic fields, showing that one cannot create an alternative image of time without crossing disciplinary boundaries.

In the context of post-dictatorship cultural production, Ana Forcinito recovers the concept of survival to point out the existence of memories situated on the margins of inherited narratives of state violence and models of justice and reconciliation. Using the figure of "intermittences" (referring to the discontinuous glow of fireflies that, according to Didi-Huberman, characterizes the work of the historical materialist), Forcinito designates the latency of a series of sediments from the recent past that exceed the official frameworks of remembrance. These are remains and residues taken up by more recent generations through new poetics of memory, which "subvert the cohesiveness or the indisputability of interpretations of the past and instead propose aesthetic and interpretive variations that make new contours of the recent past visible."[84] What underlies this analysis is the search for new frameworks of visibility, which Forcinito links to the image of the kaleidoscope used by Pilar Calveiro to portray the task of memory in the Southern Cone. It is not a puzzle in which the different fragments crystallize a totalizing image of the recent past but, instead, a random gathering of pieces that put forward unthinkable connections between heterogeneous times and spaces.[85] Likewise, Jordana Blejmar uses the concept of anachronism to examine a corpus of autofictions about the Argentinean dictatorship that display what she calls "playful memories," a heterodox treatment of the past that dissociates itself from chronological models of history. Writers use montage as a procedure that interweaves aesthetic registers and makes a series of images emerge that remained hidden in the continuum of history. "Montage," Blejmar remarks, "is used to stress the gaps and fractures that emerge when documentary film and photography try to faithfully 'document' the dictatorial past, demonstrating that there is something that cannot be shown."[86] These approaches highlight the importance of creating aesthetic devices that allow us to capture how the contemporary is constituted of durations, rhythms, and traces that draw an alternative image of history.

Conjunto vacío is structured as a heterogeneous montage of memories that illuminates the recent past of political violence and exile. Verónica, the narrator, begins by observing that she is a "collector of outsets," referring to the failed beginnings of her love life, even though the novel's first chapter revolves around an ending, that of her relationship with her boyfriend, Tordo(T). Gerber Bicecci introduces the figure of the collector to designate the task of the contemporary writer as someone who inhabits a historical moment of après-coup. "We always realize things afterwards," Verónica asserts, delineating the present as a reticular structure in which an infinity of scenes from the past flicker in the form of ruins and debris.[87] Like Forcinito and Calveiro, Bourriaud refers to our era as "a great kaleidoscope where pasts, presents and futures scintillate in furtive 'flashes.'" He defines the contemporary artist as "a collector of communal production," capable of founding new narratives and genealogies from the vestiges on which the precarious present of the new century is built.[88]

The desire to excavate the recent past indicates that children of the new generations are incapable of thinking of themselves as legitimate heirs. Instead, they experience the past as a series of fragmentary and empty narratives. Verónica's life is "a definitively unfinished landscape that stretches over flooded excavations, bare foundations, and ruined structures; an internal necropolis that has been in the early stages of construction for as long as my memory goes back."[89] In this sense, montage is the proper technique to account for the historical present as a permanent work-in-progress and to conceive of writing through new frames that capture dormant memories and lost narratives.[90]

As Verónica the narrator embarks on a vertiginous game of beginnings and endings, *Conjunto vacío* is set in an impasse, a moment in which something has died and something new has not yet finished being born. Fisher takes up Nietzsche's concept of the last man and Francis Fukuyama's thesis on the end of history (which, according to him, inhabits the cultural unconscious of contemporary societies) to point out that contemporary citizens are passive and indifferent spectators of their surrounding world.[91] In *Conjunto vacío*, Verónica assembles a collection of truncated beginnings and combats the mood of inaction and immobility generated by the inability to produce something new after the end of history, when the past has become an inaccessible temporality and the unfinished present makes it impossible to articulate alternatives for change.

Montage takes up several dimensions in *Conjunto vacío*. First, it explains the disordered configuration of chapters that, instead of obeying a chronological sequence, superimpose actions, times, and places like a kaleidoscope. This procedure delineates a time out of time that blurs the boundaries between before and after, giving rise to a temporality that is open to the irruption of involuntary memories.[92] In this sense, Gerber Bicecci shows the intervals and holes that hinder any exercise of memory, even more so when blank spaces eat away the images inherited from the past. This discontinuous relationship with the past becomes evident when Verónica begins to work in the house of an Argentinean writer named Marisa Chubut (M_x), who, like her parents, emigrated to Mexico during the last dictatorship. Verónica's job consists of sorting through the writer's archive, where she finds a series of photographs in which Chubut cut out the people portrayed, so they have become a set of silhouettes. Like memory artists who work with amnesiac apparitions, Chubut assembled a collage from the cut-out faces of these anonymous people, removing them from the places where they had been photographed.[93]

Through this renunciation of representing the real and this sharp contrast with the passport photos of the victims used by organizations such as the Mothers and Grandmothers of the Plaza de Mayo, montage becomes a visual strategy that refers not only to the dislocation of exiled subjects such as the Argentinean writer but also to the process of mourning for the disappeared. "The only thing still visible was the setting, from which the person in question was exiled, separated forever."[94] Verónica is familiar with this way of working with the past because she, as the daughter of a disappeared mother, also experiences inheritance as a silhouette without content. From this encounter with Chubut's amnesiac archive, Verónica begins to conceive of writing as working with the vestiges of the real—not so much with the past but with the consequences of living in its shadow.

The representational ethics of *Conjunto vacío* derive from the awareness that there is an unbridgeable distance between the present and the gaps, silhouettes, and blank spaces constituting Verónica's past. The distrust in the index as a strategy of representation translates into a poetics that operates through shadowing and renunciation of the real. In doing so, the book captures the consequences of uncertainty and suspicion generated by disappearance as a repressive technology. Gerber Bicecci interrogates the frameworks that bring the traumatic past into the children's present. She does not reproduce in an exact manner the historical context in which these events occurred, nor does Verónica experience her parents' past in her own flesh. Instead, she reproduces the mechanisms of forgetting and its sediments of time.[95] In this sense, Gerber Bicecci updates the aesthetic and political collective action proposed by three visual artists (Rodolfo Aguerreberry, Julio Flores, and Guillermo Kexel) in 1982, *El Siluetazo*. While this performance consisted of drawing the outlines of people's bodies to protest the disappearance of people under the military dictatorship, Gerber Bicecci uses shadows and silhouettes to represent the incapacity of fully accessing the past for members of her generation.

Gerber Bicecci sheds light on the searches of the children's generation as actors who are not usually included in the official discourses on historical memory, reconfiguring "the forms of being and the forms of visibility" of the common.[96] Referring to the war photographs promoted by the US Department of Defense during the George W. Bush administration, Judith Butler stresses that every visual frame contains forms of social and state power and that a possible solution to art's imbrication with official discourses is to make visible the frame that delimits the images: "the photograph that yields its frame to interpretation thereby opens up to critical scrutiny the restrictions on interpreting reality. It exposes and thematizes the mechanisms of restriction, and constitutes a disobedient act of seeing."[97] It is no coincidence that the various illustrations in *Conjunto vacío* show content that exceeds the imposed frames of official history: the visible Universe.

Even more relevant is the fact that Verónica adopts a procedure that is composed of Venn diagrams when the military dictatorship (as she reminds us) prohibited teaching set theory in schools. In *Conjunto vacío* Gerber Bicecci questions the aesthetic strategies that allow us to expand the sphere of the visible, break away from imposed frameworks, and erect forms of dissent and resistance in the face of centralized power. Verónica's montage technique throughout the novel reveals the condition of the children who live on the margins of history and in a shattered temporality. Her collage techniques evoke the work of several post-dictatorship artists such as the photomontages of Argentinean artist Lucila Quieto, which are based on the manipulation of photographs of family members, victims, and perpetrators to contravene the solemnity with which they are usually contemplated. These photomontage artists, according to Blejmar, "encourage us to turn our gaze to what lies 'outside the lines' and beyond the frames of what we are accustomed to seeing."[98] In the novel, Venn diagrams reconfigure the differences between the visible and the invisible, the decipherable and the unspeakable, words and noise, which is how the arts, according to Rancière, impinge on the distribution of meaning in each and every community.[99] "Venn diagrams," Verónica tells us, "are tools of the logic of sets. And from the perspective of sets, dictatorship makes no sense, because its aim is, for the most part, dispersal: separation, scattering, disunity, disappearance." What the military feared, Verónica observes, is that the Venn diagrams would lead children to the creation of community bonds and, by extension, to the collective reflection on "the contradictions of language, of the system."[100]

The procedure adopted by Verónica is intended to make visible these intangible relationships, the gathering of details from diverse origins, and the knot of antagonistic temporalities. Four years before the publication of *Conjunto vacío*, the Argentinean artist Amalia Pica exhibited at the Venice Biennale an artwork entitled *Venn Diagram (Under the Spotlight)* (2011). The work consists of two circles—one red, the other green—projected onto a blank wall and activated when visitors walk into the room. A possible source of inspiration for Gerber Bicecci's novel, Pica's work highlights the dictatorship's prohibition of communal bonds and its promotion of neoliberal subjectivities.

In the context of post-dictatorship and after the advent of a post-historical temporality, language has become an entity full of black holes of meaning, as demonstrated in the exhibition Verónica attends at the Tamayo Museum in Mexico City entitled *The Poetics of the Illegible*. Through Verónica's visual duplications of works by Ulises Carrión, Marcel Broodthaers, and Mirtha Dermisache, Gerber Bicecci shows the paradox that lies at the core of this spectral representation of the traumatic past. The poetics of erasure exhibits that which cannot be plausibly represented but simultaneously indicates that this is the only way to make it legible without transgressing the memory of the victims.[101]

Gerber Bicecci emulates this same poetics by visually displaying holes in time and representation. "There should be a three-line space here," says Verónica, evoking the procedure of un-writing, anti-writing, and non-writing that Luis Felipe Fabre examines in certain contemporary "post-poems."[102] This is Gerber Bicecci's way of visually representing the amnesiac condition of the victims' children, whose articulation of a poetics of the illegible shows a discourse that is not so much historical as hysterical.[103] Including these illegible words reveals that language, even when it has become a heap of ashes, continues to serve as a vehicle for commemorating traumatic events. It also admits the possibility that literature, understood as a mimetic record of reality, is mourning its own demise.

Conjunto vacío combines drawings, diagrams, and objets trouvés to provide the image of art outside itself. Ticio Escobar defines this type of art through its inscription within "a non-place, a place without thresholds, perhaps without a floor."[104] Gerber Bicecci describes herself as "a visual artist who writes," and in her 2010 book of essays, *Mudanza*, she traces a genealogy of her literary practice by referring to the case of artists and writers who fluidly straddle the borders between aesthetic fields. An heiress of conceptual art, Gerber Bicecci inscribes her practice in the "expanded field" of literature, proposing (as she indicates in relation to the work of Carrión) "to shift the limits of the literary event toward other disciplines."[105] In *Conjunto vacío*, where Verónica also reveals that she "wanted to be a visual artist, but visualized almost everything in words," the free circulation between disciplinary fields aims at creating new devices of visibility when the contemporary subject is conceived as an orphan of collective history and family genealogies.[106]

In combining visual and verbal language, Gerber Bicecci transforms the modes of accessing the past by focusing on the fractures in linear history. It is a matter of invoking what, in Rancière's opinion, lies at the core of the work of fiction: establishing "new relations between words and visible forms, speech and writing, a here and an elsewhere, a then and a now."[107] Using Venn diagrams, Gerber Bicecci creates a space of intersection between the children's sense of orphanhood, as demonstrated in the love affair that Verónica establishes with Chubut's son, Alonso(A), another orphan who experiences the past as an accumulation of ruins. Faced with the question of how to represent the dictatorial catastrophe in a period of endings— when, as García Canclini argues, only "de-totalized narratives, fragments of a visuality without history" survive—Gerber Bicecci uses montage to point out the impossibility of representing trauma in all its magnitude and the need to conjure these specters to forge new narratives.[108] The present thus becomes a site of orientation and a new departing point.

EVANESCENT ARCHIVES

Chubut's archive contains a palimpsest of manuscripts, photographs, and letters, a record of anonymous existences and secondary characters that allegorizes the blurred image of the past inherited by the children's generation. Chubut's housekeeper describes Verónica's work using the verb *escombrar*—which Christina MacSweeney, the novel's translator, rendered in English as "clear out," though in Spanish it specifically refers to the task of sorting out *escombros* or debris.[109] This verb characterizes the state of the archive as an accumulation of ruins in need of archaeological work and places Verónica in the same genealogy as the Trümmerfrauen, the women who devoted themselves to cleaning up German and Austrian cities after the Second World War, putting the rubble of bombed-out buildings to new uses. This is a new incarnation of Baudelaire's figure of the ragpicker who catalogs the debris of the modern city and produces original assemblages.[110]

In *Conjunto vacío*, Verónica becomes an interpreter of rubble or a "semi-onaut," as Bourriaud calls contemporary artists who propose unprecedented combinations between signs and new interpretative contexts for history, activating in the reader spectator a posture of lucidity that makes possible the continuous reactualization of the past.[111] In this sense, in *Conjunto vacío* Gerber Bicecci evokes the work of a series of contemporary artists who traverse the urban landscape and compile dynamic assemblages from the waste that people leave behind. In several of the projects by Mexican artist Gabriel Orozco, he represents a post-historical world in which garbage is the only sign that gives us a glimpse of human presence on the planet. The figure of debris in *Conjunto vacío* does not prompt Verónica to order the archive chronologically but, rather, to assemble new constellations that capture the flickering character of history, the multiplicity of times that co-exist in the same historical moment. The novel thus unfolds an alternative museum of memory that replicates its fragmentary configuration. Memory is subject to ongoing debates to ensure its construction and transmission with an eye toward the future.

Gerber Bicecci shows the need to immerse oneself in the archive to create new filiations with the past when history is experienced through the lens of orphanhood. Verónica is an orphan of history who sees in the archive the possibility not only of restoring a continuity with the past but also of summoning the presence of these anonymous lives and restoring to them some of the dignity they have lost.[112] It is a matter of combating not only her own orphanhood but also that of the archive, because, as Paul Ricœur points out, "the document sleeping in the archives is not just silent, it is an orphan."[113] Gerber Bicecci's novel is inscribed in what François Noudel-mann calls the "genealogical passion" of contemporary fiction, an attempt to revalue filiations and inscribe individuals within a historical continuum, combating their state of orphanhood and transforming the contemporary into "a sharing of generational times."[114]

In Chubut's archive, Verónica finds a link to the past that both she and her brother lack. To unearth the life of the Argentinean writer is to restitute her mother's history vicariously. Chubut's archive—especially the correspondence she maintained with a person whose code name was "S."—is in voluntary disarray, prompting Verónica to reconstruct it from scratch. She links this work to piecing together puzzles during her childhood, insofar as the loose pieces and illegible fragments convince her that "there was undoubtedly some mystery behind those vestiges," for which she must create new frames of legibility. But the figure of "S.," with whom Chubut exchanged romantic letters, becomes impossible to restore, to such an extent that Verónica compares him to the "dust suspended in the atmosphere" she reads about in the manual of a telescope.[115]

For Verónica, the writing of history consists of capturing something of these dust particles floating imperceptibly in the blinding lights of the present, which Didi-Huberman refers to through the metaphor of the flickering light of fireflies. This means that Verónica, as she immerses herself in the vastness of the archive, must avail herself of minute details and minor images to combat the destruction of experience.[116] It is no coincidence that in Chubut's archival room there is a telescope, which metaphorically designates the work of the Argentinean writer in exile. The figure of the telescope implies a spatial and temporal journey: a journey into the past through the incessant search in the archive. During moments of rest from archival work, Verónica uses the telescope to observe "details that would otherwise pass unnoticed," even penetrating the cracks in the walls in search of "possible constellations there, black holes and life forms."[117] Thus, she gradually discovers that the archivist's gaze must also perceive the fractures in linear history and the rubble of the social edifice to construct an alternative image of time, one that considers the unstable foundations on which the contemporary moment is built.[118] The telescope helps Verónica to observe details on a microscopic scale and to train her vision to that which disappears. It also helps her take the present out of the picture and see it in the *longue durée* or from a cosmic perspective. It is the same procedure of enlarging the point of view that Arendt describes in *The Human Condition* through the figure of the telescope, which allows humans "to act on the earth and within terrestrial nature as though we dispose of it from outside, from the Archimedean."[119]

This conjunction between archive and telescope becomes more apparent when Verónica watches Patricio Guzmán's *Nostalgia de la luz* with her brother. Guzmán's documentary links two different searches in the Atacama Desert: one by the women who scour the desert in search of the remains of their missing relatives and the other the astronomers who use telescopes to study celestial bodies. Verónica inscribes the search for her missing mother in this constellation of tracing. As she points out after watching the documentary, "We're all trying to find traces, or asking ourselves questions. We're all waiting for what we can't see to finally appear."[120]

In this sense, she trains her gaze to perceive the presence of other temporalities and life forms, as reflected in the illustrations that show parallel universes. As Rancière points out, "learning to see . . . means learning to subtract the gaze from its ordinary exercise . . . exposing the gaze to that which permits of no enframing, to that which acts on it, shocks it, intrigues it and that it cannot bear."[121] At a time when the notion of history as a race toward progress seems to have come to an end, in *Conjunto vacío* Gerber Bicecci transforms aesthetic form into a vehicle for subtracting the gaze from its usual frames and projecting it onto other surfaces, which reflect the apparitions and specters that haunt the contemporary imagination.

In parallel to Verónica's work in Chubut's archive, her brother is filming a documentary about high-contrast images—how they become abstract through the play of light and shadow. "He wants to describe those high contrasts," Verónica states, "as if they were found maps, cities of pixels, islands of bits hiding in the memories of computers."[122] While Verónica is obsessed with calligraphies that do not become letters and asemic forms of writing that derive meaning through interruption, her brother investigates noises that do not become sounds and stains that make images illegible.[123] Through procedures that generate presence by highlighting the absence or impossibility of transmission, Verónica and her brother conceive of the archive as a series of notes that will require future elaboration, just as Foster refers to the "anarchival impulse" of these aesthetic practices interested less in categorical origins than in obscure traces and hieroglyphic writings.[124] Verónica inscribes her own genealogy in these poetics of the illegible, expressing her desire to live in an Argentinean town called Garabato (Doodle): "Never been there, but would love to be able to say I was a Doodler: an inhabitant of, as its name in Spanish suggests, a badly drawn, illegible town."[125] The vindication of asemic writing reorganizes the archive through the literal representation of black holes, indeterminacy, and missing memory links.

In this sense, the procedure adopted by Verónica to configure the text obeys the logic of collage. Collage is central to Cristina Rivera Garza's theorization of necrowriting and disappropriation, forms of writing that displace traditional notions of authorship and posit collaborative practices to oppose the languages of global capitalism. The role of collage, Rivera Garza reminds us, is "to sustain as many versions as possible, for as long as possible, arranging them so close to each other that they provoke contrast, astonishment, pleasure. Knowledge here is not generated as a result of the random, externally imposed application of a high-contrast composition technique, but by honoring . . . the compositional principles emanating from the materials themselves."[126]

The emphasis on high contrasts corresponds to a metaphor Gerber Bicecci uses to describe her artistic practice: amblyopia or lazy eye. In the first essay of *Mudanza*, Gerber Bicecci relates how she grew up with one eye that developed normally and another that turned inward, which prompted her to be naturally drawn to "characters with amblyopic destinies, those who, in an act of conscious dementia, decide to give up, to abandon themselves to contingency to place their life, body, and work in the same indeterminate space."[127] Besides delineating the contemporary artist as someone who has arrived too late and whose gaze is turned toward the past, Gerber Bicecci uses the image of amblyopia to exhibit the traces of the archive as mysteries without resolution. These unfinished pieces of knowledge also bridge a fragmentary past and the construction of a future.

Gerber Bicecci summons reader spectators to decipher a message that is elusive even to the author herself, redefining the traditional opposition between activity and passivity and the roles of the participants in the communicative process. There are several instances in the novel when meaning is interrupted by lines of fracture, such as the insertion of Chubut's letters into the narrative, written in code to avoid being captured by the dictatorship's security agencies. We also find out that throughout her life Chubut wrote only one book, *Exile*. Her various manuscripts repeat the same text word for word. More than the consequences of geographical dislocation, Chubut's manuscripts are a symbol of the exile and banishment of language: "The only change was the writing, a firm hand becoming increasingly tremulous until it was practically illegible."[128] The decomposition of Chubut's handwriting happens concurrently with that of her memories. Handwriting is the vehicle that reveals the difficulties in representing trauma. What is striking, however, is that Verónica and Alonso, both of whom belong to the post-dictatorship generation, repeat this mechanism of concealment or postponement of meaning. The emails they exchange, like Chubut's letters, contain a coded message through word games: Verónica writes to Alonso using anagrams, and he answers with acrostics. Illegibility is the consequence of an incomplete inheritance presented to them enigmatically, pierced by their parents' inability to tell their own stories. "In my family," Verónica observes, "everyone contradicts everyone else, and in the end, the only things left are holes."[129]

Verónica searches for narrative procedures to reveal the temporal palimpsest that history has become for members of her generation. For example, she distinguishes between disguised and undisguised words, preferring disguised words since they delineate the past as a mystery to be unraveled and an inheritance to come. In *Mudanza*, Gerber Bicecci praises onomatopoeias in an essay dedicated to the Swedish artist Öyvind Fahlström who, in many of his works, creates monstrous languages based on the reproduction of animal sounds. This procedure promotes a radical estrangement from everyday language. For Gerber Bicecci, the Swedish artist "wrote impenetrable words with a known alphabet. Because even when he made ordinary language explode, even in that extreme level of hermeticism, he wanted to be read; he wanted there to be eardrums for his noises, for dissonance, cacophony, and disharmony. Ears for disagreement."[130] In *Conjunto vacío* Gerber Bicecci questions the category of words as sites of memory, just as she questions the form of the novel, which unfolds as an art installation that oscillates between the visual and the written.

The verbal games Verónica inserts in *Conjunto vacío* open the experience of language to a plurality of interpretations. By configuring the novel as a museum that blurs the boundaries between the visual and the written, Gerber Bicecci stands against the modern experience of distinction-making and portrays the contemporary as the superimposition of various orders. For Rancière, dissensus makes it possible to invent new forms of collective enunciation and redistribute the categories of the visible and the invisible, discourse and noise. "The 'loss of a steady relation' between the sensible and the intelligible is not the loss of the power of relating, but the multiplication of its forms. There is nothing that is unrepresentable in the aesthetic regime of art."[131] Dissensus disarticulates the idea that the artist is transmitting a specific knowledge or source of inspiration to the reader spectator. What one is delegating to the other is, according to Rancière, "the third thing that is owned by no one, whose meaning is owned by no one, but which subsists between them, excluding any uniform transmission, any identity of cause and effect."[132] By putting together asemic forms of writing, onomatopoeias, and word games, Gerber Bicecci takes to the extreme the suspicion about the capacity of art to transmit knowledge, experiences, and meaning. Through an aesthetics of the unrepresentable, she addresses the orphanhood of a generation that relates to the past via a rupture in the order of historical continuity.

The disordered configuration of the chapters proves that Verónica derives her vision of the past from traces and vestiges confirming the irreconcilable distance between memory and history. One senses her distrust of archival work as a calculated compilation of memory, as what Pierre Nora has called the "cult of continuity" or "the terrorism of 'historicized' memory," delineating, instead, "a memory cast in the discontinuity of history."[133] This past that is experienced as radically alien requires an appropriation of specific moments with which we have lost all connection and will allow us to reconstitute a narrative of filiation. The image of the past as a jigsaw puzzle whose pieces do not fit together into a coherent whole is dramatized through the sculpture classes of a Japanese master, who teaches not only how to sculpt but also how to deal with the outer edges of the creative process. Instead of teaching his students how to make plywood boards, the Japanese master tells them about dendrochronology, the science of calculating the age of a tree by analyzing the rings of a trunk.

In contrast to tree trunks as repositories of millenary knowledge, Verónica delineates the archive through the figure of plywood boards, which do not allow the age of a tree to be determined because they were composed by cutting the trunk diagonally. The plywood boards illustrate the impossibility of restoring stable origins and filiations when history has ceased to be experienced through genealogical continuity. Hence Verónica, while taxonomically categorizing Chubut's papers, sets out to alter the order of time: "In the bunker, there were three wooden panels with time disordered and overlapping. If only that were possible: to disorder time. I'd like to invent a science that investigates how a pine plywood board disorders time. It would be useful to relocate the moments when certain things happen, to put the endings at the beginning, for instance (or anywhere else). Or the past in a future so distant we never reach the moment of confronting it."[134]

The plywood boards serve as an analogy for the aesthetic device Verónica uses to represent the discontinuities of time and the failures in transmitting a memory of history. Chubut's illegible manuscripts address the incommensurability and incommunicability of traumatic experience, which Maurice Blanchot points out when he asserts that "the only thing worthwhile is the transmission of the untransmittable."[135] In the aesthetic configuration of *Conjunto vacío* Gerber Bicecci seeks to make visible the reception of this incoherent inheritance, this archive of documents full of blank spaces and lacunae. As an empty set, the archive becomes a paradoxical figure: it is to be distrusted but continues to be used as a paradigm for aesthetic composition.[136] The book thus becomes an incomplete, dynamic archive under permanent construction. The empty set of the title refers to those children of unknown parents, to the community of those who have no community and who devote themselves to the conformation of alternative archives. This is the children's mechanism to combat their collective orphanhood. Gerber Bicecci suggests that, in the absence of grand narratives making it possible to organize history, the only thing left to do is to disarrange time, to oppose the cult of continuity, to find in the past, in the perished and the obsolete, new paradigms of beginning.

THE END AS A STARTING POINT

Conjunto vacío is an untimely novel that deals with the theme of disappearance as a repressive technology to reconfigure our conception of the present: the disappearance of time horizons in an era of presentist orientation. As Hartog points out, presentism is a regime of historicity proper to the contemporary moment, when the production of historical time has been suspended and an elusive, immobile, and eternal present has ensued.[137] Verónica meets Tordo(T) when "the year 2000 was about to come to an end."[138] Josefina Ludmer would call *Conjunto vacío* a fiction of the year 2000, which unfolds in "the temporality of the end and the after the end times," rejecting "the organic, linear, progressive temporalities of the nation."[139] Gerber Bicecci's novel occurs when the new millennium has begun and after Verónica has separated from Tordo(T). "It soon became clear that the abruptness of the ending," Verónica remarks, "had brought things back to the beginning, to some beginning."[140]

To return to the origins, to conjure shadows and ghosts, to work with the ruins and vestiges of a past in the process of disappearing. Such is the narrative wager of *Conjunto vacío* when the new millennium is experienced as an "interregnum," the term with which Antonio Gramsci, in an entry of his prison notebooks dating from 1929–1930, described the temporal crisis that sets in when "the old is dying and the new cannot be born; in this interregnum, a great variety of morbid symptoms appear."[141] In an age of crisis and vanishing futures, Gerber Bicecci turns her gaze back to the failed utopian projects of art, history, and literature to find in them the seeds of a new paradigm, conceiving of a narrator who is a collector of outsets in a time of endings. By expanding what is traditionally understood as literature, Gerber Bicecci develops a participatory art that summons reader spectators to the elaboration of the precarious and unfinished present of the new millennium.

More than the end of history, in *Conjunto vacío* Gerber Bicecci delineates a natural history of destruction that opposes the linearity of capitalist accumulation.[142] On a return trip to Argentina to visit her grandmother, Verónica travels to Patagonia to see the glaciers and Jules Verne's Lighthouse at the End of the World. The glaciers become an analogy for the temporal intermittences that make up the contemporary, as Verónica wonders about the possibility they might melt because of global warming and that the bodies of the disappeared might appear floating, breaking the indifference that characterizes the post-historical mood. Akin to her reflections on dendrochronology and tree rings as repositories of time, Verónica indicates that in the glaciers, "the different layers of snow that have accumulated during each season are visible. It's a way of doing archaeology with ice." Taking a phrase in the guidebook that equates glaciers with "ice witnesses," Verónica wonders about her ability to make the nonhuman world speak.[143]

The same archaeological conception of time is apparent when she enters a coffee shop and orders a submarine, a traditional drink in Argentina and Uruguay consisting of a cup of hot milk with a bar of chocolate inside. Both figures—glaciers and submarines—suggest that the present is composed of geological layers that are difficult to access and that history, rather than a linear race toward the progress of enlightenment and reason, has become a dark tunnel that seems to lead nowhere.[144] It is not a confrontation with history but with the fact that we live in its absence.

In *Conjunto vacío* Gerber Bicecci posits the contemporary as a period of beginnings, a collection of outsets rather than an era of exhaustion. When Verónica visits the Lighthouse at the End of the World, the tour guide warns her that, in fact, the lighthouse is called Les Eclaireurs (Explorers) Lighthouse, and that the other one exists only in the novel by Jules Verne. Verónica is even more disappointed when the ship encircles the lighthouse, transgressing the boundaries of the world's supposed end. "I was thinking 'The End' might be a life jacket," she observes, "wanted to drop anchor there. But one way or another, things succeed in returning to the outset, to some beginning."[145] As Baudrillard suggests concerning the debates about the end of history and the passage to the year 2000, "unable to locate an end, we strive desperately to pin down a beginning," since the end must also be understood as the period when meaning is retroactively granted.[146] As Verónica discovers in The Lighthouse at the End of the World, the end is only an illusion or a state of mind—the idea that there is nothing new under the sun and everything is a repetition of the past. Gerber Bicecci shows us that what ended was a specific idea of history and literature: history as a succession of stages leading irremediably toward progress and the literary tradition as a set of works to be surpassed. In *Conjunto vacío* she delineates the contemporary writer as a melancholic subject whose gaze is turned toward the vestiges of history, noting that the only form of progress lies in the original arrangement of historical and literary materials of the past.

Postmemory theories had an ambivalent reception among scholars of the Latin American post-dictatorship. The term coined by Hirsch was seen as belonging more to the post-Holocaust European context and less directly to the Southern Cone dictatorships, in which disappearance was used as a technology of repression and family members were left in a continuous state of search. In *Tiempo pasado* (2005), Sarlo argues that all reconstructions of the past are vicarious representations of previous events, claiming that the difference between postmemory and other forms of memory is its personal and subjective character. However, as opposed to Sarlo's dismissal of postmemory through her contention that "what is unknown is not an effect of second-generation memory but a consequence of the way in which the dictatorship administered assassination," I argue that postmemory designates a particular form of writing history and conceiving the contemporary.[147]

Postmemory works derive their fragmentary status from this generation of writers' discontinuous relationship with the past, their questioning of the inherited frameworks for accessing history, and their exploration of the archive's absences. In signaling the incomplete nature of the past, these works do not align with the politics of *testimonio* nor do their authors attempt to transform readers "into witnesses who must experience the pain of others," as Di Stefano remarks in his analysis of post-dictatorship cultural production. Instead, these authors point to the inaccessible and unrepresentable quality of the dictatorial period.[148] Like Gerber Bicecci's drawing of the staircase that continues beyond the page, these writers seek less to vanish the aesthetic frame than to highlight the status of their works as artworks through illegible writing, silhouettes, and blank spaces. Latin American postmemory novels are tentative explorations of pasts that the children's generation did not experience and that these writers reproduce in the unstable format of the literary work, which oscillates between the diary, the exhibition, and the artist's notebook. More than asserting "an anticapitalist politics," as Di Stefano suggests regarding post-dictatorship novels that emphasize their condition as works of art, this insistence on negative images confronts readers with the lingering shadows of the Latin American dictatorships in our neoliberal present.[149]

Both Fuks in *A resistência* and Gerber Bicecci in *Conjunto vacío* insistently question how to access the recent past when history is experienced as a temporality devoid of absolute truths and horizons of justice. For Rancière, the issue of time's justice—the search for a temporality emancipated from the reign of presentism—becomes fundamental in the post-historical era, as the present has been transformed into "a time full of holes, increasingly marked by speed-ups and slow-downs . . . also a time when individuals live the intertwining of several heterogeneous temporalities."[150] In the works analyzed here, Fuks and Gerber Bicecci are concerned with conjuring a version of the past that distances itself from the linguistic and visual clichés imposed by presentism, conceived as a temporality that summons the past through nostalgic images and creates a paralysis in the exercise of imagining perspectives of change.[151] They seek to escape the prisons of language imposed by the condition of the end times, giving back to words their power of imagination and to images their power of reflection.[152] In *A resistência*, this translates into a poetics that spirals around itself, as Sebastián shows himself incapable of making definitive judgments about his family's history when the distance that separates him from the past has become impossible to measure. In *Conjunto vacío*, Verónica demonstrates that it is difficult to invoke a crystalline version of the past because of the mediation involved in every linguistic act, which operates from the distortion of the real. As Gerber Bicecci remarks in *Mudanza*, "every word has a thousand faces."[153] Both Sebastián and Verónica's parents are psychoanalysts. In their childhood, Sebastián and Verónica link psychoanalysis with the exercise of conjuring specters—her mother, Verónica would tell her schoolmates, taught classes about phantoms. But as adults, they become obsessed with recovering their lost cultural roots, which are imprinted as absences upon their bodies and minds. By reassembling the family archive, Fuks and Gerber Bicecci in *A resistência* and *Conjunto vacío* aim to reveal the unconscious of the present, recognizing, in dislocation and reordering, an epistemological method that is suitable to combatting the opaque condition of contemporary history.

CHAPTER 5

WAYS OF BEING CONTEMPORARY

The Novel after the End of History

The term "'contemporary' has come to designate something more than simply the art of the present moment," remarked Arthur Danto in 1997. "It designates less a period than what happens after there are no more periods in some master narrative of art, and less a style than a style of using styles."[1] More than two decades after Danto's assertion, is it still possible to claim that history has ended and, along with it, our capacity to think of ourselves in continuity with past and future generations? Is the contemporary a label that designates something more than merely the arts of the present and the most recent literary style? Might it also be a marker for the impossibility of producing new styles at a time when everything appears to have been written?[2]

Although the apocalyptic time of neoliberal societies seems to contradict Danto's claim that the contemporary is not a temporal label, the Latin American writers whose work I discuss in this chapter would agree with his assertion that "it is part of contemporary art that the art of the past is available for such use as artists care to give it."[3] After the end of the grand

156

narratives of modernity, writers have resorted to appropriation and quotation as the privileged modes to rewind the literary canon and weave new
relationships with the past once history is experienced as a series of overlapping crises. Understood as a "simulation of the past and its dead styles,"
postmodernism appears to have collapsed after the fall of the Berlin Wall
and given way to "far more political" aesthetic modes.[4] The contemporary
has emerged as a significant aesthetic, philosophical, and political category
to periodize history and literature when, according to Mathias Nilges, "the
idea of periodization no longer has meaning in a present without time, in
a moment when all we have is now."[5] When the contemporary feels like a
gathering of different pasts and futures, literature has been given over to
historicizing the multiple temporalities of our disorienting present. Paradoxically, the most salient feature of the contemporary might be its anachronism: not speculative projections into the future nor the reproduction of
presentism but the politicized return to the literary past as the only way to
build a new theory of time and literature.

In this chapter I raise the question of how to think about literature after
the end of history through the work of Mexican writer Valeria Luiselli and
Chilean writer Alejandro Zambra, both of whom conceive the present via
the exploration of the ruins, specters, and echoes of their respective national
histories and literary traditions. Faced with the void of transmission and
inheritance that characterizes the post-historical period, both writers weave
new stories of filiation that cast history against the grain of linear chronol-
ogies, putting together poetics of suspicion rather than actual restitution.
Their novels revolve around the secondary actors of history—anonymous
lives, faces in the crowd, lost children, or forgotten writers—to politicize
the present and create new starting points for literature written after the
turn of the millennium.

The work of both writers is traversed by a generalized sense of having
arrived too late, after the end of history and literature, as orphans of the
grand narratives of modernity or as castaways of the Latin American literary tradition. "I only manage to emulate my ghosts," says the narrator of
Luiselli's *Los ingrávidos* (2011; trans. 2014 as *Faces in the Crowd*), "write
the way they used to speak, not make noise, narrate our phantasmagoria."[6]
Meanwhile, Zambra conceives of writing through the silence of the archive
when he states that "the novel makes visible the silence of those who were
and are no longer. . . . The silence of the silenced. The silence of the victims and the victimizers."[7] Contemporaneity appears to these writers as a
permanent state of transition because of the experience of a generation that
grew up in the 1990s and early 2000s, when Mexico was living the failed
promises of modernity brought about by the passing of NAFTA and Chile
was living its problematic democratic experiment.[8] For both Luiselli and

Zambra, contemporaneity is a critical gesture that posits a new relationship with history: a relationship that no longer obeys the modern separation between past, present, and future, but which embraces the dissolution of temporal boundaries and the crisis of linear history models.

It is no coincidence that both Luiselli and Zambra posit the figure of the tree against the grain of the grand narratives of modernity to elaborate forms of knowledge transmission considering the uncertain future of the new millennium. As opposed to the *ombú* in Mairal's *El año del desierto* and the ceiba in Indiana's *La mucama de Omicunlé*, two emblematic trees used to dramatize the cultural imagination of the modern nation-state, the botanical metaphors appearing throughout Luiselli's and Zambra's works derive from miniature trees that allegorize the aesthetics of transplantation and appropriation of the contemporary writer. "To be radicant," Bourriaud remarks, "means setting one's roots in motion, staging them in heterogeneous contexts and formats, denying them the power to completely define one's identity, translating ideas, transcoding images, transplanting behaviors, exchanging rather than imposing."[9]

In Luiselli's *Los ingrávidos*, the narrator uses the figure of a dry tree that must be watered incessantly to create a relationship of continuity with tradition where only a void existed, dramatizing the transmission of experiences through a spectral dialogue with her literary predecessors. "Writing is like taking care of a bonsai," claims Zambra as a declaration of principles: "to write is to prune the branches until you make visible a form that was already there, lying in wait . . . to write is to read an unwritten text."[10] For both Luiselli and Zambra, the task of the contemporary writer would be to prune the tree of tradition so as to establish original relationships and to bring forth the unwritten text. What underlies their narratives is not so much a radical break with the literary past but a search for contemporaries—that is, for comrades of time, collaborators in rewriting the past and the future—through the survival of anachronistic figures.[11] Rather than following a teleological model of history, Luiselli's and Zambra's fictions are ramifications of historical materials that call to be continually reinterpreted, conceiving the return to the past not as a mere repetition but as a new beginning.

A HISTORY OF THE END OF HISTORY

Both these authors share the sensation of living after the end of history, although this is certainly not a new feeling. In the mid-twentieth century, Alexandre Kojève argued that the end of history was a phenomenon that had occurred in 1806 after Napoleon's victory at the Battle of Jena rather than a threat that lay in the future. According to Kojève, at the beginning of the nineteenth century, Homo sapiens had entered a terminal stage, and after the devastating landscape brought about by the two world wars only a couple of options remained to face our post-historical reality: the animality embodied by the American Way of Life and the snobbery of Japanese culture.[12] For Kojève, the triumph of economic activity over the other spheres of culture, the return to a primitive condition devoted to mere survival, and the lack of originality of human actions would be the main features of life after the end of history.

In the first decades of the twenty-first century, the idea that time is a permanent race toward progress—as Hegel understood it—is no longer operative. Nor has the concept of the end of history proposed by Fukuyama served as a diagnosis of the heterogeneity of times that coincide in the same historical period, because it was based on the hypothesis that, after the triumph of liberal democracies and free market economies, historical consciousness would no longer be a feasible alternative. Fukuyama's thesis presupposed that history had reached its goal or was close to it. Years later, Fukuyama himself had to retract the scope of his hypothesis and redefine the term, surrendering to the evidence of a present of such radical changes—among them, the threat of global warming, religious fundamentalisms, and terrorist attacks—that the achievements of liberal democracies ended up looking extremely fragile and the development of a consciousness of the contemporary became a necessary, if not urgent, task to preserve the survival of the human species on the planet.[13]

Instead of resigning themselves to the presentist configuration of neoliberal societies, Latin American writers conceive of time as a simultaneity of pasts, presents, and futures that move at different speeds. It is no coincidence that Terry Smith points to 1945 as a year that constitutes a "prehistory of the present," since the challenges of a world in full planetary reconstruction prefigure those faced by today's societies and, consequently, those that are part of the aesthetic imaginary of contemporary artists and writers.[14] While contemporaneity became an aesthetic and temporal category that urgently needed to be interrogated, the sense of permanent crisis translated into the impossibility of grouping the arts and literatures of the present under a single paradigm, style, or critical model. After all, the twenty-first century began with a nonevent underpinning the ubiquity of this apocalyptic imaginary: the Y2K bug of the year 2000, which threatened to wipe out storage systems on a global scale. Millenarian fears materialized with force the following year: the terrorist attack on the World Trade Center, the socioeconomic crisis in Argentina, and the recession affecting the countries of the European Union inaugurated a century that, in the traumatic passage from the old to the new, witnessed the definitive eclipse of modern utopias. In *The Literature of Catastrophe*, Carlos Fonseca argues that nowadays, "writers arrive always a bit late, when history has already ended, and what remains is the ruinous landscape of the lettered city."[15] If contemporaneity means living in a present without a past or future, writers stage a return to history after the end of history, when the links to the foundational past have been shattered and the future seems increasingly difficult to predict.

I side with Jacques Derrida's thesis of the end of history as a period characterized by the spectral and traumatic return of previous epochs, which he develops through the notion of hauntology. "After the end of history," Derrida claims in *Specters of Marx*, "the spirit comes by coming back [*revenant*], it figures *both* a dead man who comes back and a ghost whose expected return repeats itself, again and again."[16] This vision of the contemporary as a period of persistence of the repressed underlies the notion of return put forward by Hal Foster, who analyzes the retroactive reading that the neo-avant-gardes have made of the historical avant-gardes: returns that transform past artistic works into a critical poetics, creative analyses, and deconstructive examinations.[17] For Foster, the avant-garde does not come to us from the past but from the future, since it inhabits an off-kilter temporality, "a complex relay of anticipated futures and reconstructed pasts . . . a deferred action that throws over any simple scheme of before and after, cause and effect, origin and repetition."[18]

If "the end of history is just another name for the end of interpretation," as Walter Benn Michaels claims, the contemporary novel recycles critical moments of the Latin American cultural tradition in order to enact the disagreements necessary for the collective construction of the future.[19] The notion of return encompasses a resignification of the present as untimely—a time that is never entirely contemporary since it is besieged by the ghost of déjà vu or the promise of what is about to happen. Through the notion of return, I aim to show that time is the sphere par excellence in which central discussions on the politics of our present moment are occurring—discussions that seek to open the new millennium to the *longue durée* of social, political, and geological processes to pierce historical becoming and suggest new possibilities of meaning.

SPECTERS OF THE CONTEMPORARY

Valeria Luiselli's *Los ingrávidos* unfolds as a kaleidoscope that projects multiple times and spaces that converge as the narrative moves forward. At first glance, the nameless narrator recounts her life as a mother and wife in present-day Mexico City, where she takes care of her two children, a baby who is beginning to articulate her first words and an older boy who is nevertheless called *el mediano* or "the middle child" (in the English version simply "the boy"), while her marriage with a scriptwriter gradually falls apart. However, the recollection of her past as a translator at a small publishing house in New York—where she becomes obsessed with the fact that her apartment in Morningside Park is located only a few blocks from where the Mexican poet Gilberto Owen lived in the 1920s—leads to the opening of another temporal plane in which Owen recounts his life in the first person: his past as a diplomat at the Mexican Embassy in New York and his present of physical decay in Philadelphia. Despite the gradual evaporation of time frames, we can gather that the narrator's life in New York City takes place during 2001—a year that marked a radical change in our conception of time through cultural anxieties about the arrival of the new century and through the terrorist attacks on the Twin Towers and the reordering of geopolitical relations on a global scale. While the narrator's plotline culminates in a spectral version of the events that unfolded in 9/11, Owen's narrative arc ends with the Wall Street crash of 1929. As the two planes intersect, the present of the new century begins to be experienced as déjà vu or as a spectral repetition of previous catastrophes, so that the narrator reveals from the beginning the difficulty of finding "the correct tenses" to situate her own story in the present. *Los ingrávidos* can thus be read as a phantasmagoria of "fuzzy temporal boundaries" with which Luiselli, as the narrator's alter ego, conceives the task of the writer at the beginning of the twenty-first century, after several diagnoses about the end of history, temporality, and literature have been decreed.[20]

In this sense, Luiselli uses the figure of the tree to weave the different narrative planes and create a filiation narrative.[21] The temporal loans between the narrator and Gilberto Owen (including a dry tree) are an antidote to the regime of historicity of the new century, characterized by the impossibility of conceiving history chronologically. Luiselli creates a new filiation narrative, not through the image of the genealogical tree—with its dynamics of descendants, evolutions, and reversals—but of a dry tree or a portable pot that writers must water, revive, and prune in the present. In *Los ingrávidos*, Owen leaves on the rooftop of his New York building a dried orange tree that the narrator finds in the 2001 present when she visits the site where the Mexican poet lived in the 1920s. The scene encapsulates how the novel reworks literary tradition in the contemporary moment, because the narrator, through the restitution of the Mexican poet's life and work, intervenes in the present and in Owen's New York past, enacting the type of retroactive reading of literary tradition that Borges theorized in his essay "Kafka and His Precursors." "The fact is that each writer *creates* his precursors," Borges wrote in 1951. "His work modifies our conception of the past, as it will modify the future."[22] After all, to restitute, as Viart points out, "also means to give something back to someone."[23] Against the grain of the reconstruction of the past "as a sequence of events that lead to a destiny," in *Los ingrávidos* Luiselli accounts for a non-teleological, nonlinear conception of literary tradition, which allows for the elaboration of new fables of trans-mission, filiation, and inheritance.[24]

The notion of borrowing is key for Luiselli's conception of tradition as a living entity continually modified by new readings of materials thought to be outmoded. As the loans between the narrator and Owen blur the bound-aries between past and present, she inscribes the desire to resurrect what Tabarovsky calls the "ghost of the avant-garde" and "the art of speaking im-possibly with the ghost," to create a filiation narrative or a strategic alliance with the figure of Owen.[25] "The past did not arrive and the future is barely a loan," Tabarovsky observes. "In the impasse between these two times, the ghost of the avant-garde is written in the present. In a present thought as a point of view, as a strategy, as a strategy in the present, or rather, before the present, against the present."[26]

In *Los ingrávidos* Luiselli develops a notion of originality that derives from rereadings of the literary past. Specifically, she rescues a past that con-stitutes a truncated inheritance, a road abandoned or forgotten by the writ-ers of the Mexican literary field. The choice of Owen as a tutelary figure in this construction of a new myth of beginning is significant not only because he is part of "an almost secret tradition . . . close in its remoteness."[27] Owen belonged to Los Contemporáneos, that "group without a group" that inau-gurated the avant-garde in Mexico proposing to polemicize with the label of the modern used by the Latin American *modernista* generation, to establish a dialogue with the European and North American cultural scene through its homonymous magazine, and to question the assumptions involved in being contemporaries "of themselves, of their creative will."[28]

Luiselli's interest in the figure of Owen predates *Los ingrávidos* by sev-eral years, as it had already been the subject of an article she published in January 2009 in the magazine *Letras Libres* entitled "Gilberto Owen, narrador." In the article, Luiselli proposes to read Owen's work through his "preference for a type of writing outside of time. Not a timeless form of writing but one that, within the story, was free from the corset of the chronological plot." According to Luiselli, Owen's works unfold through "displacements in an effective, timeless space: immobile journeys of a per-petually stranded Sinbad," a description that refers to Owen's book of po-ems *Sindbad el varado*.[29] What Luiselli emphasizes in Owen's body of work is a poetics of simultaneity, which requires a crossover between multiple aesthetic registers. "If we read his letters," Luiselli remarks, "we are read-ing his poetry." This transfiguration of his biography into literary material makes "a blurred portrait" of people and things and composes a "faithful portrait of the gaze" that registers them.[30]

Luiselli's interest in Owen thus corresponds to this conception of con-temporaneity as a blurred portrait of the present, which calls individuals to be in several places and times simultaneously. This notion of an untimely contemporaneity, which Owen develops throughout his poetic work, is the same that dictates the form of *Los ingrávidos*.[31] It is a conception of the contemporary that, as Julio Premat maintains via Gilles Bonnet, is not a mere "repetition of the past, permanence, or plurality of times: it is also a step aside, a disorientation of time."[32] For Luiselli, the contemporary is an experience of indistinction and cooperation between formerly stable categories such as reality and fiction, past and present, the oral and the written.

Whereas critics such as Oswaldo Zavala have read Luiselli's affiliation with the figure of Owen as a strategic attitude to "integrate organically into the neoliberal present of Western culture," I show how this spectral dialogue constitutes an attempt to combat neoliberal presentism through the shadowing of old figures and genres.[33] In the face of a present that is felt as incomplete and multiple, an experience of time that Jürgen Habermas described as the unfinished project of modernity, Luiselli in *Los ingrávidos* makes visible the desire to take up forgotten trajectories in order to update them in the present.[34] The contemporary turns into a repository of multiple moments and figures of the past, which reflects the polysemic and heterogeneous character of the work of memory. By following the structure of a temporal kaleidoscope, Luiselli shows the epistemological inability to represent history as a series of evolutionary processes after a century marked by catastrophe.[35]

Contemporary writers are thus confronted with a paradoxical situation; while they experience the literary canon through a lack of continuity, they also need to turn to the past to find new filiations. As Guerrero points out, at the turn of the century, Latin American writers have tried not so much to reconstruct "a continuity, a history, or a unique story of defined filiations" as "to creatively manifest the need to seek other alternatives in the face of the temporal dislocation that marks the contemporary and places the past, the multiple pasts, in a situation of unprecedented otherness."[36] In *Los ingrávidos* Luiselli carries this slogan forward by tracing new combinations of times and conceiving the present as a kaleidoscope in which original connections are forged between the writers of the world literary canon. "We always choose . . . to rehearse the beginnings of the end," remarks the narrator regarding the novel she is writing about Owen, "beforeshocks, pretremblings."[37] Such a statement blurs the boundaries between beginnings and endings in a manner characteristic of the post-historical period. *Los ingrávidos* shows the discursive limits of history as a paradigm of temporal organization, conceiving the contemporary as a palimpsest of antithetical temporalities.

This position of untimeliness in the face of the contemporary is embodied in *Los ingrávidos* by the space of the subway, where the different historical times converge momentarily and flash up before the characters' eyes. This clash occurs when the cars of their respective trains intersect, an eloquent metaphor because, in Owen's time, the New York subway—a mode of transportation founded in October 1904—represented the modern race toward the future. By contrast, in the twenty-first century, it has become a place of obsolescence, abandonment, and homelessness: a future that never arrived. Owen was part of an avant-garde movement concerned with "the enactment of our future," as he supposedly wrote in a letter to another member of Los Contemporáneos, Xavier Villaurrutia, that is reproduced in the novel. This projection of literary posterity becomes tangible when Owen observes a woman "wearing an olive-green cloth hat and a red coat" (whom the reader comes to understand is none other than the narrator) reading his *Obras* in the New York subway, in the form of a memory of the future. For the narrator, on the other hand, the subway constitutes a chamber of echoes and returns that brings her "close to dead things; to the death of things." The New York subway crystallizes the notion of an outmoded contemporaneity, which Luiselli refers to through the image of two trains traveling in opposite directions and meeting during "just a flash."[38] This is a metaphor for the "intermittent temporalities" that, according to Bourriaud, are characteristic of our time.[39]

The New York subway system serves as the privileged space of the contemporary, understood as the return of other historical moments and experiences that still form a constituent part of the present.[40] In this way, Luiselli conceives the contemporary through the confluence of diverse and asynchronous temporalities, the meeting of several simultaneous presents that produce a paradoxical experience of historicity as a unity in conflict. Peter Osborne remarks that the contemporary is "a coming together not simply 'in' time, but *of* times."[41] This conception of the present as a multitude of temporalities in dispute is not alien to Los Contemporáneos, who rejoiced in the experience of simultaneity offered by the emerging media of technological modernity, such as the montage of parallel sequences in early films. Pedro Ángel Palou points out that, in Owen's work, the New York subway system serves as a figure of cinema, so long as it represents an experience of temporal simultaneity that turns the poetic voice of a text like *Sindbad el varado* into "a fragmented being" who becomes "a distiller of times and discourses."[42]

In *Los ingrávidos*, the subway is where the contemporary translates into a continuous updating of the past, becoming a true site of memory. Unlike history as a mere portrait of the past, Nora says, "memory is a perpetually actual phenomenon, a bond tying us to the eternal present."[43] In other words, the subway system materializes the absences of transmission and forces the narrator to develop a critical gaze that does not reproduce the inertia of the melancholic subject: the "past that does not pass by . . . overinflated, hyperbolic" that, according to Julia Kristeva, defines the perspective of melancholic people.[44] As opposed to dwelling nostalgically in the bygone days of literary modernism and urban modernity, Luiselli focuses on the past's future in order to highlight its importance for creating a community in the present.

If we consider the narrator's inability to form communal ties, *Los ingrávidos* becomes a novel about the temporal annihilation that characterizes contemporary societies. The narrator inhabits a time when fragmentation emerges as the only strategy to write the present. This lack of time results from her being the mother of two small children at home in Mexico City. The flashbacks to her life as a single woman in New York City plunge us into the 24/7 temporality of contemporary capitalism, which imposes nonstop production as the only life goal. This is a historical condition that Jonathan Crary associates with the end of sleep, the "duration without pauses," and the "capitalist mirage of post-history."[45] It is unsurprising that the narrator embodies this sleep-deprived citizen in various ways, for according to the fictional Owen, she is "a woman with a brown face and dark shadows under her eyes."[46]

Her life is marked by the inability to create authentic connections with others, form a community of contemporaries, and conceive long-term undertakings. While her work in the publishing house triggers a series of forgeries that blur the differences between copy and original, her love life unfolds as an accumulation of sexual adventures with men with whom she shares no affective ties. Since the narrative occurs in 2001, the narrator's apathy and indifference could be thought of as symptoms of what Virno has described as the post-historical state of mind. "Since the present is dressed in the clothes of an irrevocable past," Virno remarks, "these people must renounce any influence on how the present plays out."[47] Consequently, the condition that characterizes the narrator is simulacrum, as if the present was detached from other historical periods and she could not intervene in the production of the future.

The metaphor of weightlessness that gives *Los ingrávidos* its Spanish title designates the paradox with which the novel portrays the post-historical condition: one cannot escape the past, which continually returns in the form of déjà vus and untimely specters, but it is necessary to engage in a conversation with it so as to open up future horizons. First, weightlessness is the metaphor that encapsulates the narrator's life in New York City, dictated by a routine she abides by with the indifference of a zombie. It is a way of designating what French philosopher Gilles Lipovetsky defines as "the floating life" of the contemporary world, whose main features are apathy and "emotional emptiness, the indifferent weightlessness in which social operations unfold."[48] The narrator's life embodies this era of emptiness on both an affective level and a material one, since her New York apartment is barely furnished and serves as a temporary dwelling. "In that apartment there were only five pieces of furniture: bed, kitchen table, bookcase, desk, and chair."[49] As the narrator establishes a transtemporal conversation with Owen's ghost, however, her apartment becomes a site of memory populated by furniture and objects from the outside world, which points to a continuous reactualization of the past.

Likewise, the novel shifts from portraying Owen as a ghostly figure who experiences a progressive loss of weight each time he descends into the New York subway—"as if I were hollowing out," the fictional Owen remarks, "while my shell remained intact"—to depicting him as an obese old man who can barely leave the confines of his apartment.[50] It is the same operation that Luiselli carries over to the novel's narrative configuration, as the narrator's voice gives way to Owen's until the two become indistinguishable. As the narrator reactivates Owen's voice in the present, Luiselli creates a new filiation narrative. Owen, as the embodiment of a literary past to which one wants to belong, begins to exert a progressive influence on the configuration of the contemporary.

In *Los ingrávidos* Luiselli portrays the turn-of-the-century present through the phantasmagoric return of scenes and discourses belonging to other moments of crisis. Luiselli posits a new conception of history in which the past can only be envisioned from the vantage point of the present, delineating the end of history as a state of trauma and mourning for the lack of prospects. According to Ruffel, the contemporary can be thought of as "a mode of historical approach that is not historicist," which entails "a hypertrophied present, a crisis involving the future or progress, an invasion of the present into the past which can only be seen through the lens of the present, an end to linear time but by no means a return to cyclical time."[51] The end of history is reflected in the weightlessness that the novel's characters inhabit, dying not once but several times, becoming receptacles for echoes, specters, and mirages of the past. This spectrality invokes a traumatic past that, in Kristeva's words, "blocks the horizon of depressive temporality or rather removes any horizon, any perspective."[52] Luiselli establishes a vertiginous dialogue between past and present that serves as a portrait of the unconscious of the contemporary. She introduces images of a world in suspense that undo a linear conception of history, as recorded in the metaphor used by Owen to describe the evaporation of narrative times: "a sort of pitiless boomerang that flies back and knocks out your teeth, your enthusiasm, and your balls."[53] The narrator experiences the crisis through déjà vus or memories of the present, and Owen realizes that his memories come from the future, in a conversation that delineates the contemporary, not through the harmonious coexistence of several historical times but as a palimpsest of contested temporalities.

In this way, Luiselli raises the question of how to write the present in an era of endings, when the teleology of progress has given way to the spectral repetition of critical events in social history. Contrary to a representation of time as a line that leads only forward, she portrays the end of history as a temporal palimpsest. As Owen's character declares in a statement that could refer to the aesthetic configuration of the novel, "nothing ever finishes finishing."[54] This jarring statement helps explain the interplay that the narrator and Owen establish between the idea of a horizontal and a vertical novel. While the narrator seeks to write "a horizontal novel, told vertically," Owen wants to work on "a vertical novel told horizontally."[55] Through this visual conundrum, this temporal interweaving that undoes "linear and ascending" historicity and disorients both Owen and the narrator, Luiselli conveys the difficulties posed by the writing of history in periods of crisis, when the arrows of clocks have broken down and given way to the asynchronous metabolization of various historical moments.[56]

If the fragmentary structure of *Los ingrávidos* reflects the idea of "a horizontal novel" through the image of the subway, which evokes the concept of arcades put forward by Benjamin, it is possible to perceive verticality in several images of falls that occur toward the end of the novel: Mexican dancer José Limón at a performance of *Othello*, the stock market crash of 1929, and the suicide of a man who jumps from the New York Stock Exchange building that prefigures the one that would occur in 2001 (the Falling Man who jumped from the upper floors of the North Tower). Through these "spectral figures" who fall from up high and impact the ground without making a sound, like ghosts that metamorphose over time and come back to haunt the present, Luiselli conveys literature's inability to insert the contemporary within a historical continuum and, even more so, to imagine future perspectives.[57]

Luiselli recycles the specters that mutate throughout social history and the aesthetic forms and figures of the literary past. In *Los ingrávidos* she interrogates how to begin literature anew at a time when various discourses on the end of the literary prevail in the cultural sphere. Luiselli inscribes in the present forgotten or outmoded aesthetic formats that allow her to restore the possibility of historical transmission. This is a shadowing procedure adopted by certain currents of contemporary art, film, and literature that repurpose old literary genres or aesthetic formats.[58] Luiselli inscribes this shadowing procedure through the avant-garde slogans of fragmentation, simultaneity, and montage that Owen employed in works such as *Novela como nube*, but she subjects them to a series of formal transformations that fit the historical conjuncture of the new millennium.[59]

For Owen, montage and simultaneity implied aligning himself with the discourse of the cinematograph as the privileged medium of the future. In contrast, Luiselli employs the montage procedure in *Los ingrávidos* to reveal the post-historical condition of the artist who has arrived too late, whose function is to revisit the utopias and collective illusions of the previous century. Luiselli does not create a pastiche from styles and quotations from the literary past. Instead she conceives models of orientation in the present, a new sensorium of the contemporary that serves as an antithesis to the passive culture of presentism and consumerism.[60] In *Los ingrávidos* Luiselli returns to the historical avant-garde to construct a critical strategy that allows her to situate herself in the twenty-first-century present.[61]

Luiselli makes an archaeological portrait of the present through the re-elaboration of literary tradition in this sociocultural context populated by the ruins of failed modernizing projects. When the narrator visits the rooftop of Owen's former apartment and picks up the flowerpot that she links to the poet of Los Contemporáneos, she turns into a ghost. Her body becomes a receptacle for Owen's return to the literary scene, just as Luiselli reanimates the ghost of the avant-garde through an homage-laden narrative procedure. Faced with a regime of historicity that privileges the immediate and the ephemeral, the narrator concentrates on weaving an anachronistic narrative that would allow her to conceive "an aleatory vision of History affirming that everything could have happened differently." Contemporary artists, according to Bourriaud, use "the slightest clue, the meagrest fragment . . . [to] found new narratives."[62]

At the level of plot, Luiselli in *Los ingrávidos* sets out to establish a new narrative by putting artists who inhabited the same time period and the same city, such as Owen, Federico García Lorca, and Louis Zukofsky into a conversation, even though the historical record indicates that they never met in person.[63] In turn, she reproduces this estrangement effect in the novel through its formal elements, because, as spaces, times, and voices converge on the same narrative plane, it becomes difficult to ascertain whether it is Owen or the narrator who intends to found a new beginning. She thus transforms the lack of time of contemporary societies into an excess of time and turns a marginal figure of the Latin American literary canon such as Gilberto Owen into "a collaborator, a comrade of time, [a] true contemporary."[64]

Luiselli foregrounds the figure of the ghostwriter, the counterfeiter, or the pirate who creates new filiation narratives after the turn of the millennium. She seeks to delineate the writer as an active agent who inscribes her literary text within a catalog of existing works, thus standing against the overproduction and passivity of consumerist culture.[65] The narrator is writing two books: on the one hand, she writes "a book about Gilberto

Owen's ghost," and, on the other, she forges a book by Owen supposedly translated by Zukofsky, becoming a ghostwriter of the Mexican poet—that is, a ghostwriter of the writer who is a ghost, in one of the various riddles, inside jokes, and hidden symbols that the reader must learn to navigate as the novel progresses.[66] Just as the characters in the novel, "the original and the ghost, go on living, each in his own right," Luiselli conjures a new archive of tradition that blurs the differences between original and copy while mistrusting the classic categories of periodization according to generations, groups, and movements.[67] It is no coincidence that Luiselli has chosen Los Contemporáneos, a "group without a group," to construct this phantasmagoria of tradition, in which it becomes extremely difficult to determine whether it is the narrator who is representing an apocryphal version of Owen's life or whether the fragments of the poet's correspondence that are inserted into the narrative via Post-it notes are true or false. As Sarah Booker suggests, "in her reimagining of Owen's life, [the narrator] is enacting a sort of translation in the way that she rewrites his story."[68] As a translator, the narrator updates the literary tradition so as to create new filiation narratives, rendering tangible the old aphorism that delineates the translator as a traitor or a forger of the original text.

In addition to embracing a position of illegality vis-à-vis literary tradition, Luiselli demonstrates the obsolescence of the figure of the family tree in accounting for the contemporary writer's work. Novels of genealogy are based on the linear and progressive family tree model, narrating in detail the founding of a lineage and its generational evolution.[69] On the other hand, contemporary stories of filiation begin with the impossibility of situating the subject in a relationship of continuity with the past and, therefore, narrate the attempts to restore a truncated inheritance through search and reminiscence.[70]

In this novel Luiselli proposes a new filiation with the literary past through the figure of the tree, which is no longer the repository of a lineage that allows writers to project themselves into the future but, rather, a dry plant that must be watered and revitalized by the new generations. It is also a portable plant, which materializes the various transhistorical loans between Owen and the narrator, thus aligning with Bourriaud's notion of "works that set themselves the task of effacing their origin in favor of a multitude of simultaneous or successive enrootings."[71] In this way, she depicts the state of orphanhood of the contemporary writer, who must spin tales from the revival of tradition and oppose the modernist telos that points to the search for the new as the ultimate end of artistic production.[72] The category of the new is inoperative at the turn of the millennium. Originality derives from exploring the literary tradition and inventing an apocryphal narrative, as demonstrated through Owen's spectral voice. His voice invades the narrative to recount, among other episodes, his encounters with Federico García Lorca and Louis Zukofsky in 1920s New York City, despite the narrator's admitting that such encounters were impossible.

By blurring the boundaries between past and present, original and copy, Luiselli portrays the archive of tradition as composed of "false papers," to invoke the Spanish title (*Papeles falsos*) of Luiselli's book of essays, translated as *Sidewalks*. The affinity with the figure of Owen derives from the rise of a whole publishing industry around forgeries and apocryphal manuscripts, taking advantage of the warm reception of Bolaño's work in the United States. "That's the way literary recognition works," the narrator tells us. "It's all a matter of rumor, a rumor that multiplies like a virus until it becomes a collective affinity."[73]

This exercise of de-writing tradition operates at the heart of Luiselli's procedure: erasing the boundaries between truth and lies, history and literature. It is the same exercise that Fabre perceives in contemporary "works pierced by holes, works that welcome within them absences that are the product of un-writing, anti-writing, or non-writing."[74] The narrator conceives the form of the novel as notes lightly articulated in a narrative totality. "Scaffoldings, structures, empty houses" are the graphic figures she employs to designate the emptying out of the narrative structure: "a structure full of holes."[75] In *Los ingrávidos* she turns aesthetic form into a vessel that welcomes the specters, the remains, and the echoes of tradition that populate the apocalyptic landscape of contemporary culture. Luiselli repurposes outmoded aesthetic practices and lost moments in social history in order to restore the possibility of starting art and life anew after the death of the grand narratives of modernity.

The novel's denouement builds a world of coexistence between the living and the dead in which both perceive each other as insects, making the nonhuman a repository of echoes, traces, and untimely specters. Earlier in the novel, the fictional Owen sends a letter to Mexican playwright Celestino Gorostiza in which he describes Manhattan as "an hour, or a century, with the woodworm of the subways boring through it, eating it away, second by second."[76] As in the work of the German writer W. G. Sebald, moths become figures of what Eric Santner calls "creaturely life," nonhuman lives or presences that invite us to think of that which survives the natural history of destruction.[77] Whereas the narrator and her children coexist with Owen, Lorca, and Zukofsky who have returned as cockroaches, for Owen the future arrives in the form of mosquitoes. The boy—whose nickname in Spanish, *el mediano*, hints at his role as a medium or intermediary between the different temporal planes—is interested in the afterlife of cockroaches: "if you cut a cockroach's head off," he says, "it goes on living for two weeks."[78] This reflection tangentially refers to Owen's posthumous fame, whose ghost inserts itself into the present almost despite himself through the publishing success of a series of apocryphal manuscripts.

In this way, a novel concerned with the spectral survival of writers, figures, and spaces from the past becomes an empty structure that accommodates a multiplicity of spatiotemporal horizons. It is Luiselli's way of broadening "the fraternal spaces of coexistence of places and times, of experiences and sentences," which is how fiction, according to Rancière, can posit other temporal cartographies disregarding the chain of causes and effects.[79] In *Los ingrávidos* Luiselli invents a new sensorium of the contemporary in which the coexistence between the living and the dead, the archaic and the current, pierces the hypertrophied present of the new millennium and restores the possibility of transmission.

THE REMAINS OF LITERATURE

The work of Chilean writer Alejandro Zambra weaves a fragile relationship with the contemporary by recounting the recent political past through the perspective of children, considered the secondary characters of the last military dictatorship. Zambra's first novel, *Bonsái* (2006; trans. 2008 as *Bonsai*), tells a story of love and family ties through the procedure of montage, which, as in *Los ingrávidos*, clearly delineates the post-historical condition of fragmentation that ensued after the collapse of the past century's utopian visions of progress.[80] Through characters who occupy a subsidiary space in History with a capital H, *Bonsái* portrays how the new generations are forced to confront an inheritance that was not completely or successfully passed down to them. The secondary characters of this novel are schematic beings whose lives contain fractures of experience, lapses of personal memory, and the absence of transmission of a family or collective story.

For Chilean writers of the post-dictatorship, writing thus becomes an exploration of what Richard calls "the potholes of meaning, the opacities of representation," that did not fit comfortably within the "present chronologically programmed as 'transition,'" the "light present" that was the product of a change of power between the members of the military junta and the Christian Democratic government of Patricio Aylwin in 1990.[81] However, unlike the artistic and literary practices that dominated the Chilean cultural scene in the 1990s, in *Bonsái* Zambra does not work with evidence that can be presented in court, with newspaper clippings or archival materials that are inscribed in searches for justice and reconciliation. He works instead with minor affective orientations, unstable names, and traces of historical experience that delineate the contemporary as a temporal impasse: a time of waiting and anxiety in which several attempts are made to give meaning to inherited discourses. Zambra seeks to restore a filiation narrative and weave a new relationship with previous generations and the traumatic events that marked recent Chilean history so that it becomes possible to transmit experiences in the present and into the future.[82]

In this sense, I examine *Bonsái* as a text about the end of history whose author insistently asks how to begin literature from scratch during a time of endings, when everything seems to have been written and the contemporary is experienced as an impasse. After the end of history, the writer is expected to put together historical materials in unprecedented ways, through assemblages that shed new light on a story that is only partially known. The absence of temporal markers turns *Bonsái* into a representation of a time when history has ceased to make sense. This is what Rancière indicates with respect to the end of history, a period in which we have buried "the belief that time carried a meaning and a promise."[83] "The 'end of history,'" Rancière argues, "is the end of an era in which we believed in 'history,' in time marching towards a goal, towards the manifestation of a truth or the accomplishment of an emancipation. Ends of centuries in general lend themselves to the task of burying the past."[84]

In *Bonsái* Zambra exposes language and literature to a temporality of survivals, inscribed in the contemporary as enigmas to be deciphered through search and restitution. As Didi-Huberman points out, "because it is woven of long stretches of time and of critical moments, of ageless latencies and of brutal resurgences, survival ends up by *anachronizing history*."[85] Zambra depicts the contemporary through the procedure of montage, which opens the present to another sense of time in which history becomes anachronistic and ceases to be subordinated to the logic of continuities and ruptures.

Bonsái is the story of the breakup between Julio and Emilia, two literature students who meet at the university and gradually weave a universe of affinities based on shared readings and non-readings.[86] The relationship follows a dynamic of imposture and simulacra through their mutual love of reading, when Julio and Emilia pretend to have read the seven volumes of Marcel Proust's *In Search of Lost Time*. The choice of *In Search of Lost Time* does not seem casual, since it is a novel that unfolds as an atlas of a person's intimacy, an infinite chain of memory images prompted by a sensorial experience of everyday life. On the contrary, *Bonsái* is a short narrative that could be either a novel or a short story and that reproduces the idea of the Chilean transition as a time in which the old has not died and the new is yet to be born. More than a love epic, *Bonsái* is the narrative of the brief itinerary of anonymous lives and secondary characters who bear an unstable name and belong to a generation shaped by forgetfulness and imposture. The novel's structure turns this space of unknowingness (which can be thought of alongside Zambra's strategy of non-reading as posited in *No leer*) into a productive terrain, unfolding the totality of life out of fragments that do not seem to fit into a coherent whole. The novel is an assemblage of details that "turn out to be meaningful only when they are bearers of incertitude, of non-knowing, of disorientation."[87] This is also how Didi-Huberman describes the *Mnemosyne Atlas* by art historian Aby Warburg, which aimed to reveal how each historical moment is an "anachronistic puzzle" traversed by the survival of earlier times.[88] As opposed to Proust's memory epic, Zambra's novella narrates the trajectory of the post-dictatorship generation by assembling minimal scenes of everyday life and stories that seem unworthy of being told, which calls into question the idea of generation as a stable temporal marker.

The notion of survival corresponds to a word that recurs frequently throughout *Bonsái* and which produces various constellations of meaning: *el resto*, which in Megan McDowell's English translation is rendered both as "rest" and "everyone else." To speak of remainders is a way of designating the gaps in the transmission of knowledge that people face when they want to delve into their parents' past, since children cannot fully experience reality or perceive the surrounding world as a meaning-bearing signifier. "The rest is literature," the narrator remarks in the first paragraph, encapsulating the novel's aesthetic procedure.[89] At the end of the twentieth century, which is the novel's temporal setting, the writer is someone who must work with the remains of the real, the voids of transmission, and the ruins of revolutionary discourses shattered by the military dictatorship.

I use the notion of the remainder as articulated by Mario Cámara in relation to a series of contemporary aesthetic practices that work with the ruins of epic forms and projects that shaped the twentieth century. For Cámara, the remainder is the recursive time that entangles "pasts and presents in a perpetual back-and-forth movement that makes them dense and plural."[90] In *Bonsái*, the characters move through the Chilean present as survivors of a shipwreck. Considering the events of the last military dictatorship, the phrase "the rest" invokes a series of signifiers related to the practices of torture and disappearance as repressive technologies used against political dissidents: corpses, ashes, and residues. However, Zambra strips the word "rest" of its political charge—which belongs to the testimonial discourse of the parents' generation—and inscribes it in everyday life. Julio and Emilia experience "the violent complacency of those who believe themselves better and purer than others, than that immense and detestable group called *everyone else*."[91] As exemplified in the scenes in which the narrator does not reveal the name of a character but offers several options from which to choose, *Bonsái* is a temporal montage that punctures language and opens the present to the survival of images and times that ceaselessly return.

While secondary characters such as Julio and Emilia move in a temporal impasse that seems to be outside of history, language becomes a space where the present surrenders to the influence of other temporalities. As Didi-Huberman points out, montage creates a time of repetitions in which ideas and discourses return from the past, but not completely; they return only as remains or specters of what they once were, inciting readers and spectators to build new perspectives with them.[92] Other chapters of *Bonsái* are titled after terms that, like the word *restos*, form a constellation of the untimely: *Bulto* ("entity," though a more literal translation would be "lump" or "bulk") and *Sobras* ("leftovers"). The word *bulto* also evokes the political context of the tortured and the disappeared, traumatic events that Chilean society has not yet atoned for and which haunt the present in the form of specters. Rather than exceptional characters, Julio and Emilia are young people who move in a light or weightless present. They talk or read quietly and cannot find an occupation to fill their time. As the narrator reminds us in the first pages, *Bonsái* is "a light tale that becomes heavy," as Julio and Emilia manage to create an affective community in the present.[93] By emptying the term *bulto* of the traumatic content that links it to Chile's recent history, Zambra performs a semantic operation through which he transforms the punctured time of the end of history into an inclusive time: "a time of coexistence," as Rancière indicates about transitional periods, "in which moments interpenetrate and persist by spreading out in larger and larger circles; a shared time that no longer knows any hierarchy between those who live in it."[94] A time, in other words, in which secondary characters come to exert influence in the construction of a community, in which they cease to speak in a low voice and begin to develop an autonomous discourse. By introducing the events of the military dictatorship as a latent presence, *Bonsái* unfolds a time of leftovers in which language has fallen prey to acts of destruction so dramatic that it needs to be rebuilt from scratch.

Bonsái is a novel about selecting a suitable aesthetic form to narrate the present and, by extension, to elaborate a non-teleological and unprecedented relationship with tradition. To learn about the care of bonsais, Julio reads technical manuals in which he finds a definition that becomes applicable to the work of gardening and to the modus operandi of the literature of post-dictatorship as developed by Zambra: "'The selection of a right pot for a tree is almost an art form in itself,' he thinks. . . . He is ashamed, then, of *Bonsai*, his improvised novel, his unnecessary novel, whose protagonist doesn't even know that the choice of a container is an art form in itself."[95] Di Stefano points out that *Bonsái* seeks to reveal the container in which it has been composed. "Zambra's text is essentially about the flowerpot," Di Stefano argues, "it's about what makes a bonsai different from a tree."[96]

The word "bonsai" refers to both the tree and the pot that contains it; one is inseparable from the other. The act of pruning the bonsai's roots becomes an attempt to reduce the world's content at a time of cultural saturation. The metaphor of writing as caring for a bonsai does not seek to break with tradition or add branches to the family tree but, rather, to prune and build with what has already been written in the past. That is why Zambra uses the metaphor of carving and pruning several times, including in the novel's epigraph from Gonzalo Millán: "Pain is inscribed and described."[97] Writing unfolds in the margins of what has already been produced, creating new assemblages and constellations with the material used or discarded by previous generations.

Consequently, terms such as "remains," "leftovers," and "entities" take on an unusual importance in *Bonsái*, both because they are part of the resignification of language that operates at the core of the literature of the children and because they designate the state of literary tradition after the end of history. For the children of post-dictatorship, literature and language have perished along with the notion of history as an arrow pointing forward. Writing is now an exercise in selecting the proper receptacle, choosing certain affiliations, discarding others, and looking back to seek strategies for bringing something new to the surface. As Premat argues, Zambra's writing is situated in an interstitial time, between an oppressive and alien past and a past that one wishes to recover: "In that interstice, one passes from the blank page to writing, from a 'bonsai of a novel' to a 'novel-novel,' from an imposed filiation to a chosen identity."[98] Grínor Rojo perceives in the Chilean post-dictatorship novel, especially the literature of the children, "a subtraction aesthetic."[99] According to Rojo, these works explore "the depth of the gap that separates the generational experience of children who were not yet born when the coup took place, or who were born immediately after, from the experience of their elders."[100] At a time when the present is experienced as incomplete and discontinuous, Zambra explores the holes of memory and language through an aesthetic form that manages to spread them out in all their complexity.

The fact that the bonsai is inside a portable container sets it apart from a tree planted in the ground and posits a genealogical relationship with the past. Rather than a dynamic of continuities and ruptures, tradition becomes fertile ground for the appropriation and assembly of divergent temporalities, texts, and contexts through the figure of the bonsai. Compared with the rooted tree, the bonsai renders any attempt at periodizing literary history impossible. Through the bonsai, Zambra conceives tradition via anachronism and the disorientation of temporal coordinates. "It's a tree on the edge," the narrator remarks after including Julio's drawing in the narrative, evoking those edges of time in which subjects move after the end of history: a time oversaturated with history and, consequently, outside of chronological time, in which individuals have become mere spectators of their own actions.[101] Although Fukuyama's thesis about the end of history and the triumph of liberal democracies has been scorned, Fisher warns us, "it is accepted, even assumed, at the level of the cultural unconscious."[102] The bonsai is a tree that seems to be growing on a precipice, and in many cases its roots are in plain sight. Like the mangrove and *ombú* roots used by Rita Indiana and Pedro Mairal as metaphors for tradition, this display of intertwined roots shows that there is no single origin but, rather, several simultaneous enrootings. The bonsai as a tree on the edge serves as a metaphor for writing at the end of history, when alternative times are needed to counteract the detachment from the present and the excess of history that Fisher ties to the condition of Nietzsche's Last Man: the illusion that one has seen everything and there is nothing new under the sun.

In this sense, *Bonsái* could be read as a rewriting or an appropriation of "Tantalia" (1930), the short story by Argentinean writer Macedonio Fernández that Julio and Emilia read in bed. It tells the story of a couple who buy a plant to celebrate their anniversary and then realize that the relationship will end as soon as the plant dies.[103] The tale seems to be an omen for romantic estrangement and the end of Zambra's novel, which weaves content and form so that one becomes indistinguishable from the other. "Tantalia," like *Bonsái*, walks us through five moments in a couple's life. The Argentinean writer is, in this sense, the specter of the avant-garde that is inscribed in the impasse of the present: the ghost of the avant-garde, Tabarovsky observes, returns in the form of "remains, pieces that arrive empty, loose, almost in an immanent way: the text reaches us, no longer the epoch," settling "in the crack, in the earthquake, in the storm, in the whirlpool, which changes everything from one instant to the next."[104] As we can see in Luiselli's repurposing of Owen's poetic work, the montage technique at the turn of the twenty-first century entails both an appropriation and a distancing from the original text, as if tradition has been swept away by a computer virus and turned into a series of distorted remains: the *tantalia*, a fictional plant in Macedonio's short story, becomes a bonsai in Zambra's novel.[105] Through the reinterpretation of Macedonio's "Tantalia," the ghost of the avant-garde returns to offer temporal alternatives to a present that is experienced as edge and precipice.

As in *Los ingrávidos*, loans play a fundamental role in how Zambra positions *Bonsái* vis-à-vis tradition. The novel's third chapter is entitled "Loans." The appropriation of cultural objects from the literary past, such as Macedonio Fernández's short story, posits the idea of a precarious and wandering artist who moves outside of legal frameworks and resorts to "the world of criminal vagrancy: petty theft, poaching, robbery, and a refusal to seek paid employment."[106] For this reason, in *Bonsái* Zambra incorporates the concept of the loan into his lexicon of the contemporary, as the characters gradually form affective and communal bonds based on the objects they traffic among themselves: in the case of Emilia and her friend Anita, the exchange begins during their childhood through clothing items, a book on origami, and a rice-filled doll and continues with cultural objects such as the magazine *Tú* or tapes of Duran Duran and Miguel Bosé, among other artists. As Rancière writes about the films of Béla Tarr, a filmmaker whose work he situates at the edge of time, "it is not the individuals who live in places and make use of things. It is the things that first come to them, that surround, penetrate, or reject them."[107]

The narrator of *Bonsái* shows how people enter and leave the narrative plane to the rhythm of things, which pass from hand to hand as if they were part of a clandestine trade network. Simultaneously, the exchange of identities between the different characters exposes reality as a mere simulacrum. For example, Anita lends Emilia her husband—we do not know whether his name is Andrés or Leonardo—so that she can get a job as a Spanish teacher, for which she had pretended to be married.

However, the most important loans are the books circulating from hand to hand, which become palimpsests of cross-readings containing interventions in the margins and anonymous rewritings. Julio buys the manuals and specialized magazines on bonsai with the money he collects from selling his books at Santiago's Plaza Italia. In Zambra's work, reading is a way of seeing how another person has read the same book, as in "Erasing the Reader," an article he wrote about his underlined and annotated copy of Chilean writer Mauricio Wacquez's novel *Toda la luz del mediodía*, in which Zambra confesses he has spent a whole afternoon "imagining that noisy reader, deciding on his features, his interests."[108]

In a fragmented world where products acquire new forms as they move away from their place of origin, the writer establishes unusual connections and creates precarious assemblages by tracing the path of cultural signs. Zambra does not adhere to the neoliberal aesthetics that Luis E. Cárcamo-Huechante perceived in 1990s' Chilean novels by authors such as Alberto Fuguet, "writer-consumers" who resorted to "a sentimental economy of reading: nostalgia for past, remote, or lost references."[109] In *Bonsái,* books and literary quotations are part of collaborative networks of exchange that oppose hierarchical copyright structures and highlight the communal experience of art. In this sense, he proposes a communitarian writing strategy reproducing the informal economic practices that Gago links to the subversion of the neoliberal city. "The communitarian," Gago observes, regarding Buenos Aires's Mercado de La Salada, "becomes a source of pragmatic versatility that crosses borders and is capable of adaptation and invention."[110] Zambra challenges neoliberalism's passive culture by creating new itineraries through literary history and by turning his forebears into co-creators.

Furthermore, by being attentive to the survival of traumatic moments that modify the texture of the present, Zambra inscribes his works in the vestiges of various aesthetic genres. Zambra writes books that could be novels, short stories, or poems in order to depict memory as "an excellent *assembler*": the gathering of heterogeneous elements, the erosions in the continuum of history, and the interaction between different times and places.[111] Zambra mixes discursive fields in order to question how to represent the past when it is experienced through discontinuities and fractures.[112] By positing an expanded notion of literature that moves between forms and genres, he reflects on the time it will take readers to consume each work from start to finish.[113] In *Bonsái*, the growth or death of a tree defines the structure of the text and the trajectory of its protagonists, and in "I Smoked Very Well," one of the short stories of *My Documents*, the image of a cigarette that is consumed in a specific time-lapse ("It lasted six minutes and seven seconds") runs parallel to the reading of the text itself.[114] The comparison between the story and the cigarette highlights the duration of the reading process, which lasts—or seems to last—as long as it takes the character to smoke the cigarette. Zambra's works revolve around what Rancière calls "time-images, images from which duration is made manifest—the very stuff of which those individualities, which we call situations or characters, are woven."[115]

Zambra writes fictions of obsolescence or object narratives that, from the very first lines, announce the moment of their expiration, such as the death of Emilia.[116] In *Bonsái*, the eponymous novel composed by Julio is written to resemble (or supplant) that of a novelist who belongs to his parents' generation. The indeterminacy of Zambra's texts is the direct consequence of the suspension of meaning and aesthetic specificity during Chile's democratic transition, which oscillated between presence and absence, between the push for a globalized future and the pull of a traumatic past that never ceases to pass. *Bonsái* demands an act not so much of reading as of non-reading. As Zambra argues in one of the articles in *No leer*: "Books say no to literature. Some. Others, the majority, say yes. They obey the market or the holy spirit of governments. Or the placid idea of a generation. Or the even more placid idea of a tradition. I prefer books that say no. Sometimes, even, I prefer the books that don't know what they are saying."[117]

The poetics of negativity embraced by Zambra implies, as Rancière points out, an opening that allows readers to reorganize the intersections between art and technology, between that which counts as art and that which does not.[118] Similarly, authors writing against the grain of a stable notion of authorship or generation seek to pierce the assumptions on which the contemporary is built, as they recognize that ideas such as tradition and transmission are composed of oversights and that, in many cases, they conform to the need for classification imposed by the publishing market. Zambra posits the figure of the writer as a stutterer, as someone who does not know what he or she is saying or who must repeat it countless times in order to be understood. *Bonsái* and *La vida privada de los árboles*, its follow-up from 2007 (trans. 2010 as *The Private Lives of Trees*), are two hypothetical works that revolve around the same theme: incomplete searches that open stories to future constellations of meaning.[119]

Like Bellatin's *El jardín de la señora Murakami*, which also cannibalizes Japanese culture, *Bonsái* is the translation of an imaginary book.[120] Julio writes a novel that seeks to imitate the one written by Gazmuri, an author from his parents' generation who could be read as a fictionalized version of the Chilean historian Cristián Gazmuri. Whereas the real-life Gazmuri has written extensively on the Pinochet dictatorship and the democratic transition, the fictional Gazmuri is a writer who "has published six or seven novels that together comprise a series on Chile's recent history" and who intended to hire Julio to transcribe an untitled novel.[121] However, the deal finally falls through because of financial differences. Julio ends up transcribing an apocryphal novel, which he conceives through the parameters he has heard from Gazmuri ("I'll summarize it a little," Gazmuri tells him, "A guy finds out that a girlfriend from his youth is dead") and of which he only knows the title: *Bonsai*, although Gazmuri's final version will be called *Leftovers*.[122]

In addition to conceiving the exercise of transcribing a fictional manuscript as a way of conjuring the condition of coming after, Julio imitates Gazmuri even in the procedure of manual writing. Instead of writing on a computer, Julio writes with a pencil in the Colón notebooks used by Gazmuri, "in a handwriting that isn't his." To suppress any trace of imposture, Julio accentuates the materiality of the novel by smearing the manuscript: "He smudges a few paragraphs, spills coffee on the pages, and even scatters some ashes over the manuscript."[123] The case of Julio in *Bonsái* shows in a subtle way how the children have erected their literature in the shadow of the discourse of the parents, either questioning that discourse or simply giving voice to the characters who did not occupy a predominant place during the dictatorial period and who now form an essential part of the Chilean present. As Rivera Garza argues regarding the poetics of contemporary rewriting and appropriation opposing the notion of private property put forward by global capitalism: "Writing, in this context, is always rewriting, a going-back to what others have put into words and sentences, a practice that delays and belabors the finished version of any text. An exercise in unfinishedness."[124] If Julio chooses to write the novel he imagines Gazmuri to be writing, he does so not to overcome the anxiety of influence à la Harold Bloom but, rather, to appropriate the language of previous generations so as to construct new ways of being in community in the present.[125]

In *Bonsái* Zambra conjures the ghost of the preceding generation by demystifying the figure of the canonical writer and questioning the realist aesthetics of human rights restitution as suitable for events that escape the realm of the visible. Even though Gazmuri does not hire him to transcribe the novel, Julio sets up a farce by telling his new girlfriend, María, that he is still meeting with the famous author. However, like those in Fernández's "Tantalia," the characters in Gazmuri's novel that Julio imagines have no names: "The characters? Gazmuri didn't give them names. He says it's better that way, and I agree: they're He and She, John and Jane Doe, they don't have names and they might not have faces either."[126]

Zambra's texts often resist subjectification—their protagonists are nameless or bear unstable names, standing against the need for indexicality that characterized post-dictatorship testimonies. In *Bonsái*, there is an attempt to question proper names from the outset: "Let's say her name is or was Emilia and that his name is, was, and will be Julio."[127] For Zambra's narrators, last names would seem to belong to the testimonial discourses of the parents—which are based on the accuracy of data because they are, at the same time, literary texts and legal documents—while the literature of the children moves in the terrain of anonymity and autofiction. Significantly, the only character whose name resembles a surname is Gazmuri, a representative of a generation that still believed in literature's capacity to articulate utopian discourses and grand narratives of knowledge legitimization.[128]

In the new century, as Bourriaud argues, there are no longer any great historical or mythical narratives; therefore, "no people and no proletariat" can claim the role of hero.[129] Zambra's characters are castaways of the grand narratives of modernity at a time when social discourses and aesthetic forms circulate in extreme volatility. Gazmuri distrusts Julio when the latter confesses that he writes on a computer instead of writing by hand, which the author of total novels about Chilean history associates with contemporary literature's brief and fragmentary format. "Do you write novels, those forty-page novels with short chapters that are so in fashion?"[130] Besides revealing the porosity of identities through characters without last names, in *Bonsái* Zambra demonstrates that, in the new century, aesthetic forms are constituted in a state of precariousness and vagueness, as fleeting constellations that admit the possibility of being continually reconstructed or updated.

Bonsái appeals to a nonlinear history model through its characters' wandering and displaced itineraries, antithetical to the idea of the root. Like the portable products of contemporary culture, the characters in *Bonsái* move in a floating world in which identities are in continuous mutation, in such a way that it becomes difficult to determine what prompts them to enter and leave the narrative plane. In the last chapter, for example, characters cross paths without interacting with one another. These failed encounters give the sense of a generation that embodies the privatization measures adopted by the Chilean neoliberal democracy: emotional disengagement, lack of motivation, and indifference to interpersonal communication. María is in Madrid when Emilia dies in circumstances that are never fully clarified. Gazmuri and Andrés find themselves in the same clinic without talking to each other, exemplifying the inability to build connections among members of different generations that causes the incomplete transmission of the dictatorship's memories.

The characters in *Bonsái* grow parallel to the miniature tree: in a certain direction, trapped with wires. The bonsai that Julio takes care of must resemble the one he has previously drawn: "The tree follows the course set by the wire. Sometime in the coming years, Julio figures, it will look, finally, like the drawing."[131] The forced growth of the bonsai could be read as a metonymy for the children's generation, who were educated in the context of a privatized school system set up by the dictatorship. Zambra's characters are children of neoliberalism whose lives and names are interchangeable because the system has lumped them all together.

The bonsai is also a portable tree that, toward the end of the novel, comes to designate a poetics of wandering or what Bourriaud refers to as radicant aesthetics. "The individual of these early years of the twenty-first century," Bourriaud observes, "resembles those plants that do not depend on a single root for their growth but advance in all directions on whatever surfaces present themselves by attaching multiple hooks to them, as ivy does."[132] This is how Zambra moves from describing a generation of children who were molded under the influence of wires to showing a series of uprooted adults whose trajectories have no origin or end. Upon learning of Emilia's suicide, Julio gets into a cab and asks the driver to "go any direction, go in circles, diagonally, doesn't matter."[133]

Like the impossible encounters between characters who do not know each other, the random cab ride obeys a movement contrary to the bonsai tree's restricted growth. The cab ride that gives the novel its anticlimactic ending disarticulates the teleological, revolutionary, and utopian time inhabited by the parents' generation. In *Bonsái* Zambra captures the predicament of the post-dictatorship generation, caught between remembrance and uprootedness, isolation and the need to connect with others. Oscillating between a novel and a short story, *Bonsái* takes up an aesthetic format resembling the unfinished identity of the children's generation. It puts together a nomadic way of thinking that inhabits, like Zambra's characters, the neoliberal period, marked by austerity, privatization, and the abandonment of long-term goals.

Literary form captures the contradictions of Latin America's insertion into the global order. The precarious form of these novels corresponds to the unfinished present that Latin American citizens experienced at the beginning of the millennium following the region's adoption of neoliberal economic policies. Valeria Luiselli represents the instability of the globalized present by creating a seamless exchange between New York City in the 1920s and Mexico City in the twenty-first century, between the possibility of a stable future that fell apart in 1929 and a present still haunted by the ghosts of modernity's failed promises symbolized by the momentous year of 2001. Alejandro Zambra reflects on the incomplete memory of the post-dictatorship generation through short texts that replicate the gaps in historical knowledge and characters with interchangeable names who struggle to make sense of the heavy burden passed down to them by their parents' generation. Both writers illustrate the inability of Latin American societies to move into the new century when they are still dealing with the ghosts of the recent past. Moreover, they depict cultures of oversaturation, which call writers to combine already existing signs in order to conjure the different futures—for society as well as for literature—that lie hidden in the past. By transforming the home from a familiar space into a topography of forgotten dramas and traumas, Luiselli and Zambra posit the estrangement of the past as the only possible way of inhabiting the present.

I started this book with the image of the ceiba and the *ombú* tree as metaphors for how Latin American writers are returning to the roots of the modern nation-state at a time of interlocked crises and unimaginable futures. In this chapter, I take the bonsai and the unnamed dry plant as metaphors for the Latin American literary tradition: how can literature dramatize transmission when history appears to have ended? According to the Spanish writer Enrique Vila-Matas, whom Luiselli and Zambra recognize as an important figure in the current revival of the avant-garde, "only those who write with an awareness of the end of literature can ensure its survival."[134] At a time of endings both writers update modernism's passion for the root, the clean slate, and the new beginning. In *Bonsái*, Zambra uses the modernist strategy of "pruning, purifying, eliminating, subtracting, returning to first principles." Similarly, Luiselli's wandering narrators inhabit tradition like nomadic subjects, using "preexisting structures" but "modifying them more or less extensively."[135] These writers break away from the image of tradition as a succession of ancestors and descendants, conceiving the past as an assembly table of discontinuous moments and heterogeneous materials. Both writers inscribe the modernist longing for the root within a globalized world cluttered with signs and floating signifiers. The imaginary of global translation gives way to texts that reproduce the dialogues between disparate locations, such as Zambra's adaptation of Japanese aesthetics through the figure of the bonsai.

By rescuing forgotten voices, anonymous lives, and minor events, Luiselli's and Zambra's novels are filiation narratives that show what lies in the folds of contemporary history. More than any other historical period, the present of the new millennium is experienced as a dead end, as a false recognition or déjà vu that incessantly repeats various moments of the past and, therefore, blocks any possibility of projecting one's gaze into the future. In contrast to the obsession with the future that characterized modernity, Hartog points out that contemporary societies move between amnesia and the desire to remember all the moments of the past without hierarchies or selective criteria, turning culture into a series of museum pieces.[136]

On the contrary, Luiselli and Zambra begin with the premise that restoring the past in all its plurality is impossible, configuring poetics of suspicion that destabilize our conception of the present by opposing linear narratives. In these novels they focus on the secondary actors of history, who experience the past as an enigma to be unraveled through archives composed of inherited stories, memories, and materials of diverse origins.[137] They produce hypothetical works that assemble kaleidoscopic visions of the past, conjuring it with the aim to produce an original narrative. For contemporary writers such as Luiselli and Zambra, searching for origins and restoring the transmission of part of a heritage experienced as an absence becomes the answer to how to reconceive literature after the end of history.

HISTORY IN THE PRESENT TENSE

In this study I have traced the diverse ways in which twenty-first-century Latin American novelists are weaving nonlinear relationships with history in order to escape apocalyptic discourses and the presentist organization of contemporary societies. In times of proliferating borders, economic imperialism, global epidemics, and religious fundamentalisms, the literary artists of the present have much to tell us about the mobile figures—migrants, refugees, and stateless people—who embody the vulnerability of those who do not enjoy the right to citizenship. In a different novel, one of the authors studied here takes up the concern to create new ways of relating to the past in order to perceive the futures that did not materialize and those that lie dormant in front of us.

Published in 2019, Valeria Luiselli's *Lost Children Archive* recounts a family's road trip from New York City to Apachería, where, in the second half of the nineteenth century, the Apache Indigenous tribes fought against the armed forces of the United States. This return to the past in times of temporal crisis evokes Rita Indiana's *La mucama de Omicunlé* and Pedro

Mairal's *El año del desierto*, in which these authors review and rewrite the history of their countries in a dystopian key so as to conjure the unfinished fabric of the nation-building past, which is a way of opening horizons of possibility in the face of our precarious present and uncertain future. In *Lost Children Archive*, the journey takes place against the backdrop of the Donald Trump administration's policies for the incarceration and deportation of migrant children at the United States–Mexico border. The parents want to form an "inventory of echoes" about the last Apaches and their leader Geronimo, while one of the two children riding in the car's back seat is learning to document the American landscape with a Polaroid camera.

In a section entitled "Future Present," the boy questions his mother about the meaning of documenting and what aspects of the landscape merit the camera's focus. The narrator raises her doubts about whether documenting means collecting "the present for posterity" when posterity, in the early decades of the twenty-first century, is no longer something to be taken for granted:

> Something changed in the world. Not too long ago, it changed, and we know it. We don't know how to explain it yet, but I think we all can feel it, somewhere deep in our gut or in our brain circuits. We feel time differently. No one has quite been able to capture what is happening or say why. Perhaps it's just that we sense an absence of future, because the present has become too overwhelming, so the future has become unimaginable. And without future, time feels like only an accumulation. An accumulation of months, days, natural disasters, television series, terrorist attacks, divorces, mass migrations, birthdays, photographs, sunrises. We haven't understood the exact way we are now experiencing time. And maybe the boy's frustration at not knowing what to take a picture of, or how to frame and focus the things he sees as we all sit inside the car, driving across this strange, beautiful, dark country, is simply a sign of how our ways of documenting the world have fallen short.[1]

This passage encapsulates the task of conceiving the present against the grain that is shared by the other authors in this study, who posit ways of thinking about the contemporary by resolving its ruptures with the past and the future.

Luiselli's novel conjures a new relationship with the archive, which is no longer experienced as a site closed to the public but, rather, as an open-air repository of materials organized in a non-hierarchical manner—unlike Borges's Library of Babel, which served as an image of modernity. Through the sound archaeology practiced by the narrator and her husband and the "linguistic archaeology" of the children, in *Lost Children Archive* Luiselli situates the precarious situation of migrant children in the *longue durée* of the crimes committed against the Apaches and the abuses against the environment.[2] The desert becomes an archive that transcends the realm of the human and the chronological conception of history through the material traces of the last Apaches and the objects with which to reconstruct the life and journey of the migrant children. Like the Argentinean countryside in Samanta Schweblin's *Distancia de rescate* or the Mexico City subway in Guadalupe Nettel's *El huésped*, the desert in *Lost Children Archive* is an archive of destruction that must be thoroughly inspected in order to build collective memories from which to derive new futures.

In *Lost Children Archive* Luiselli shares another of the fundamental attributes of the literatures of the present, which, at a time when book publishing is migrating toward digital formats, emphasize the materiality of writing and the book as a medium. Several of the novels I have analyzed in this study reveal the mechanisms of their own construction and turn the narrators into historical materialists who glimpse the potentiality of a fragmented and incomplete history. This is the case of the narrator of Luiselli's *Los ingrávidos*, who accumulates Post-it notes on which she registers her communion with the ghost of Gilberto Owen; the narrator of Verónica Gerber Bicecci's *Conjunto vacío*, who transforms the blank page into an artist's notebook; the narrator of Julián Fuks's *A resistência*, who uses ekphrastic writing to reproduce photographs of the disappeared; and the narrator of Alejandro Zambra's *Bonsái*, who spills coffee on the novel he is writing so as to highlight its material condition.

One of the narrators of *Lost Children Archive* compiles bibliographies, photo albums, and newspaper clippings like a detective who, in traces of the past, perceives new ways of ordering the future. Two central figures of Benjamin's *The Arcades Project* appear in *Lost Children Archive*: the collector and the child. On the one hand, Luiselli has constructed the novel from brief fragments resembling index cards and from boxes containing maps, photographs, and mortality reports of migrants, which form a patchwork of references or productive chaos. On the other hand, she raises the issue of the intergenerational transmission of experience through the children as "anthropologists studying cosmogonic narratives" and delving into family genealogies to construct their own stories of filiation.[3]

Many of the novels I have analyzed here can be read through the interplay between the deep time of geological scales and nation-building and the more recent past of dictatorial violence and neoliberal crisis. To provide a brief example, the mothers' quest for environmental justice in Schweblin's *Distancia de rescate* can be read along two axes. On the one hand, the novel can be interpreted through the lens of nineteenth-century state formation and the legacy of the racial whitening policies embraced by the fathers of the Argentinean nation. This reading underscores land distribution among a few wealthy families of European origin, the creation of the myth of a white Argentina, and the extermination of Indigenous communities in order to repopulate the pampas and bring industrial capitalism. On the other hand, the novel echoes the search for human rights carried out by the Mothers and Grandmothers of Plaza de Mayo since the 1970s and by the Grupos de Madres de Barrio Ituzaingó Anexo since 2001. Besides the still unfulfilled search for the remains of the disappeared carried out by several mothers and grandmothers, Latin America's necropolitical present is populated by the struggles for environmental justice concerning the drift of toxic agrochemicals in marginalized neighborhoods. This reading of *Distancia de rescate* considers the adoption of soy monocultures in the early 2000s as the engine of the national economy—what Leguizamón calls the *sojiización* (soyification) of Argentinean agricultural production.[4] In both readings, the novel puts together forms of thinking about the nation-state through the perspective of female guardians who prioritize long-term care for both the children and the land in an effort to remediate the effects of short-term policies of economic growth. Schweblin combines both temporal scales in her novel and delineates the contemporary as the point that metabolizes the modern nation's pasts, presents, and futures.

The collective construction of a lexicon on the contemporary becomes evident when the narrator of *Lost Children Archive* talks about the "rescue distance" that separates her from her daughter. "A friend of mine calls this 'the rescue distance'—the constant equation operating in a parent's mind, where time and distance are factored in to calculate whether it would be possible to save a child from danger."[5] This explicit reference to Schweblin's novel also appears in books that are representative of what Zambra calls the literature of the children.

Consider Nona Fernández's *La dimensión desconocida* (trans. 2021 as *The Twilight Zone*), in which she documents the unfinished present of the Chilean post-dictatorship period through the testimony of a man who tortured political dissidents during the Pinochet regime. More than reconstructing the torturer's story, Fernández uses his testimony to piece together the surviving fragments of the victims' lives. In the Chilean post-dictatorship present, Fernández recontextualizes many of the expressions and words used by Schweblin to dramatize the effects of environmental toxicity, such as "rescue distance" and the metaphor of a loose thread. The narrator imagines the last minutes of a disappeared person using the conditional tense, speculating on "the unbroken thread of history" that unites the children of post-dictatorship and penetrating "that place beyond rescue distance" that ties together the torturer's victims.[6] Like Fuks's *A resistência* and Gerber Bicecci's *Conjunto vacío*, *La dimensión desconocida* reflects on literature's capacity to access the "hidden dimension" of the victims' experience. Besides turning to photography, Fernández resorts to verse to make sense of the torturer's words, "searching for clues—remarks the narrator—that might help me decipher their message."[7] Fernández assembles a museum of post-dictatorial memory and converses with Zambra through their joint account of significant historical events in Pinochet's Chile, such as the appearance of the Mexican comedian Chespirito in 1977 at the Estadio Nacional when the stadium still served as a concentration camp for political prisoners. This event is a recurrent motif in the Chilean post-dictatorship because it points to the hidden reality of the Pinochet years, which children can access only retroactively.

Finally, Luiselli's turn toward English-language writing reveals unprecedented hemispheric dialogues and the formation of a shared vocabulary for our neoliberal end times. Luiselli has spearheaded a recent trend that sees US Latino novels engaging with diverse Latin American literary traditions in order to consider the continent as a platform for the aesthetic and political imagination of crisis. Among these works, Michael Zapata's *The Lost Book of Adana Moreau* (2020) is an apocalyptic novel that takes the circum-Caribbean—the region stretching from the Dominican Republic to New Orleans—as "a stage setting for the Americas."[8] Hurricane Katrina serves as backdrop for a contemporary history of disaster that the narrator traces to the Pinochet dictatorship and the Argentinean Great Recession. For Zapata's narrator, disaster is "the infrastructure of the world," which is exemplified by "the Lago Agrio oil fields in Ecuador, the Tepito neighborhood of Mexico City[,] . . . the collapsing financial center of Buenos Aires, the aftermath of the great deluge of New Orleans."[9]

In *The Lost Book* Zapata connects the Americas through the shared experience of the end times brought about by extractivism, socioeconomic precariousness, and environmental catastrophe—all symptoms of the continent's embrace of neoliberal economic policies. More important, he does so by taking up the Latin American tradition of books within books cemented by Borges and Bolaño: Adana Moreau, the author of an early and forgotten sci-fi novel, is the ghost of the avant-garde that returns to redefine the contours of the present. As in Indiana's *La mucama de Omicunlé*, Zapata foregrounds the strong purchase of the weird and H. P. Lovecraft's works in the Caribbean, where reality is made up of "multiple dimensions" and the end of the world emerges from the depths of the sea. In *The Lost Book* he conceives the planetary imagination out of the impossibility of utopian thinking in an age of ecological catastrophe, not through Latin America's dreams of integration into the global economy, depicting the contemporary as "that fragile space between the past and the future."[10]

The narrator of *Lost Children Archive* observes that it is difficult to differentiate the present from the past or future at a time of continual commodity renewal and programmed obsolescence. "Beginnings," she says, "get confused with endings."[11] Contemporary Latin American authors are constructing fables of beginnings that are distanced from apocalyptic discourses about the end times. As they engage in the search for future presents and past futures, the readers of these fictions become direct participants in the history of the present. As I write the last lines of this book, the COVID-19 pandemic has caused the deaths of thousands of people, the most significant recession in history, the closing of borders, and the mandatory confinement of one-third of the planet. Faced with a time devoid of prospects and horizons of justice, the literary artists of the present stand against the end times and give humanity back its tools for critical thinking.

NOTES

INTRODUCTION: THE RETURN OF THE CONTEMPORARY

1. Klein, *Shock Doctrine*, 104.

2. "Había un engaño de que estábamos en el primer mundo. Se aceleraron las historias de deterioro. Todo se terminó de romper." Mairal quoted in Gutiérrez, "Pedro Mairal, escritor." Unless otherwise indicated, henceforth all translations from sources in languages other than English will be my own. When an English translation is available, I will give the source reference for the quote in English.

3. Despite this turn away from irony and pastiche as privileged aesthetic modes, Latin American writers continue to use postmodern strategies to make sense of the region's outstanding debts with its violent past. For example, the post-dictatorship novels that I analyze in the book's second part are examples of what Linda Hutcheon calls "historiographic metafiction." She contends that "the past is only known to us today through its textualized traces (which, like all texts, are always open to interpretation)." Hutcheon, *Politics of Postmodernism*, 78. I am not suggesting that postmodernism is inherently apolitical since, as John Beverley and José Oviedo remarked, postmodern aesthetic experience can be "both a place of resistance to actually existing forms of domination and exploitation and an enactment of new forms of community." Beverley and Oviedo, "Introduction," 11.

4. This archeological stance against the present is in line with Michel Foucault's notion of the archeology of knowledge. For him, archival work presupposes an attempt to make visible "the border of time that surrounds our presence, which overhangs it, and which indicates it in its otherness; it is that which, outside ourselves, delimits us." Foucault, *Archaeology of Knowledge*, 130.

5. Hartog, *Regimes of Historicity*, 204.

6. Virno, *Déjà Vu and the End of History*, 40.

7. The authors whose work I analyze throughout this book share the turn toward the untimely that Idelber Avelar diagnosed in his groundbreaking book, *The Untimely Present: Postdictatorial Latin American Fiction and the Task of Mourning*.

Avelar argues that post-dictatorial Latin American writers put together allegories of defeat in which "the untimely takes distance from the present, estranges itself from it by carrying and caring for the seeds of time. An untimely reading of the present will, then, at the same time rescue past defeats out of oblivion and remain open to an as yet unimaginable future." Avelar, *Untimely Present*, 20–21. As opposed to the authors of the immediate post-dictatorship, however, contemporary Latin American writers reflect less on defeat than on the irrecoverable traces of the post-dictatorial archive, since they were only children when the military regimes rose to power in the 1970s and 1980s.

8. Zambra, *Bonsai*, 62.

9. Lerner, *Leaving the Atocha Station*, 8.

10. McCarthy, *Satin Island*, 116.

11. Lerner, *Topeka School*, 271.

12. See Héctor Hoyos, *Beyond Bolaño: The Global Latin American Novel*; Ignacio Sánchez Prado, *Strategic Occidentalism: On Mexican Fiction, the Neoliberal Book Market, and the Question of World Literature*; Mariano Siskind, *Cosmopolitan Desires: Global Modernity and World Literature in Latin America*; Gesine Müller, *How Is World Literature Made? The Global Circulations of Latin American Literature*.

13. Smith, *What Is Contemporary Art?*, 3–4.

14. The notion of "expanded field" in contemporary Latin American literature has been explored in depth by Florencia Garramuño and Reinaldo Laddaga. Garramuño speaks of the "worlds in common" of contemporary aesthetic practices that stand "contra la propia noción de campo como espacio estático y cerrado." Florencia Garramuño, *Mundos en común: ensayos sobre la inespecificidad en el arte*, 43. Laddaga, borrowing a phrase from César Aira's *Las noches de Flores*, refers to the "espectáculos de realidad" that contemporary fictions mount through "dispositivos de exhibición de fragmentos de mundo." Laddaga, *Espectáculos de realidad*, 14.

15. See Rancière, *El reparto de lo sensible*, 20.

16. "De la página al cuerpo, de la palabra al espacio, al lugar; de la frase al suceso, a la acción; de la novela a la vida escenificada." Gerber Bicecci, *Mudanza*, 17–18.

17. Bourriaud, *Relational Aesthetics*, 13. When using the concept of relational aesthetics, I am less focused on "the 'relations' that are produced by relational art works" (which Claire Bishop has sharply critiqued) than on the links between open-ended formats and the positing of history as a contested space that is pregnant with possibilities. Bishop, "Antagonism and Relational Aesthetics," 64.

18. Bourriaud, *Exform*, x.

19. Bourriaud, *Postproduction*, 17; Bourriaud, *Radicant*, 22.

20. Bourriaud, *Radicant*, 19.

21. Bourriaud, *Postproduction*, 18.

22. Bourriaud, *Relational Aesthetics*, 15.

23. Ruffel, *Brouhaha*, 92.

24. The Second World War had immediate consequences in the field of history, since it inaugurated a new contemporaneity marked by pessimism and melancholy. According to Henry Rousso, contemporaneity must be measured on the basis of the most recent catastrophe since "our own regime of historicity is defined in great part by the difficulty of getting over the memory of the recent major catastrophes, hence of reestablishing a certain historical continuity of longer duration." Rousso, *Latest Catastrophe*, 12.

25. Giunta, *¿Cúando empieza el arte contemporáneo?*, 118.

26. Bishop, *Artificial Hells*, 9. Enrique Vila-Matas points out that some installations by French artist Dominique Gonzalez-Foerster belong to the field of expanded literature, which he defines in the following terms: "Me gusta sentir que he hecho algo que se ha situado en los límites al buscar profundizar en las posibilidades, que sé amplísimas, del propio término de novela. . . . DGF se comporta con sus escenografías de un modo parecido. Todo a priori le parece susceptible de entrar a formar parte de la obra, como si pensara que para crear hay que tirar de un hilo, y después de otro. . . . De hecho, ella—tal como dijera la ensayista Ana Pato—ha encontrado 'otras formas de escribir novelas' y viene practicando desde hace tiempo el arte de la literatura expandida." Vila-Matas, *Marienbad eléctrico*, 36.

27. See Smith, *What Is Contemporary Art?*, 5.

28. See Smith, *Art to Come*, 301.

29. Koselleck, *Sediments of Time*, 7.

30. Gerstle, *Rise and Fall*, 2.

31. Gerstle, *Rise and Fall*, 73.

32. Klein, *Shock Doctrine*, 8.

33. For an analysis of artistic and literary responses to Chilean neoliberalism, especially through the lens of moral and sexual perversion, see Blanco, *Neoliberal Bonds*.

34. Gerstle, *Rise and Fall*, 279.

35. In revisiting the notion of postmodernism, Fredric Jameson argues that, more than a style as such, postmodernity is a historical period that came to replace the modern era: "Modernity, in the sense of modernization and progress, or *telos*, was now definitely over." Jameson, "Aesthetics of Singularity," 104.

36. In conceiving the strategy of return as an antidote to neoliberalism's crisis of futurity, I draw from Dan Sinykin's concept of neoliberal apocalypse. "Apocalypse is a political literary form," Sinykin argues, "[that] writers adopted . . . in an attempt to resolve what felt like insurmountable crises for political agency[,] . . . the attempts are an indispensable archive that reveal the textures of life, and the meanings of literature, under neoliberalism." Sinykin, *American Literature and the Long Downturn*, 2.

37. The term "Anthropocene" was coined by the ecologist Eugene Stoermer in the 1980s and popularized in the 2000s by the chemist Paul Crutzen. For a definition of the concept of the Anthropocene, see Crutzen, "Geology of Mankind," 23. According to Dipesh Chakrabarty, "the Anthropocene requires us to think on two different scales of time that earth history and world history respectively involve: the tens of millions of years that a geological epoch usually encompasses . . . versus the five hundred years at most that can be said to constitute the history of capitalism." Chakrabarty, *Climate of History in a Planetary Age*, 156.

38. Pratt, *Planetary Longings*, 61.

39. See Gerstle, *Rise and Fall*, 237–40.

40. See Pratt, *Planetary Longings*, 66.

41. Rancière, *Modern Times*, 18.

42. Arendt, *Between Past and Future*, 4. René Char's aphorism first appeared in *Feuillets d'Hypnos* (1946), a collection of epigrammatic texts that he wrote during the Nazi Occupation of France. For the original source, see Char, *Feuillets d'Hypnos*, 190. For an interpretation of Arendt's reading of Char, see Hartog, *Regimes of Historicity*, 4.

43. Didi-Huberman is in the tradition of Henri Focillon and George Kubler, who also thought about the relationship between image and history dialectically and anachronistically. More recently, Alexander Nagel and Christopher Wood complexify the models of time through which the history of images is studied by considering the layered temporality of Renaissance artifacts and artworks. See Focillon, *Life of Forms in Art*; Kubler, *Shape of Things*; Nagel and Wood, *Anachronic Renaissance*; Nagel, *Medieval Modern*.

44. Didi-Huberman, *Surviving Image*, 318.

45. "Los debates actuales sobre el 'fin de la historia' y—paralelamente—sobre el fin del arte, son burdos y están mal planteados." Didi-Huberman, *Ante el tiempo*, 48.

46. Didi-Huberman, *Ante el tiempo*, 64.

47. Didi-Huberman, *Surviving Image*, 49.

48. Didi-Huberman, *Surviving Image*, 308.

49. For Franco "Bifo" Berardi, the collapse of the welfare state signified the arrival of an era of impotence, characterized by paralysis, the proliferation of dystopian imaginaries, and the feeling that "our suffering cannot be relieved by political projects, but only by psychopharmacology." Berardi, *Futurability*, 44.

50. "Nuevo mundo"; "los moldes, géneros y especies"; "la fábrica de la realidad." Ludmer, *Aquí América Latina*, 9, 12.

51. The notion of "cognitive mapping" was coined by Jameson to refer to the process by which individuals situate themselves within an "unrepresentable totality." Jameson, *Postmodernism*, 51. The disorienting historicity of the postmodern age derives from the recent conquering of two realms that remained untouched by the reign of capital: nature and the unconscious. Cognitive mapping allows

people to bridge the gap between past and present, thus enabling a critique of the global system.

52. "Laguna temporal"; "comienzo del fin"; "el presente es memoria y *déjà vu*: una duplicación del pasado." Ludmer, *Aquí América Latina*, 25.

53. José Donoso referred to the Boom writers as orphans who embraced global influences in national contexts promoting realist aesthetics. "Éramos huérfanos," he observes, "pero esta orfandad, esta posición de rechazo a lo forzadamente 'nuestro' en que nos pusieron los novelistas que nos precedieron, produjo en nosotros un vacío. . . . Me parece que nada ha enriquecido tanto a mi generación como esta falta de padres literarios propios." Donoso, *Historia personal del "boom"*, 27.

54. González Echevarría, *Myth and Archive*, 18, 181.

55. González Echevarría, *Myth and Archive*, 183.

56. Ruffel, *Brouhaha*, 159.

57. Blanco, *Ghost-Watching American Modernity*, 4. Similarly, Jobst Welge and Juliane Tauchnitz argue that literary studies scholars need to approach novels through spatiotemporal perspectives to conceive "landscape as historically layered, haunted, marked by material ruins, and filtered through previous cultural representations or literary models." Welge and Tauchnitz, "Introduction," 2.

58. Borges, "Library of Babel," 85.

59. Boym, *Future of Nostalgia*, 41.

60. Luiselli, *Faces in the Crowd*, 88.

61. In this sense, they stand against the critique of memory discourse put forward by Charles Hatfield, who raises suspicions about the politics of memory and its "affective identification with people in the past at the expense of a class-based identification with people in the present." He considers "memory as an epiphenomenon of neoliberalism rather than a mode of resistance to it." Hatfield, *Limits of Identity*, 80.

62. Wylie, *Poetics of Plants in Spanish American Literature*, 4; Vieira, "*Phytographia*," 215. Italics in the original.

63. "Un libro es una forma de regreso: una refamiliarización y una reparación." Rivera Garza, *Autobiografía del algodón*, 202.

64. Premat, *Érase esta vez*; Premat, *Non nova sed nove*.

65. "Una exterioridad, una diferenciación, una distancia, como únicas maneras de pensarlo y de participar en él." Premat, *Non nova sed nove*, 67–68.

66. "Configuraciones todavía inaccesibles a otros lenguajes." Speranza, *Cronografías*, 20.

67. Ruffel, *Brouhaha*, 24; Brouillette, Nilges, and Sauri, "Contemporaneity," xvii.

68. The contemporaries share more than one trait with the group of writers that Antoine Compagnon has called antimoderns, even though the term "antimodern" suggests a relationship of continuity with modernism and modernity.

Members of a constellation that goes from François-René de Chateaubriand to Julien Gracq, passing through Joris-Karl Huysmans, the antimoderns are subjects who place themselves in a position out of phase with respect to their own epoch, in what Barthes called "the rear guard of the avant-garde." Barthes, "Responses," 262. According to Compagnon, the most outstanding features of the antimoderns are "le doute, l'ambivalence, la nostalgie," which is why even today "nous tendons à voir les antimodernes comme plus modernes que les modernes et que les avant-gardes historiques: en quelque sorte ultramodernes, ils ont maintenant l'air plus contemporains et proches de nous parce qu'ils étaient plus désabusés." Compagnon, *Les antimodernes*, 11–12.

69. See Nietzsche, *Untimely Meditations*, 83.

70. Agamben, "What Is the Contemporary?," 47.

71. Agamben, "What Is the Contemporary?," 44. The gender specific pronoun appears in the original but refers to all genders.

72. See Smith, *Art to Come*, 282.

73. Nietzsche, *Untimely Meditations*, 75, 83.

74. Nietzsche, *Untimely Meditations*, 76.

75. "Un concepto historiográfico (como 'Barroco' o 'Renacimiento') con implicaciones metodológicas . . . más flexible y útil que el de 'posmoderno,' empleado para caracterizar una especie de superación de la modernidad." Domínguez Hernández, Fernández, Giraldo, and Tobón, "Presentación," 7.

76. "Un mosaico, un caleidoscopio de tiempos diferidos." Thayer, "Para un concepto heterocrónico de lo contemporáneo," 21.

77. Pedrosa, Klinger, Wolff, and Cámara, *Indiccionario de lo contemporáneo*, 191.

78. Hoyos and Librandi-Rocha, "Theories of the Contemporary in South America," 97, 99.

79. See Didi-Huberman, *Ante el tiempo*, 204.

80. Bloch, *Heritage of Our Times*, 3.

CHAPTER 1: THE RETURN OF NATURE

1. Although the 2001 socioeconomic meltdown is a landmark moment in the history of pot-banging as a form of protest, *cacerolazos* were used in Chile in the 1970s to protest food shortages during the Salvador Allende administration and later, in the 1980s, to stand against Pinochet's regime in the countdown to the 1988 national plebiscite, which led to the country's return to democracy.

2. "Desigualdad del tiempo." *Real Academia Española*, 23rd ed. (Madrid: Espasa, 2016), s.v. "Intemperie."

3. Elsa Drucaroff coined the expression "narraciones de la intemperie" to refer to the fictions that were written in light of the 2001 crisis in Argentina, which, in her words, embraced "la intemperie como condición latente de la escritura, de

la existencia, del país, incluso de cualquier construcción posible de algo nuevo." Drucaroff, "Narraciones de la intemperie."

4. For a comprehensive analysis of the notion of intemperie in contemporary aesthetic practices, see La Rocca and Neuburger, *Figuras de la intemperie.* Julio Ariza captures the transversal nature of the word *intemperie* when, in his analysis of the post-2001 Argentinean novel, he remarks that "en 'intemperie' podemos encontrar un aspecto espacial (estar afuera), climático (estar a merced de elementos naturales hostiles), y afectivo (sentirse a la intemperie, abandonado a ese afuera cambiante, inmoderado)." Ariza, *El abandono,* 101.

5. Although I refer to the book's Spanish title, I quote from the English translation of Indiana's novel.

6. Pratt gives the example of states in the western United States that in May 2001 "seemed to be turning back into the frontier: Euro-Americans were migrating out, and the land was reverting to an uncultivated state. Buffalo were making a comeback." Pratt, *Planetary Longings,* 70. This return to the American frontier (as will become clear throughout my analysis of *El año del desierto*) also resonates with the imagination of crisis in post-2001 Argentina.

7. Through an analysis of the texts of the Zapatista movement, whose authors propose paradoxical temporal figures such as "advancing backwards," Robin posits this strategy of non-contemporaneity as "indispensable para quebrar la ilusión del fin de la historia y reabrir la perspectiva de un porvenir que no sea la repetición del presente." Robin, *La memoria saturada,* 54.

8. "Las adivinas nos agarraban la mano y podían adivinarnos todos los detalles de nuestro pasado, pero no eran capaces ni de decirnos si nos íbamos a morir al día siguiente." Mairal, *El año del desierto,* 141.

9. In this sense, *El año del desierto* should be placed alongside a series of works that in the 1990s gave an account of such changes in the social acceleration of time: among them, *Por favor, rebobinar* (1994) by Alberto Fuguet and *La velocidad de las cosas* (1998) by Rodrigo Fresán. For a critical theory of social acceleration in late-stage capitalism, see Rosa, *Alienación y aceleración,* 15–65.

10. For contemporary debates about the end of literature, see Premat, *Non nova sed nove,* 106.

11. "Precios superpuestos." Mairal, *El año del desierto,* 27.

12. Steiner, *Grammars of Creation,* 6–7.

13. Ruffel, *Brouhaha,* 13.

14. Virno, *Déjà vu,* 8. Italics in the original.

15. Brown, *Undoing the Demos,* 37.

16. "Capitalismo salvaje." Mairal, *El año del desierto,* 199.

17. Ursula K. Heise situates *El año del desierto* within a larger corpus of Latin American novels that document vanishing cities as a result of climate change and socio-environmental injustice. Some of these works include Ignácio de Loyola Brandão's *Não verás país nenhum* (1981) and Gioconda Belli's *Waslala* (1996),

which she reads as political allegories of Latin America's urban crises. Of particular interest is her analysis of María's dog, which has cameos throughout the narrative, as an example of what she calls "multispecies justice." Moreover, Heise compares *El año del desierto*'s slow apocalypse with the imagination of spectacular destruction featured in North American literary works. Heise, "Vanishing Metropolis," 91–92.

18. For an analysis of the dialectical images posited by Mairal's novel, see Zimmer, "Year in Rewind."

19. "Un hormiguero de tipos hambrientos." Mairal, *El año del desierto*, 268.

20. "Morocho, con rasgos fuertes." Mairal, *El año del desierto*, 10.

21. "Años de espejismo." Mairal, *El año del desierto*, 13.

22. "Fenómeno duradero." Mairal, *El año del desierto*, 13–14.

23. "Algún día [la relación] se iba a terminar porque no podía durar siendo los dos tan distintos." Mairal, *El año del desierto*, 22.

24. For an analysis of the novel through the derangements of scale brought about by the Anthropocene, see Knobloch, "Globalization Reversed."

25. "Sentía que los cuerpos que lavaba y cuidaba eran siempre el mismo cuerpo. Un mismo cuerpo que ayudaba a curar para que pudiera irse y reaparecía enfermo, baleado, humillado, sucio, y otra vez había que limpiarlo, desinfectarlo, atenderlo para que volviera a salir y lo volvieran a mandar destrozado." Mairal, *El año del desierto*, 84.

26. Virno, *Déjà vu*, 7–8.

27. "Contiene todos los pasados y también el futuro, que 'ya fue.'" Ludmer, *Aquí América Latina*, 96.

28. "Cuando un cuerpo padece, sale del tiempo de la historia, pierde su posibilidad de proyectarse hacia adelante, borra las señales de sus recuerdos." Sarlo, *Tiempo presente*, 17.

29. "Mapa de la desidia." Mairal, *El año del desierto*, 78.

30. *Cocoliche* is a slang that mixes Spanish with Italian from northern and southern Italy, created as a result of the long waves of Italian immigration that arrived in Argentina between 1880 and 1930. Many of these words and expressions are still part of the Spanish spoken in Río de la Plata today.

31. "Meditación de lo viejo en lo nuevo, de la vejez en lo contemporáneo." Martínez Estrada, *Sarmiento*, 112. "Conquistador venido a menos." Martínez Estrada, *Radiografía de la pampa*, 32. "Ocultas fuerzas tectónicas." Martínez Estrada, *Sarmiento*, 54.

32. "Debajo de la ciudad, siempre había estado latente el descampado." Mairal, *El año del desierto*, 156.

33. Hans Ulrich Gumbrecht uses the notion of "broad present" to describe the "expanding" or "spreading" time that we are currently inhabiting; a present that, by absorbing all the pasts of recent history, has been transformed into a temporality without defined contours. Gumbrecht, *Our Broad Present*, xiii.

34. Sarlo, *Tiempo presente*, 114.

35. "Una sociedad volcada a revolver en sus basuras." Gorelik, *Miradas sobre Buenos Aires*, 247.

36. According to Hartog, presentism (as opposed to the modern imaginary of Italian futurism) is the regime of historicity proper to the contemporary world, an omnivorous present in which only immediacy has value. On the other hand, Hartog links presentism to the situation of mass unemployment in contemporary societies, which has established a time without past or future. Hartog, *Regimes of Historicity*, xviii, 113. Jonathan Crary argues that neoliberal capitalism has established a temporality of continuous functioning and duration without pauses, rendering obsolete the "distinctions between day and night, between light and dark, and between action and repose." Crary, *24/7*, 17.

37. "Irreconocible, mugriento, hecho harapos." Mairal, *El año del desierto*, 271.

38. Agamben, "What Is the Contemporary?," 49.

39. Premat, "La literatura hoy," 338.

40. "La constitución del Estado como un proceso lineal orientado por las fuerzas del progreso." Rodríguez, *Un desierto para la nación*, 362.

41. Martín-Barbero, "Dislocaciones del tiempo y nuevas topografías de la memoria," 142.

42. Huyssen, *Twilight Memories*, 6–7.

43. Huyssen, *Twilight Memories*, 7.

44. García Márquez, *One Hundred Years of Solitude*, 43–44.

45. García Márquez, *One Hundred Years of Solitude*, 48.

46. García Márquez, *One Hundred Years of Solitude*, 47.

47. "Coma catódico"; "televidentes compulsivos." Mairal, *El año del desierto*, 76.

48. "Nostalgia de lo contemporáneo, de un presente que adopta la textura de lo que se halla al borde de su extinción." Montoya Juárez, "Hacia una arqueología del presente," 281.

49. "A la tumba de los electrodomésticos toda la memoria de vida." Mairal, *El año del desierto*, 12.

50. Gago, *Neoliberalism from Below*, 6.

51. Bourriaud, *Postproduction*, 29, 28.

52. "Situarnos en un momento cultural marcado por la inestabilidad, la superposición y la rapidez." Premat, *Érase esta vez*, 12.

53. "A veces tengo que encerrarme acá para hablar sin que me vean, sin que me oigan, tengo que decir frases que había perdido y que ahora reaparecen y me ayudan a cubrir el pastizal, a superponer la luz de mi lengua natal sobre esta luz traducida donde respiro cada día. Y es como volver sin moverme, volver en castellano, entrar de nuevo a casa. Eso no se deshizo, no se perdió; el desierto no me comió la lengua." Mairal, *El año del desierto*, 8.

54. Huyssen, *After the Great Divide*, 162.

55. "Catedrales y castillos"; "fuera de tiempo"; "las cosas no cambian." Mairal, *El año del desierto*, 7–8.

56. "Salvación." Gersende, "El oficio de traducir," 451. Several critics have explored the idea of the end of literature in relation to the emergence of other apocalyptic discourses such as the end of the book, of the humanities, and more broadly, of Western civilization. See Viart and Demanze, *Fins de la littérature*. Likewise, the end of literature (or of a certain type of literature) has been explored in discussions about the return of the real or the return of experience. See Premat, *Non nova*.

57. Dabove and Hallstead, "Introducción," xvii.

58. "La imagen de una generación sin maestros, que crece en una suerte de intemperie simbólica, o la de un grupo de imberbes Robinsones que sobreviven al naufragio del siglo XX y deben empezarlo todo otra vez." Guerrero, *Paisajes en movimiento*, 45.

59. For an analysis of this group of writers as a displaced generation, see Pérez, "El payador absoluto."

60. "A un estado de vacilación, de tartamudeo, de paradoja. A un exilio permanente, a la duda sobre la propia noción de original"; "La exterioridad como experiencia literaria." Tabarovsky, *Literatura de izquierda*, 37, 39.

61. Bourriaud, *Postproduction*, 18.

62. The fact that María is a woman and that she travels both in time and space is relevant, since modern republics were represented with the image of a woman. The name María, moreover, is easily translatable into the Irish Catholic Mary/Mery. In this sense, Drucaroff points out, the fact that María is a woman reverses the nineteenth-century travelers' accounts, since "ni por asomo la protagonista de semejante periplo hubiera sido una mujer en el imaginario de los siglos anteriores." Drucaroff, *Los prisioneros de la torre*, 487.

63. "Pertenece a la literatura de la comunidad inoperante, integra la comunidad de los que no tienen comunidad." Tabarovsky, *Literatura de izquierda*, 20.

64. "Desherencia." Premat, *Non nova*, 71–72.

65. "Fabricar presente." Ludmer, *Aquí América Latina*, 149; Virno, *Déjà vu*, 189.

66. "Hubiera querido que el ombú me tragara, que las raíces se cerraran sobre mí, como en los cuentos para chicos. . . . Quería quedarme en el árbol, hacer del árbol mi casa." Mairal, *El año del desierto*, 127.

67. The passage from *La cautiva* describes the *ombú* as the home of all types of birds that live in the middle of the desert: "Fórmale grata techumbre / La copa extensa y tupida / de un ombú donde se anida / la altiva águila real; / y la varia muchedumbre / de aves que cría el desierto / se pone en ella a cubierto / del frío y sol estival." Echeverría, *Poemas varios*, 134.

68. "Un sistema errático." Glissant, *Filosofía de la relación*, 67.

69. Glissant, *Caribbean Discourse*, 64, 65.

70. See DeLoughrey, *Allegories of the Anthropocene*, 18.

71. Indiana, *Tentacle*, 12, 47.

72. Ramírez, *Colonial Phantoms*, 6.

73. García-Peña, *Borders of Dominicanidad*, 10.

74. Indiana, *Tentacle*, 17.

75. Indiana, *Tentacle*, 15.

76. Hartog, *Regimes of Historicity*, 3.

77. Indiana, *Tentacle*, 55.

78. Haraway, *Staying with the Trouble*, 101.

79. Haraway, *Staying with the Trouble*, 31.

80. "La identidad caribeña lleva 500 años sin terminar de coagular y sigue absorbiendo elementos. Es una materia esponjosa y viva." "No hace falta ser Nostradamus para adivinar el futuro, basta ser Rita Indiana."

81. Indiana, *Tentacle*, 128.

82. Indiana, *Tentacle*, 132.

83. Indiana, *Tentacle*, 98, 99.

84. Indiana, *Tentacle*, 99, 100.

85. Benítez-Rojo, *Repeating Island*, 11.

86. Indiana, *Tentacle*, 105.

87. Deckard and Oloff, "'One Who Comes from the Sea,'" 9.

88. Haraway, *Staying with the Trouble*, 52.

89. Haraway, *Staying with the Trouble*, 51.

90. García-Peña, *Borders of Dominicanidad*, 157.

91. Cabrera, "Ceiba Tree," 234. Charlotte Rogers explores the tribute that Indiana pays Cabrera through the appearance of an apocryphal manuscript penned by the Cuban ethnographer and the importance of queerness and Santería in the novel: "both Cabrera and Indiana produce queer, polyphonic texts that draw deeply on Santería and valorize peoples excluded from the upper classes of white heterosexual Hispanic Caribbean society." Rogers, "Rita Indiana's Queer Interspecies Caribbean."

92. del Cid, "Descuido y vegetación amenazan la Ceiba de Colón."

93. Glissant, *Caribbean Discourse*, 62. Indiana is not the only Caribbean writer who has used the figure of intemperie to refer to the temporal dispossession of contemporary subjects. Eduardo Lalo develops a fragmented writing style that reflects the experience of walking the streets of San Juan, Puerto Rico, while feeling like a "náufrago" and seeking "una vida fuera de las estructuras de dominio para vivir a la intemperie." Lalo, *Intemperie*, 31.

94. Ginwala and Ziherl, "Sensing Grounds."

95. Indiana, *Tentacle*, 124.

96. "Reciclaje barroco." Rogers, "'El ágora entre manglares,'" 292.

97. Glissant, *Caribbean Discourse*, 14.

98. Bourriaud, *Radicant*, 22.

99. Vazquez, "Learning to Live in Miami," 860.

100. Indiana, *Tentacle*, 116, 115.

101. Lauro and Embry, "Zombie Manifesto," 90.

102. Glissant, *Poetics of Relation*, 32.

103. As Mimi Sheller points out, the island of Hispaniola "faces common ecological crises connected to global warming, deforestation, soil loss, depleted coral reefs and mangrove forests, growing intensity of hurricanes due to sea surface warming, and threats to biodiversity. These issues are likely only to worsen as climate change continues to affect the entire Caribbean region." However, Haitians are especially at risk because their side of the island is more densely populated and suffers from greater income inequality. Sheller, *Island Futures*, 108.

104. Indiana, *Tentacle*, 58.

105. Benjamin, *Arcades Project*, 473.

106. Garrido Castellano, *Literary Fictions of the Contemporary Art System*, 111.

107. Indiana, *Tentacle*, 64.

108. Smith, *Art to Come*, 324.

109. Indiana, *Tentacle*, 111.

110. Foster, *Bad New Days*, 34.

111. Shklovsky, *Viktor Shklovsky*, 352.

112. Wall, "Visual Dimension of *El siglo de las luces*," 156.

113. Indiana, *Tentacle*, 112.

114. Foster, *Bad New Days*, 52.

115. Indiana, *Tentacle*, 113.

116. Indiana, *Tentacle*, 117, 119.

117. According to Marjorie Perloff, contemporary poetry is characterized by a series of procedures (appropriation, quotation, copying, and reproduction) that destabilize the notions of originality and artistic genius and that have their precedents in the aesthetic practice of Marcel Duchamp, the concrete art movement of the 1950s and 1960s, Oulipo (*Ouvroir de littérature potentielle*), and the translational poetics of works such as Ezra Pound's *Cantos*. These are aesthetic practices that, according to Perloff, have their own "momentum and inventio" and call for "dissociating the word original from its partner genius." Perloff, *Unoriginal Genius*, 21. In the same way, Kenneth Goldsmith shows how certain contemporary practices, including his own, displace the concept of creativity by working with digital culture's own procedures such as sampling: "perhaps the best authors of the future will be the ones who can write the best programs with which to manipulate, parse and distribute language-based practices." Goldsmith, *Uncreative Writing*, 11. Finally, Patrick Greaney argues that these "quotational practices" are inscribed in the allegorical tradition of Benjamin's *Arcades Project* through their conception of the present against the grain. By attempting to repeat the past,

"artists and writers may be attempting to repeat that past's unrealized futures." Greaney, *Quotational Practices*, x.

118. See Bourriaud, *Postproduction*, 43.

119. Indiana, *Tentacle*, 128.

120. "Cuerpos cuya materialidad da cuenta de la inestabilidad y de las posibilidades de resistencia con las que operan los sujetos y las corporalidades que habitan en la deriva del discurso hegemónico." Vera-Rojas, "¡Se armó el juidero!," 211–12.

121. Gonzenbach Perkins, "Queer Materiality, Contestatory Histories, and Disperse Bodies," 52–53.

122. Vera-Rojas, "¡Se armó el juidero!," 209.

123. Halberstam, *In a Queer Time and Place*, 2.

124. "El cuerpo-cosa de las mujeres." Segato, *Contra-pedagogías de la crueldad*, 13.

125. In this context, I am using the term *intemperie* following Segato's argument that it is impossible to think about the violence against women in Latin America today without taking into account "la situación de intemperie de la vida" caused by new forms of war via gangs, *maras*, hit men, and armed corporations. Segato, *Contra-pedagogías*, 16.

126. Escobar, *Pluriversal Politics*, xiii.

127. Halberstam, *In a Queer Time and Place*, 1; Muñoz, *Cruising Utopia*, 12.

128. Muñoz, *Cruising Utopia*, 187.

129. Halberstam, *In a Queer Time and Place*, 4–5.

130. Indiana, *Tentacle*, 91, 92.

131. Indiana, *Tentacle*, 96.

132. Segato, *Contra-pedagogías*, 17. In a later novel that could be read as a follow-up to *La mucama*, entitled *Hecho en Saturno* (2018), Argenis's father pays for him to travel to Cuba so he can run his presidential campaign without interference from his son, whose LSD addiction has led to a psychotic breakdown that ruined his marriage and artistic career. The figure of Goya appears yet again in a reference to the Spanish artist's work *Saturn Devouring His Son*, which is repurposed in the context of the extractive rationality of Dominican politicians such as Argenis's father.

133. Indiana, *Tentacle*, 101.

134. Freeman, *Time Binds*, 64.

135. Indiana, *Tentacle*, 11.

136. Indiana, *Tentacle*, 101.

137. Indiana, *Tentacle*, 53.

138. Jens Andermann analyzes Mendieta's *Silueta* series within the framework of the Cuban artist's "condición exílica": "una contestación tardía, excéntrica, pero marcada por el mismo contexto de guerra fría y de violencia contrainsurgente desencadenada por la metrópolis capitalista y sus clientes regionales como,

digamos, las intervenciones corporales en la escena pública de Antonio Manuel o de Artur Barrio en Brasil o las acciones del CADA en el Chile de la dictadura pinochetista." Andermann, *Tierras en trance*, 334.

139. Haraway, *Staying with the Trouble*, 53–54.

140. Bourriaud, *Relational Aesthetics*, 26.

CHAPTER 2: A TOXIC HISTORY OF THE PRESENT

1. Latin America is among the world's most dangerous regions for environmental activists according to figures provided by Global Witness. Brazil, Colombia, and Mexico have stood out in recent years, with twenty-six murders occurring in Brazil, thirty-three in Colombia, and fifty-four in Mexico in 2021 alone.

2. I conceive the notion of "literary affect" following Lawrence Buell's theoretical category of "ecoglobalist affect," which he describes as "an emotion-laden preoccupation with a finite, near-at-hand physical environment defined, at least in part, by an imagined inextricable linkage of some sort between that specific site and a context of planetary reach." Lawrence Buell, "Ecoglobalist Affects: The Emergence of U.S. Environmental Imagination on a Planetary Scale," 232. I also draw from Heather Houser's argument that the formal dimension of literary texts about ecosickness convey particular emotions that lead "individuals from information to awareness and ethics." Houser, *Ecosickness in Contemporary U.S. Fiction*, 7.

3. Ngai, *Ugly Feelings*, 3.

4. Tidwell and Soles, *Fear and Nature*, 3.

5. Tidwell and Soles, *Fear and Nature*, 4; Virno, *Déjà vu*, 21.

6. Buell coined the term "toxic discourse" to account for the "expressed anxiety arising from perceived threat of environmental hazard due to chemical modification by human agency." Buell, *Writing for an Endangered World*, 31.

7. Although I refer to the book's Spanish title, I quote from the English translation of Schweblin's novel.

8. Halberstam, *Skin Shows*, 17.

9. The list of Latin American novels that address the climate crisis from a dystopian lens is lengthy and includes *Plop* (2002) by Argentinean writer Rafael Pinedo, *Poso Wells* (2007) by Ecuadorian writer Gabriela Alemán, *Después de la ira* (2018) by Colombian writer Cristian Romero, and *La Compañía* (2019) by Mexican writer Verónica Gerber Bicecci.

10. Oloff, "'Monstrous Head' and the 'Mouth of Hell,'" 79.

11. Anderson, "Dimensions of Crisis," xviii.

12. Nixon, *Slow Violence and the Environmentalism of the Poor*, 2.

13. Danowski and Viveiros de Castro, *Ends of the World*, 5, 8.

14. Hartog, *Regimes of Historicity*, 113.

15. For an explanation of these three topoi in contemporary environmental

narratives, see Heffes, *Políticas de la destrucción / Poéticas de la preservación*, 15–73. Heffes examines contemporary cultural products that are creating a "nuevo archivo epistemológico." In her view, these literary works are crafting original reflections around the issue of the "distribución desigual de recursos naturales" and the "incremento de la escala económica como productora de desechos, la falta de acceso a servicios y bienes sanitarios o la cantidad desproporcionada de contaminación en los sectores poblacionales marginados." Heffes, *Políticas de la destrucción*, 72. Laura Barbas-Rhoden has analyzed the crisis of futurity in contemporary Latin American fiction, showing how novels by Homero Aridjis and Gioconda Belli have diagnosed a present on the brink of collapse and how they have explored "ancient and recent Latin American history for alternative models of being and regeneration." Barbas-Rhoden, *Ecological Imaginations in Latin American Fiction*, 139.

16. Houser, *Ecosickness*, 3.

17. Heise, *Imagining Extinction*, 35.

18. Ghosh, *Great Derangement*, 9.

19. Ganguly, "Catastrophic Form and Planetary Realism," 421.

20. Gago, *Feminist International*, 85.

21. Nixon, *Slow Violence*, 4; Martinez-Alier, *Environmentalism of the Poor*.

22. García Canclini, "Aesthetic Moments of Latin Americanism," 23.

23. Blindness is the central concern of Nettel's *El cuerpo en que nací* (2011), a semi-autobiographical account in which she relates the difficulties of growing up with a birthmark on the cornea of her left eye.

24. "Historias de desdoblamientos." Guadalupe Nettel, *El huésped*, 13.

25. Bruno Latour argues that modern thought has established a stark contrast between nature and culture, carrying out a strategy of purification that has relegated other nature-cultures to a premodern order. Latour, *We Have Never Been Modern*, 37–39.

26. "Solamente esperaba que esa otra cosa, LA COSA urbana, no permeara a los subsuelos, para que al menos quedara en la ciudad ese espacio libre como a mí me quedaría la memoria." Nettel, *El huésped*, 176.

27. See Danowski and Viveiros de Castro, *Ends of the World*, 29.

28. Wolfenzon, "El fantasma que nos habita," 43; Ferrero Cárdenas, "Geografía en el cuerpo," 56.

29. González, "La potencia de los cuerpos corrompidos," 99, 112.

30. Oloff, "Monstrous Head," 79, 80.

31. Dávila, *Houseguest and Other Stories*, 14.

32. Other dystopian works that address the socioecological issues of Mexico City include *La leyenda de los soles* (1993), *¿En quién piensas mientras haces el amor?* (1996) and *Ciudad de zombis* (2004) by Homero Aridjis; *Las verdades infames* (2019) by Damián Comas; and *Desagüe* (2019) by Diego Rodríguez Landeros.

33. Anderson, "Grounds of Crisis and the Geopolitics of Depth."

34. For a historical account on the drainage project in colonial Mexico City, see Candiani, *Dreaming of Dry Land*, 1–14. A photographic and sculptural installation by Maria Thereza Alves has depicted the drainage of Lake Chalco by an extractive corporation. The installation conveys a sustainable aesthetics through "the reactivation of a *chinampa*, an artificial island of pre-Hispanic design used for hydro-agriculture." Alves, *El retorno de un lago (The Return of a Lake)*, 12. For an analysis of Alves's work, see Andermann, *Tierras en trance*, 411–12.

35. Anderson, "Grounds of Crisis," 111.

36. "Atemporalmente . . . con la voracidad de una bulímica, como si fuera la última vez." Nettel, *El huésped*, 128.

37. Bonfil Batalla, *México profundo*, xvii. Juan Villoro traces this connection between the underground of Mexico City and Bonfil Batalla's concept by observing that "the dead and our origin are buried underground." Villoro, "Metro," 127. On the other hand, Anderson points to the underground of the city as a space of popular resistance through the metaphor of "los de abajo" or "the underdogs," the characters of Mariano Azuela's homonymous novel about the Mexican Revolution. Anderson, "Grounds of Crisis," 112.

38. Bonfil Batalla, *México profundo*, 156.

39. del Valle, "On Shaky Ground," 213.

40. del Valle, "On Shaky Ground," 198.

41. Halberstam, *Skin Shows*, 15.

42. "La amenaza [de La Cosa] era una constante, un factor inmutable de la atmósfera como el smog o la lluvia ácida del verano en la ciudad de México." Nettel, *El huésped*, 29–30.

43. In *The Natural Contract*, Michel Serres points out that human beings have a contract of "admiring attention, reciprocity, contemplation, and respect" with nature, which indicates that both parties are meant to sustain themselves mutually. For Serres, however, humans have not only broken the contract by ignoring the language of nature and promoting short-term environmental thinking but have established a parasitic natural contract: "a parasite—which is what we are now—condemns to death the one he pillages and inhabits, not realizing that in the long run he's condemning himself to death too." Serres, *Natural Contract*, 38.

44. Houser, *Ecosickness*, 222.

45. "Yo, que desde hacía tantos años llevaba un parásito dentro, lo sabía mejor que nadie; también la ciudad se estaba desdoblando, también ella empezaba a cambiar de piel y de ojos." Nettel, *El huésped*, 175–76.

46. Anderson, "Grounds of Crisis," 110.

47. Wolfenzon, "El fantasma que nos habita," 44.

48. "En la *longue durée* (comenzando, quizá, por el proceso de drenar la cuenca de México, que ha llevado siglos)." Lomnitz, "La depreciación de la vida en la Ciudad de México circa 1985," 158.

49. Agamben, "What Is the Contemporary?," 51, 44.

50. Agamben, "What Is the Contemporary?," 50.

51. "Insectos microscópicos que se comen nuestra grasa y más tarde devorarán nuestros restos." Nettel, *El huésped*, 27. In this sense, we can connect Nettel's work to the field of posthumanism and new materialisms. For an analysis of posthumanism as a disciplinary field, see Alaimo, *Bodily Natures*. For an analysis of new materialisms, see Bennett, *Vibrant Matter*; Hoyos, *Things with a History*.

52. Nettel, *Body Where I Was Born*, 82. The narrator of Nettel's short story "War in the Trash Cans," which appears in her collection *Natural Histories*, is a biologist who specializes in insects and who describes cockroaches as beings that preserve the genealogical memory of humankind: "Those animals were the first inhabitants of Earth and even if the world were to end tomorrow, they would survive. They are the memory of our ancestors. They are our grandparents and our descendants." Nettel, *Natural Histories*, 57–58.

53. Pérez Limón, "Visualizing the Nonnormative Body," 212.

54. Didi-Huberman, *Survival of the Fireflies*, 11, 34.

55. One could mention movements such as La Vía Campesina, which opposes agribusiness; the activism of the *seringueiros* (or rubber tappers) who in the 1980s stood against extractive corporations in the Amazon rainforest; or the campaign "Sin maíz no hay país" (No Corn, No Country) in Mexico, which asks for the renegotiation of the agricultural chapter of NAFTA. For an analysis of the concept of environmentalism of the poor, see Martinez-Alier, *Environmentalism of the Poor*.

56. "A los ciegos de estos movimientos los ha guiado siempre la fuerza de la ira, la venganza colectiva, no un proyecto." Nettel, *El huésped*, 131.

57. Virno, *Déjà vu*, 8.

58. "Conservar en la memoria todas las imágenes posibles, construir una recuerdoteca, era hacer un homenaje de mí misma." Nettel, *El huésped*, 56. The idea of a memory library evokes a number of contemporary artistic projects that stand against the temporal logic of the Anthropocene, such as the "temporama" by French artist Dominique Gonzalez-Foerster, who reflects on the insignificance of human time when compared to the scales of the planet or the cosmos. As Speranza points out, Gonzalez-Foerster's artistic project involves "una meditada relocalización emocional de objetos y copias de medios, tiempos y espacios diversos, recuperados y extrañados en el 'aquí y ahora' de un espacio alternativo, ficticio y a la vez real, mental y físico, que mueve a imaginar otros mundos posibles." Speranza, *Cronografías*, 62.

59. Virno, *Déjà vu*, 52, 55.

60. "Coleccionar recuerdos, como quien almacena una reserva de víveres, para resistir a la catástrofe inminente." Nettel, *El huésped*, 55.

61. See Danowski and Viveiros de Castro, *Ends of the World*, 18.

62. See Heffes, *Políticas de la destrucción*, 97.

63. For a history of the underground in Western literature and culture, see Toth, *Mole People*, 169–79. For a comparative analysis of the sewer system and the metro in Mexico City, see Biron, "Paisajes de la (in)seguridad."

64. Houser, *Ecosickness*, 120.

65. "La ciudad es una fachada hueca que cubre los escombros de todos nuestros temblores." Nettel, *El huésped*, 175.

66. Koolhaas, *Generic City*, 1250; Hartog, *Regimes of Historicity*, xix. For Koolhaas, the term "Junkspace" points to the waste that humanity leaves behind once it embarks on modernizing processes, because "generic cities" demand to be remodeled using new materials: "Junkspace is what remains after modernization has run its course, or, more precisely, what coagulates while modernization is in progress, its fallout. Modernization had a rational program: to share the blessings of science, universally. Junkspace is its apotheosis, or meltdown." Koolhaas, *Junkspace with Running Room*, 3.

67. "En la ciudad, las calles están llenas de casas, anuncios, gente y sin embargo tan vacías, pintadas de ese moho percudido que lo impregna todo. Los olores de la ciudad se han convertido en un tufo único y nauseabundo. Constantemente, el espacio deja de existir y la gente, obstinada en negarlo, sigue hablando de edificios, estatuas, cines que hace mucho derrumbaron; sigue mencionando calles que ya no son calles sino ejes viales y no tienen ya el mismo nombre, avenidas donde los camellones son sólo el recuerdo colectivo de un tiempo más apacible y menos vertiginoso." Nettel, *El huésped*, 174–75.

68. Benjamin, "Work of Art in the Age of Its Technological Reproducibility," 27.

69. "Los desagües constipados." Nettel, *El huésped*, 175.

70. Villoro, *Horizontal Vertigo*, 285.

71. "Hubiera deseado . . . integrarme poco a poco a la flora submarina como un alga más; conocer la enigmática felicidad de los ahogados; vivir para toda la eternidad debajo de una roca como un caracol, como un fósil milenario." Nettel, *El huésped*, 184.

72. Giorgi, "Paisajes de sobrevida," 135.

73. For an account of the cases of death and intoxication caused by Monsanto's synthetic pesticides in Argentina, Brazil, and Paraguay, see Robin, *World according to Monsanto*, 273–89.

74. Bett, "Poisoned World." Since the publication of *Distancia de rescate* in 2015, several books have revolved around cases of pesticide poisoning in rural populations. See Fernanda Sández's journalistic essay *La Argentina fumigada: agroquímicos, enfermedad y alimentos en un país envenenado* and María Inés Krimer's detective novel *Noxa*, both published in 2016.

75. Valencia, *Gore Capitalism*, 20.

76. Robin, *El glifosato en el banquillo*, 31.

77. Leguizamón, *Seeds of Power*, 96.

78. For an account of contemporary Argentinean gothic literature, see Inés Ordiz, "Civilization and Barbarism and Zombies: Argentina's Contemporary Gothic." Mariana Enriquez, C. E. Feiling, and Leandro Ávalos Blacha are among the authors who belong in this category. Fernando J. Rosenberg argues that the characters in *Distancia de rescate* inhabit a zombie-like state of consciousness: "sus personajes parecen transitar entre la vida y una especie de estado entre zombi y visionario." Rosenberg, "Toxicidad y narrativa," 913.

79. Other texts by Argentinean authors that address the topic of motherhood through the horror genre include "Como una buena madre" (2001) by Ana María Shua and "Una madre protectora" (2013) by Guillermo Martínez. For a book-length analysis about representations of motherhood in Argentinean literature, see Domínguez, *De donde vienen los niños*.

80. Leguizamón, *Seeds of Power*, 146. Italics in the original.

81. Leguizamón, *Seeds of Power*, 86, see also 18–19.

82. Wallace, *Female Gothic Histories*, 2.

83. Mutis, "Monsters and Agritoxins," 49.

84. "Un cuento que no funcionaba." Pavón, "Samanta Schweblin."

85. "No pertenencia a la especificidad de un arte en particular, pero también, y sobre todo, no pertenencia a la idea del arte como una práctica específica." Garramuño, *Mundos en común*, 26.

86. According to Esposito's paradigm, "the common is not characterized by what is proper but by what is improper, or even more drastically, by the other; by a voiding [*svuotamento*], be it partial or whole, of property into its negative; by removing what is properly one's own [*depropiazione*] that invests and decenters the proprietary subject, forcing him to take leave . . . of himself, to alter himself." Esposito, *Communitas*, 7.

87. The unbounded nature of *Distancia de rescate*'s literary genre as well as its location in the Argentinean pampas evoke the fictional work of Manuel Puig, who—according to César Aira—wrote novels in which "el estilo es lo que se oculta y mimetiza" because "historia y estilo son lo mismo." César Aira, "El sultán," 28.

88. Kurnick, *Empty Houses*, 9; Halberstam, *Skin Shows*, 11.

89. In this sense, the narrative structure of *Distancia de rescate* points to the notion of "transgenic art" espoused by Brazilian artist Eduardo Kac and groups of activist performance such as "Puesto Amaranto," which from 2013 onward has opposed the establishment of a Monsanto transgenic seeds factory in a small Argentinean town. See Andermann, *Tierras en trance*, 415–18.

90. Morton, "Ecology without the Present," 234.

91. "Un nuevo relato rural, *agusanado*, contado a dos voces, cruzado por distintas temporalidades, marcado por los ritmos de la intoxicación." de Leone, "Imaginaciones rurales argentinas," 199.

92. Buell, *Writing for an Endangered World*, 30–31.

93. Buell, *Writing for an Endangered World*, 31.

94. "Dar marcha atrás." Pratt, "Globalización," 27.

95. Pratt, "Globalización," 27.

96. "La destemporalización del presente." Ludmer, *Aquí América Latina*, 91.

97. "Necesitamos una política de conquista sobre la soledad y el desierto." Alberdi, *Bases y puntos*, 200.

98. Pratt, "Globalización," 27.

99. Schweblin, *Fever Dream*, 122. In this sense, *Distancia de rescate* could be read as a racial gothic fiction, if we understand the decomposition of whiteness as an ominous inversion of the nineteenth-century governmental project of populating the pampas with European immigrants. For a theorization of racial gothic fictions, see Malchow, *Gothic Images of Race in Nineteenth-Century Britain*.

100. Žižek, *Looking Awry*, 23.

101. Schweblin, *Fever Dream*, 162.

102. Žižek, "Discipline between Two Freedoms," 100.

103. Schweblin, *Fever Dream*, 13.

104. "Lo que une a un zombi y otro zombi es que no tienen nada que hacer el uno para con el otro . . . Se instaura así una comunidad de seres singularmente separados, una comunidad de la no-comunidad, no comunicación, no union, no mezcla." Fernández Gonzalo, *Filosofía zombi*, 115.

105. Sández, *La Argentina fumigada*, 15.

106. Fisher, *Weird and the Eerie*, 77.

107. Fisher, *Weird and the Eerie*, 11.

108. Schweblin, *Fever Dream*, 180.

109. "Cultivo inmunológico." De Leone, "Campos que matan," 64.

110. Schweblin, *Fever Dream*, 81.

111. Schweblin, *Fever Dream*, 137.

112. Schweblin, *Fever Dream*, 19.

113. Punter, "Shape and Shadow," 258.

114. Ruffel, *Brouhaha*, 20.

115. Schweblin, *Fever Dream*, 57–58.

116. Schweblin, *Fever Dream*, 90, 183, 183.

117. Houser, *Ecosickness*, 3–4.

118. Fisher, *Vehement Passions*, 95.

119. Schweblin, *Fever Dream*, 131.

120. Punter, "Ghost of a History," 5.

121. See Jagoe, *End of the World as They Knew It*, 50.

122. Schweblin, *Fever Dream*, 81.

123. Serres, *Natural Contract*, 33.

124. Buell, *Environmental Imagination*, 285.

125. Hartog, *Regimes of Historicity*, 189.

126. Smith, *What Is Contemporary Art?*, 267.

CHAPTER 3: THE CONTEMPORARY PLANTATION

1. Fernandes, *Millôr definitivo*, 30. In several interviews about his novel *Torto arado*, Brazilian author Itamar Vieira Junior has quoted Fernandes's phrase to refer to the structural racism that is still present in Brazilian society more than a century after the abolition of slavery. Vieira Junior argues that freedom was a sociohistorical construction and that, even today, "o racismo estrutural permeia tudo, desde a força policial em comunidades predominantemente negras nas grandes cidades brasileiras até o impacto de uma pandemia na vida da população, que não é o mesmo para todos." Peres, "'Há muita história soterrada.'"

2. Drescher, "Brazilian Abolition in Comparative Perspective," 53.

3. Two prominent examples of Latin American slave narratives are *The Autobiography of a Slave / Autobiografía de un esclavo* (1835) by Juan Francisco Manzano (1797–1854) and *Biografía de un cimarrón* (1966) by Miguel Barnet about the life of fugitive slave Esteban Montejo (1860–1973).

4. Although I refer to the book's Portuguese title, I quote from the English translation of Vieira Junior's novel.

5. Vieira Junior, *Crooked Plow*, 276.

6. Here I am echoing the words of Ariella Aïsha Azoulay, who argues that "in between Europe and its offshore outposts, a new template for political regimes emerged early on—one based on a differential body politic." Azoulay refers to the ways in which imperial actors forced populations throughout the world to change their cultural traditions and therefore stripped them of their right "to feel at home." Azoulay, *Potential History*, 35.

7. Taussig, *Devil and Commodity Fetishism*, 10. In an interview about *Elástico de sombra*, Cárdenas makes this connection between the contemporary figure of the DJ and the classic literary trope of listening to the stories of others: "Un DJ es una persona que mantiene una actitud de escucha, es una persona que es capaz de juntar músicas de distintas procedencias en una sesión. Pero también tiene una tradición muy fuerte con la manera en la que la literatura clásica se hizo. La mitad de la literatura mundial se ha hecho así. Desde el *Decamerón* hasta *Las mil y una noches*." de Narváez, "El mundo de mierda."

8. Free indirect style refers to a narrative device introduced by nineteenth-century novelists like Gustave Flaubert and Jane Austen. It reveals a character's thoughts by combining third-person narration with first-person speech, thus collapsing interior and exterior perspectives. Moreover, it produces the illusion that the third-person narrator has access to the character's interior life.

9. Wynter, "Novel and History, Plot and Plantation," 291, 293.

10. Levine, *Black Culture and Black Consciousness*, 30.

11. Wynter, "Novel and History," 295.

12. Wynter, "Novel and History," 297.

13. "Letra muerta"; "personajes vivos de la historia que camina"; "Ajeno[s] a

la cultural nacional"; "Fuerza bruta." Zapata Olivella, *Africanidad, indianidad, multiculturalidad*, 131–32.

14. "El 'Muntú' concibe la familia como la suma de los difuntos (ancestros) y los vivos, unidos por la palabra a los animales, a los árboles, a los minerales (tierra, agua, fuego, estrellas) y a las herramientas, en un nudo indisoluble" Zapata Olivella, *Africanidad, indianidad, multiculturalidad*, 80.

15. See de Friedemann, *La saga del negro*, 97.

16. "Esconde muchos secretos no revelados por la ciencia"; "Sobrevivencia, historia y fuerza creadora, pensante, en el momento en que se investiga." Zapata Olivella, *Africanidad, indianidad, multiculturalidad*, 31, 131.

17. Levine, "Great Unwritten," 219.

18. In this sense, novels like *Elástico de sombra* and *Torto arado* form part of an alternative history of modernity that is in line with Paul Gilroy's call "for the primal history of modernity to be reconstructed from the slaves' point of view." Arguing that Western rationality was complicit with racial terror, Gilroy challenges writers and historians to use "the memory of slavery as an interpretive device." Gilroy, *Black Atlantic*, 55.

19. Ruffel, *Brouhaha*, 13.

20. Wood, *How Fiction Works*, 9; Bewes, *Free Indirect*, 2.

21. "No es un Dios como en Macondo"; "es una especie de fantasma, una voz fantasmal que no coincide con ninguna, pero está más pegada a los personajes, se transforma en las voces." "Juan Cárdenas y Dolores Reyes."

22. In Cárdenas's *El diablo de las provincias* (2017), the hacienda is a symbol of power but also of decadence. Cárdenas explores the idea of nature as a cultural and historical construction. He also posits hacienda literature as a distinct literary tradition in Latin America, composed of key works by Jorge Isaacs and Aluísio Azevedo, among others. The proliferation of monocultures in the Cauca Valley appears as a negation of historical time. "El monocultivo niega el tiempo, lo cancela. Para el monocultivo no hay historia, ni hombres, solo eternidad, o sea, la nada absoluta. El monocultivo es la voluntad de Dios en la tierra. Una tierra sin tierra." Cárdenas, *El diablo de las provincias*, 89.

23. "El último gran machetero." Cárdenas, *Elástico de sombra*, 39.

24. "Esos conocimientos perdidos que, según decían los viejos, voj [*sic*] guardás como un tesoro . . . las paradas de esgrima de machete desaparecidas." Cárdenas, *Elástico de sombra*, 28–29.

25. Desch-Obi, "*Peinillas* and Popular Participation," 154.

26. Desch-Obi, "*Peinillas* and Popular Participation," 149.

27. Wynter, "Against a One-Dimensional Course," 590.

28. "La memoria perdida del cuerpo." Cárdenas, *Elástico de sombra*, 46.

29. "La memoria perdida de los ancestros"; "El ritmo es el temblor del tiempo humano." Cárdenas, *Elástico de sombra*, 45, 110.

30. Giorgi, "'Temblor del tiempo humano.'"

31. "El mundo perdido vuelve a empezar"; "nuevo mundo negro." Cárdenas, *Elástico de sombra*, 47.

32. Glissant, *Caribbean Discourse*, 144.

33. Glissant, *Caribbean Discourse*, 161.

34. "El proyecto más urgente de la cultura universal, a saber, la aniquilación definitiva del Hombre Blanco." Cárdenas, *Elástico de sombra*, 7.

35. "Escribidor blanquito, así medio cafeconleche"; "ladrón y apropiadorcista de lo ajeno." Cárdenas, *Elástico de sombra*, 11.

36. Camilo Malagón reads the name Cero as reflecting Cárdenas's antipatriarchal and antiracist stance against the White Man, arguing that it is a rhetorical strategy because Cerón is Cárdenas's maternal last name. Malagón, "El *intelectual implicado*," 60.

37. "Alguien que lleva y trae cosas de un lado al otro, brincándose y en últimas tratando de borrar las fronteras raciales que el hombre blanco inventa para garantizar su derecho de dominación, para marcar el terreno con su sistema de medidas." Cárdenas, *Elástico de sombra*, 73.

38. Hartman, "Venus in Two Acts," 2.

39. "El misterio de lo Incomunicable . . . adonde ninguna computadora podrá llegar nunca." Cárdenas, *Elástico de sombra*, 35.

40. Glissant, *Caribbean Discourse*, 85.

41. Glissant, *Caribbean Discourse*, 87.

42. "Archivos vivientes donde se depositan memorias populares, saberes acumulados de luchas políticas y, sobre todo, historias. Cuentos, leyendas, mitos, anécdotas, chistes, décimas." Cárdenas quoted in Bermeo Gamboa, "Odisea caucana."

43. Taussig, *Devil and Commodity Fetishism*, 13.

44. According to Taussig, "societies on the threshold of capitalist development necessarily interpret that development in terms of precapitalist beliefs and practices." Taussig, *Devil and Commodity Fetishism*, 11. An example would be the Indigenous miners in Bolivia who created group prayers to the devil, thought to be the true owner of the tin mines.

45. Taussig, *Devil and Commodity Fetishism*, 15, 43.

46. "De las que hacen hablar a las piedras, de las que rezan al revés, de las que voltean la lengua ajena, de las que saben volar y hacer conjuro de amor, conjuro de odio y hasta hechizo pa ganar las elecciones departamentales." Cárdenas, *Elástico de sombra*, 18.

47. "La cosa es que Nubia me obligó a dejar el trabajo, me obligó a vender un pedacito de tierra que tenía a la orilla de El Palo y me dejó sin cinco, luego me obligó a pelearme con mi familia, me obligó a odiar a mis amigos." Cárdenas, *Elástico de sombra*, 19.

48. Federici, *Caliban and the Witch*, 174.

49. Glissant, *Devil and Commodity Fetishism*, 147.

50. Cárdenas, "Teoría del escombro," 184.

51. Tsing, *Mushroom at the End of the World*, 40.

52. "El hechizo del mercado"; "la mano invisible blanca que mueve todas las manos pardas." Cárdenas, *Elástico de sombra*, 46.

53. Achille Mbembe defines necropolitics as the rise of the modern paradigm of biopolitical control over bodies and territories, considering how "the plantation system and its consequences express the emblematic and paradoxical figure of the state of exception." Mbembe, *Necropolitics*, 74.

54. McKittrick, "Plantation Futures," 7.

55. "Ninguno era capaz de decir nada. Hay cosas que no admiten comentario." Cárdenas, *Elástico de sombra*, 43.

56. "En estas montañas estamos peleando dos guerras, la del siglo XIX y la del siglo XXI." Cárdenas, *Elástico de sombra*, 82.

57. Miguel Rocha Vivas theorizes what the Pasto Indigenous community calls "word mingas" or "thought mingas": the communal creation of creative texts, which can adopt a variety of forms. Rocha Vivas coins the term "oralitegraphies" to designate the "textual intersections among diverse systems of oral, literary, and graphic-visual communication." An example that he uses is the map of Colombia created by the Intercultural Minga of Indigenous Peoples, showing the country through centuries-old Indigenous ideograms that undermine the idea of the nation and the centrality of the written word as the privileged medium of communication. Rocha Vivas, *Word Mingas*, 25.

58. "Compañeros y compañeras, decía Francia, son siglos, siglos de lucha por estos territorios. Yo he estado varias veces en el archivo histórico del Cauca, en la Casa Mosquera, revisando esos mamotretos. Y allí consta que, al menos desde 1632, nuestros ancestros consiguieron asentarse aquí para barequear oro en el río y trabajar la tierra, cuidando el agua, el bosque, la montaña. . . . No somos los propietarios, somos los cuidadores, los guardianes de estas tierras. Los que sabemos cuidar de la vida. Y por eso nos atacan, por eso nos persiguen, por eso nos desplazan y por eso nos matan. Porque ellos, este Gobierno, donde encontraron guarida los descendientes de quienes esclavizaron a nuestros tatarabuelos hace cuatro siglos, hoy son agentes al servicio de una gran máquina global de muerte, una máquina automática que produce muerte, que subsiste gracias a la producción de muerte. . . . Y ojo muchachos, esta máquina de muerte no está por allá lejos, en las capitales del mundo, esa máquina de muerte es astuta porque trabaja dentro de cada cuerpo, de cada alma. La máquina de muerte coloniza nuestro lenguaje y nos domina hasta que consigue hablar por nosotros, en nuestro nombre." Cárdenas, *Elástico de sombra*, 64–66.

59. "Un arroyo artificial, de esos que los ingenios de caña usan para irrigar su vagabundería y chuparles la sangre a los ríos." Cárdenas, *Elástico de sombra*, 33.

60. Márquez, "Francia Márquez en el Centro Cultural Kirchner."

61. "Una máquina de fachadas blanqueadas donde durante siglos se legalizó, se naturalizó y hasta se embelleció el despojo." Cárdenas, *Elástico de sombra*, 87.

62. "Mantienen viva la llama de la historia." Cárdenas, *Elástico de sombra*, 79.

63. "Huellas de africanía." de Friedemann, *La saga del negro*, 92.

64. "Contra la muerte y el olvido sistemático, contra el olvido impuesto desde arriba." Cárdenas, *Elástico de sombra*, 79.

65. According to Walter Fraga, masters gave slaves subsistence plots as a way to appease them and ensure order on the plantation. Masters strictly regulated how much time the slaves could spend cultivating these lands. Conflicts about the ownership of subsistence plots frequently emerged between planters and slaves. By selling their products in local markets, slaves became acquainted with people from outside the plantation who helped them to reflect on the illegitimate nature of their enslavement. Fraga, *Crossroads of Freedom*, 18.

66. For an analysis of provision grounds in eighteenth- and nineteenth-century Bahia, see Barickman, "'Bit of Land, Which They Call Roça.'" Barickman focuses his attention on the Bahian Recôncavo region, which is much closer to urban centers than the remote Bahian *sertão* in which *Torto arado* takes place.

67. Federici, *Caliban and the Witch*, 113.

68. José Martins Catharino distinguishes three periods in the history of mining in the Chapada Diamantina: a first stage in which Black slaves made up the majority of the workforce, a second phase of free workers using rudimentary mining techniques, and a third period of large-scale corporate mining. This clear-cut historical division does not mean, however, that the introduction of machines came to replace artisanal mining practices completely since there are still clashes between artisanal miners and corporate actors. Martins Catharino, *Garimpo—Garimpeiro—Garimpagem*, 49.

69. Rinaldo Walcott provides a state-of-the-art analysis of how neoliberal capitalism continues to undermine Black freedom of movement. More specifically, Walcott argues that "the logics of transatlantic slavery continue to shape Black movement and, therefore, Black belonging globally." Walcott, *Long Emancipation*, 36.

70. Vieira Junior, *Crooked Plow*, 4.

71. Vieira Junior, *Crooked Plow*, 133. Karl Erik Schøllhammer's analysis of *Torto arado* foregrounds "the weight of an archaic inheritance" on the characters, who continue to experience forms of colonial violence that their ancestors suffered decades before. In this sense, Schøllhammer places *Torto arado* in conversation with Juan Rulfo's works about land dispossession in postrevolutionary Mexico. Schøllhammer, "Predicament of Contemporary Brazilian Fiction," 83.

72. Vieira Junior, *Crooked Plow*, 26.

73. Vallejo, *Papyrus*, 156.

74. The concept of bodies-territories derives from the struggles of ecofeminist activists throughout the Americas (see chapter 2). Gago remarks that the concept of body-territory "says that it is impossible to cut apart and isolate the individual body from the collective body, the human body from the territory and landscape." Gago, *Feminist International*, 86.

75. In my reading, I echo Robin Wall Kimmerer's stories about the destruction of her Indigenous heritage. She describes this trauma as "a knot of sorrow I've carried like a stone buried in my heart" and conceives her relationship with the land as essential to reweave the broken fragments of the past, "like ash splints . . . into a new whole." Wall Kimmerer, *Braiding Sweetgrass*, 264, 266.

76. Vieira Junior, *Crooked Plow*, 177.

77. Banaggia, *As forças do jarê*, 292–93, 294.

78. Vieira Junior, *Crooked Plow*, 42.

79. Vieira Junior, *Crooked Plow*, 172.

80. Vieira Junior, *Crooked Plow*, 48, 69.

81. Lins do Rego, *Plantation Boy*, 50.

82. In his depiction of contemporary peasants living and working in conditions resembling the pre-abolition plantation, Vieira Junior rewrites Freyre's sociological treatise *Casa-Grande & Senzala* (1933). Freyre described the landowners' routine as a monotonous accumulation of days filled with idleness and sexual debauchery, which contributed to his idea of Brazilian society as being not so much a civilization as a "syphilization": a sick society without a future. For the slaveholders and their wives, according to Freyre, "os dias se sucediam iguais; a mesma modorra; a mesma vida de rede, banzeira, sensual. E os homens e as mulheres, amarelos, de tanto viverem deitados dentro de casa e de tanto andarem de rede e palanquim." Freyre, *Casa-Grande & Senzala*, 519. In *Torto arado*, on the contrary, it is the slaves and not the masters who are the victims of the modern nation-state turning into a factory of sick bodies.

83. Vieira Junior, *Crooked Plow*, 33.

84. One such origin story is recounted by Leonice de Jesus Silva and Raquel Souzas in an article about the village of Rio de Contas, which revolves around how the Black communities of the Chapada Diamantina arrived in the region before the *bandeirantes* (the Portuguese explorers or flag-carriers) and the garimpeiros. When the ship that brought them to Bahia ran aground, the slaves escaped through the Contas River. Silva and Souza, "Re(existências) quilombolas em Rio de Contas," 90.

85. Vieira Junior, *Crooked Plow*, 183, 186.

86. Vieira Junior, *Crooked Plow*, 242.

87. Vieira Junior, *Crooked Plow*, 128.

88. Vieira Junior, *Crooked Plow*, 31–32.

89. Vieira Junior, *Crooked Plow*, 127.

90. Sweet, *Domingos Álvares, African Healing*, 124.

91. Macfarlane, *Underland*, 15–16.

92. Vieira Junior, *Crooked Plow*, 213.

93. Morrison, "Site of Memory," 238, 243.

94. Hartman, "Venus in Two Acts," 11.

95. In this sense, *Torto arado* could be read as a rewriting of Rachel de Queiroz's *O quinze* (1930), the story of a rural family in northeast Brazil who flees their home following the 1915 drought.

96. Vieira Junior, *Crooked Plow*, 129, 96, 99.

97. Ochoa Gautier, *Aurality*, 61.

98. Vieira Junior, *Crooked Plow*, 261.

99. Vieira Junior, *Crooked Plow*, 130, 86.

100. Azoulay argues that classification is part and parcel of the imperial archival regime. According to her, "the materialization of violence on bodies, objects, and environments is the inaugural imperial act. . . . From the system of *encomienda* to the regime of enslavement, examples of the way in which people were differentiated abound, starting with those members who were endowed with the power of collecting, documenting, and processing information about others, matching these records to concrete people differentiated into 'populations'—women, young men, old—capable of different tasks and exposed to different forms of exploitation." Azoulay, *Potential History*, 172.

101. Serres, *Natural Contract*, 3.

102. Vieira Junior, *Crooked Plow*, 234, 137.

103. Goyal, *Runaway Genres*, 3–4.

104. "Racial capitalism" was a term first espoused by Cedric Robinson to refer to "the legitimation and corroboration of social organization as natural by reference to the 'racial' components of its elements," specifically in "the social structures emergent from capitalism." Robinson, *Black Marxism*, 2.

105. Ruffel, *Brouhaha*, 150.

106. My reading of the knotting in these novels owes much to Rafael Pérez-Torres's reading of Toni Morrison's *Beloved* (1987) through the interweaving of oral narratives, styles, and marginalized discourses. Pérez-Torres concludes that "the 'not' signified by blackness becomes for Morrison a means by which to weave her tale," whereas readers "form an 'is' out of the 'nots,' help untie the tangled threads by which Morrison knits together her novel." Pérez-Torres, "Knitting and Knotting the Narrative Thread," 691.

107. Gates, "Criticism in De Jungle," 626.

108. Azoulay, *Potential History*, 347.

109. "La historia de Colombia ha funcionado a partir de unas máquinas de olvidos impuestas." Cárdenas quoted in de Narváez, "El mundo de mierda."

CHAPTER 4: THE CHILDREN RETURN

1. Bloch, *Heritage of Our Times*, 3.

2. "El umbral del presente." Benjamin quoted in Didi-Huberman, *Cuando las imágenes toman posición*, 121.

3. Although I refer to the books' Portuguese and Spanish titles, I quote from the English translation of both novels.

4. Hirsch, *Family Frames*, 22.

5. Fuks, *Resistance*, 82–83; Gerber Bicecci, *Empty Set*, 133.

6. Hirsch, *Generation of Postmemory*, 42.

7. Walkowitz, *Cosmopolitan Style*, 79.

8. Beverley, *Testimonio*, 32.

9. Di Stefano, *Vanishing Frame*, 3.

10. Moyn, *Last Utopia*, 5.

11. The epigraph comes from Ernesto Sabato's book of the same name, *La resistencia* (2000): "Creo que hay que resistir: éste ha sido mi lema. Pero hoy, cuántas veces me he preguntado cómo encarnar esta palabra." Sabato, *La resistencia*, 103.

12. Rebecca Atencio discusses the process of transformation of the DEOPS building, first into a "site of culture" under the name Memorial da Liberdade and, following the protest of various political groups, into the current Memorial da Resistência consecrated to the collective work of memory. Atencio, *Memory's Turn*, 116–21.

13. The novel was translated into Spanish by Fuks himself and published under the Literatura Random House imprint in 2018. On the other hand, Fuks is not the only Brazilian writer born to Argentinean parents who has written about the legacy of the last military dictatorship. The novel *Mar azul* (2012) by Paloma Vidal, a writer born in Buenos Aires in 1975, also addresses the subject. Carola Saavedra's novel *O inventário das coisas ausentes* (2014) reflects on dictatorship, memory, and exile from the perspective of a Brazilian writer born in Santiago de Chile in the wake of Pinochet's rise to power.

14. Fuks, *Resistance*, 77.

15. Fuks, *Resistance*, 123.

16. Fuks, *Resistance*, 17.

17. "Un sentido único." Sarlo, *Tiempo pasado*, 68.

18. Fuks, *Resistance*, 66.

19. Luz Horne highlights this same feature—slowness—in the photographic writing of other contemporary Latin American writers, such as Sergio Chejfec and João Gilberto Noll. Situating her intervention within the discussion on new realisms, Horne observes that Chejfec's writing incorporates the register of the image to "construir un retrato de lo contemporáneo." Horne, "Fotografía y retrato de lo contemporáneo," 126.

20. Hirsch, *Family Frames*, 7.

21. Fuks, *Resistance*, 115.

22. Hirsch, *Family Frames*, 118.

23. Azoulay, "Potential History," 556.

24. Azoulay, "Potential History," 565.

25. Nouzeilles, "Postmemory Cinema and the Future of the Past," 268. Cinema vérité (or reality cinema) is a style of documentary filmmaking based on the authenticity of dialogue, the participation of the filmmaker as a subjective observer, and the awareness that the camera serves as a mediator of reality. Cinema vérité emerged in the 1960s and is often linked to the work of French filmmakers Jean Rouch and Chris Marker.

26. Azoulay, *Civil Contract of Photography*, 104.

27. Reati, "El monumento de papel," 168.

28. For an analysis of the concept of citizenship in recent Brazilian literature, see Lehnen, *Citizenship and Crisis*, 1–21.

29. Sontag, *Regarding the Pain of Others*, 89.

30. Richard, *Eruptions of Memory*, 78.

31. Fuks, *Resistance*, 101–2.

32. Sontag, *Regarding the Pain of Others*, 102.

33. Nussbaum, "Patriotism and Cosmopolitanism," 9, 7.

34. Appiah, "Cosmopolitan Patriots," 621, 624.

35. Sontag, *Regarding the Pain of Others*, 46.

36. Fuks, *Resistance*, 27, 11–12.

37. Fuks, *Resistance*, 11.

38. Siskind, "Towards a Cosmopolitanism of Loss," 223.

39. Fuks, *Resistance*, 146.

40. Pieter Vermeulen examines the figure of the fugueur in the novel *Open City* (2011) by Nigerian American writer Teju Cole. For Vermeulen, the figure of the fugueur appears in contemporary fiction to effect a critique of the cosmopolitan imagination, a discourse that promises global change based on empathy and cultural exchange. Vermeulen, "Flights of Memory," 42.

41. A novel by Argentinean writer María Sonia Cristoff, *Mal de época* (2017), takes up even more explicitly the figure of the fugueur to account for the dislocated condition of contemporary subjects.

42. Hacking, *Mad Travelers*, 30, see also 8, 123.

43. Fuks, *Resistance*, 143.

44. Fuks, *Resistance*, 105, 106.

45. Fuks, *Resistance*, 105.

46. Appiah, *Cosmopolitanism*, 30.

47. "Sensação de ilegitimidade." Vidal, "A literatura como resistência."

48. Walkowitz, *Cosmopolitan Style*, 2.

49. Fuks, *Resistance*, 138, 151–52.

50. "Adyacencias traumáticas"; "despidos y cancelaciones." Richard, "Introducción," 9–10.

51. Rousso, *Latest Catastrophe*, 3.

52. For an analysis of the field of recent history in Argentina, see Franco and Lvovich, "Historia reciente."

53. Rousso, *Latest Catastrophe*, 9, 152.

54. Fuks, *Resistance*, 99.

55. Hartog, *Regimes of Historicity*, 113.

56. Rousso, *Latest Catastrophe*, 157.

57. Fuks, *Resistance*, 143.

58. "Directamente afectadas." Sosa, "Filiaciones virales," 133.

59. Nora, "Between Memory and History," 8.

60. Huyssen, *Present Pasts*, 101–2.

61. Fuks, *Resistance*, 145.

62. Ruffel, *Brouhaha*, 13.

63. Rousso, *Latest Catastrophe*, 10, 11–12.

64. "Se o romance se constrói hoje com as sobras de sua própria destruição e se o que se cria a partir das sobras só se cria para que seja destruído depois." Fuks, "A era da pós-ficção," 85.

65. Fuks's intervention can be found in a collection of essays entitled *Ética e pós-verdade* (2017). "Post-truth" became a widely used adjective in 2016, when Oxford Dictionaries declared it "word of the year." Its emergence was linked to the Brexit referendum and Donald Trump's election campaign. According to Lee McIntyre, post-truth "amounts to a form of ideological supremacy, whereby its practitioners are trying to compel someone to believe in something whether there is good evidence for it or not." McIntyre, *Post-truth*, 13.

66. Sarlo, *Tiempo pasado*, 74.

67. "Imaginación reflexiva." Sarlo, *Tiempo pasado*, 54.

68. "La verdad de la experiencia"; "un narrador siempre piensa *desde afuera* de la experiencia, como si los humanos pudieran apoderarse de la pesadilla y no sólo padecerla" Sarlo, *Tiempo pasado*, 49, 166.

69. Fuks, *Resistance*, 82, 80, 83.

70. Fuks, *Resistance*, 153, 97.

71. This is what Garramuño observes in relation to a series of contemporary fictions (which she inscribes in the category of "literature outside itself" or unspecific art), characterized by the will to "mostrar la materialidad de esos restos [del archivo], la obstinada conservación de los vestigios y residuos que en la preservación e insistencia conducen al surgimiento de otras historias." Garramuño, *Mundos en común*, 65. On the other hand, as an expression of a distrust of the concept of truth, *A resistência* would fall within what Ludmer called "post-autonomous literatures," meaning a reformulation of the category of reality: "una

realidad que no quiere ser representada porque ya es pura representación." Ludmer, *Aquí América Latina*, 151.

72. In an article published in the *Guardian* on October 31, 2018, a few days after Bolsonaro's victory, Fuks points out that Brazil's present is made up of regressive values that recall the last dictatorships of the Southern Cone, the Nazi Germany from which his grandparents fled, and by extension, a dystopian future. "This past-laden future," Fuks writes, "is made up of countless threats: the persecution of political adversaries, the wiping out of activism, the criminalising of social movements as terrorist organisations." Fuks, "I Never Thought Dark Forces Might Make Me Leave Brazil."

73. "Resistência como algo negativo, como uma recusa a alcançar algo ou, pelo contrário, como um ato de força, de posicionamento diante de uma situação que exige uma tomada de posição. Eu gosto de pensar a literatura como capaz de fazer essa transição." Pires, "'O Brasil é incapaz de refletir.'"

74. For a comparative analysis of *Conjunto vacío* and other works of postmemory throughout Latin America such as José Carlos Agüero's *Persona* (2017), see Renker, "'Generation After' Talks Back."

75. Gerber Bicecci, *Empty Set*, 2–3. Emilia Deffis analyzes the novel through its positing of "an internal necropolis," a metaphor of the suspended state of mourning inhabited by the children of exiled or disappeared parents. Deffis, "'La necrópolis interior.'"

76. Gerber Bicecci, *Empty Set*, 3, 11.

77. See Saltzman, *Making Memory Matter*, 83.

78. For an analysis of *Conjunto vacío* and its intermedial strategies, see Schmitter, "Contar con todo."

79. Fisher, *Capitalist Realism*, 7.

80. "Un manifiesto debería estarse manifestando, en gerundio, en su presente infinito. Por ejemplo: no es lo mismo desaparecer que estar desapareciendo todos los días, todo el tiempo." Gerber Bicecci, "Manifiesto evanescente," 143.

81. Gerber Bicecci, *Empty Set*, 7.

82. "Lo que el síntoma-tiempo interrumpe no es otra cosa que el curso de la historia cronológica. Pero lo que contraría, también lo sostiene: se lo podría pensar bajo el ángulo de un inconsciente de la historia." Didi-Huberman, *Ante el tiempo*, 64.

83. Didi-Huberman, *Surviving Image*, 326.

84. Forcinito, *Intermittences*, 6.

85. According to Pilar Calveiro, the task of memory consists of "no acallar las voces discordantes con la propia, sino sumarlas para ir armando, en lugar de un puzzle en el que cada pieza tiene un solo lugar, una especie de caleidoscopio que reconoce distintas figuras posibles." Calveiro, *Política y/o violencia*, 17. See also Forcinito, *Intermittences*, 7.

86. Blejmar, *Playful Memories*, 26.

87. Gerber Bicecci, *Empty Set*, 1, 138.

88. Bourriaud, *Exform*, 51, 55.

89. Gerber Bicecci, *Empty Set*, 1. In an analysis of montage, Benjamin Buchloh points out that mnemonic desire arises with greater strength in historical moments of discontinuity between time horizons: "Mnemonic desire . . . is activated especially in those moments of extreme duress in which the traditional material bonds between subjects, between subjects and objects, and between objects and their representation appear to be on the verge of displacement, if not outright disappearance." Buchloh, "Gerhard Richter's Atlas," 95.

90. Vivian Abenshushan also uses montage to account for the unfinished present of the new millennium. She even more explicitly displaces the traditional notion of authorship—what Foucault called "the author function"—by presenting herself as an author among many. The work is conceived, in Abenshushan's words, as a "libro/fichero/algoritmo de internet." Abenshushan, *Permanente obra negra*, 6.

91. Fisher, *Capitalist Realism*, 6–7.

92. For montage as a crystallization of multiple temporalities, see Didi-Huberman, *Ante el tiempo*, 43–44.

93. For an overview of contemporary art that uses silhouettes, shadows, and projections as vehicles to reference memory work, see Saltzman, *Making Memory Matter*, 1–24. Saltzman analyzes the work of American artist Kara Walker, British artist Rachel Whiteread, and South African artist William Kentridge, among others.

94. Gerber Bicecci, *Empty Set*, 81.

95. For an analysis of second-generation poetics of memory and forgetting, see Robin, *La memoria saturada*, 360–61.

96. "Las formas de ser y las formas de visibilidad." Rancière, *El reparto*, 20. See also Forcinito, *Intermittences*, 8–9.

97. Butler, *Frames of War*, 71–72.

98. Blejmar, *Playful Memories*, 140.

99. Rancière, *El reparto*, 20.

100. Gerber Bicecci, *Empty Set*, 82, 83.

101. See Saltzman, *Making Memory Matter*, 53.

102. Gerber Bicecci, *Empty Set*, 41. See Fabre, *Leyendo agujeros*, 12.

103. Saltzman, *Making Memory Matter*, 17.

104. "Un no-lugar, un deslugar sin umbrales, tal vez sin suelo." Escobar, *El arte fuera de sí*, 152.

105. Gerber Bicecci, *Mudanza*, 17, 43.

106. Gerber Bicecci, *Empty Set*, 26.

107. Rancière, *Emancipated Spectator*, 102.

108. "Relatos destotalizados, fragmentos de una visualidad sin historia." García Canclini, *La sociedad sin relato*, 21–22.

109. Gerber Bicecci, *Empty Set*, 75.

110. See Robin, *La memoria saturada*, 58–59.

111. Bourriaud, *Exform*, 47.

112. See Rancière, *Edges of Fiction*, 117–118; Viart, "El relato de filiación."

113. Ricœur, *Memory, History, Forgetting*, 169.

114. "La passion généalogique"; "le partage du temps générationnel." Noudelmann, "Le contemporain sans époque: une affaire de rythmes," 63.

115. Gerber Bicecci, *Empty Set*, 132, 177.

116. Arlette Farge refers to archival work as diving into an infinite ocean of documents: "When working in the archive you will often find yourself thinking of this exploration as a dive, a submersion, perhaps even a drowning . . . you feel immersed in something vast, oceanic." Farge, *Allure of the Archives*, 4.

117. Gerber Bicecci, *Empty Set*, 74, 61.

118. Bourriaud, *Exform*, 58.

119. Arendt, *Human Condition*, 262.

120. Gerber Bicecci, *Empty Set*, 47.

121. Rancière, *Edges of Fiction*, 47–48.

122. Gerber Bicecci, *Empty Set*, 170.

123. Sergio Chejfec closely examines a series of material practices and conceptual modes of writing, among them the asemic writing practice of Argentinean artist Mirtha Dermisache, whose work Gerber Bicecci pays tribute to (*Empty Set*, 108). "Quizá la misma disposición sémica de la escritura se confabule contra las posibilidades afectivas de la composición caligráfica; y, en este sentido, la escritura asémica de Dermisache apostaría a mostrar esa potencialidad eventualmente liberada de los mandatos de transmisión de significado." Chejfec, *Últimas noticias de la escritura*, 101.

124. Foster, "Archival Impulse," 5.

125. Gerber Bicecci, *Empty Set*, 64.

126. Rivera Garza, *Restless Dead*, 96.

127. "Personajes con destinos ambliopes, aquellos que, en una demencia consciente, deciden renunciar, abandonarse a la contingencia para poner su vida, cuerpo y trabajo en el mismo espacio de indeterminación." Gerber Bicecci, *Mudanza*, 16.

128. Gerber Bicecci, *Empty Set*, 100.

129. Gerber Bicecci, *Empty Set*, 24.

130. "Escribió palabras impenetrables con un alfabeto conocido. Porque aún cuando dinamitaba el lenguaje común y corriente, aún en ese extremo del hermetismo quería ser leído, quería que hubiera tímpanos para sus ruidos, para el desentono, la cacofonía y la desarmonía. Oídos para el desacuerdo." Gerber Bicecci, *Mudanza*, 96.

131. Rancière, *Dissensus*, 139.

132. Rancière, *Emancipated Spectator*, 15.

133. Nora, "Between Memory and History," 16, 14, 17.

134. Gerber Bicecci, *Empty Set*, 32.

135. Blanchot, *Unavowable Community*, 18.

136. See Garramuño, "Obsolescencia, archivo."

137. Hartog, *Regimes of Historicity*, 17–18.

138. Gerber Bicecci, *Empty Set*, 67.

139. "La temporalidad del fin y del después del fin . . . el relato orgánico, lineal, progresivo, de las temporalidades de la nación." Ludmer, *Aquí América Latina*, 91.

140. Gerber Bicecci, *Empty Set*, 3.

141. Gramsci, *Selections from the Prison Notebooks*, 276.

142. The phrase "natural history of destruction" belongs to the German writer W. G. Sebald, author of *On the Natural History of Destruction*. In "Dr. Henry Selwyn," a story included in *The Emigrants*, Sebald's narrator tells the story of a mountaineer trapped in the ice for decades, ever since an accident occurred before the Great War, until his body was discovered in 1980 after the melting of the glacier: "And so they are ever returning to us, the dead. At times they come back from the ice more than seven decades later and are found at the edge of the moraine, a few polished bones and a pair of hobnailed boots." Sebald, *Emigrants*, 23.

143. Gerber Bicecci, *Empty Set*, 168.

144. As Sergio Villalobos-Ruminott claims, we are currently experiencing the contours of an era of disappearance, marked not only by the biopolitical abandonment into which the bodies of citizens have fallen but also by "la desaparición de la misma desaparición de la cual el cadáver daba testimonio y, así[,] . . . marcada por la desaparición del cadáver como signo último de una lengua que ya no promete un acceso al sentido." Villalobos-Ruminott, *Heterografías de la violencia*, 200.

145. Gerber Bicecci, *Empty Set*, 170.

146. Baudrillard, *Passwords*, 60.

147. "Lo que se desconoce no es un efecto de la memoria de segunda generación sino una consecuencia del modo en que la dictadura administró el asesinato." Sarlo, *Tiempo pasado*, 157.

148. Di Stefano, *Vanishing Frame*, 15.

149. Di Stefano, *Vanishing Frame*, 12.

150. Rancière, *Modern Times*, 27.

151. See Jameson, "Aesthetics of Singularity," 120.

152. See Didi-Huberman, *Cuando las imágenes*, 170.

153. "Cada palabra tiene mil caras." Gerber Bicecci, *Mudanza*, 82.

CHAPTER 5: WAYS OF BEING CONTEMPORARY

1. Danto, *After the End of Art*, 10.

2. For a discussion of post-historical returns to the past in contemporary

art and literature, see Foster, *Design and Crime (and Other Diatribes)*, 123–43; García Canclini, *La sociedad sin relato*, 58.

3. Danto, *After the End of Art*, 5.

4. Jameson, "Aesthetics of Singularity," 106, 104. Peter Osborne argues "that 'contemporary' emerges as a critical category, within an internationalized theoretical discourse, only in the course of the 1990s, in the wake of the rapid collapse in the plausibility of the concept of the postmodern after '1989'—a collapse almost as sudden as that of the Berlin Wall itself." Osborne, *Crisis as Form*, 4.

5. Nilges, *How to Read a Moment*, 174. The discussion about the exhaustion and afterlife of postmodernism lies beyond the scope of this chapter. For an account of the exhaustion of postmodernism vis-à-vis its implication with the main structures of neoliberalism, see Nilges, *How to Read a Moment*, 176–90. Echoing Jameson's arguments in "Aesthetics of Singularity" about the end of postmodernism and the continuation of postmodernity, Nilges argues that the main tenets of postmodernity still hold true in describing our contemporary political and socioeconomic reality.

6. Luiselli, *Faces in the Crowd*, 11. Although I refer to the book's Spanish title, I quote from the English translation of Luiselli's novel.

7. Zambra, *Not to Read*, 59. To be sure, Zambra is writing here about Daniel Alarcón's novel *Lost City Radio* (2007), but he is also implicitly referring to the stakes of his own literary project, as will become clear throughout this chapter.

8. Although *Los ingrávidos* does not deal directly with the passing of NAFTA and the subsequent Zapatista uprising, the consequences of this treaty for Mexico's insertion in the global economy runs through Luiselli's body of work. Both of her books on Central American and Mexican migration to the United States— *Tell Me How It Ends* (2017) and *Lost Children Archive* (2019)—address the paradox that the NAFTA agreement "has allowed for freer trade of merchandise across the border, and less freedom of movement for people." Luiselli, "Wild West Meets the Southern Border." In an autobiographical essay, Luiselli has related how her mother moved to the town of La Realidad in the state of Chiapas to assist the Zapatista movement, especially in the education of children and young women. Luiselli, "Difficult Forgiveness."

9. Bourriaud, *Radicant*, 22.

10. Zambra, *Not to Read*, 216.

11. See Groys, "Comrades of Time."

12. See Kojève, *Introduction to the Reading of Hegel*, 161; Agamben, *Creation and Anarchy*, 1–2; Groys, *Introduction to Antiphilosophy*, 146.

13. Fukuyama argues that the master concept that articulates such dissimilar contemporary phenomena as the triumph of Donald Trump, the movement against systemic racism (Black Lives Matter), or the rise of the terrorist group ISIS is the "desire for recognition" or *thymos*. This is another rereading of the notion of the end of history according to Hegel, who argued that human history was

traversed by a series of struggles for the recognition of one's own identity. Today, according to Fukuyama, the emergence of identity politics constitutes a threat to liberal democracies since its demands cannot be satisfied by large-scale political or economic reforms. Fukuyama, *Identity*, 113.

14. Smith, *Art to Come*, 2.

15. Fonseca, *Literature of Catastrophe*, 168.

16. Derrida, *Specters of Marx*, 10.

17. Foster, *Return of the Real*, 24.

18. Foster, *Return of the Real*, 29. In Latin America, Tabarovsky has theorized the notion of return through his definitions of "literature of the left" and "ghost of the avant-garde." In contrast to Argentinean literature of the 1990s (which according to him was docile to the demands of the market), Tabarovsky advocates for a spectral return to the historical avant-gardes. Returning to the avant-gardes allows writers to shatter the postulates of our neoliberal present. For Tabarovsky, as for Foster: "El fantasma de la vanguardia viene del futuro. Es el fantasma de lo que no nació aún, de lo que está por llegar, de lo que hay que ir a buscar." Tabarovsky, *Fantasma de la vanguardia*, 27.

19. Michaels, *Shape of the Signifier*, 81.

20. Luiselli, *Faces in the Crowd*, 1, 12.

21. For a definition of filiation narratives, see Viart, "El relato de filiación." Filiation narratives seek to amend an incomplete transmission of memory through the inspection of archives, objects, or stories that allow writers to decipher the past. In many cases, filiation narratives explore the minor lives of actors excluded by hegemonic histories, as in the discipline of microhistory pioneered by the Italian historian Carlo Ginzburg.

22. Borges, "Kafka and His Precursors," 236. Italics in the original.

23. "Restituir significa también devolver algo a alguien." Viart, "El relato de filiación."

24. Luiselli, *Faces in the Crowd*, 124.

25. "Fantasma de la vanguardia"; "el arte de hablar de un modo imposible con el fantasma." Tabarovsky, *Fantasma de la vanguardia*, 11.

26. "El pasado no llegó y el futuro es apenas un préstamo. En el *impasse* entre esos dos tiempos, la vanguardia del fantasma se escribe en presente. En un presente pensado como punto de vista, como estrategia, como estrategia en el presente, o mejor dicho, ante el presente, contra el presente." Tabarovsky, *Fantasma de la vanguardia*, 20. Tabarovsky's notion is similar to that elaborated by Foster in *The Return of the Real* (1996), where he points out that the potential of the avant-garde comes from the future. "For even as the avant-garde recedes into the past, it also returns from the future, repositioned by innovative art in the present." Foster, *Return of the Real*, x. For a reading of *Los ingrávidos* through the notion of "traumatic realism" put forward by Foster, see Pape, "El pasaje como *modus operandi*."

27. "Una tradición secreta . . . cercana en su lejanía." García Ponce, "La noche y la llama," 4.

28. Sheridan, *Los Contemporáneos ayer*, 203, 205. *Los ingrávidos* is not the first novel to fictionalize a figure from the Contemporáneos group. Two writers of the Crack generation, Jorge Volpi and Pedro Ángel Palou, had already written novels about poets that belonged to this same avant-garde group: *A pesar del oscuro silencio* (1992) by Volpi rescues the figure of Jorge Cuesta, while *En la alcoba de un mundo* (1992) by Palou does the same with Xavier Villaurrutia. According to Ignacio Sánchez Prado, "this tactic allows Crack writers to trace a lineage to the past in such a way that legitimizes their attempt to reconstitute the Mexican literary field." Sánchez Prado, *Strategic Occidentalism*, 93.

29. "La preferencia por una escritura ajena al tiempo. No una que fuera intemporal sino una que, en el interior del relato, estuviera libre del corsé de la trama cronológica"; "Y es que así son las novelas de Owen, desplazamientos en un espacio efectivo, sin tiempo: viajes inmóviles de un Simbad perpetuamente varado." Luiselli, "Gilberto Owen."

30. "Si leemos sus cartas estamos leyendo su poesía"; "un retrato desenfocado"; "retrato fiel de la mirada." Luiselli, "Gilberto Owen."

31. The theme of blurred photographs is a leitmotif throughout Owen's work. See Sheridan, *Los Contemporáneos*, 253.

32. "Repetición del pasado, permanencia o pluralidad de tiempos: es también un paso a un lado, una desorientación del tiempo." Premat, *Non nova sed nove*, 67.

33. "Integrarse orgánicamente al presente neoliberal de la cultura occidental." Zavala, *Volver a la modernidad*, 161. Zavala's reading aligns with the notion of postmodern pastiche as theorized by Fredric Jameson: "a collective loss of historicity in such a way that the future fades away as unthinkable or unimaginable, while the past itself turns into dusty images and Hollywood-type pictures of actors in wigs and the like." Jameson, "Aesthetics of Singularity," 120. In fact, Zavala compares *Los ingrávidos* with Woody Allen's *Midnight in Paris* (2011) for their mutual depiction of the past through a depoliticized use of nostalgia. Zavala, *Volver a la modernidad*, 163.

34. See Habermas, "Modernity—An Incomplete Project"; Burges and Elias, "Time Studies Today," 11.

35. See Saltzman, *Making Memory Matter*, 6.

36. "Una continuidad, una historia o un relato único de filiaciones definidas"; "de poner de manifiesto creativamente la necesidad de buscar otras alternativas ante la dislocación temporal que signa lo contemporáneo y sitúa al pasado, a los pasados, en una situación de alteridad inédita." Guerrero, *Paisajes en movimiento*, 61–62.

37. Luiselli, *Faces in the Crowd*, 51.

38. Luiselli, *Faces in the Crowd*, 107, 60, 120.

39. Bourriaud, *Exform*, 51.

40. For Marc Augé, the subway is an emblematic space for the perception of what is contemporary of a given epoch, because of the changes in mentality that can be perceived through material culture (for example, advertisements and fashion). The frequent use of the metro, according to Augé, raises a series of questions about the notion of the contemporary: "¿En qué piensan mis contemporáneos?, ¿qué sienten?, ¿quiénes son? . . . ¿Qué caracteriza a una época?, ¿con relación a qué podría apreciarse el hecho de pertenecer todavía o no a ella?." Augé, *El metro revisitado*, 85, 101–2.

41. Osborne, *Anywhere or Not at All*, 17. Emphasis in the original.

42. "Un ser fragmentado"; "destilador de tiempos y discursos." Palou, *La casa del silencio*, 339.

43. Nora, "Between Memory and History," 8.

44. Kristeva, *Black Sun*, 60.

45. Crary, *24/7*, 8–9.

46. Luiselli, *Faces in the Crowd*, 89.

47. Virno, *Déjà vu*, 8.

48. "La vida flotante"; "el vacío emocional, la ingravidez indiferente en la que se despliegan las operaciones sociales." Lipovetsky, *La era del vacío*, 36.

49. Luiselli, *Faces in the Crowd*, 3.

50. Luiselli, *Faces in the Crowd*, 62. This weightlessness corresponds with Owen's own body of work, in which, according to Guillermo Sheridan, the figure of "cuerpos sin sombra" appears as an important leitmotif. Sheridan, *Los Contemporáneos*, 236.

51. Ruffel, *Brouhaha*, 154.

52. Kristeva, *Black Sun*, 60.

53. Luiselli, *Faces in the Crowd*, 72.

54. Luiselli, *Faces in the Crowd*, 129.

55. Luiselli, *Faces in the Crowd*, 61, 122.

56. Luiselli, *Faces in the Crowd*, 72.

57. Luiselli, *Faces in the Crowd*, 129.

58. Foster, *Design and Crime*, 134.

59. According to Palou, "El simultaneísmo le permite [a Owen] difuminar el tiempo—quizá el descubrimiento mayor de la prosa oweniana: detener el tiempo narrativo, descronologizarlo." Palou, *La casa del silencio*, 287. This statement corresponds with various phrases pronounced by Owen throughout *Los ingrávidos*, which refer to the act of folding or freezing time. For example, "If you dedicate your life to writing novels, you're dedicating yourself to folding time," or "I think it's more a matter of freezing time without stopping the movement of things, a bit like when you're on a train, looking out of the window." Luiselli, *Faces in the Crowd*, 115.

60. I draw on Eugenio Di Stefano and Emilio Sauri's analysis of Nicolás Cabral's *Catálogo de formas*, which, according to them, "insists not simply on

narrating the end of history, but on imagining a space in which . . . 'history be-gins,' and from which the possibility of thinking art and the literary emerges as well." Di Stefano and Sauri, "'La furia de la materia,'" 157.

61. Foster, *Design and Crime*, 134. In her analysis of *Los ingrávidos*, Cecily Raynor highlights Luiselli's distancing from the postmodern ethos. She argues that "Luiselli's fixation is not on the impossibility of representing the present but rather on a celebration of the text as an open, polyvocal, iterative means of narrat-ing the world. Luiselli reveals the author not as a distant figure who speaks from afar to transmit watertight representations of a contemporary present but as some-one who lives within a world of collaborations and chance encounters that later emerge in writing." Raynor, *Latin American Literature at the Millennium*, 114.

62. Bourriaud, *Exform*, 58, 57.

63. For a speculative history of Owen's relationship with García Lorca in 1920s New York, see Sheridan, *Tres ensayos sobre Gilberto Owen*, 105–27.

64. Groys, "Comrades of Time."

65. See Bourriaud, *Postproduction*, 10–11; Speranza, *Cronografías*, 170.

66. Luiselli, *Faces in the Crowd*, 57.

67. Luiselli, *Faces in the Crowd*, 112.

68. Booker, "On Mediation and Fragmentation," 281.

69. Premat, "Fin de los tiempos, comienzos de la literatura," 117.

70. Viart, "El relato de filiación."

71. Bourriaud, *Radicant*, 22.

72. Bourriaud, *Postproduction*, 42–43.

73. Luiselli, *Faces in the Crowd*, 35.

74. "Obras atravesadas por agujeros, obras que acogen en su interior ausen-cias producto de una (des)escritura o de una antiescritura o de una no escritura." Fabre, *Leyendo agujeros*, 12.

75. Luiselli, *Faces in the Crowd*, 4, 10.

76. Luiselli, *Faces in the Crowd*, 120.

77. Santner, *On Creaturely Life*, 112.

78. Luiselli, *Faces in the Crowd*, 142.

79. Rancière, *Edges of Fiction*, 124.

80. Although I refer to the book's Spanish title, I quote from the English translation of Zambra's novel. María Belén Contreras and Rodrigo Zamorano Muñoz have traced several correspondences between the works of Luiselli and Zambra since both authors write "prosas minimalistas, de 'voz baja,' en las que se retratan las vidas íntimas de escritores." Contreras and Muñoz, "Autor, autoridad y policía," 67. The notion of literature written in a low voice (*en voz baja*) is in-debted to the Chilean writer Alejandra Costamagna, author of the homonymous novel *En voz baja* (1996). Moreover, both Luiselli and Zambra have written about each other's work, to such an extent that a character by the name of Alejandro Zambra makes a cameo appearance in Luiselli's *La historia de mis dientes*. See

Zambra, *No leer*, 65–71; Luiselli, *Sidewalks*, 78; and Luiselli, *Story of My Teeth*, 135–36.

81. "Los baches de sentido, las opacidades de la representación"; "presente cronológicamente programado como 'transición'"; "presente liviano." Richard, *Crítica de la memoria (1990–2010)*, 182, 184.

82. My reading of *Bonsái* aligns with that proposed by Lorena Amaro, who has examined Zambra's work through Viart's concept of "filiation narrative." For Amaro, Zambra's novels "no sólo van a la caza de la memoria infantil y una herencia familiar, sino que entrañan también interrogantes sobre la herencia literaria, lo que hace la búsqueda doblemente interesante." Amaro Castro, "Formas de salir de casa," 111. Similarly, Sergio Rojas highlights the way in which Zambra's novels, in parallel to those of other Chilean writers such as Nona Fernández and Álvaro Bisama, put forward "memorias individuales huérfanas de comunidad" and "un pasado que al no ingresar en la historia, permanece en su inmanencia." Rojas, "Profunda superficie," 235, 236. Paradoxically, the idea of a community of sons and daughters of post-dictatorship depends on the condition of orphanhood of its members, who experience history as a discontinuous timeline. Premat analyzes Zambra's works through the figure of the writer "que llegó después, que recibe parcialmente una experiencia trágica, que intenta definir una posición personal ante el monumento memorial que constituye la dictadura con sus relatos, sus héroes, sus dramas." Premat, *"Yo tendré mis árboles,"* 93.

83. Rancière, *"Fin de Siècle,"* 8.

84. Rancière, *"Fin de Siècle,"* 8–9.

85. Didi-Huberman, *Surviving Image*, 49. Italics in the original.

86. *Bonsái* can be read alongside a series of contemporary fictions that articulate the relationship between crisis, end of history, and romantic breakup. In Argentina, novels such as *El aire* (1992) by Sergio Chejfec, *El pasado* (2003) by Alan Pauls, and *Ida* (2008) by Oliverio Coelho, in addition to *El año del desierto* by Pedro Mairal, narrate the advent of socioeconomic crisis through romantic breakups and the impossibility of forming long-term affective bonds. For a study of these fictions and the ways in which they link romantic breakup and social crisis, see Ariza, *El abandono*.

87. Didi-Huberman, *Surviving Image*, 324.

88. Didi-Huberman, *Surviving Image*, 313.

89. Zambra, *Bonsai*, 3.

90. "Enmarañando pasados y presentes en un movimiento de vaivén perpetuo que los torna densos y plurales." Cámara, *Restos épicos*, 16–17.

91. Zambra, *Bonsai*, 13. Italics in the original.

92. Didi-Huberman, *Surviving Image*, 308.

93. Zambra, *Bonsai*, 13.

94. Rancière, *Edges of Fiction*, 134.

95. Zambra, *Bonsai*, 71.

96. Di Stefano, *Vanishing Frame*, 119.

97. Zambra, *Bonsai*. Page number is not provided.

98. "En ese intersticio se pasa de la página en blanco a la escritura, de un 'bonsái de novela' a una 'novela-novela,' de una filiación impuesta a una identidad elegida." Premat, *"Yo tendré,"* 103.

99. "Una estética por substracción." Rojo, *Las novelas de la dictadura*, 127.

100. "La profundidad de la brecha que separa la experiencia generacional de unos vástagos que no habían nacido aún cuando sobrevino el golpe de estado, o que nacieron inmediatamente después, respecto de la experiencia de sus mayores." Rojo, *Las novelas de la dictadura*, 130.

101. Zambra, *Bonsai*, 69.

102. Fisher, *Capitalist Realism*, 6.

103. In *No leer*, Zambra rescues the figure of Macedonio as a writer of unfinished drafts: "As many critics have noted, in the end Macedonio was a draft of Borges. And sometimes—every other year—we like drafts more than the clean version." Zambra, *Not to Read*, 130. Additionally, he points to his discovery of Macedonio as an encounter with a new type of writing practice that he contrasts with the mandatory readings of the Ercilla Library, a collection of the "best books in world literature" that he found in his family library: "My generation grew up believing that Chilean literature was brown, and that there was no such thing as Latin American literature." Zambra, *Not to Read*, 225.

104. "Restos, trozos que llegan vacíos, sueltos, casi de un modo inmanente: nos llega el texto, ya no la época"; "en la grieta, en el terremoto, en la tormenta, en el remolino, que todo lo cambia de un instante a otro." Tabarovsky, *Fantasma de la vanguardia*, 19–20.

105. For an analysis of techniques of appropriation and disappropriation used by contemporary writers, see Rivera Garza, *Restless Dead*, 43–79. Rivera Garza analyzes works that use appropriation and montage as techniques to make the dead speak in contexts of necropolitical violence such as Mexico's War on Drugs and the escalation of crimes against women. "Disappropriation," according to Rivera Garza, "forces us to discern the material traces of those who were *there*, and those who are *here* as I write: specters, apparitions, memories, accompaniment." Rivera Garza, *Restless Dead*, 53. Italics in the original.

106. Bourriaud, *Radicant*, 98.

107. Rancière, *Béla Tarr, the Time After*, 27.

108. Zambra, *Bonsai*, 35–36.

109. "Escritores-consumidores"; "una economía sentimental de lectura: la nostalgia por referentes pasados, remotos o perdidos." Cárcamo-Huechante, *Tramas del mercado*, 52–53.

110. Gago, *Neoliberalism from Below*, 188.

111. Didi-Huberman, *Surviving Image*, 329.

112. Influenced by Rosalind Krauss's notion of sculpture in an expanded

field, Garramuño defines nonspecific works of art and literature through the idea of "un campo expansivo . . . que en su inestabilidad y ebullición atenta incluso contra la propia noción de campo como espacio estático y cerrado." Garramuño, *Mundos en común*, 43.

113. For example, in Zambra's *Facsímil* (2014; trans. 2016 as *Multiple Choice*), students are asked to complete a university exam (the Prueba de Aptitud Académica, used for enrollment in Chilean universities between 1966 and 2002) under certain temporal parameters.

114. Zambra, *My Documents*, 135.

115. Rancière, *Béla Tarr*, 34–35.

116. Héctor Hoyos points to obsolescence and the politics of nostalgia as some of Zambra's recurring themes through a reading of his short story "Memories of a Personal Computer." "Zambra's core intervention [is] his re-appropriation of the motif of obsolescence as the cornerstone of a 'new' politics of nostalgia. This politics speaks to the experience of shock in Chile but also to the peculiar historical situation of an emerging global middle class. As such, Zambra's writings offer a window into the affective life of contemporary capitalism and raise important questions about its subjects' disjointed, easily coopted assimilation of experience." Hoyos, "Telltale Computer," 109. In a reelaboration of this reading, Hoyos highlights the role of the computer as "an assemblage of human and non-human elements," standing against contemporary capitalism's ever shorter cycles of production and obsolescence. Hoyos, *Things with a History*, 179.

117. Zambra, *Not to Read*, 223.

118. Rancière, "What a Medium Can Mean," 42.

119. *La vida privada de los árboles* takes place during a single night, while its protagonist, Julián (an alter ego of Julio), puts his stepdaughter to sleep and awaits the arrival of his wife.

120. Bellatin in his novel creates a fictional Japan through imagined words and cultural products. Other fictional renderings of East Asia in contemporary Latin American literature include César Aira's *Una novela china* (1987) and Eduardo Berti's *El país imaginado* (2011; trans. 2018 as *The Imagined Land*). For an analysis of *Bonsái* through the concept of *japonisme*, see Romero, "Japonismo."

121. Zambra, *Bonsai*, 49.

122. Zambra, *Bonsai*, 52.

123. Zambra, *Bonsai*, 62.

124. Rivera Garza, *Restless Dead*, 48.

125. In fact, in an interview with Argentinean writer Mauro Libertella, Zambra declared: "Estoy muy en contra de la angustia de las influencias. Creo que si las influencias te angustian es porque eres un pelotudo." Libertella, *El estilo de los otros*, 73. According to Wilfrido H. Corral, who analyzes Zambra's statement: "Si hoy no se lee como en 1996 o 2018, no es porque la novela actual es mejor o peor sino porque la experiencia y tradición acumuladas exigen más, aun al volver

a leer una obra admirada." Corral, *Discípulos y maestros 2.0*, 11. In this sense, Zambra's works align with Foster's assertion that shadowing as a procedure in contemporary art "operates formally at the level of genre or medium. The shadowing I have in mind has little of the 'anxiety of influence' described by Harold Bloom in modernist poetry; yet neither is there much 'ecstasy of influence' along the postmodernist lines of the high-spirited meta-fiction of university novelists like John Barth and Robert Coover, or of the homage-laden neo-genre cinema of film-school directors like Martin Scorsese and Brian de Palma. The shadowing in play today is more muted, a sort of outlining and shading, in the manner that *Mrs. Dalloway* (1925) outlines and shades *The Hours* (1998) by Michael Cunningham." Foster, *Design and Crime*, 134.

126. Zambra, *Bonsai*, 62.

127. Zambra, *Bonsai*, 3.

128. According to Jean-François Lyotard, the postmodern condition derives from the process of delegitimization of the grand narratives of modernity. "The grand narrative has lost its credibility," Lyotard argues, "regardless of what mode of legitimization it uses, regardless of whether it is a speculative narrative or a narrative of emancipation." Lyotard, *Postmodern Condition*, 37.

129. Bourriaud, *Radicant*, 104.

130. Zambra, *Bonsai*, 50.

131. Zambra, *Bonsai*, 75.

132. Bourriaud, *Radicant*, 51.

133. Zambra, *Bonsai*, 79.

134. "Sólo quienes escriben conscientes del fin de la literatura pueden lograr que ésta sobreviva." Iglesia, *Ese famoso abismo*, 25.

135. Bourriaud, *Radicant*, 44, 56.

136. Hartog, *Regimes of Historicity*, 185.

137. Viart, "El relato de filiación."

CONCLUSION: HISTORY IN THE PRESENT TENSE

1. Luiselli, *Lost Children Archive*, 103.

2. Luiselli, *Lost Children Archive*, 29.

3. Luiselli, *Lost Children Archive*, 8.

4. Leguizamón, *Seeds of Power*, 49.

5. Luiselli, *Lost Children Archive*, 106.

6. Fernández, *Twilight Zone*, 139, 187.

7. Fernández, *Twilight Zone*, 136, 57.

8. Zapata, *Lost Book of Adana Moreau*, 44.

9. Zapata, *Lost Book of Adana Moreau*, 153.

10. Zapata, *Lost Book of Adana Moreau*, 16, 98.

11. Luiselli, *Lost Children Archive*, 60.

BIBLIOGRAPHY

Abenshushan, Vivian. *Permanente obra negra*. Mexico City: Sexto Piso, 2019.

Agamben, Giorgio. *Creation and Anarchy: The Work of Art and the Religion of Capitalism*. Translated by Adam Kotsko. Stanford, CA: Stanford University Press, 2019.

Agamben, Giorgio. "What Is the Contemporary?" In *What Is an Apparatus?* Translated by David Kishik and Stefan Pedatella, 39–54. Stanford, CA: Stanford University Press, 2009.

Agüero, José Carlos. *Persona*. Lima: Fondo de Cultura Económica, 2017.

Aira, César. *Las noches de Flores*. Barcelona: Random House Mondadori, 2004.

Aira, César. "El sultán." *Paradoxa* 6, no. 6 (1991): 27–29.

Aira, César. *El vestido rosa/Las ovejas*. Buenos Aires: Ada Korn Editora, 1984.

Alaimo, Stacy. *Bodily Natures: Science, Environment, and the Material Self.* Bloomington: Indiana University Press, 2010.

Alberdi, Juan Bautista. *Bases y puntos de partida para la organización política de la República Argentina*. Buenos Aires: Biblioteca del Congreso de la Nación, 2017.

Alemán, Gabriela. *Poso Wells*. Quito: Eskeletra Editorial, 2007.

Alves, Maria Thereza. *El retorno de un lago (The Return of a Lake)*. Mexico City: MUAC, 2014.

Amaro Castro, Lorena. "Formas de salir de casa, o cómo escapar del Ogro: relatos de filiación en la literatura chilena reciente." *Literatura y Lingüística* 29 (2014): 109–29.

Andermann, Jens. *Tierras en trance: arte y naturaleza después del paisaje*. Santiago de Chile: Metales Pesados, 2018.

Anderson, Mark. "The Grounds of Crisis and the Geopolitics of Depth: Mexico City in the Anthropocene." In *Ecological Crisis and Cultural Representation in Latin America: Ecocritical Perspectives on Art, Film, and Literature*, edited by Mark Anderson and Zélia M. Bora, 99–123. Lanham, MD: Lexington Books, 2016

Anderson, Mark. "Introduction: The Dimensions of Crisis." In *Ecological Crisis and Cultural Representation in Latin America: Ecocritical Perspectives on Art,*

Film, and Literature, edited by Mark Anderson and Zélia M. Bora, ix–xxxii. Lanham, MD: Lexington Books, 2016.

Appiah, Kwame Anthony. *Cosmopolitanism: Ethics in a World of Strangers.* New York: W. W. Norton, 2006.

Appiah, Kwame Anthony. "Cosmopolitan Patriots." *Critical Inquiry* 23, no. 3 (1997): 617–39.

Arendt, Hannah. *Between Past and Future: Six Exercises in Political Thought.* 1954. New York: Viking Press, 1961.

Arendt, Hannah. *The Human Condition.* Chicago: University of Chicago Press, 1998.

Ariza, Julio. *El abandono: abismo amoroso y crisis social en la reciente literatura argentina.* Rosario, Argentina: Beatriz Viterbo Editora, 2018.

Atencio, Rebecca. *Memory's Turn: Reckoning with Dictatorship in Brazil.* Madison: University of Wisconsin Press, 2014.

Augé, Marc. *El metro revisitado: el viajero subterráneo veinte años después.* Translated by Rosa Bertran and Marta Bertran. Madrid: Paidós, 2010.

Avelar, Idelber. *The Untimely Present: Postdictatorial Latin American Fiction and the Task of Mourning.* Durham, NC: Duke University Press, 1999.

Azoulay, Ariella Aïsha. *The Civil Contract of Photography.* Translated by Rela Mazali and Ruvik Danieli. New York: Zone Books, 2008.

Azoulay, Ariella Aïsha. "Potential History." *Critical Inquiry* 39, no. 3 (2013): 548–74.

Azoulay, Ariella Aïsha. *Potential History: Unlearning Imperialism.* London: Verso, 2019.

Banaggia, Gabriel. *As forças do jarê: religião de matriz africana da Chapada Diamantina.* Rio de Janeiro: Garamond, 2015.

Barbas-Rhoden, Laura. *Ecological Imaginations in Latin American Fiction.* Gainesville: University Press of Florida, 2011.

Barickman, B. J. "'A Bit of Land, Which They Call Roça': Slave Provision Grounds in the Bahian Recôncavo, 1780–1860." *Hispanic American Historical Review* 74, no. 4 (1994): 649–87.

Barnet, Miguel. *Biografía de un cimarrón.* 1966. Madrid: Siruela, 2020.

Barthes, Roland. "Interview with *Tel Quel.*" Translated by Vérène Grieshaber. In *The Tel Quel Reader,* edited by Patrick ffrench and Roland-François Lack, 249–67. London: Routledge, 1998.

Barthes, Roland. *Roland Barthes by Roland Barthes.* Translated by Richard Howard. New York: Hill and Wang, 2010.

Baudrillard, Jean. *Passwords.* Translated by Chris Turner. London: Verso, 2003.

Belli, Gioconda. *Waslala: memorial del futuro.* Managua: anamá Ediciones Centroamericanas, 1996.

Benítez-Rojo, Antonio. *The Repeating Island: The Caribbean and the Postmodern Perspective*. Translated by James E. Maraniss. Durham, NC: Duke University Press, 1996.

Benjamin, Walter. *The Arcades Project*. Translated by Howard Eiland and Kevin McLaughlin. Cambridge, MA: Harvard University Press, 2002.

Benjamin, Walter. "The Work of Art in the Age of Its Technological Reproducibility." In *The Work of Art in the Age of Its Technological Reproducibility and Other Writings on Media*, edited by Michael W. Jennings, Brigid Doherty, and Thomas Y. Levin, translated by Harry Zohn, 19–55. Cambridge, MA: Harvard University Press, 2008.

Bennett, Jane. *Vibrant Matter: A Political Ecology of Things*. Durham, NC: Duke University Press, 2010.

Berardi, Franco "Bifo." *Futurability: The Age of Impotence and the Horizon of Possibility*. London: Verso, 2019.

Bermeo Gamboa, L. C. "Odisea caucana." *El País Colombia*, October 23, 2020. https://www.elpais.com.co/cultura/gaceta/odisea-caucana-entrevista-con-el -escritor-juan-cardenas-sobre-su-novela-elastico-de-sombra.html.

Bett, Alan. "Poisoned World: Samanta Schweblin on *Fever Dream*." *The Skinny*, October 16, 2017. https://www.theskinny.co.uk/books/features/samanta -schweblin-on-fever-dream.

Beverley, John. *Testimonio: On the Politics of Truth*. Minneapolis: University of Minnesota Press, 2004.

Beverley, John, and José Oviedo. "Introduction." In *The Postmodernism Debate in Latin America*, edited by John Beverley, Michael Aronna, and José Oviedo, 1–17. Durham, NC: Duke University Press, 1995.

Bewes, Timothy. *Free Indirect: The Novel in a Postfictional Age*. New York: Columbia University Press, 2022.

Biron, Rebecca E. "Paisajes de la (in)seguridad: circuitos del miedo en la Ciudad de México." In *Utopías urbanas: geopolíticas del deseo en América Latina*, edited by Gisela Heffes, 87–111. Madrid: Iberoamericana Vervuert, 2013.

Bishop, Claire. "Antagonism and Relational Aesthetics." *October* 110 (Fall 2004): 51–79.

Bishop, Claire. *Artificial Hells: Participatory Art and the Politics of Spectatorship*. London: Verso, 2012.

Blanchot, Maurice. *The Unavowable Community*. Translated by Pierre Joris. Barrytown, NY: Station Hill Press, 1988.

Blanco, Fernando. *Neoliberal Bonds: Undoing Memory in Chilean Art and Literature*. Columbus: Ohio State University Press, 2015.

Blanco, María del Pilar. *Ghost-Watching American Modernity: Haunting, Landscape, and the Hemispheric Imagination*. New York: Fordham University Press, 2012.

Blejmar, Jordana. *Playful Memories: The Autofictional Turn in Post-dictatorship Argentina*. Cham, Switzerland: Palgrave Macmillan, 2016.

Bloch, Ernst. *Heritage of Our Times*. Translated by Neville and Stephen Plaice. Cambridge, UK: Polity Press, 1991.

Bonfil Batalla, Guillermo. *México profundo: Reclaiming a Civilization*. Translated by Philip A. Dennis. Austin: University of Texas Press, 1996.

Booker, Sarah K. "On Mediation and Fragmentation: The Translator in Valeria Luiselli's *Los ingrávidos*." *Revista Canadiense de Estudios Hispánicos* 41, no. 2 (Winter 2017): 273–95.

Borges, Jorge Luis. *Borges on Writing*. Edited by Norman Thomas Di Giovanni, Daniel Halpern, and Frank MacShane. New Jersey: Ecco Press, 1994.

Borges, Jorge Luis. "Kafka and His Precursors." In *Labyrinths: Selected Stories and Other Writings*, edited by Donald A. Yates and James E. Irby, 234–36. New York: Penguin Books, 1970.

Borges, Jorge Luis. "The Library of Babel." In *Labyrinths: Selected Stories and Other Writings*, edited by Donald A. Yates and James E. Irby, 78–86. New York: Penguin Books, 1970.

Borges, Jorge Luis, and Adolfo Bioy Casares. "La fiesta del monstruo." In *Jorge Luis Borges: obras completas en colaboración*, 453–66. 1972. Madrid: Alianza Editorial, 1981.

Bourriaud, Nicolas. *The Exform*. Translated by Erik Butler. London: Verso, 2016.

Bourriaud, Nicolas. *Postproduction. Culture as Screenplay: How Art Reprograms the World*. Translated by Jeanine Herman. New York: Sternberg Press, 2006.

Bourriaud, Nicolas. *The Radicant*. Translated by James Gussen and Lili Porten. New York: Sternberg Press, 2009.

Bourriaud, Nicolas. *Relational Aesthetics*. Translated by Simon Pleasance and Fronza Woods. Dijon: Les presses du réel, 2002.

Boym, Svetlana. *The Future of Nostalgia*. New York: Basic Books, 2001.

Brouillette, Sarah, Mathias Nilges, and Emilio Sauri. "Introduction. Contemporaneity: On Refusing to Live in the Moment." In *Literature and the Global Contemporary*, edited by Sarah Brouillette, Mathias Nilges, and Emilio Sauri, xv–xxxviii. Cham, Switzerland: Palgrave Macmillan, 2017.

Brown, Wendy. *Undoing the Demos: Neoliberalism's Stealth Revolution*. New York: Zone Books, 2016.

Buchloh, Benjamin. "Gerhard Richter's Atlas: The Anomic Archive." In *The Archive*, edited by Charles Merewether, 85–102. London: Whitechapel Gallery/ MIT Press, 2006.

Buell, Lawrence. "Ecoglobalist Affects: The Emergence of U.S. Environmental Imagination on a Planetary Scale." In *Shades of the Planet: American Literature as World Literature*, edited by Wai Chee Dimock and Lawrence Buell, 227–48. Princeton, NJ: Princeton University Press, 2007.

Buell, Lawrence. *The Environmental Imagination: Thoreau, Nature Writing, and the Formation of American Culture*. Cambridge, MA: Harvard University Press, 1995.

Buell, Lawrence. *Writing for an Endangered World: Literature, Culture, and Environment in the U.S. and Beyond*. Cambridge, MA: Harvard University Press, 2001.

Burges, Joel, and Amy J. Elias. "Introduction: Time Studies Today." In *Time: A Vocabulary of the Present*, edited by Joel Burges and Amy J. Elias, 1–32. New York: New York University Press, 2016.

Butler, Judith. *Frames of War: When Is Life Grievable?* London: Verso, 2009.

Cabrera, Lydia. "The Ceiba Tree." Translated by Patricia González. In *The Latin American Ecocultural Reader*, edited by Gisela Heffes and Jennifer French, 234–38. Evanston, IL: Northwestern University Press, 2020.

Calveiro, Pilar. *Política y/o violencia: una aproximación a la guerrilla de los años setenta*. Buenos Aires: Siglo XXI, 2013.

Cámara, Mario. *Restos épicos: la literatura y el arte en el cambio de época*. Buenos Aires: Libraria, 2017.

Camenen, Gersende. "El oficio de traducir: de algunos traductores en la narrativa argentina de los años noventa y primera década del siglo XXI." *Cuadernos de Literatura* 20, no. 40 (July–December 2016): 449–64.

Candiani, Vera S. *Dreaming of Dry Land: Environmental Transformation in Colonial Mexico City*. Stanford, CA: Stanford University Press, 2014.

Cárcamo-Huechante, Luis E. *Tramas del mercado: imaginación económica, cultura pública y literatura en el Chile de fines del siglo veinte*. Santiago de Chile: Cuarto Propio, 2007.

Cárdenas, Juan. *El diablo de las provincias: fábula en miniaturas*. Cáceres, Spain: Periférica, 2017.

Cárdenas, Juan. *Elástico de sombra*. Mexico City: Sexto Piso, 2020.

Cárdenas, Juan. "Teoría del escombro: una fábula bioluminiscente sobre el futuro del arte." In *En una orilla brumosa: cinco rutas para repensar los futuros de las artes visuales y la literatura*, edited by Verónica Gerber Bicecci, 181–203. Querétaro, Mexico: Gris Tormenta, 2021.

Carpentier, Alejo. *Viaje a la semilla*. Havana: Ucar, García, y Cía, 1944.

Chakrabarty, Dipesh. *The Climate of History in a Planetary Age*. Chicago: University of Chicago Press, 2021.

Char, René. *Feuillets d'Hypnos: œuvres complètes*. Paris: Gallimard, 1983.

Chejfec, Sergio. *Últimas noticias de la escritura*. Buenos Aires: Entropía, 2015.

Compagnon, Antoine. *Les antimodernes: de Joseph de Maistre à Roland Barthes*. Paris: Gallimard, 2016.

Contreras, María Belén, and Rodrigo Zamorano Muñoz. "Autor, autoridad y policía en *Formas de volver a casa* de Alejandro Zambra." *Mester* 44, no. 1 (2016): 51–72.

Corral, Wilfrido H. *Discípulos y maestros 2.0: novela hispanoamericana hoy*. Madrid: Iberoamericana Vervuert, 2019.

Cortázar, Julio. "Casa tomada." In *Cuentos completos 1*, 131–36. Mexico City: Santillana, 2011.

Cortázar, Julio. "La noche boca arriba." In *Cuentos completos 1*, 523–31. Mexico City: Santillana, 2011.

Crary, Jonathan. *24/7: Late Capitalism and the Ends of Sleep*. London: Verso, 2014.

Cristoff, María Sonia. *Mal de época*. Buenos Aires: Mardulce, 2017.

Crutzen, Paul. "Geology of Mankind." *Nature* 415 (2002): 23.

Dabove, Juan Pablo, and Susan Hallstead. "Introducción." In Pedro Mairal, *El año del desierto*, vii–xiii. Doral, FL: Stockcero, 2012.

Danowski, Déborah, and Eduardo Viveiros de Castro. *The Ends of the World*. Translated by Rodrigo Nunes. Malden, MA: Polity, 2017.

Danto, Arthur. *After the End of Art: Contemporary Art and the Pale of History*. Princeton, NJ: Princeton University Press, 1997.

Dávila, Amparo. *The Houseguest and Other Stories*. Translated by Audrey Harris and Matthew Gleeson. New York: New Directions, 2018.

Deckard, Sharae, and Kerstin Oloff. "'The One Who Comes from the Sea': Marine Crisis and the New Oceanic Weird in Rita Indiana's *La mucama de Omicunlé* (2015)." *Humanities* 9, no. 86 (2020): 1–14.

Deffis, Emilia. "'La necrópolis interior' en *Conjunto vacío* de Verónica Gerber Bicecci." *Anclajes* 24, no. 2 (2020): 17–32.

de Friedemann, Nina S. *La saga del negro: presencia africana en Colombia*. Bogotá: Pontificia Universidad Javeriana, 1993.

del Cid, Marvin. "Descuido y vegetación amenazan la Ceiba de Colón." *Diario Libre*, October 22, 2020. https://www.diariolibre.com/actualidad/medio ambiente/descuido-y-vegetacion-amenazan-la-ceiba-de-colon-GC22209816.

De Leone, Lucía. "Campos que matan: espacios, tiempos y narración en *Distancia de rescate* de Samanta Schweblin." *452ºF* 16 (2017): 62–76.

de Leone, Lucía. "Imaginaciones rurales argentinas: el campo como zona de cruce en expresiones artísticas contemporáneas." *Cuadernos de Literatura* 20, no. 40 (2016): 181–203.

DeLoughrey, Elizabeth. *Allegories of the Anthropocene*. Durham, NC: Duke University Press, 2019.

del Valle, Ivonne. "On Shaky Ground: Hydraulics, State Formation, and Colonialism in Sixteenth-Century Mexico." *Hispanic Review* 77, no. 2 (2009): 197–220.

de Narváez, Santiago A. "El mundo de mierda en el que estamos es obra del Hombre Blanco." *Pacifista!*, February 4, 2020. https://pacifista.tv/notas/juan -cardenas-mundo-mierda-estamos-obra-hombre-blanco-entrevista-elastico -sombra.

Derrida, Jacques. *Specters of Marx: The State of the Debt, the Work of Mourning and the New International.* Translated by Peggy Kamuf. London: Routledge, 1994.

Desch-Obi, T. J. "*Peinillas* and Popular Participation: Machete Fighting in Haiti, Cuba, and Colombia." *Memorias: Revista Digital de Historia y Arqueología desde el Caribe Colombiano* 6, no. 11 (November 2009): 144–72.

Di Benedetto, Antonio. *Zama.* 1956. Buenos Aires: Adriana Hidalgo, 2022.

Didi-Huberman, Georges. *Ante el tiempo: historia del arte y anacronismo de las imágenes.* Translated by Antonio Oviedo. Buenos Aires: Adriana Hidalgo, 2011.

Didi-Huberman, Georges. *Confronting Images: Questioning the Ends of a Certain History of Art.* Translated by John Goodman. University Park, PA: Penn State University Press, 2005.

Didi-Huberman, Georges. *Cuando las imágenes toman posición: el ojo de la historia, 1.* Translated by Inés Bértolo. Madrid: Antonio Machado Libros, 2008.

Didi-Huberman, Georges. *Survival of the Fireflies.* Translated by Lia Swope Mitchell. Minneapolis: University of Minnesota Press, 2018.

Didi-Huberman, Georges. *The Surviving Image. Phantoms of Time and Time of Phantoms: Aby Warburg's History of Art.* Translated by Harvey L. Mendelsohn. University Park, PA: Penn State University Press, 2017.

Di Stefano, Eugenio. *The Vanishing Frame: Latin American Culture and Theory in the Postdictatorial Era.* Austin: University of Texas Press, 2018.

Di Stefano, Eugenio, and Emilio Sauri. "'La furia de la materia': On the Non-contemporaneity of Modernism in Latin America." In *The Contemporaneity of Modernism: Literature, Media, Culture,* edited by Michael D'Arcy and Mathias Nilges, 148–62. New York: Routledge, 2016.

Domínguez, Nora. *De donde vienen los niños: maternidad y escritura en la cultura argentina.* Rosario, Argentina: Beatriz Viterbo Editora, 2007.

Domínguez Hernández, Javier, Carlos Arturo Fernández, Efrén Giraldo, and Daniel Jerónimo Tobón. "Presentación." In *Moderno/Contemporáneo: un debate de horizontes,* edited by Javier Domínguez Hernández, Carlos Arturo Fernández, Efrén Giraldo, and Daniel Jerónimo Tobón, 7–10. Medellín, Colombia: La Carreta Editores/Universidad de Antioquia, 2008.

Donoso, José. *Historia personal del "boom."* Barcelona: Anagrama, 1972.

Drescher, Seymour. "Brazilian Abolition in Comparative Perspective." In *The Abolition of Slavery and the Aftermath of Emancipation in Brazil,* edited by Rebecca J. Scott, Seymour Drescher, Hebe Maria Mattos de Castro, George Reid Andrews, and Robert M. Levine, 23–54. Durham, NC: Duke University Press, 1988.

Drucaroff, Elsa. "Narraciones de la intemperie." *El interpretador* 27, June 6, 2006. http://elinterpretador.net/27ElsaDrucaroff-NarracionesDeLaIntemperie.html.

Drucaroff, Elsa. *Los prisioneros de la torre*. Buenos Aires: Emecé, 2011.

Echeverría, Esteban. *Obras completas. Tomo 1. Poemas varios*. Buenos Aires: Imprenta y Librería de Mayo, 1870.

Escobar, Arturo. *Pluriversal Politics: The Real and the Possible*. Translated by David Frye. Durham, NC: Duke University Press, 2020.

Escobar, Ticio. *El arte fuera de sí*. Asunción, Paraguay: FONDEC, 2004.

Esposito, Roberto. *Communitas: The Origin and Destiny of Community*. Translated by Timothy Campbell. Stanford, CA: Stanford University Press, 2006.

Fabre, Luis Felipe. *Leyendo agujeros: ensayos sobre (des)escritura, antiescritura y no escritura*. Mexico City: Fondo Editorial Tierra Adentro, 2005.

Farge, Arlette. *The Allure of the Archives*. Translated by Thomas Scott-Railton. New Haven, CT: Yale University Press, 2013.

Federici, Silvia. *Caliban and the Witch: Women, the Body and Primitive Accumulation*. Brooklyn, NY: Autonomedia, 2014.

Fernandes, Millôr. *Millôr definitivo: a bíblia do caos*. Porto Alegre, Brazil: L&PM Editores, 1994.

Fernández, Nona. *The Twilight Zone*. Translated by Natasha Wimmer. Minneapolis, MN: Graywolf Press, 2021.

Fernández Gonzalo, Jorge. *Filosofía zombi*. Barcelona: Anagrama, 2011.

Ferrero Cárdenas, Inés. "Geografía en el cuerpo: el otro yo en *El huésped*, de Guadalupe Nettel." *Revista de Literatura Mexicana Contemporánea* 41, no. 15 (2009): 55–62.

Fisher, Mark. *Capitalist Realism: Is There No Alternative?* London: Zero Books, 2009.

Fisher, Mark. *The Weird and the Eerie*. London: Repeater, 2016.

Fisher, Philip. *The Vehement Passions*. Princeton, NJ: Princeton University Press, 2002.

Focillon, Henri. *The Life of Forms in Art*. Translated by Charles B. Hogan and George Kubler. 1934. New York: Zone Books, 1992.

Fogwill, Rodolfo Enrique. *Los pichiciegos*. Cáceres, Spain: Periférica, 2010.

Fonseca, Carlos. *The Literature of Catastrophe: Nature, Disaster, and Revolution in Latin America*. New York: Bloomsbury, 2020.

Forcinito, Ana. *Intermittences: Memory, Justice, and the Poetics of the Visible in Uruguay*. Pittsburgh, PA: University of Pittsburgh Press, 2019.

Foster, Hal. "An Archival Impulse." *October* 110 (2004): 3–22.

Foster, Hal. *Bad New Days: Art, Criticism, Emergency*. London: Verso, 2015.

Foster, Hal. *Design and Crime (and Other Diatribes)*. London: Verso, 2002.

Foster, Hal. *The Return of the Real: The Avant-Garde at the End of the Century*. Cambridge, MA: MIT Press, 1996.

Foucault, Michel. *The Archaeology of Knowledge and the Discourse on Language*. Translated by A. M. Sheridan Smith. New York: Pantheon Books, 1972.

Fraga, Walter. *Crossroads of Freedom: Slaves and Freed People in Bahia, Brazil, 1870–1910*. Durham, NC: Duke University Press, 2016.

Franco, Marina, and Daniel Lvovich. "Historia reciente: apuntes sobre un campo de investigación en expansion." *Boletín del Instituto de Historia Argentina y Americana* 47 (2017): 190–217.

Freeman, Elizabeth. *Time Binds: Queer Temporalities, Queer Histories*. Durham, NC: Duke University Press, 2010.

Fresán, Rodrigo. *La velocidad de las cosas*. 1998. Barcelona: Literatura Random House, 2002.

Freyre, Gilberto. *Casa-Grande & Senzala: formação da família brasileira sob o regime da economia patriarcal*. São Paulo: Global, 2003.

Fuguet, Alberto. *Por favor, rebobinar*. 1994. Buenos Aires: Alfaguara, 1998.

Fuks, Julián. "A era da pós-ficção: notas sobre a insuficiência da fabulação no romance contemporáneo." In *Ética e pós-verdade*, 73–93. Porto Alegre, Brazil: Dublinense, 2017.

Fuks, Julián. *A resistência*. São Paulo: Companhia das Letras, 2015.

Fuks, Julián. "I Never Thought Dark Forces Might Make Me Leave Brazil." *The Guardian*, October 31, 2018. https://www.theguardian.com/books/2018/oct/31/brazil-jair-bolsonaro-cultural-political-resistance-julian-fuks.

Fuks, Julián. *Resistance*. Translated by Daniel Hahn. Edinburgh: Charco Press, 2018.

Fukuyama, Francis. *Identity: The Demand for Dignity and the Politics of Resentment*. New York: Farrar, Straus and Giroux, 2018.

Gago, Verónica. *Feminist International: How to Change Everything*. Translated by Liz Mason-Deese. London: Verso, 2020.

Gago, Verónica. *Neoliberalism from Below: Popular Pragmatics and Baroque Economies*. Translated by Liz Mason-Deese. Durham, NC: Duke University Press, 2017.

Ganguly, Debjani. "Catastrophic Form and Planetary Realism." *New Literary History* 51, no. 2 (2020): 419–53.

García Canclini, Néstor. "Aesthetic Moments of Latin Americanism." *Radical History Review* 89 (2004): 13–24.

García Canclini, Néstor. *La sociedad sin relato: antropología y estética de la inminencia*. Buenos Aires: Katz Editores, 2010.

García Márquez, Gabriel. *One Hundred Years of Solitude*. Translated by Gregory Rabassa. New York: Harper Perennial, 2006.

García-Peña, Lorgia. *The Borders of Dominicanidad: Race, Nation, and Archives of Contradiction*. Durham, NC: Duke University Press, 2016.

García Ponce, Juan. "La noche y la llama." *Revista de la Universidad de México* 21, no. 5 (January 1967): 4.

Garramuño, Florencia. *Mundos en común: ensayos sobre la inespecificidad en el arte*. Buenos Aires: Fondo de Cultura Económica, 2015.

Garramuño, Florencia. "Obsolescencia, archivo: políticas de la supervivencia en el arte contemporáneo." *Cuadernos de Literatura* 20, no. 40 (July–December 2016): 56–68.

Garrido Castellano, Carlos. *Literary Fictions of the Contemporary Art System: Global Perspectives in Spanish and Portuguese.* New York: Routledge, 2022.

Gates, Henry Louis, Jr. "Introduction: Criticism in De Jungle." *African American Review* 50, no. 4 (Winter 2017): 625–29.

Gerber Bicecci, Verónica. *La compañía.* Mexico City: Almadía, 2019.

Gerber Bicecci, Verónica. *Conjunto vacío.* Mexico City: Almadía, 2015.

Gerber Bicecci, Verónica. *Empty Set.* Translated by Christina MacSweeney. Minneapolis, MN: Coffee House Press, 2018.

Gerber Bicecci, Verónica. "Manifiesto evanescente." In *Inventar lo posible: manifiestos mexicanos contemporáneos,* edited by Luciano Concheiro, 139–44. Mexico City: Taurus, 2017.

Gerber Bicecci, Verónica. *Mudanza.* Mexico City: Almadía, 2017.

Gerstle, Gary. *The Rise and Fall of the Neoliberal Order: America and the World in the Free Market Era.* Oxford: Oxford University Press, 2022.

Ghosh, Amitav. *The Great Derangement: Climate Change and the Unthinkable.* Chicago: University of Chicago Press, 2016.

Gilroy, Paul. *The Black Atlantic: Modernity and Double-Consciousness.* Cambridge, MA: Harvard University Press, 1995.

Ginwala, Natasha, and Vivian Ziherl. "Sensing Grounds: Mangroves, Unauthentic Belonging, Extra-Territoriality." *e-flux* 45, May 2013. https://www.e-flux.com/journal/45/60128/sensing-grounds-mangroves-unauthentic-belonging-extra-territoriality.

Giorgi, Gabriel. "Paisajes de sobrevida." *Catedral Tomada: Revista de Crítica Literaria Latinoamericana* 4, no. 7 (2016): 126–41.

Giorgi, Gabriel. "'Temblor del tiempo humano': política de la novela en Juan Cárdenas." *Cuadernos de Literatura* 24 (2020).

Giunta, Andrea. *¿Cúando empieza el arte contemporáneo? When Does Contemporary Art Begin?* Translated by Tamara Stuby. Buenos Aires: Fundación arteBA, 2014.

Glissant, Édouard. *Caribbean Discourse: Selected Essays.* Translated by J. Michael Dash. Charlottesville: University of Virginia Press, 1999.

Glissant, Édouard. *Filosofía de la relación: poesía en extensión.* Translated by Sol Gil. Buenos Aires: Miluno, 2019.

Glissant, Édouard. *Poetics of Relation.* Translated by Betsy Wing. Ann Arbor: University of Michigan Press, 1997.

Goldsmith, Kenneth. *Uncreative Writing: Managing Language in the Digital Age.* New York: Columbia University Press, 2011.

González, Carina. "La potencia de los cuerpos corrompidos: *El huésped* como *bildungs* político." *Hispanófila* 174 (2015): 97–115.

González Echevarría, Roberto. *Myth and Archive: A Theory of Latin American Narrative*. Cambridge, UK: Cambridge University Press, 1990.

Gonzenbach Perkins, Alexandra. "Queer Materiality, Contestatory Histories, and Disperse Bodies in *La mucama de Omicunlé*." *Journal of Latin American Cultural Studies* 30, no. 1 (2021): 47–60.

Gorelik, Adrián. *Miradas sobre Buenos Aires: historia cultural y crítica urbana*. Buenos Aires: Siglo XXI, 2004.

Goyal, Yogita. *Runaway Genres: The Global Afterlives of Slavery*. New York: New York University Press, 2019.

Gramsci, Antonio. *Selections from the Prison Notebooks of Antonio Gramsci*. Edited and translated by Quintin Hoare and Geoffrey Nowell-Smith. London: Lawrence and Wishart, 1971.

Greaney, Patrick. *Quotational Practices: Repeating the Future in Contemporary Art*. Minneapolis: University of Minnesota Press, 2014.

Groys, Boris. "Comrades of Time." *e-flux* 11, December 2009. https://www.e-flux.com/journal/11/61345/comrades-of-time.

Groys, Boris. *Introduction to Antiphilosophy*. Translated by David Fernbach. London: Verso, 2012.

Guerrero, Gustavo. *Paisajes en movimiento: literatura y cambio cultural entre dos siglos*. Buenos Aires: Eterna Cadencia, 2018.

Gumbrecht, Hans Ulrich. *Our Broad Present: Time and Contemporary Culture*. New York: Columbia University Press, 2014.

Gutiérrez, Bernardo. "Pedro Mairal, escritor: 'Por el hecho de tener hijos, tengo la responsabilidad de no ser pesimista.'" *El Periódico de España*, April 5, 2023. https://www.epe.es/es/cultura/20230405/pedro-mairal-entrevista-ano-desierto-85574977.

Habermas, Jürgen. "Modernity—An Incomplete Project." In *The Anti-aesthetic: Essays on Postmodern Culture*, edited by Hal Foster, 3–15. Port Townsend, WA: Bay Press, 1983.

Hacking, Ian. *Mad Travelers: Reflections on the Reality of Transient Mental Illnesses*. Charlottesville: University of Virginia Press, 1998.

Halberstam, Jack. *In a Queer Time and Place: Transgender Bodies, Subcultural Lives*. New York: New York University Press, 2005.

Halberstam, Jack. *Skin Shows: Gothic Horror and the Technology of Monsters*. Durham, NC: Duke University Press, 1995.

Haraway, Donna J. *Staying with the Trouble: Making Kin in the Chthulucene*. Durham, NC: Duke University Press, 2016.

Hartman, Saidiya. "Venus in Two Acts." *Small Axe* 12, no. 2 (June 2008): 1–14.

Hartog, François. *Regimes of Historicity: Presentism and Experiences of Time*. Translated by Saskia Brown. New York: Columbia University Press, 2015.

Hatfield, Charles. *The Limits of Identity: Politics and Poetics in Latin America*. Austin: University of Texas Press, 2015.

Heffes, Gisela. *Políticas de la destrucción / Poéticas de la preservación: apuntes para una lectura (eco) crítica del medio ambiente en América Latina*. Rosario, Argentina: Beatriz Viterbo Editora, 2013.

Heise, Ursula K. *Imagining Extinction: The Cultural Meaning of Endangered Species*. Chicago: University of Chicago Press, 2016.

Heise, Ursula K. "The Vanishing Metropolis: Environmental Justice and Urban Narrative in Latin America." In *Post-Global Aesthetics: 21st Century Latin American Literatures and Cultures*, edited by Gesine Müller and Benjamin Loy, 77–94. Berlin/Boston: De Gruyter, 2023.

Hirsch, Marianne. *Family Frames: Photography, Narrative, and Memory*. Cambridge, MA: Harvard University Press, 1997.

Hirsch, Marianne. *The Generation of Postmemory: Writing and Visual Culture after the Holocaust*. New York: Columbia University Press, 2012.

Horne, Luz. "Fotografía y retrato de lo contemporáneo en *El aire* y otras novelas de Chejfec." In *Sergio Chejfec: trayectorias de una escritura (ensayos críticos)*, edited by Dianna C. Niebylski, 123–46. Pittsburgh, PA: IILI, 2012.

Hoyos, Héctor. *Beyond Bolaño: The Global Latin American Novel*. New York: Columbia University Press, 2015.

Hoyos, Héctor. "The Telltale Computer: Obsolescence and Nostalgia in Chile after Alejandro Zambra." In *Technology, Literature, and Digital Culture in Latin America: Mediatized Sensibilities in a Globalized Era*, edited by Matthew Bush and Tania Gentic, 109–24. New York: Routledge, 2016.

Hoyos, Héctor. *Things with a History: Transcultural Materialism and the Literatures of Extraction in Contemporary Latin America*. New York: Columbia University Press, 2019.

Hoyos, Héctor, and Marília Librandi-Rocha. "Theories of the Contemporary in South America." *Revista de Estudios Hispánicos* 48, no. 1 (2014): 97–103.

Houser, Heather. *Ecosickness in Contemporary U.S. Fiction: Environment and Affect*. New York: Columbia University Press, 2014.

Hutcheon, Linda. *The Politics of Postmodernism*. London: Routledge, 1989.

Huyssen, Andreas. *After the Great Divide: Modernism, Mass Culture, Postmodernism*. Bloomington: Indiana University Press, 1986.

Huyssen, Andreas. *Present Pasts: Urban Palimpsests and the Politics of Memory*. Stanford, CA: Stanford University Press, 2003.

Huyssen, Andreas. *Twilight Memories: Marking Time in a Culture of Amnesia*. New York: Routledge, 1995.

Iglesia, Anna María. *Ese famoso abismo: conversaciones con Enrique Vila-Matas*. Terrades, Spain: Wunderkammer, 2020.

Indiana, Rita. *La mucama de Omicunlé*. Cáceres, Spain: Periférica, 2015.

Indiana, Rita. *Tentacle*. Translated by Achy Obejas. New York: And Other Stories, 2018.

"Intemperie." *Real Academia Española*. 23rd ed. Madrid: Espasa, 2016, s.v.

Jameson, Fredric. "The Aesthetics of Singularity." *New Left Review* 92 (2015): 101–32.

Jameson, Fredric. *Postmodernism, or, The Cultural Logic of Late Capitalism.* Durham, NC: Duke University Press, 1991.

"Juan Cárdenas y Dolores Reyes: 'La realidad no se mete en los libros, los libros construyen realidad.'" *WMagazín*, September 10, 2020. https://wmagazin .com/relatos/juan-cardenas-y-dolores-reyes-la-realidad-no-se-mete-en-los-li bros-los-libros-construyen-realidad.

Klein, Naomi. *The Shock Doctrine: The Rise of Disaster Capitalism.* New York: Picador, 2007.

Knobloch, Jan. "Globalization Reversed: Reading Scales of Collapse in Pedro Mairal's *El año del desierto.*" In *Post-Global Aesthetics: 21st Century Latin American Literatures and Cultures*, edited by Gesine Müller and Benjamin Loy, 169–87. Berlin/Boston: De Gruyter, 2023.

Kojève, Alexandre. *Introduction to the Reading of Hegel: Lectures on the Phenomenology of Spirit.* Translated by James H. Nichols Jr. Ithaca, NY: Cornell University Press, 1980.

Koolhaas, Rem. *The Generic City.* New York: Monacelli Press, 1998.

Koolhaas, Rem. *Junkspace with Running Room.* London: Notting Hill Editions, 2013.

Koselleck, Reinhart. *Sediments of Time: On Possible Histories.* Translated by Sean Franzel and Stefan-Ludwig Hoffmann. Stanford, CA: Stanford University Press, 2018.

Krimer, María Inés. *Noxa.* Buenos Aires: Revólver, 2016.

Kristeva, Julia. *Black Sun: Depression and Melancholia.* Translated by Leon S. Roudiez. New York: Columbia University Press, 1989.

Kubler, George. *The Shape of Things: Remarks on the History of Things.* New Haven: Yale University Press, 1962.

Kurnick, David. *Empty Houses: Theatrical Failure and the Novel.* Princeton, NJ: Princeton University Press, 2012.

Laddaga, Reinaldo. *Espectáculos de realidad: ensayo sobre la narrativa latinoamericana de las últimas dos décadas.* Rosario, Argentina: Beatriz Viterbo Editora, 2007.

Lalo, Eduardo. *Intemperie.* Buenos Aires: Corregidor, 2016.

La Rocca, Paula, and Ana Neuburger, eds. *Figuras de la intemperie: panorámica de estéticas contemporáneas.* Córdoba: Universidad Nacional de Córdoba, 2019.

Latour, Bruno. *We Have Never Been Modern.* Translated by Catherine Porter. Cambridge, MA: Harvard University Press, 1993.

Lauro, Sarah Juliet, and Karen Embry. "A Zombie Manifesto: The Nonhuman Condition in the Era of Advanced Capitalism." *boundary 2* 35, no. 2 (2008): 85–108.

Leguizamón, Amalia. *Seeds of Power: Environmental Injustice and Genetically Modified Soybeans in Argentina*. Durham, NC: Duke University Press, 2020.

Lehnen, Leila. *Citizenship and Crisis in Contemporary Brazilian Literature*. New York: Palgrave Macmillan, 2013.

Lerner, Ben. *Leaving the Atocha Station*. Minneapolis, MN: Coffee House Press, 2011.

Lerner, Ben. *The Topeka School*. New York: Farrar, Straus and Giroux, 2019.

Levine, Caroline. "The Great Unwritten: World Literature and the Effacement of Orality." *Modern Language Quarterly* 74, no. 2 (June 2013): 217–37.

Levine, Lawrence W. *Black Culture and Black Consciousness: Afro-American Folk Thought from Slavery to Freedom*. Oxford: Oxford University Press, 2007.

Libertella, Mauro. *El estilo de los otros: conversaciones con escritores contemporáneos de América Latina*. Santiago de Chile: Ediciones UDP, 2015.

Lins do Rego, José. *Plantation Boy*. Translated by Emmi Baum. New York: Alfred A. Knopf, 1966.

Lipovetsky, Gilles. *La era del vacío: ensayos sobre el individualismo contemporáneo*. Translated by Joan Vinyoli and Michèle Pendanx. Barcelona: Anagrama, 2003.

Lomnitz, Claudio. "La depreciación de la vida en la Ciudad de México circa 1985." In *La nación desdibujada: México en trece ensayos*. Translated by Marianela Santoveña, 157–84. Barcelona: Malpaso, 2016.

Loyola Brandão, Ignácio. *Não verás país nenhum: Memorial descritivo*. Rio de Janeiro: Codecri, 1981.

Ludmer, Josefina. *Aquí América Latina*. Buenos Aires: Eterna Cadencia, 2010.

Luiselli, Valeria. "Difficult Forgiveness." *Guernica*, December 12, 2016. https://www.guernicamag.com/difficult-forgiveness.

Luiselli, Valeria. *Faces in the Crowd*. Translated by Christina MacSweeney. Minneapolis, MN: Coffee House Press, 2014.

Luiselli, Valeria. "Gilberto Owen, narrador." *Letras Libres*, January 31, 2009. https://letraslibres.com/revista-mexico/gilberto-owen-narrador.

Luiselli, Valeria. *Los ingrávidos*. Mexico City: Sexto Piso, 2011.

Luiselli, Valeria. *Lost Children Archive*. New York: Alfred A. Knopf, 2019.

Luiselli, Valeria. *Sidewalks*. Translated by Christina MacSweeney. Minneapolis, MN: Coffee House Press, 2013.

Luiselli, Valeria. *The Story of My Teeth*. Translated by Christina MacSweeney. Minneapolis, MN: Coffee House Press, 2015.

Luiselli, Valeria. "The Wild West Meets the Southern Border." *New Yorker*, June 3, 2019. https://www.newyorker.com/magazine/2019/06/10/the-wild-west-meets-the-southern-border.

Lyotard, Jean-François. *The Postmodern Condition: A Report on Knowledge*. Translated by Geoff Bennington and Brian Massumi. Minneapolis: University of Minnesota Press, 1984.

Macfarlane, Robert. *Underland: A Deep Time Journey*. New York: W. W. Norton, 2019.

Mairal, Pedro. *El año del desierto*. Buenos Aires: Interzona, 2005.

Malagón, Camilo. "El *intelectual implicado*: violencia y narrativa colombiana a finales del siglo XX y comienzos del siglo XXI." *A Contracorriente: Una Revista de Estudios Latinoamericanos* 20, no. 1 (Fall 2022): 40–66.

Malchow, H. L. *Gothic Images of Race in Nineteenth-Century Britain*. Stanford, CA: Stanford University Press, 1996.

Manzano, Juan Francisco. *Autobiography of a Slave/Autobiografía de un esclavo*. Translated by Evelyn Picon Garfield. Detroit: Wayne State University Press, 1996.

Márquez, Francia. "Francia Márquez en el Centro Cultural Kirchner." Filmed 2022, YouTube video, 1:28:12. https://www.youtube.com/watch?v =yrsWq-JTNZY.

Martín-Barbero, Jesús. "Dislocaciones del tiempo y nuevas topografías de la memoria." In *Artelatina: cultura, globalização e identidades cosmopolitas*, edited by Heloisa Buarque de Hollanda and Beatriz Resende, 139–69. Rio de Janeiro: Aeroplano Editora, 2000.

Martinez-Alier, Joan. *The Environmentalism of the Poor: A Study of Ecological Conflicts and Valuation*. Cheltenham, UK: Edward Elgar, 2002.

Martínez Estrada, Ezequiel. *Radiografía de la pampa*. Buenos Aires: ALLCA XX, 1996.

Martínez Estrada, Ezequiel. *Sarmiento / Meditaciones sarmientinas / Los invariantes históricos en el Facundo*. Rosario, Argentina: Beatriz Viterbo Editora, 2001.

Martins Catharino, José. *Garimpo—Garimpeiro—Garimpagem: Chapada Diamantina, Bahia*. Salvador, Brazil: Philobiblion, 1986.

Mbembe, Achille. *Necropolitics*. Translated by Steven Corcoran. Durham, NC: Duke University Press, 2019.

McCarthy, Tom. *Satin Island*. London: Vintage, 2015.

McIntyre, Lee. *Post-truth*. Boston: MIT Press, 2018.

McKittrick, Katherine. "Plantation Futures." *Small Axe* 17, no. 3 (November 2013): 1–15.

Michaels, Walter Benn. *The Shape of the Signifier: 1967 to the End of History*. Princeton, NJ: Princeton University Press, 2004.

Montoya Juárez, Jesús. "Hacia una arqueología del presente: cultura material, tecnología y obsolescencia." *Cuadernos de Literatura* 20, no 40 (2016): 276–93.

Morrison, Toni. "The Site of Memory." In *The Source of Self-Regard: Selected Essays, Speeches, and Meditations*, 233–45. New York: Alfred A. Knopf, 2019.

Morton, Timothy. "Ecology without the Present." *Oxford Literary Review* 34, no. 2 (2012): 229–38.

Moyn, Samuel. *The Last Utopia: Human Rights in History*. Cambridge, MA: Harvard University Press, 2010.

Müller, Gesine. *How Is World Literature Made? The Global Circulations of Latin American Literature*. Berlin/Boston: De Gruyter, 2021.

Muñoz, José Esteban. *Cruising Utopia: The Then and There of Queer Futurity*. New York: New York University Press, 2019.

Mutis, Ana María. "Monsters and Agritoxins: The Environmental Gothic in Samanta Schweblin's *Distancia de rescate*." In *Ecofictions, Ecorealities, and Slow Violence in Latin America and the Latinx World*, edited by Ilka Kressner, Ana María Mutis, and Elizabeth Pettinaroli, 39–54. New York: Routledge, 2019.

Nagel, Alexander. *Medieval Modern: Art Out of Time*. New York: Thames and Hudson, 2012.

Nagel, Alexander, and Christopher Wood. *Anachronic Renaissance*. New York: Zone Books, 2010.

Nettel, Guadalupe. *The Body Where I Was Born*. Translated by J. T. Lichtenstein. New York: Seven Stories Press, 2015.

Nettel, Guadalupe. *El huésped*. Barcelona: Anagrama, 2006.

Nettel, Guadalupe. *Natural Histories*. Translated by J. T. Lichtenstein. New York: Seven Stories Press, 2015.

Ngai, Sianne. *Ugly Feelings*. Cambridge, MA: Harvard University Press, 2005.

Nietzsche, Friedrich. *Untimely Meditations*. Translated by R. J. Hollingdale. 1876. Cambridge, UK: Cambridge University Press, 2018.

Nilges, Mathias. *How to Read a Moment: The American Novel and the Crisis of the Present*. Evanston, IL: Northwestern University Press, 2021.

Nixon, Rob. *Slow Violence and the Environmentalism of the Poor*. Cambridge, MA: Harvard University Press, 2013.

"No hace falta ser Nostradamus para adivinar el futuro, basta ser Rita Indiana." *VICE Colombia*, April 27, 2015. https://www.vice.com/es/article/kwv9nx/entrevista-rita-indiana.

Nora, Pierre. "Between Memory and History: *Les Lieux de Mémoire*." *Representations* 26 (Spring 1989): 7–24.

Noudelmann, François. "Le contemporain sans époque: une affaire de rythmes." In *Qu'est-ce que le contemporain?*, edited by Lionel Ruffel, 59–75. Nantes: Éditions Cécile Defaut, 2010.

Nouzeilles, Gabriela. "Postmemory Cinema and the Future of the Past in Albertina Carri's *Los rubios*." *Journal of Latin American Cultural Studies* 14, no. 3 (2005): 263–78.

Nussbaum, Martha C. "Patriotism and Cosmopolitanism." In *For Love of Country: Debating the Limits of Patriotism*, edited by Joshua Cohen, 2–17. Boston: Beacon Press Books, 1996.

Ochoa Gautier, Ana Maria. *Aurality: Listening and Knowledge in Nineteenth-Century Colombia*. Durham, NC: Duke University Press, 2014.

Oloff, Kerstin. "The 'Monstruous Head' and the 'Mouth of Hell': The Gothic Ecologies of the 'Mexican Miracle.'" In *Ecological Crisis and Cultural Representation in Latin America: Ecocritical Perspectives on Art, Film, and Literature*, edited by Mark Anderson and Zélia M. Bora, 79–98. Lanham, MD: Lexington Books, 2016.

Ordiz, Inés. "Civilization and Barbarism and Zombies: Argentina's Contemporary Gothic." In *Latin American Gothic in Literature and Culture*, edited by Sandra Casanova-Vizcaíno and Inés Ordiz, 15–26. New York: Routledge, 2018.

Osborne, Peter. *Anywhere or Not at All: Philosophy of Contemporary Art*. London: Verso, 2013.

Osborne, Peter. *Crisis as Form*. London: Verso, 2022.

Palou, Pedro Ángel. *La casa del silencio: aproximación en tres tiempos a Contemporáneos*. Zamora, Spain: El Colegio de Michoacán, 1997.

Pape, Maria. "El pasaje como *modus operandi*: perspectivas simultáneas y recíprocamente excluyentes en *Los ingrávidos* de Valeria Luiselli." *Revista Chilena de Literatura* 90 (September 2015): 171–95.

Pavón, Héctor. "Samanta Schweblin: algo malo está por suceder." *Clarín*, December 10, 2014. https://www.clarin.com/literatura/samanta-schweblin-distancia-rescate_0_HJ_EpFv9P7e.html.

Pedrosa, Celia, Diana Klinger, Jorge Wolff, and Mario Cámara. *Indiccionario de lo contemporáneo*. La Plata, Argentina: EME Editorial, 2021.

Peres, Ana Cláudia. "'Há muita história soterrada,' diz Itamar Vieira, autor de *Torto arado*." *Vermelho*, June 4, 2021. https://vermelho.org.br/2021/06/04/ha-muita-historia-soterrada-diz-itamar-vieira-autor-de-torto-arado.

Pérez, Martín. "El payador absoluto." *Página 12*, July 21, 2023. https://www.pagina12.com.ar/diario/suplementos/libros/10-5081-2013-07-21.html.

Pérez Limón, Lilia Adriana. "Visualizing the Nonnormative Body in Guadalupe Nettel's *El cuerpo en que nací*." In *Mexican Literature in Theory*, edited by Ignacio M. Sánchez Prado, 211–26. New York: Bloomsbury, 2018.

Pérez-Torres, Rafael. "Knitting and Knotting the Narrative Thread—*Beloved* as Postmodern Novel." *Modern Fiction Studies* 39, no. 3/4 (Fall/Winter 1993): 689–707.

Perloff, Marjorie. *Unoriginal Genius: Poetry by Other Means in the New Century*. Chicago: University of Chicago Press, 2010.

Pinedo, Rafael. *Plop*. 2002. Buenos Aires: Interzona, 2013.

Pires, Paula. "'O Brasil é incapaz de refletir sobre seu passado,' diz Julián Fuks." *Revista CULT*, November 7, 2018. https://revistacult.uol.com.br/home/o-brasil-e-incapaz-de-refletir-sobre-seu-passado-diz-julian-fuks.

Pratt, Mary Louise. "Globalización, desmodernización y el retorno de los monstruos." *Revista de História* 156, no. 1 (2007): 13–29.

Pratt, Mary Louise. *Planetary Longings*. Durham, NC: Duke University Press, 2022.

Premat, Julio. *Érase esta vez: relatos de comienzo.* Sáenz Peña, Argentina: EDUN-TREF, 2016.

Premat, Julio. "Fin de los tiempos, comienzos de la literatura." *Eidos: Revista de Filosofía de la Universidad del Norte* 24 (2016): 104–23.

Premat, Julio. "La literatura hoy: de nuevo lo nuevo. Notas sobre *Una belleza vulgar* de Damián Tabarovsky." In *Mil hojas: formas contemporáneas de la literatura,* edited by Carlos Walker, 315–42. Santiago de Chile: Hueders, 2017.

Premat, Julio. *Non nova sed nove: inactualidades, anacronismos, resistencias en la literatura contemporánea.* Macerata, Italy: Quodlibet, 2018.

Premat, Julio. "*Yo tendré mis árboles*: Los comienzos en Zambra." *Taller de Letras* 60 (2017): 87–105.

Punter, David. "Introduction: The Ghost of a History." In *A New Companion to the Gothic,* edited by David Punter, 1–9. Malden, MA: Wiley Blackwell, 2015.

Punter, David. "Shape and Shadow: On Poetry and the Uncanny." In *A New Companion to the Gothic,* edited by David Punter, 252–64. Malden, MA: Wiley Blackwell, 2015.

Ramírez, Dixa. *Colonial Phantoms: Belonging and Refusal in the Dominican Americas, from the 19th Century to the Present.* New York: New York University Press, 2018.

Rancière, Jacques. *Béla Tarr, the Time After.* Translated by Erik Beranek. Minneapolis: University of Minnesota Press, 2013.

Rancière, Jacques. *Dissensus: On Politics and Aesthetics.* Translated by Steven Corcoran. London: Bloomsbury, 2015.

Rancière, Jacques. *The Edges of Fiction.* Translated by Steve Corcoran. Cambridge, UK: Polity Press, 2020.

Rancière, Jacques. *The Emancipated Spectator.* Translated by Gregory Elliott. London: Verso, 2009.

Rancière, Jacques. "*Fin de Siècle* and New Millennium, May 1996." In *Chronicles of Consensual Times.* Translated by Steven Corcoran, 8–11. London: Continuum, 2010.

Rancière, Jacques. *Modern Times.* Translated by Gregory Elliott. London: Verso, 2022.

Rancière, Jacques. *El reparto de lo sensible: estética y política.* Translated by Mónica Padró. Buenos Aires: Prometeo, 2014.

Rancière, Jacques. "What a Medium Can Mean." Translated by Steven Corcoran. *Parrhesia* 11 (2011): 35–43.

Raynor, Cecily. *Latin American Literature at the Millennium: Local Lives, Global Spaces.* Lewisburg, PA: Bucknell University Press, 2021.

Reati, Fernando. "El monumento de papel: La construcción de una memoria colectiva en los recordatorios de los desaparecidos." In *Políticas de la memoria:*

tensiones en la palabra y la imagen, edited by Sandra Lorenzano and Ralph Buchenhorst, 159–70. Mexico City: Universidad del Claustro de Sor Juana, 2007.

Renker, Tess. "The 'Generation After' Talks Back: Contestations of Postmemory in Recent Latin American Literature." *Chasqui: Revista de Literatura Latino-americana* 51, no. 1 (May 2022): 113–33.

Richard, Nelly. *Crítica de la memoria (1990–2010)*. Santiago de Chile: Ediciones UDP, 2010.

Richard, Nelly. *Eruptions of Memory: The Critique of Memory in Chile, 1990–2015*. Translated by Andrew Ascherl. Cambridge, UK: Polity Press, 2019.

Richard, Nelly. "Introducción." In *Pensar en/la postdictadura*, edited by Nelly Richard and Alberto Moreiras, 9–20. Santiago de Chile: Cuarto Propio, 2001.

Ricœur, Paul. *Memory, History, Forgetting*. Translated by Kathleen Blamey and David Pellauer. Chicago: University of Chicago Press, 2004.

Rivera, José Eustasio. *La vorágine*. 1924. Madrid: Cátedra, 2006.

Rivera Garza, Cristina. *Autobiografía del algodón*. Buenos Aires: Literatura Random House, 2020.

Rivera Garza, Cristina. *The Restless Dead: Necrowriting and Disappropriation*. Translated by Robin Myers. Nashville: Vanderbilt University Press, 2020.

Robin, Marie-Monique. *El glifosato en el banquillo*. Translated by Margarita Merbilhaá. La Plata: De la Campana, 2018.

Robin, Marie-Monique. *The World according to Monsanto: Pollution, Corruption, and the Control of the World's Food Supply*. Translated by George Holoch. New York: New Press, 2010.

Robin, Régine. *La memoria saturada*. Translated by Víctor Goldstein. Buenos Aires: Waldhuter Editores, 2012.

Robinson, Cedric J. *Black Marxism: The Making of the Black Radical Tradition*. Chapel Hill: University of North Carolina Press, 1983.

Rocha Vivas, Miguel. *Word Mingas: Oralitegraphies and Mirrored Visions on Oralitures and Indigenous Contemporary Literatures*. Translated by Paul M. Worley and Melissa Birkhofer. Chapel Hill: University of North Carolina Press, 2021.

Rodríguez, Fermín A. *Un desierto para la nación: la escritura del vacío*. Buenos Aires: Eterna Cadencia, 2010.

Rogers, Charlotte. "'El ágora entre manglares': la arquitectura griega en *El siglo de las luces* de Alejo Carpentier." *Revista de Estudios Hispánicos* 53, no. 1 (2019): 283–303.

Rogers, Charlotte. "Rita Indiana's Queer Interspecies Caribbean and the Hispanic Literary Tradition." *Small Axe Salon*, July 30, 2020. http://small axe.net/sxsalon/discussions/rita-indianas-queer-interspecies-caribbean-and -hispanic-literary-tradition.

Rojas, Sergio. "Profunda superficie: memoria de lo cotidiano en la literatura chilena." *Revista Chilena de Literatura* 89 (2015): 231–56.

Rojo, Grínor. *Las novelas de la dictadura y la postdictadura chilena: ¿qué y cómo leer?* Santiago de Chile: LOM, 2016.

Romero, Berenice. "Japonismo: otra forma de leer a Alejandro Zambra." *Taller de Letras* 59 (2016): 11–18.

Romero, Cristian. *Después de la ira.* Bogotá: Alfaguara, 2018.

Rosa, Hartmut. *Alienación y aceleración: hacia una teoría crítica de la temporalidad en la modernidad tardía.* Translated by Centro de Investigaciones Interdisciplinarias en Ciencias y Humanidades (CEIICH), Universidad Nacional Autónoma de México (UNAM). Buenos Aires: Katz Editores, 2016.

Rosenberg, Fernando J. "Toxicidad y narrativa: *Los suicidas del fin del mundo* de Leila Guerriero, *Cromo* de Lucía Puenzo, y *Distancia de rescate* de Samanta Schweblin." *Revista Iberoamericana* 85, no. 268 (2019): 901–22.

Rousso, Henry. *The Latest Catastrophe: History, the Present, the Contemporary.* Translated by Jane Marie Todd. Chicago: University of Chicago Press, 2016.

Ruffel, Lionel. *Brouhaha: Worlds of the Contemporary.* Translated by Raymond N. MacKenzie. Minneapolis: University of Minnesota Press, 2018.

Rulfo, Juan. *Pedro Páramo.* 1955. Madrid: Cátedra, 2005.

Saavedra, Carola. *O inventário das coisas ausentes.* São Paulo: Companhia das Letras, 2014.

Sabato, Ernesto. *La resistencia.* Buenos Aires: Seix Barral, 2002.

Saer, Juan José. *El entenado.* 1983. Barcelona: Rayo Verde, 2013.

Saltzman, Lisa. *Making Memory Matter: Strategies of Remembrance in Contemporary Art.* Chicago: University of Chicago Press, 2006.

Sánchez Prado, Ignacio M. *Strategic Occidentalism: On Mexican Fiction, the Neoliberal Book Market, and the Question of World Literature.* Evanston, IL: Northwestern University Press, 2018.

Sández, Fernanda. *La Argentina fumigada: agroquímicos, enfermedad y alimentos en un país envenenado.* Buenos Aires: Planeta, 2016.

Santner, Eric L. *On Creaturely Life: Rilke, Benjamin, Sebald.* Chicago: University of Chicago Press, 2006.

Sarlo, Beatriz. *Tiempo pasado: cultura de la memoria y giro subjetivo (una discusión).* Buenos Aires: Siglo XXI, 2012.

Sarlo, Beatriz. *Tiempo presente: notas sobre el cambio de una cultura.* Buenos Aires: Siglo XXI, 2001.

Schmitter, Gianna. "Contar con todo: análisis de las estrategias intermediales en la novela *Conjunto vacío,* de Verónica Gerber Bicecci." *Bellaterra Journal of Teaching & Learning Language & Literature* 14, no. 1 (2021): 1–27.

Schøllhammer, Karl Erik. "The Predicament of Contemporary Brazilian Fiction and Its Spatiotemporal Modalities." *Portuguese Studies* 37, no. 1 (2021): 75–87.

Schweblin, Samanta. *Distancia de rescate*. Buenos Aires: Literatura Random House, 2014.

Schweblin, Samanta. *Fever Dream*. Translated by Megan McDowell. New York: Riverhead Books, 2017.

Sebald, W. G. *The Emigrants*. Translated by Michael Hulse. New York: New Directions, 1997.

Sebald, W. G. *The Rings of Saturn*. Translated by Michael Hulse. New York: New Directions, 2016.

Segato, Rita. *Contra-pedagogías de la crueldad*. Buenos Aires: Prometeo, 2018.

Serres, Michel. *The Natural Contract*. Translated by Elizabeth MacArthur and William Paulson. Ann Arbor: University of Michigan Press, 1995.

Sheller, Mimi. *Island Futures: Caribbean Survival in the Anthropocene*. Durham, NC: Duke University Press, 2020.

Sheridan, Guillermo. *Los Contemporáneos ayer*. Mexico City: Fondo de Cultura Económica, 1985.

Sheridan, Guillermo. *Tres ensayos sobre Gilberto Owen*. Mexico City: Universidad Nacional Autónoma de México, 2008.

Shklovsky, Viktor. *Viktor Shklovsky: A Reader*. Translated by Alexandra Berlina. New York: Bloomsbury, 2016.

Silva, Leonice de Jesus, and Raquel Souza. "Re(existências) quilombolas em Rio de Contas na Chapada Diamantina-Bahia." In *Comunidades quilombolas: outras formas de (re)existências*, edited by Ana Angélica Leal Barbosa, 85–96. Curitiba, Brazil: Appris, 2020.

Sinykin, Dan. *American Literature and the Long Downturn: Neoliberal Apocalypse*. Oxford: Oxford University Press, 2020.

Siskind, Mariano. *Cosmopolitan Desires: Global Modernity and World Literature in Latin America*. Evanston, IL: Northwestern University Press, 2014.

Siskind, Mariano. "Towards a Cosmopolitanism of Loss: An Essay about the End of the World." In *World Literature, Cosmopolitanism, Globality: Beyond, Against, Post, Otherwise*, edited by Gesine Müller and Mariano Siskind, 205–35. Berlin: De Gruyter, 2019.

Smith, Terry. *Art to Come: Histories of Contemporary Art*. Durham, NC: Duke University Press, 2019.

Smith, Terry. *What Is Contemporary Art?* Chicago: University of Chicago Press, 2009.

Sontag, Susan. *Regarding the Pain of Others*. New York: Picador, 2003.

Sosa, Cecilia. "Filiaciones virales: Facebook, efemérides y una poética *queer* de la memoria." In *El pasado inasequible: desaparecidos, hijos y combatientes en el arte y la literatura del nuevo milenio*, edited by Jordana Blejmar, Silvana Mandolessi, and Mariana Eva Pérez, 127–46. Buenos Aires: Eudeba, 2017.

Speranza, Graciela. *Cronografías: arte y ficciones de un tiempo sin tiempo*. Barcelona: Anagrama, 2017.

Steiner, George. *Grammars of Creation*. New Haven, CT: Yale University Press, 2001.

Sweet, James H. *Domingos Álvares, African Healing, and the Intellectual History of the Atlantic World*. Chapel Hill: University of North Carolina Press, 2011.

Tabarovsky, Damián. *Fantasma de la vanguardia*. Buenos Aires: Mardulce, 2018.

Tabarovsky, Damián. *Literatura de izquierda*. Rosario, Argentina: Beatriz Viterbo Editora, 2011.

Taussig, Michael T. *The Devil and Commodity Fetishism in South America*. Chapel Hill: University of North Carolina Press, 2010.

Thayer, Willy. "Para un concepto heterocrónico de lo contemporáneo." In *¿Qué es lo contemporáneo? Actualidad, tiempo histórico, utopías del presente*, edited by Miguel Valderrama, 13–24. Santiago de Chile: Ediciones Universidad Finis Terrae, 2011.

Tidwell, Christy, and Carter Soles, eds. *Fear and Nature: Ecohorror Studies in the Anthropocene*. University Park, PA: Penn State University Press, 2021.

Toth, Jennifer. *The Mole People: Life in the Tunnels beneath New York City*. Chicago: Chicago Review Press, 1993.

Tsing, Anna Lowenhaupt. *The Mushroom at the End of the World: On the Possibility of Life in Capitalist Ruins*. Princeton, NJ: Princeton University Press, 2015.

Valencia, Sayak. *Gore Capitalism*. Translated by John Pluecker. Cambridge, MA: Semiotext(e), 2018.

Vallejo, Irene. *Papyrus: The Invention of Books in the Ancient World*. Translated by Charlotte Whittle. New York: Alfred A. Knopf, 2022.

Vazquez, Alexandra T. "Learning to Live in Miami." *American Quarterly* 66, no. 3 (2014): 853–73.

Vera-Rojas, María Teresa. "¡Se armó el juidero! Cartografías imprecisas, cuerpos disidentes, sexualidades transgresoras: hacia una lectura queer de Rita Indiana Hernández." In *Rita Indiana: Archivos*, edited by Fernanda Bustamante Escalona, 207–30. Santo Domingo: Cielonaranja, 2017.

Vermeulen, Pieter. "Flights of Memory: Teju Cole's *Open City* and the Limits of Aesthetic Cosmopolitanism." *Journal of Modern Literature* 37, no. 1 (2013): 40–57.

Viart, Dominique. "El relato de filiación. Ética de la restitución contra deber de memoria en la literatura contemporánea." Translated by Macarena Miranda. *Cuadernos LIRICO* 20 (August 2019). https://journals.openedition.org/lirico/8883.

Viart, Dominique, and Laurent Demanze, eds. *Fins de la littérature: esthétique et discours de la fin. Tome I*. Paris: Armand Colin, 2011.

Vidal, Paloma. "A literatura como resistência no romance de Julián Fuks." *O Globo*, December 5, 2015. https://oglobo.globo.com/cultura/livros/a-literatura-como-resistencia-no-romance-de-julian-fuks-18220517.

Vidal, Paloma. *Mar azul*. Rio de Janeiro: Editora Rocco, 2012.

Vieira, Patrícia. "*Phytographia*: Literature as Plant Writing." *Environmental Philosophy* 12, no. 2 (2015): 205–20.

Vieira Junior, Itamar. *Crooked Plow*. Translated by Johnny Lorenz. New York: Verso, 2023.

Vieira Junior, Itamar. *Torto arado*. São Paulo: Todavia, 2019.

Vila-Matas, Enrique. *Marienbad eléctrico*. Buenos Aires: Caja Negra, 2015.

Villalobos-Ruminott, Sergio. *Heterografías de la violencia: historia nihilismo destrucción*. Adrogué, Argentina: Ediciones La Cebra, 2016.

Villoro, Juan. *Horizontal Vertigo: A City Called Mexico*. Translated by Alfred MacAdam. New York: Pantheon Books, 2021.

Villoro, Juan. "The Metro." In *The Mexico City Reader*, edited by Rubén Gallo, Translated by Lorna Scott Fox and Rubén Gallo, 123–32. Madison: University of Wisconsin Press, 2004.

Virno, Paolo. *Déjà Vu and the End of History*. Translated by David Broder. London: Verso, 2015.

Walcott, Rinaldo. *The Long Emancipation: Moving toward Black Freedom*. Durham, NC: Duke University Press, 2021.

Walkowitz, Rebecca L. *Cosmopolitan Style: Modernism beyond the Nation*. New York: Columbia University Press, 2007.

Wall, Catherine E. "The Visual Dimension of *El siglo de las luces*: Goya and *Explosión en una catedral*." *Revista Canadiense de Estudios Hispánicos* 13, no. 1 (1988): 148–57.

Wallace, Diana. *Female Gothic Histories: Gender, History and the Gothic*. Cardiff: University of Wales Press, 2013.

Wall Kimmerer, Robin. *Braiding Sweetgrass: Indigenous Wisdom, Scientific Knowledge, and the Teachings of Plants*. Minneapolis, MN: Milkweed Editions, 2013.

Welge, Jobst, and Juliane Tauchnitz. "Introduction." In *Literary Landscapes of Time: Multiple Temporalities and Spaces in Latin American and Caribbean Literatures*, edited by Welge and Tauchnitz, 1–15. Berlin/Boston: De Gruyter, 2023.

Wolfe, Cary. *What Is Posthumanism?* Minneapolis: University of Minnesota Press, 2010.

Wolfenzon, Carolyn. "El fantasma que nos habita: *El huésped* y *El cuerpo en que nací* de Guadalupe Nettel como espejo político de México." *Latin American Literary Review* 44, no. 88 (2017): 41–50.

Wood, James. *How Fiction Works*. New York: Picador, 2018.

Wylie, Lesley. *The Poetics of Plants in Spanish American Literature*. Pittsburgh, PA: University of Pittsburgh Press, 2020.

Wynter, Sylvia. "Against a One-Dimensional Course." In *We Must Learn to Sit Down and Talk about a Little Culture: Decolonising Essays, 1967–1984*, edited by Demetrius L. Eudell, 585–623. Leeds, UK: Peepal Tree, 2022.

Wynter, Sylvia. "Novel and History, Plot and Plantation." In *We Must Learn to Sit Down and Talk about a Little Culture: Decolonising Essays, 1967–1984*, edited by Demetrius L. Eudell, 291–99. Leeds, UK: Peepal Tree, 2022.

Zambra, Alejandro. *Bonsái*. Barcelona: Anagrama, 2006.

Zambra, Alejandro. *Bonsai*. Translated by Megan McDowell. New York: Penguin, 2022.

Zambra, Alejandro. *My Documents*. Translated by Megan McDowell. San Francisco: McSweeney's, 2015.

Zambra, Alejandro. *No leer: crónicas y ensayos sobre literatura*. Barcelona: Anagrama, 2018.

Zambra, Alejandro. *Not to Read*. Translated by Megan McDowell. London: Fitzcarraldo Editions, 2020.

Zapata, Michael. *The Lost Book of Adana Moreau*. Toronto: Hanover Square Press, 2020.

Zapata Olivella, Manuel. *Africanidad, indianidad, multiculturalidad*. Edited by William Mina Aragón. Santiago de Cali, Colombia: Universidad del Valle, 2011.

Zavala, Oswaldo. *Volver a la modernidad: genealogías de la literatura mexicana de fin de siglo*. Valencia: Albatros, 2017.

Zimmer, Zac. "A Year in Rewind, and Five Centuries of Continuity: *El año del desierto*'s Dialectical Image." *MLN* 128, no. 2 (March 2013): 373–83.

Žižek, Slavoj. "Discipline between Two Freedoms—Madness and Habit in German Idealism." In *Mythology, Madness, and Laughter: Subjectivity in German Idealism*, edited by Markus Gabriel and Slavoj Žižek, 95–121. London: Continuum, 2009.

Žižek, Slavoj. *Looking Awry: An Introduction to Jacques Lacan through Popular Culture*. Cambridge, MA: MIT Press, 1991.

INDEX